Routledge Revivals

Growth and Fluctuations 1870-1913

In this title, first published in 1978, Sir Arthur Lewis considers the development of the international economy in the forty years leading up to the First World War, with the adoption of the gold standard, a rapid growth in world trade, the opening up of the continents by the railways, vast emigration from Europe, India and China, and large-scale international investment.

The book contrasts the relationship between prices, industrial fluctuations, agricultural output, and the stock of monetary gold, considering both the varying patterns of leading economies and then their net combined effect on the rest of the world.

Growth and Fluctuations 1870-1913

W. Arthur Lewis

Routledge
Taylor & Francis Group
Routledge Revivals

First published in 1978
by George Allen & Unwin Ltd.

This edition first published in 2010 by Routledge
2 Park Square, Milton Park, Abingdon, Oxon, OX14 4RN

Simultaneously published in the USA and Canada
by Routledge
270 Madison Avenue, New York, NY 10016

Routledge is an imprint of the Taylor & Francis Group, an informa business

ISBN 13: 978-0-415-56344-4 (hbk)
ISBN 13: 978-0-415-56783-1 (pbk)
ISBN 13: 978-0-203-09261-3 (ebk)

ISBN 10: 0-415-56344-5 (hbk)
ISBN 10: 0-415-56783-1 (pbk)
ISBN 10: 0-203-09261-9 (ebk)

Growth and Fluctuations 1870–1913

Also by W. Arthur Lewis

Economic Survey, 1919–1939
Principles of Economic Planning
Overhead Costs
Development Planning
Politics in West Africa
The Theory of Economic Growth
Some Aspects of Economic Development

Growth and Fluctuations 1870–1913

W. Arthur Lewis
James Madison Professor of Political Economy, Princeton University

London
GEORGE ALLEN & UNWIN
Boston Sydney

First published in 1978

ISBN 0 04 300072 X Hardback

Printed in Great Britain
in 10 on 11 point Times
by University Press, Cambridge

Preface

I have come to this subject from an interest in the problems of our own time, some of which began in this period (such as the economic development of the tropical countries, or the economic difficulties of Britain) and others of which show marked correspondences (such as twenty years of worldwide inflation, international recessions, the struggle of even the richest countries to maintain fixed exchange rates for their currencies). This interest declares itself in brief comments scattered through the book comparing then and now. However, my main purpose has been to try to find out what actually happened – a difficult enough task – and I hope that the reader will not be distracted by the occasional reference to the preoccupations of our own times.

The chapters are of varying technical difficulty. Chapter 1 is intended as a simple introduction for people who are not familiar with the history of trade cycle analysis; others will find all they need in the synopsis which precedes the chapter. There are many places where the flow of the argument is interrupted for intensive discussion of some particular problem. The device of preceding each chapter with a synopsis is intended to help the reader to recognise the sequence of ideas in each section.

In writing this book the hardest and most time-consuming task has been to assemble the statistical appendices, without which it could not have been written. As the reader will see, I have remade the British index of industrial production, and made a new index of British real income. I have also had to make certain revisions of the available indexes for France, Germany and the United States. Since other writers will be continuing this process long after this book is finished, as well as producing similar series for other countries, I am only too well aware how tentative are the conclusions I offer here, and apologise in advance for the number of times that they are introduced by 'conceivably' or some similar evasion.

There is no separate bibliography. A bibliography of materials relevant to the expansion of the world economy would fill a book this size, and take years to prepare. Instead the Notes and Appendices contain extensive references to the materials used, which are further identified in an Index of Authors.

How does one record one's intellectual debts after nearly forty years of reading, teaching and listening to other economists, and non-economists as well? All I know I have learnt from other people, and from reflecting on what they have said. This manuscript has been read by two of my colleagues at Princeton University, Professors W. J. Baumol and Wallace Oates whose penetrating advice I am glad to acknowledge, without committing them to what has emerged. I have had wonderful secretarial and technical assistance in the Princeton Research Program in Development Studies from Geraldine Kavanagh, Alice Anne Navin, Wanda Prorock and Dorothy Rieger. I have relied on Marion O'Connor for information on wheat production, and her paper on this subject appears as an appendix.

W.A.L.

Princeton
December 1976

Contents

List of Tables in the Text

List of Tables in the Appendices

Charts

Chapter 1

Prospectus

SYNOPSIS: 1.00 The book is written around three interlocking themes: (a) the speed and regularity of growth of the four industrial core countries; (b) the Kondratiev swing in prices, downwards to 1895 and upwards thereafter; and (c) the differing degrees of response of countries at the periphery to the possible adoption of new technology and to opportunities to trade.

1.01 There are marked fluctuations in industrial production in the core countries. 1.02 The best known is the Juglar fluctuation, averaging about eight years. 1.03 The shorter Kitchin fluctuation is not relevant to our themes. 1.04 The Kuznets fluctuation turns on great depressions occurring about once every seventeen years. All four countries experienced such great depressions though not always simultaneously. The great depressions were associated with long swings in construction. We shall inquire whether there is a connection between great depressions and the Kondratiev swing in prices.

1.05 This long downswing followed by a long upswing is found in most price series or in their rates of change. 1.06 We shall inquire whether there was a corresponding change in the rate of growth of production. 1.07 In the downswing the terms of trade moved against farmers in both the core and the peripheral countries, stimulating political activism. The great outburst of urban radicalism at this time has also been attributed to falling prices, but the onset of the series of great depressions is a more probable cause.

1.08 The core contributed to the peripheral countries not only example but also technology, capital and migrant labour. Countries could adopt the new technology or could trade. 1.09 We shall consider why some peripheral countries responded with greater alacrity than others. 1.10 In doing so we will have to take political relationships (the colonial system) into account.

1.00 The idea of continuous economic growth from year to year is relatively new in human history; it belongs only to the period since the industrial revolution. Before that there had been long periods of economic fluctuation, including in Western Europe several low patches between 1600 and 1700. But after 1800 output per head had begun to rise steadily, and by 1900 the idea of an annual increment had joined the list of natural human rights.[1]

The process of continuous growth began in England, spread during the first half of the nineteenth century to the United States, France, Belgium and Germany, in that order, and thereafter set out to conquer the whole world. For the believer in cultural diffusion, a more appropriate metaphor is that of an escalator, taking countries to ever higher levels of output per head. Countries get on to the escalator at different dates – only half a dozen before 1870, perhaps another fifteen before the First World War, another fifteen between the two world wars, and somewhat more than twenty between 1950 and 1970. The list includes peoples of all creeds, races and continents, and continues to grow.[2]

During the nineteenth century the escalator moved upwards at a speed of about one and a half per cent per annum (in terms of growth of output per head) but the countries on it – like the individuals on an escalator – can move faster or slower, by stepping up or down. It is also possible to fall off the escalator – to grow for a while and then to stagnate; to remain on the escalator is to have achieved the conditions for 'sustained growth'.

Our study originates from interest in the proposition that the upward movement of those already on the escalator helps to pull more and more countries into the moving company. This proposition is not obvious, and its opposite – that it is the enrichment of the rich that impoverishes the poor – is perhaps even more widely held in one form or another. Our purpose is to study the extent and mechanisms of the spread of 'sustained growth' during one period of time, namely the forty years before the First World War.

The theory of international trade, as the classical economists developed it, did not provide for the transmission of sustained growth (or its opposite) from one country to another, since it simply did not deal with growth: technologies are given, and neither labour nor capital migrates. The 'dependency' relation was introduced into economics during the inter-war period by Canadians interested in the 'staple' (or as we would now say, 'export-led growth'),[3] by Australians interested in the multiplier effects of an adverse balance of payments[4] and by Englishmen blaming the great depression of the 1930s on US failure to maintain its own prosperity.[5]

The words we now use we owe to Dennis Robertson and to Raoul Prebisch. Robertson, writing in 1938, referred to international trade as 'the engine of growth', and Prebisch writing twelve years later referred to the relations between the industrial world and the 'periphery'.[6] These writers had their own definitions. In this study we shall divide the world into 'core' countries and the 'periphery'.[7] The four core countries will be Great Britain, France, Germany and the United States. The 'engine of growth' is the industrial sector of the core countries taken together. Our prime concern is therefore the response of the periphery to the engine of growth in the core. This atrocious mixing of metaphors may perhaps symbolise the confusion of the subject matter itself.

Core and periphery together add up to the whole world, but we are not equipped to write about the whole world, so our picture of the periphery will be general and illustrative. Furthermore, we are not writing general economic history; our focus is on rates of growth and their interactions. Even this is further restricted, since what we are seeking is the causes of growth rather than its consequences. We are taking from history only that part which seems necessary to explain core–periphery economic relations from 1870 to 1913.

What follows is thus not a systematic exposition, but a series of discussions around these three questions:

(1) How fast and regular was the engine of growth (industrial production in the four core countries)?
(2) What accounts for the 'Kondratiev' price swing, down from 1873 to 1895, and up from 1895 to 1913?
(3) How does one account for the differential response of the peripheral countries?

THE ENGINE OF GROWTH AND ITS PULSATIONS

1.01 Our engine of growth is the combined industrial production of Britain, France, Germany and the United States. According to Hilgerdt[8] this sum, by value added, was 72 per cent of world industrial production in 1913. The next two countries in size were Russia (5·5 per cent) and Italy (2·7 per cent). Our coverage seems sufficient for our purpose.

The progress of industrial production in each of these four countries is shown on semi-logarithmic scale in Chart 1.1. These indexes combine manufacturing, mining and building. They are themselves controversial, and have had to be double checked before they could be used. The derivation of the British figures is explained in Appendix I, and the derivation of the others in Appendix II.

The curves are all drawn on the same scale, so their growth rates can be compared. But they are not additive, and their relative positions on the vertical scale is without significance.

Each series is shown with a line running along the top, connecting as many peaks as will fit on to a straight line. It is a peculiarity of volume series (i.e. series corrected for or not incorporating changes in price) belonging to the period 1870 to 1913 that their peaks tend to run in straight lines of this kind; this does not happen with earlier nineteenth-century series, or with series for the period between the two world wars. Even in Chart 1.1 nearly half the peaks are not strictly in line, but accuracy within one or two per cent is not to be expected of indexes of industrial production.

The line is not a trend in the statistician's sense. It does not measure the average rate of growth of actual output, but, if anything, indicates the long-run average growth of industrial capacity.[9] Since a straight line on a semi-logarithmic scale represents a constant annual rate of growth, the closeness of fit suggests that the fundamental determinants of industrial capacity were growing at constant rates in the four countries over these particular decades. However, we do not take this for granted; it is one of the things we want to find out.

Ultimately we shall be combining our four series to see the behaviour of the core as a whole; but since we shall not understand what happens to the whole unless we first understand what has happened to the parts, we shall first spend some time studying each of our countries individually.

First, it is obvious from the graph that the four countries grow at very different speeds. The slopes of the straight lines translate into: France 1·8 per cent per annum, UK 2·2 per cent per annum, Germany 3·9 per cent per annum, and USA 4·9 per cent per annum. Why these rates were so different is a puzzle we shall be probing.[10]

The graph also reveals pronounced wave-like movements in the rate of

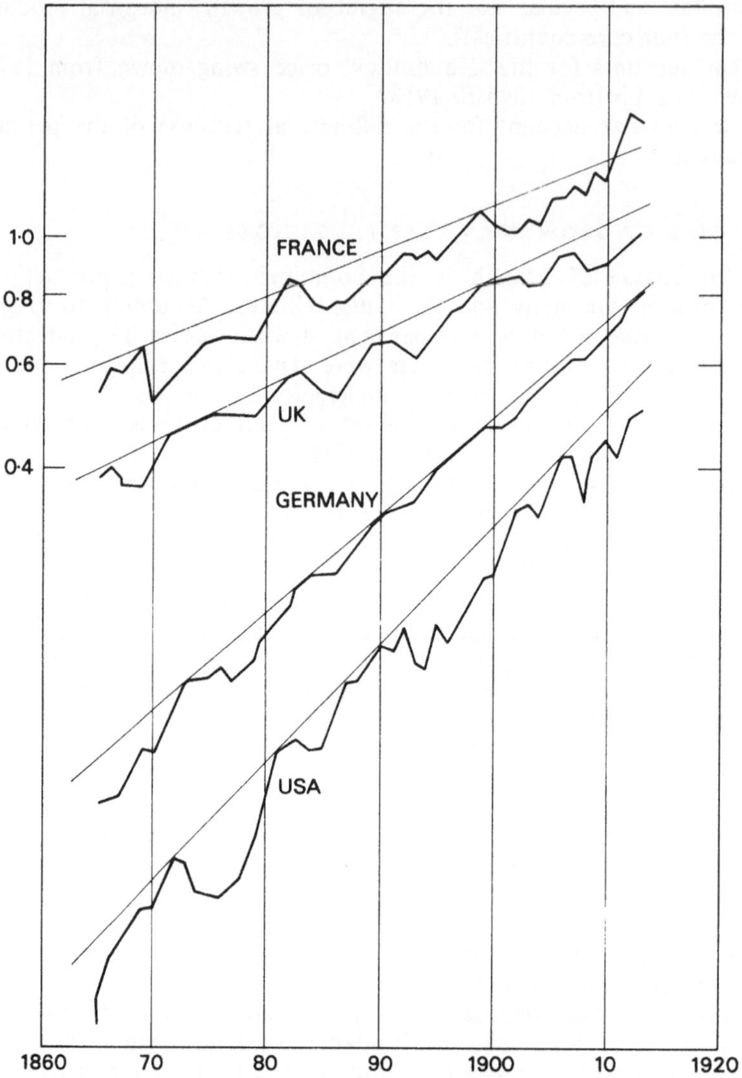

Chart 1.1 Industrial Production

growth, which we used to call 'cycles'. Economists have devoted an enormous literature to the study of such movements, most of it designed to show how a market economy has a built-in tendency to generate production cycles (as in the rest of economics, empirical studies are only a small fraction of the trade cycle literature). This approach is now unpopular, not because the mathematical logic is suspect, but because the models, while they explain the past satisfactorily, always fail to predict the future with reasonable accuracy. If the term 'cycle' is to be confined to a movement whose future can be predicted from its own past, then the movements of industrial production, though wave-like, are not cycles; and the models which can explain them backwards but not predict them forwards have to be viewed with suspicion.

It does not follow that we should abandon trade cycle theory. Meteorologists can explain the path which a hurricane has taken, but cannot predict its future direction without a wide margin of error. One day they may have mastered prediction. The same may happen to economists, or it may not. To predict the course of the trade cycle requires predicting not only human behaviour, but also the physical events (such as the weather) to which human beings will have to react. So economics may always be a trade which explains the past without predicting the future. Since it is both useful and entertaining to study the past, such an exercise is not entirely without merit.

In this book we shall not be attempting to give formal or complete explanations of why fluctuations occurred. In the periphery these fluctuations came as acts of God. We shall have to know when they occurred, how intense they were, and how they affected other matters which interest us, like the volume and terms of trade, or the willingness to migrate or to invest abroad. Like the captain of a ship navigating in stormy seas we shall need to identify the waves, without needing an exhaustive theory of what causes waves.

When analysing these fluctuations economists have identified four different cycles, distinguished by length of periodicity, each of which is named after the economist who first wrote about it: the Kitchin (about three years), the Juglar (about nine years), the Kuznets (about twenty years), and the Kondratiev (about fifty years).

Since cycles are identified by dating their peaks or troughs we must first say something about this process.

First, since our engine of growth is industrial production, in this work our peaks and troughs will be those of industrial production. This yields a set of dates differing by a year or more from those yielded by other series. The traditional dating of cycles in the history books derives from financial panics – either bank failures or stock exchange collapses. This is partly because monthly and even annual data of production were scarce when trade cycle studies began in the nineteenth century, whereas financial crises are exciting and spectacular events. But it also followed from the original investigators' belief that cycles were essentially financial phenomena, caused by fluctuations in the supply of money or credit. This approach was temporarily abandoned in the 1930s and 1940s, in favour of 'real' causes – especially fluctuations in investment opportunities – although it is now again in favour in some circles. Some confusion results. Since some financial crises occur after the physical changes which have occasioned them, output and financial data do not always yield the same peaks, and it is somewhat jarring to be told, for example, that the crisis of 1873 – one of the widest and best known – actually occurred in 1872! The idea that changes in stock exchange prices always precede real changes in the economy is a modern myth. It should be noted specifically that our peaks and troughs are not the same as those of the National Bureau of Economic Research, which constructs its reference cycles by averaging out many different financial and physical series (with the useful by-product that it can single out those which consistently lead, and use them as forecasters for the short term – say the next six months – though not for years ahead).

Secondly, a peak year has to stand out above its neighbours; but by how much? Most historians go by average levels; year 6 qualifies as a peak if it exceeds both years 5 and 7. This is not satisfactory in an economy where the labour force is growing all the time, and where investment plans presuppose built-in growth of demand. In such an economy a year which grows by less than the average will be a disappointing year; unemployment will mount, and profit expectations will be frustrated. For students of growth a peak year must exceed its predecessor by at least the normal rate of growth. As a corollary it follows that year 6 may be a peak year even if it lies below year 7. The definition of 'normal' will vary according to context; in the context of Chart 1.1 it is given by the slopes of the straight lines.

1.02 The standard cycle is the Juglar cycle, of about nine years' duration. This was the first to be identified,[11] and since it held the field alone for about sixty years it monopolised the title of 'the trade cycle', and is what most people mean when they speak of 'the cycle'. In the context of Chart 1.1 it is defined by two conditions to distinguish it from minor fluctuations:

(1) Its peak is higher than all preceding points. For example, 1894 is not a Juglar peak for France. And,
(2) Travelling forward from the peak, it takes more than two years to reach a year whose output exceeds that of the peak by more than two years of normal growth. (A line drawn from the peak parallel to the capacity straight line must take more than two years to touch the curve again.) Thus for France 1903 is not a Juglar peak.

On this definition the dates of the Juglar peaks are roughly: 1872/3, 1882/4, 1889/92, 1899, 1906/7 and 1912/13. It is also possible to treat 1875/6 as an extra Juglar peak for France and Germany, with some UK interest. We are not absolutely certain that 1913 would have proved to be a Juglar peak if the Great War had not erupted in 1914, but it is usually included in the list of Juglars.

One needs the double dates because the peaks do not coincide in these four countries. Naturally the countries react to each other's fluctuations, but each has its own momentum, which yields its own timing. One must be wary of taking these figures too seriously. We are talking about differences of one per cent above or below a line, and they are not sufficiently accurate for reliable deductions in this range. Nevertheless, for what they are worth, they indicate that no single country consistently leads the others into recession. This can be seen by examining our twin peak years to see which countries turn around in the first twin year. The list is:

1872	USA
1882	France (? USA)
1889	UK
1906	(? USA)
1912	France

Each country takes its turn except Germany.

An even more remarkable sign of independence is that France, Germany and the USA all escape one or more Juglar recessions; France those of 1872 and 1907, Germany that of 1907, and the USA that of 1899. Since each of those recessions was quite severe in the other countries, the autonomous elements in each country were obviously powerful.[12]

1.03 Kitchin peaks are the Juglar peaks, plus those that were eliminated by the definition of a Juglar peak. Kitchins do not show up well in data of industrial production. They are thought to originate primarily in fluctuations in inventories and bank credit, and can be traced back to the eighteenth century, when industrial production was still small. Using again the indexes of manufacturing and mining only, one can add for the USA 1895, 1899, 1903 and 1910. US Kitchin lists usually include 1887 and 1890, which were indeed years of financial excitement, but these flurries make small dents in the industrial index. For France one can add 1872, 1889, 1894, 1903, 1907 and 1909. Our two other countries seem to have been less nervous than France and the United States. The British add only 1902, and the Germans add only 1907.

Kitchins do not help to answer any of our three basic questions, so we shall pay no more attention to them.

1.04 Kuznets cycles were identified by observing that alternate Juglar depressions in the United States were particularly severe. This was true of the years following 1872, 1892 and 1907 – intervals of twenty years and fifteen years respectively. Carried forward, the series includes 1929, some twenty-two years later. Taken backwards, it is interrupted by the Civil War, which will have broken the sequence, if there was a regular sequence. Prior to that the next recession to qualify as a 'great depression' is that of 1837 and the early 1840s. Earlier than that it is hardly profitable to go, since industry and investment would be too small in relation to national income for their fluctuations to produce great depressions.

Here we must pause a moment to avoid semantic confusion. American writers give the title 'great depression' to any depression of great severity, and specifically to the five we have just enumerated: 1837, 1872, 1893, 1907 and 1929. British writers sometimes use the term for the whole of the long period of falling prices, 1873 to 1896. In this book the term is used in the American sense.

The severity of recessions is measured in various ways. A recession has two dimensions, its length and its depth. A simple way to measure its length is to count from the peak the number of years it takes to achieve two years normal growth of output, measuring normal growth as say the rate of growth between the two preceding peaks. Depth is concerned with the percentage fall from peak to trough. A recession may be shallow but long, like that starting in Britain in 1873; or deep but short, like that which succeeded it in 1883. A measure that combines length and depth is obtained by projecting a straight line forward from one Juglar peak to the next, and calculating the proportionate area between the straight line of potential capacity and the curve of actual output.

Great depressions were not confined to the United States. All our other core countries experienced them, but at their own dates. Germany underwent a great depression starting in 1876; this was mild by comparison with other countries' great depressions, but very severe by Germany's own average performance. France started great depressions in 1882 and 1899; Britain in 1883 and 1907.

What all these great depressions have in common is that they coincide with the ending of construction booms in their respective countries. This can be seen in Chart 1.2. Construction series are unreliable and hard to find; the struggle involved in preparing those which are used in this study can be seen in Appendixes I and II. What appears in Chart 1.2 are percentage deviations from semi-logarithmic straight line trends.[13]

Fluctuations in construction do not follow the pattern of Juglar cycles either in length or in depth. The stereotype is of a fluctuation which covers two Juglars, but this is a perfect fit only for France. US construction may also be said to have covered two Juglars, but the fit is not perfect; first because, as we have noted, the US skipped the Juglar recession of 1899, in favour of one long upswing from 1894 to 1907; and secondly because there were sizable flurries of construction activity between 1895 and 1897, past the onset of the great depression of 1893; and again between 1909 and 1912, past the great depression of 1907 – these flurries being no doubt part of the reason why the great depressions of 1893 and 1907 were not as severe as those of 1873 and 1929. Britain is also hard to fit into an alternating pattern of mild and severe Juglars, since the recessions starting in 1883 and in 1889 were both bad, and the next two (1899 and 1907), though mild in themselves, were on a declining trend which produced heavy unemployment and emigration after 1907. Only France has the typical pattern of alternation, since its great depressions started in 1882 and 1899. If we date British great depressions as starting in 1883 and 1907, we find that in the four countries not only the dates but also the intervals were different (USA twenty years and fifteen years, France seventeen years, UK twenty-four years and Germany no repetition).

The fluctuations in construction which run with these great depressions are much wider than those in manufacturing. The strength of the long construction boom accounts for the mildness of those Juglar recessions which lie on their backs; while the depth of their valleys is what gives us the great depressions of the Kuznets cycle.

We can avoid a semantic debate. Some economists deny that there was a Juglar cycle in the United States; they see only Kitchin and Kuznets depressions – this is inherent in the National Bureau's reference cycle pattern. One could also take the same line for France, by treating 1892 as a Kitchin and not a Juglar peak. This argument is not necessary for our present purpose, because we shall care only whether a recession was a great depression or not; so it is the underlying construction cycle which sets our pattern.

In identifying Juglar cycles we touched on the question of the mutual interdependence of the core countries. This question has been raised even more acutely for building cycles. Here the starting point is not the coincidence of peaks, as in manufacturing, but rather the fact that the American construction booms appear to alternate with those in Western Europe. Thus

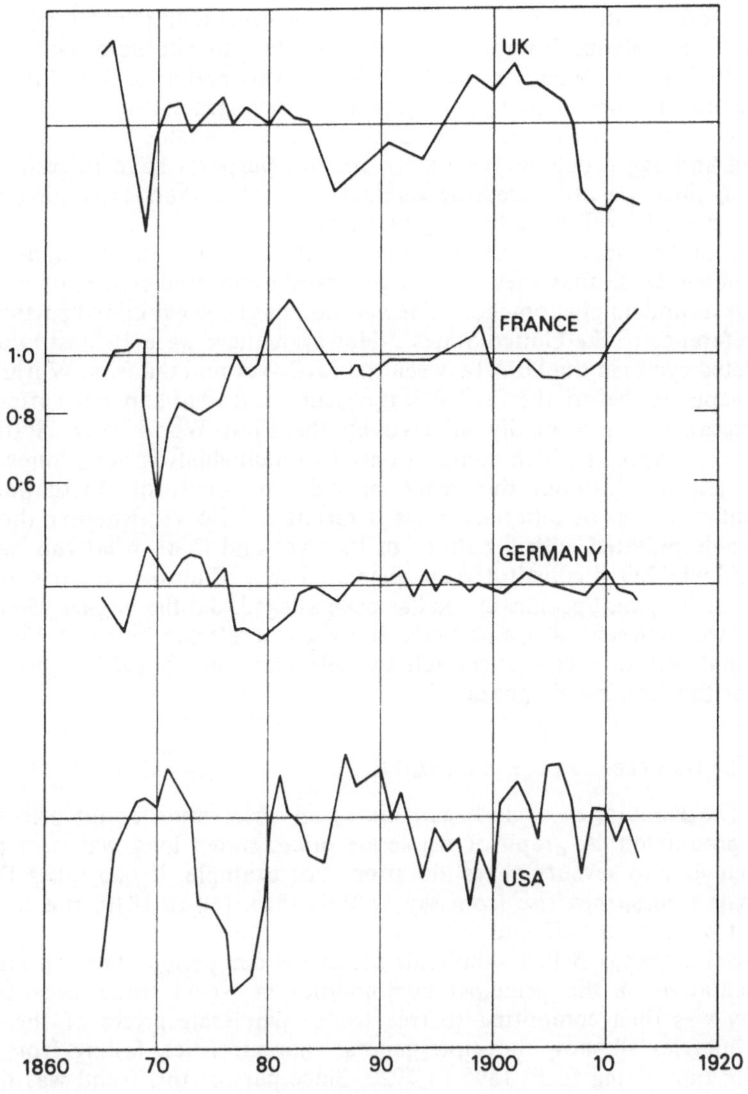

Chart 1.2 Construction

US construction edged out[11] in 1873, German in 1876, British in 1883, French in 1884. US construction edged out again in 1892, French in 1899, British in 1906 (Germany passes). US construction edged out again in 1910 when France was just launching what would have been a major new effort.

This spreading out of the times of construction booms could be purely accidental; Brinley Thomas argues the opposite case.[15] He sees the American building boom as needing and reflecting the immigration of persons and capital from Europe. This took place in long waves. On this view, during the American upswing domestic investment was reduced in Europe, whether for lack of capital, or for lack of demand (slower growth of numbers to be housed and employed in towns), or for lack of labour (slower growth of labour force). Hence European construction had to alternate with that of the United States. Whether the USA forced this pattern upon Europe, or whether the European pattern originated in demographic cycles in Europe and then forced itself upon the United States, contains elements of the chicken and egg problem. We do not for our purposes have to settle these disputes, since we are accepting fluctuations rather than explaining them, but our material will have bearing on them.

None of this involves the question whether building fluctuations are a cycle, in the sense that they are self-generating and predictable, or whether they are a random phenomenon. The question has been examined particularly with reference to the United States.[16] However, there were at most two such completed cycles in the USA between the Civil War and the First World War. What happened before the Civil War is obscure, and what happened after 1913 was presumably profoundly affected by the First World War. Statistical analysis of a species which contains only two individuals is not promising.

Our journey through this maze of different kinds of fluctuations in different countries at different times is meant to discover whether the core as a whole pulsated with a pattern of its own; and if so, what this pattern was, and whether it constituted an accidental sum of unrelated parts, or had a unity of its own. Specifically, as has been alleged, did the engine of growth slow down between 1873 and 1895, and then accelerate between 1895 and 1913; and was this why prices fell to 1895 and rose to 1913? This is the heart of the Kondratiev puzzle.

THE KONDRATIEV PRICE SWING

1.05 The Kondratiev cycle began life as an observation about prices, not about production. A graph of wholesale prices shows long waves in prices of about fifty to seventy years' duration. For example, if one takes British wholesale prices, they rise from say 1770 to 1813, fall to 1849, rise to 1873, fall to 1896, rise to 1920 and fall to 1933.

Chart 1.3 graphs British wholesale prices for our period. These prices are representative of the principal commodities in world trade because the country was then committed to free trade. Wholesale prices of the other core countries all show the same general characteristics, falling from 1873 to 1895, then rising from 1895 to 1920. Since part of this trend was due to the fall in shipping freights, also shown in this chart, a curve is also given which represents wholesale prices minus shipping freights.[17]

This price swing is all-pervasive. It does not apply to all commodities, but will be found in most. It is found in money income; 'gross domestic product deflators' have a turning point in the middle 1890s. Money wages fall in the 1870s, and start rising again in the 1880s; their turning point comes earlier than most. Interest rates and share prices fall, then rise again after 1895.

1.06 The Kondratiev price swing is central to our interests for several reasons. In the first place we want to know how it relates to the pace of growth of the core, whether as cause or as effect.

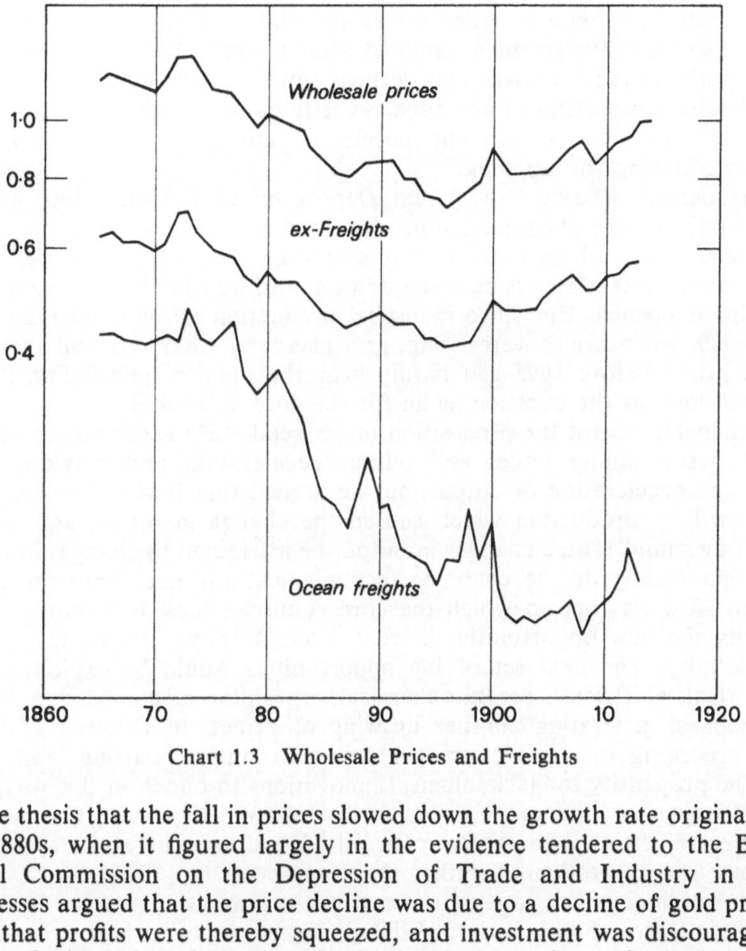

Chart 1.3 Wholesale Prices and Freights

The thesis that the fall in prices slowed down the growth rate originated in the 1880s, when it figured largely in the evidence tendered to the British Royal Commission on the Depression of Trade and Industry in 1884. Witnesses argued that the price decline was due to a decline of gold production; that profits were thereby squeezed, and investment was discouraged.

That falling prices depress profits in the short run is not in doubt; profits fall in the Juglar downswing and rise in the Juglar upswing. This is because money wages and other contractual payments adjust to changes in price only after a lapse of time. They do, however, adjust; and their adjustment is facilitated by the continued increase in productivity, which makes it possible to raise (or lower) the absolute level of wages without changing its relative share. What we need to know is what happens to the long-run share of profits over two decades of rising or falling prices, and this we shall have to explore.

However, even if price changes did not affect the share of profits, a downturn of prices could depress investment psychology by turning the terms of trade against debtors in favour of creditors. Debtors' calculations are upset because the debt charges (interest plus repayment of the loan) now absorb a larger share of their real output than was expected. Bankruptcy rates therefore increase, and the investing community (as distinct from the financial and lending communities) retreats to lick its wounds. To be sure, interest rates then fall – the association between falling prices and low interest rates and between rising prices and high interest rates is well established – so that investment is resumed after a while. But if we are talking about price movements over two decades (up or down) this lag occupies a considerable proportion of the time, so it is quite conceivable that such a movement will see investment decelerate during the downswing and accelerate during the upswing.

The question whether 'the Great Depression of 1873 to 1896' was for Britain only a price phenomenon or also a period of decelerating growth has been debated for a long time in what is now an enormous literature.[18] That the economy decelerated is beyond question, and we shall later be examining why this happened. But since industrial production decelerated even more after 1900, when prices were rising, as a glance at Chart 1.1 will show, the fall in prices before 1895 can hardly bear the main responsibility, if any. We shall look as the question again for the core as a whole.

Schumpeter turned the proposition on its head.[19] He accepted the association between falling prices and output deceleration and between rising prices and acceleration of output, but he argued that it was the changes in the growth of production which caused the change in prices, and not the other way round. These changes in output he attributed to changes in investment opportunity due to changing technological advance. Thus the period 1850 to 1870 was one in which the core countries took to a state of near maturity the new opportunities in coal, iron, railways, steamships, textiles and clothing. The next set of big opportunities would be exploited after 1890: steel, electricity, organic chemicals, the internal combustion engine, automobiles; generating another upswing of prices. In between 1870 and 1890, according to this version, the core was simply coasting, and prices fell. The propensity for technological innovations to bunch in this way, with twenty-five years of voracious investment followed by twenty-five years of somnolent digestion, Schumpeter called the Kondratiev fifty-year cycle, with the emphasis on production rather than on prices.

Now Schumpeter was one of our greatest economists, with an extremely subtle mind, stored with historical data, so one cannot in half a paragraph do justice either to his argument or to the wealth of material with which it is illustrated over two large volumes. The reader must savour this pleasure on his own. We introduce this brief statement of the theme only in our process of laying out the ground which we shall be having to cover.

Our interest in Schumpeter's story is not in the logic of his model, but in how well it fits the facts. First, did the industrial growth of the core decelerate and accelerate as described? And secondly, if it did, was this due to some common element working its way through the whole system? For it is conceivable that with each country going its own way the sum of their activities could nevertheless add to a pattern of two decades of deceleration followed by two decades of acceleration, even though none of the four showed this pattern in itself. The key to this is to study the set of Kuznets great depressions and their alleged inter-relationships. This is why we begin by examining in detail how the individual countries fared, before tackling the movement of the core as a whole.

1.07 The Kondratiev price swing is of interest, secondly, because it was accompanied by a change in the terms of trade between agriculture and industry. Agricultural prices fell more to 1895, and then rose, relative to industrial prices, to 1913.

The burden of the downswing fell upon the farmers both in the core countries and in the peripheral countries – this being one of the places where our three questions come together (about the pulse of the core, the Kondratiev price swing, and core–periphery relationships).

Farmers in the core countries suffered a double burden. The fall in prices would have hurt them as debtors even if industrial prices had fallen equally; the widened gap between industry and agriculture was an additional blow. In Western Europe the main result was to push agricultural tariffs upwards everywhere except in Britain, starting from the German tariff of 1879 and the French tariff of 1881. A tariff could not help the US farmers. They mounted a general attack on 'monopolies' which maintained prices against them, especially on the railways, on the industrial mergers and trusts, and on the banks; they became free traders, spearheading the attack on industrial tariffs, and their associations provided the solid foundation of the populist political movement which surged in the last quarter of the century. They also became involved in the demand for reflation, and therefore with the interests who sought to increase the coinage of silver. Whereas in Europe 'radicalism' was an urban, potentially working-class phenomenon, in the United States the large farm population, still 43 per cent of the labour force in 1890, was the foundation for mass democratic politics.

It is true that not all farmers were affected equally. For example British livestock farmers benefited from the fall in grain prices and the accompanying pressure on rents; some regions therefore prospered more because of falling prices. Similarly in the United States mid-western farmers may have gained as much from the fall in railway rates plus falling industrial prices as they lost from the lower price of wheat; not to mention the substantial increase in output per man deriving from mechanisation. But enough farmers were damaged to make a big protest movement, and well-organised protest movements attract large followings.

Then after 1895 agricultural prices turned around, and the burden fell on the urban working class. Real wages did not rise in Britain after 1899 until the 1920s, having risen around 40 per cent over the preceding two decades. Real wages continued to rise in Germany and the USA, but the rate of growth was sharply cut. So the first dozen years of the twentieth century saw great industrial turbulence, reaching its pitch in Britain, where the Edwardian era is one of great industrial turmoil, matched only by the years 1920 to 1926 and by current times (since the mid-1960s). The membership of trade unions rose between 1900 and 1913 from 2·0 to 4·1 million in Britain, from 0·1 to 1·0 million in France, from 0·9 to 3·0 million in Germany, and from 0·8 to 2·7 million in the USA. Perhaps if figures were available extending these numbers back to 1870 the growth rate might prove to have been fairly constant, but in union struggles it is numbers that count, and growth from one hundred to three hundred is not of the same order as growth from one million to three million.

In fact the years of the preceding Kondratiev price downswing were by no means quiescent industrially, despite improving terms of trade for the urban population. Industrial relations in the 1850s and 1860s had been quiescent, following the industrial and political turbulence of the 'hungry forties' that had culminated in the revolutions of 1848. However, from 1870 onwards organised hostility to 'pure' capitalism or to the unregulated market economy mounted steadily. This was not confined to the workers with their trade unions and burgeoning political institutions, nor to the farmers. All classes of society sniffed the wind. The industrialists abandoned free trade, which had been spreading widely in the middle of the century. The last triumph of free trade was the Anglo-French Treaty of 1860; after 1873 the tide turned, and tariffs began their steady upward march towards their peak in the 1950s. Industrialists also repudiated the gospel of free competition in the home market, and began a movement towards associations, cartels, mergers, combines and trusts, of which the celebrated 'multinational company' is only the latest phase. The middle classes also moved leftwards, tasting Fabianism, Populism and Social Democracy. The welfare state was spawned, fathered by of all people the German chancellor, Bismarck. The trend was compounded by the economists' abandonment of Malthusian political economy, whose more dismal adherents had taught that attempts to raise working-class living standards were doomed to frustration. By 1880 the economists' long march into algebra had already begun, and with it, until the temporary glamour of the Keynesian system, disappeared their intellectual prestige.

To disciples of Schumpeter, this transformation of economic and social ideas seems a natural accompaniment of the Kondratiev downswing.[20] This is not, however, obvious. The change of temper cannot have been due to falling prices, since prices turned the terms of trade in favour of urban communities. It was probably associated with the series of great depressions. It is hard to maintain faith in an unregulated market system which puts worthy artisans out of work for years and brings bankruptcy to thousands of respected business people, large and small. True, there had been a great depression in the forties, but that was thirty years before, and the industrial population had been quite small then in relation to total population, except in Britain. To enter after 1870 into a period (which would last to 1940) where no decade would pass without a great depression in one or other of the four leading industrial countries would prove to be a shock which the free market ideology could not possibly survive, except in isolated ideological enclaves. However, it is not clear that this owed anything to the long swing in prices. Great depressions occurred after 1900, when prices were rising, just as they had before. Probably the main explanation is that as the industrial system spread, drawing in more and more people, its recurring harshness came to be more widely felt and understood, and all classes of the community organised to protect themselves and to extend help to those with whom they sympathised.

The political effects of the Kondratiev swing are outside our field; we mention them only to indicate the social importance of this price phenomenon. Hereafter we shall keep to the economic story in so far as we can separate it out.

CHALLENGE AND RESPONSE

1.08 The 1870s are a good starting point for our inquiry because most of the countries of the periphery outside Europe trace the quickening of their rates of growth to that decade or after. Many had of course been in the world market long before 1870, but if we ask in how many real income per head grew by 10 per cent over two decades, our answer would yield only Ceylon, starting in the 1830s, Brazil and Australia in the 1850s and Argentina in the 1860s. The rest were yet to experience significant growth per head.

The reason for this is the rapid growth of their foreign trade after 1870. World trade was growing quite rapidly in the middle of the nineteenth century, but this growth was confined primarily to trade on the North-West Europe–United States axis. More distant trade depended on the great fall in transport costs which occurred after 1870. Shipping freights had been falling for a couple of decades, as iron and steam displaced wood and sail, but the downturn after 1873 was spectacular. According to Cairncross,[21] the index of inward freight rates to the United Kingdom fell 73 per cent from 1873 to its lowest point in 1908. With lower freights, distant countries could now compete in the markets of Europe and North America; and the heavier commodities – heavy in relation to value – now moved into international trade.

Also important in lowering transport costs inside the peripheral countries themselves was the building of railways inwards from their ports. Western Europe and North America in 1870 were already relatively well off for internal transportation. Not only had they been building railways for forty years, but they had already experienced their first transport revolution – the building of canals and of metalled roads which began in the second half of the eighteenth century. This first transport revolution had largely by-passed the rest of the world, which moreover did not begin extensive railway building until well into the second half of the nineteenth century, when international lending for this purpose began to increase.

The core countries contributed to the development of the countries at the periphery in three separate ways.

First, they offered a new and highly productive technology. The essence of the industrial and agricultural revolutions in the first three-quarters of the nineteenth century was in new ways of doing old things – of making iron, textiles and clothes, of growing cereals, and of transporting goods and services. In the last quarter of the nineteenth century the revolution added a new twist – that of making new commodities: telephones, gramophones, typewriters, cameras, automobiles and so on, a seemingly endless process whose latest twentieth-century additions include aeroplanes, radios, refrigerators, washing machines, television sets and pleasure boats. Thus a rich man in 1870 did not possess anything that a rich man of 1770 had not possessed; he might have more or larger houses, more clothes, more pictures, more horses and carriages, or more furniture than say a school teacher possessed, but as likely as not, his riches were displayed in the number of servants whom he employed rather than in his personal use of commodities.

The point is relevant because we are sometimes told that the revolution was a revolution in mass consumption, and could take hold only in countries sufficiently egalitarian in their income structure for their masses to be in a position to buy all the new commodities which the revolution would produce. This is not so. The revolution consisted of cheaper ways of making already existing things, and was therefore immediately available to any country which was already producing iron, textiles or clothes, or growing cereals – be it Sweden or Russia, Brazil, China, Japan or India. One should note, for example, that India opened its first modern textile mills in the 1850s, and its first modern ironworks in the 1870s. Why some countries adopted the new technology quickly while others held back, is a fascinating question.

Secondly, the core countries contributed resources – specifically capital and people. Private international investment in the periphery (i.e. excluding the USA) was small in the middle of the century, moving upwards to a peak just before the First World War, at a level which it would not again attain (in real terms) until the 1960s. This was also the great age of international migration, not only from all over Europe into 'the countries of new settlement', the Americas and Australasia, but also from India and China into countries throughout the tropical world.

The reasons for this movement have been much explored. Why did people leave Europe or India? How large were the 'pull' and the 'push' factors respectively? Was the investment of capital abroad due to declining profits at home? Why was it so large in the 1880s when the prices of primary commodities were falling?

Thirdly, the core contributed its own markets; it was willing to buy some of the products of the periphery. This, however, was a limited opportunity. One of the myths of this subject is the belief that the industrial revolution of the core depended on importing raw materials from the periphery. The raw materials of the industrial revolution were coal, iron ore, cotton and wool; the foodstuff was wheat. All these the core produced for itself in abundance, with the United States and Europe complementing each other. Their chief deficiency was in wool, through which Argentina and Australia received their stimuli. Apart from this the core's principal imports in 1850 were palm oil, furs, hides and skins, a little timber, tea, coffee and other commodities in small quantities. It is hardly an exaggeration to say that the industrial revolution in the core did not depend on the periphery.

The situation changed as the nineteenth century drew to a close. New technology demanded copper for electric wiring, rubber for bicycle and motor car wheels, oil for the internal combustion engine, and nitrates for the wheatfields; it also created new trades in refrigerated meat and bananas. The population explosion, coupled with rising incomes, increased the demand for tea, coffee, cocoa, vegetable oils, raw silk and jute. The closing of the American agricultural frontier gave new opportunities to the wheatfields of Argentina, Australia, Canada and Eastern Europe. In addition the periphery created one new international trade internal to itself – the big demand for rice in the new tropical market economies.

Many peripheral countries had very little industry of their own to start with. As they expanded their exports, their demand for manufactures grew. This presented an opportunity for what we now call import substitution.

This feature is common to the history of every country since the industrial revolution. France, Germany and the USA felt the impact of the British industrial revolution early in the century through mounting imports; they were substituting for imports of textiles down to the 1850s and for imports of iron down to the 1880s. Since then, import substitution has been adopted by every developing country in the world. The first stage of industrialisation in any country is either to process raw materials for export or to substitute for imports.

1.09 To divide the world into a core and a periphery is helpful, because the technology, resources and markets of the core countries played essential roles in the development of the periphery. But it is also misleading if it suggests that the countries of the periphery were a single category. The main interest of the subject lies in assessing why the peripheral countries responded at different speeds. Their geographical resources – minerals, soils, climate – were quite different. Some had already developed further than others by 1870, having more infrastructure and education, and higher levels of technology. Moreover there were great institutional differences as regards the status of labour, the extent of the market economy, financial institutions and government systems. The effect of these differences is not always obvious; even in our own time the fastest growing among the less developed countries are not always those with the best material resources, the highest levels of education, the highest per capita income or the strongest governments. We can learn something about such matters from studying development in our period.

1.10 Finally core–periphery relations were not only technological and economic but also political. The imperialists tell us that the finest contribution of the core to peripheral countries was good government. The anti-imperialists argue variously that empire was good, but in due course outlived its time; that it was irrelevant to development; that it actually held back development, by prohibiting certain activities or channelling them into spheres of limited potential; or that it de-developed, in the sense of actually reducing living standards or even killing people. Since colonies were governed very differently – 'the colonial system' is another myth – one could nominate at least one colony to fit each of these categories, from best to worst. In addition anti-imperialists emphasise that the urge to acquire empire came from commercial imperatives – the search for markets, raw materials or investment opportunities, or the desire to avoid being excluded by others – and was part of the inner logic of capitalism rather than an adventure to bring civilisation and religion to backward peoples such as is portrayed in the children's history books.

The colonial empires had for the most part been carved out long before 1870 – the principal exceptions being parts of Africa, Indochina, the Pacific Islands, and the territories acquired by the USA from Spain in 1898. Indeed large parts of the imperial system had been acquired long before the industrial revolution began. So while the causes of empire building are a fascinating question, an explanation cannot lie within the confines of this study.

Our concern is rather with the influence of empires on growth or retardation. But here the answers are more numerous than the number of imperial powers, for not only did the imperial powers differ among themselves, but the same power pursued different policies in different colonies – the most spectacular example being the diametrically opposed policies of Britain in Kenya and in neighbouring Uganda. Hence, when seeking the causes of growth or retardation, one has to look at each colony separately, instead of trying to fit all colonies into a unique colonial pattern. No colonial power helped its colony to industrialise, but in everything else that might help or hinder development – education, alienation of land, encouragement of small farming, discrimination in employment, investment in infrastructure – their policies were very diverse, and ranged as widely as those of self-governing countries in the periphery.

So much by way of setting out the questions that we shall be investigating. Now we can begin to look for the answers.

Chapter 2

The Juglar Pattern

SYNOPSIS: 2.00 The main purpose of this chapter is to establish whether there was a Kondratiev swing in core industrial production corresponding to the Kondratiev swing in prices.

2.01 Our survey opens with the great boom of 1873. 2.02 The boom was followed by a great depression. 2.03 In Britain, France and Germany this depression was long rather than deep. 2.04 In the USA it was both deep and long. 2.05 The cumulative effect was that core production did not decline but stood still for six years, during which the gap between actual and potential production widened to an extent not again experienced until the 1930s.

2.06 Prices may have fallen in the 1870s and 1890s because of great depressions, but why did prices fall in the 1880s? 2.07 The USA experienced almost unbroken prosperity in the 1880s. 2.08 So also did Germany. 2.09 But France went into a great decline after 1882. This is usually attributed to agricultural depression, but the abrupt cut in government expenditures, following the abandonment of the Freycinet Plan, is a more likely cause. 2.10 Britain also went into a decline. The suggestion that this was due to the pull of US prosperity on British capital and labour is not tenable. It was due to the low profitability of manufacturing resulting from deceleration of exports and acceleration of imports.

2.11 All four countries went into Juglar recession early in the 1890s. But while Britain, France and Germany were very prosperous in the second half of the 1890s, the USA plunged into another deep and long depression. 2.12 Balance of payments problems and a drain of gold plagued the USA in the first half of the 1890s, but were overcome in the second half. Also railway investment, which had led earlier recoveries, was now more hesitant as the main railway network neared completion.

2.13 The upswing of prices from 1895 had no common effect on growth or fluctuations of the four core countries. Their diversity continued. After a slight setback in 1900, Germany resumed its almost unbroken prosperity. 2.14 The US recovery continued until 1906/7, whereupon a new great depression began. 2.15 France progressed to a superboom in 1899, followed by a great depression, and then to another superboom culminating in 1912. 2.16 The UK was very prosperous to 1899, then languished.

2.17 Each country has its own unique pattern of superbooms and great depressions. The pattern obtained from adding the four together has no independent explanation of its own.

2.00 In this chapter we shall study Juglar and Kuznets fluctuations, mainly with an eye to discovering whether they contribute to explaining the Kondratiev swing in prices.

This chapter has become somewhat long because, originally planned as a general review, it now has embedded within itself (in order to controvert some conventional wisdom) detailed essays on Britain and France in the 1880s, and the USA in the 1890s. The general reader is therefore invited to skip sections 2.09, 2.10 and 2.12, unless specially interested in their subject matter.

THE SEVENTIES

2.01 Our period begins with the great boom that culminated in the great depression of 1873.

One distinguishing feature of the boom, which stands out in Chart 1.2, is that this would be the last time for eighty years that all four countries in the core would be having a construction boom simultaneously. The synchronisation was not perfect. France and the USA started first, and finished first; France because its economy was completely stunned by the Franco-Prussian War. Britain and Germany started a little later but went on much longer; Britain delayed by the slump in railway building following its minor recession of 1866, and Germany set back slightly by war in 1870.

In the United States the boom was clearly making up for time lost during the Civil War. Immigration was resumed, but this was not the main feature of the boom, since the average annual number of immigrants, over the most intense five-year period, 1869/73, although slightly larger than that of the preceding peak of 1850/4, namely 385,000 compared with 382,000, was considerably smaller in relation to population.[1] The housing boom also was not abnormal. Gottlieb's number of 'new housekeeping units' built[2] averages 171,000 over its biggest five-year cluster 1869/73, as compared with 137,000 over the period 1853/7; but this growth rate of 1·4 per cent per annum does not compare with the 4·8 per cent per annum growth of urban population between 1860 and 1870. More impressive is the leap of manufacturing production, which grew by 32 per cent in the six years 1860–6, rising to 48 per cent between 1866 and 1872. But most impressive of all is the contribution made by railway investment; railway mileage operated more than doubled between 1865 and 1873 (from 35,000 to 70,000 miles); this was the heart of the US boom.

The other spectacular boom was in Germany. Here also industrial production leapt spectacularly, led by pig iron, which doubled between 1860 and 1866, and doubled again between 1866 and 1873, and by the cotton industry which, somnolent during the US Civil War, also now doubled its output between 1866 and 1873: thus the cessation of the US Civil War promoted not only the US boom in manufacturing, but also similar booms elsewhere.[3] In Germany an enormous influx into the towns[4] set off a housing boom, which would last until 1876. Here too railway building was important, the mileage open doubling between 1867 and 1876. Helping to finance this boom, of course, was the reparations payment of five thousand million francs received from France in gold between 1871 and 1872.

2.02 Booms come to an end, but for the purpose of this book it is not necessary to investigate the mechanism, whether by means of econometric equations or by giving a blow by blow account.[5]

The United States exhibited all the usual phenomena. Railway building slowed, and many companies went bankrupt. Immigration declined, as did the building of houses. Three hundred banks collapsed. Industrial production fell sharply. Unemployment mounted. The depth of this depression displays itself in Chart 1.1, where at the trough of 1876 industrial production is 40 per cent below the potential capacity line. No other depression before that of 1929 shows such an enormous gap. According to rumour some three million persons were unemployed. This is highly implausible since, although it would only represent 23 per cent of the labour force compared with 25 per cent in 1932, it would also amount to three-quarters of the entire industrial population of the day. The rumour testifies to the deep impression which was made on contemporaries by the misery all around them.

As usual the first public sign was the financial crisis. Stock exchange prices fell sharply and banks collapsed. Simultaneously commodity prices came rushing down. The volatility of banks at this time is particularly important, not only in the USA but everywhere in the core. The United States had no central bank, and would not acquire one until the Federal Reserve System was established in 1914. Elsewhere, the central banks were still learning their business, and in particular had not yet fully accepted a responsibility to prevent commercial banks or other financial institutions from going bankrupt. The Bank of England's decision to rescue Baring Brothers in 1890 would be strongly contrasted with its refusal to rescue Overend, Gurney & Company in 1866. At this time there were still hundreds – in the United States thousands – of banks, since the movement to merge was only now gathering strength. The most vulnerable financial houses would be those which lent to farmers or railway promoters in the United States, and those which dealt in foreign government bonds in Britain and France.

The Bank of England prided itself on its warning system. Over-expansion of credit by the commercial banks led to an outflow of gold from the country. As soon as the Bank's reserves fell to danger level, it would raise Bank Rate, and use other means to influence the commercial banks to restrict their lending.[6] Unfortunately the Bank of England's gold reserve was very small. In the 1870s it considered the danger point to be £10,000,000, and since its average holding in the first week of each December of the 1870s was only £12·8 million, the Bank was continuously apprehensive.[7] In effect, whenever there was a Juglar upswing the country began to lose gold, partly because commodity imports rose faster than exports, but partly also because foreign lending increased, and such part of it as did not directly finance purchases from Britain, but returned indirectly via purchases elsewhere, might temporarily occasion a loss of gold. So the Bank of England always stood ready to cut short a Juglar upswing, in the interest of its gold reserve, whether or not there was still unused industrial capacity or domestic financial hazard. Hawtrey makes the same point with regard to Bank actions during recession, pinpointing 1876–8 and 1884–6 as depression years in which the Bank held back recovery by maintaining high Bank Rates in the interest of its gold reserve.[8] It is of course arguable that changes in Bank Rate made little difference to industrial production, since at this time British industry was not relying on financial institutions for its capital. The City serviced mainly the railways, the government and foreign investment, and it was these that bore the brunt of the volatility of gold. Defenders of the Bank of England would argue that its raising of interest rates did not cause recession, but merely recognised trouble that was already in process. But the more promptly the Bank acted, the greater the likelihood that its actions would accelerate the downturn or inhibit the recovery.

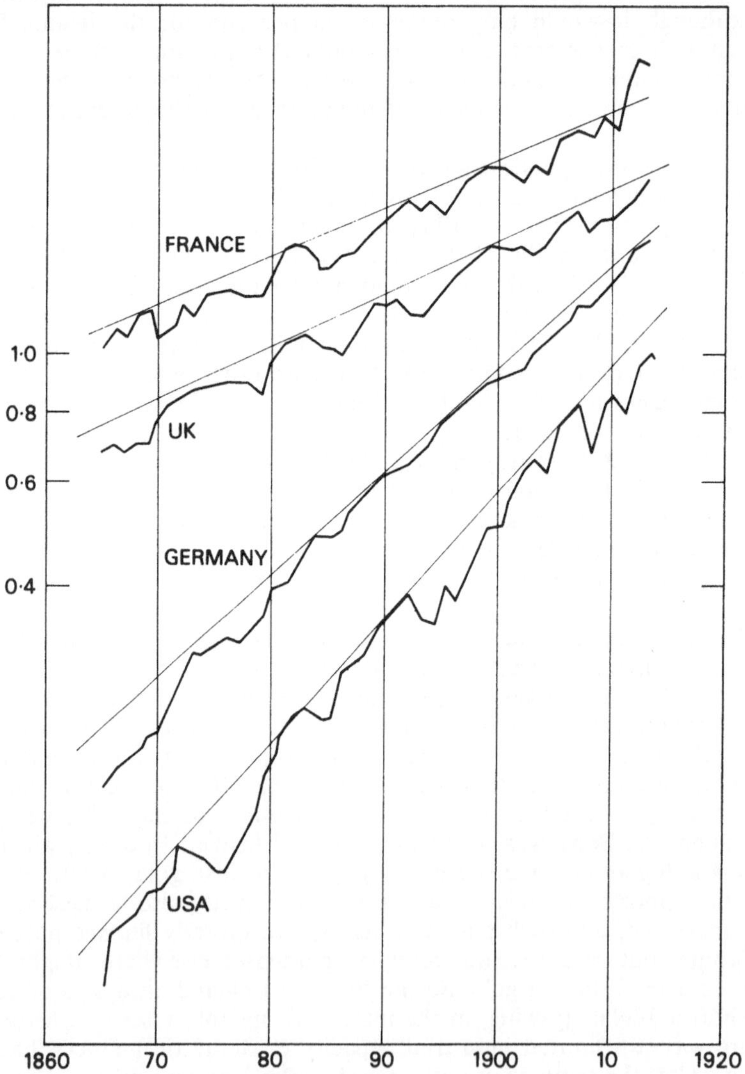

Chart 2.1 Manufacturing and Mining (without Building)

Commercial bank failures, so marked in the United States, deepened a recession: directly because they contracted credit; indirectly because they undermined investors' confidence. Perhaps this was only a short-term phenomenon. The banking crisis was over in six months; if thereafter the economy could pick itself up again, then the quicker and more intensive the liquidation, the sooner the economy would resume its upward course. This is not so obvious. Nowadays governments and central banks go to great lengths to prevent commercial bank failures because these are thought to depress the economy. If they are right, then the insecurity of financial institutions before 1914 may be one reason why Juglar depressions were so severe in that period, compared with those since 1950.

2.03 The United States went down resoundingly in 1873, while France, Britain and Germany merely paused.

Calamity had come to France in 1870, with war and defeat. Manufacturing and mining picked up rapidly, and but for a slight reverse in 1873, continued to grow until 1876. During that interval it was construction that delayed. Chart 2.1 shows manufacturing and mining output, without construction.

Britain and Germany were both sustained by building booms which retained their vigour until 1876. Indeed in the British case, though housebuilding turned down in 1876, other construction was active, so the construction boom in effect continued until 1883. Indeed, in both these countries it is sometimes said that there were two recessions in the seventies, one in 1873 and one in 1876. Germany then recovered quickly, moving up sharply from 1877, while Britain went down until 1879. Thus, if the United States was unique in the core in moving downwards every year until 1876, Britain was unique in having a second downturn which lasted until 1879, including even its own minor financial crisis, the failure in 1878 of the City of Glasgow Bank.[9]

Why did the British economy do badly in the second half of the seventies? The decline of housebuilding is a frequent answer, but British construction recovered, while German construction did not. There are two more plausible answers.

One is concerned with the collapse of foreign investment, which fell from £73 million a year for 1870/8, to £28 million a year for 1875/9.[10] This is accompanied by stagnation of exports of domestic produce, which, using Schlote's figures in constant prices, grew from £209 million a year in 1870/4 to only £215 million a year in 1875/9, instead of at the normal rate of growth of about 15 per cent over five years.[11]

Lending to the USA collapsed because, although US manufacturing output rose fast from 1876, construction moved slowly until 1880, for reasons which we shall come to in a moment. Other overseas borrowers were depressed by the sharp fall in prices – the British wholesale index fell 25 per cent between 1873 and 1879. The terms of trade probably moved in the borrower's favour; partly because freight rates fell heavily – thereby reducing the gap between their import and their export prices – and partly because the prices of British manufactures fell by more than the prices of primary products. This phenomenon seems curious today, but in the nineteenth century the prices of coal and iron were as volatile as agricultural prices, and it is only after 1880 that the British terms of trade can be relied on to improve in a recession and deteriorate in a boom. It was not the terms of trade that embarrassed the overseas borrowers, but the growing real burden of debt charges contracted at higher price levels. This set off a series of defaults, or, as we would now say, requests for rescheduling.[12] Defaults halt international lending, by destroying confidence. Promoters of international loans have short memories, and will come back again within a decade, but for a while the market is depressed.

The second explanation of the British depression in the second half of the 1870s is plausible, but more controversial; namely the Bank of England's struggle to maintain its gold reserves. To see this in perspective we must go back a little earlier.

It was in the 1870s that the gold standard came into its own. Germany ceased to coin silver from 1871. Its sale of silver and purchase of gold drove down the price of silver, thereby embarrassing bimetallic countries all over the world (i.e. countries which coined both gold and silver, and maintained constant price ratios between gold and silver). An important group of countries, linked since 1867 as the Latin Union (France, Belgium, Switzerland, Italy), therefore also ceased coining silver, and effectively joined the gold standard in 1872. The United States, which had printed large quantities of paper currency since the Civil War also decided in 1873 to demonetise silver, and in 1875 further resolved to return to the gold standard in 1879.

All this increased the demand for gold in the face of declining supply. Average annual production of gold, which had peaked in 1852/7 at £30 million, was £27 million over 1865/9, and averaged £24 million over 1870/9. Germany bought £50 million of gold in 1871–3 plus another £20 million in 1875–9. France started in 1874, and during the next five years absorbed £83 million. The United States increased its stock between 1876 and 1879 by £25 million.[13]

The worst years for the Bank of England were 1876 and 1878, and Hawtrey believed that the pressures then exercised by the Bank to keep gold in the country were the main reason that recovery was delayed until 1879. What casts doubt on the argument is the maintenance of construction activity at this time, especially railway and local authority expenditure.[14] The delay in recovery was therefore due not so much to failure of domestic investment, as to the lack of export demand, stemming from the decline in overseas investment.

2.04 One final question remains: why did United States construction slump so heavily after 1871? Chart 1.2 shows very clearly the abnormality of this event, even for a great depression. The highest five-year average for construction, in the neighbourhood of 1873, is that for 1869–73. This average exceeds that of the next five years, 1874–8, by 34 per cent. Similar calculations in the neighbourhood of 1893 show that the average for 1888–92 is only 6 per cent above that for 1895–9, and the average for 1903–7 is actually below that for 1908–12. As explained in Appendix II, the series we are using probably exaggerate the decline of construction in the second half of the

1870s. Nevertheless it seems very plausible that the great depression of 1873 compared only with that of 1929 in the depth of the gulf between successive construction booms.[15]

Was this because the preceding boom was exceptionally vigorous? Hardly so. We have seen that neither immigration nor housebuilding was exceptionally large when compared with similar activity in the 1850s. Manufacturing activity increased by 6·8 per cent per annum between 1866 and 1872, and with an average rate over the next forty years of 5·1 per cent, this certainly called for extra forces in factory building. But the only unusual effort occurred in railway building, which now slumped very heavily. 'Consumption of rails' fell from 1·4 million tons in 1872 to 0·7 million in 1877, and 0·8 million in 1878, and did not take off again until 1879.

The trough in manufacturing came in 1876. After this, recovery was vigorous and did not have to wait for the big wheat export of 1879, as we are sometimes told. The question we have to answer is why 1874 to 1876 were such bleak years.

If the decline of railway construction is not a sufficient answer, the solution may lie in the decision to return to the gold standard at the prewar parity. Prices had run very high during the Civil War. Warren and Pearson's index (1910/14 = 100) falls from 193 in 1864, past 136 in 1872, to 90 in 1879 – a fall of more than half.[16] By 1864 the dollar had lost more than half its value in the foreign exchange market; and although it had recovered sharply after the war, it was still 12 per cent below par in 1873.[17] The decision made in 1875 to return to the prewar parity in 1879 involved considerable deflation.

Background to this downward movement was a continued surplus of Federal receipts over expenditures.[18] Federal expenditure had averaged only $68 million a year in the second half of the 1850s. In the last year of the war it had risen to $1,298 million. It then fell swiftly, by more than government receipts. There would be a budget surplus every year from 1866 to 1894. This averaged $62m. during 1866/9, $83m. during 1870/3, and $21m. during 1874/7.

As can be seen in Table 2.1, wages resisted the deflation. The industrial conflicts of 1877 surpassed in bitterness all that had gone before, and heralded the creation of an organised labour movement within the next decade. Money wages fell by 7 per cent between 1873 and 1876 (more than they would ever fall again until the depression of 1929), but this was reduced to 5 per cent by the appreciation of the dollar. The rest of the fall,

Table 2.1 *USA: Wages in Manufacturing, 1873–9*[19]

	Money wages	*Wages in gold*	*Real wages*
1873	100	100	100
1874	98	101	100
1875	95	94	102
1876	93	95	103
1877	90	97	100
1878	87	98	103
1879	86	98	104

between 1876 and 1879, was more than compensated by the further appreciation of the dollar. Real wages never fell below the level of 1873. We cannot deduce what happened to the relative share of profits in industrial output, since the buoyancy of real wages was partly due to the terms of trade moving against agriculture. Nevertheless it is plausible to suppose that manufacturing was squeezed by industrial prices in gold falling faster than wages in gold, as the dollar appreciated, in much the same way as British profits were squeezed when Britain returned to the gold standard at the old parity in 1925.

2.05 From the standpoint of the periphery, what mattered most was the performance of the core taken as a whole, though some trading partnerships were closer than others. The curve in Chart 2.2 is an index of industrial production for the core, which adds together the four indexes shown in Chart 1.1 (for derivation and weights, see Appendix II).

The picture presented is one of prolonged boom to 1872 followed by prolonged slump. The strength of the boom shows in how closely the curve hugs the capacity line from 1866 to 1872. This will have prevented accumulation of surplus stocks of food or raw materials. Hence it is not surprising that the last two years of the boom sent prices rocketing skywards.

The great depression which followed was long but not deep. In those days US industry only represented about 30 per cent of the core, not 46 per cent

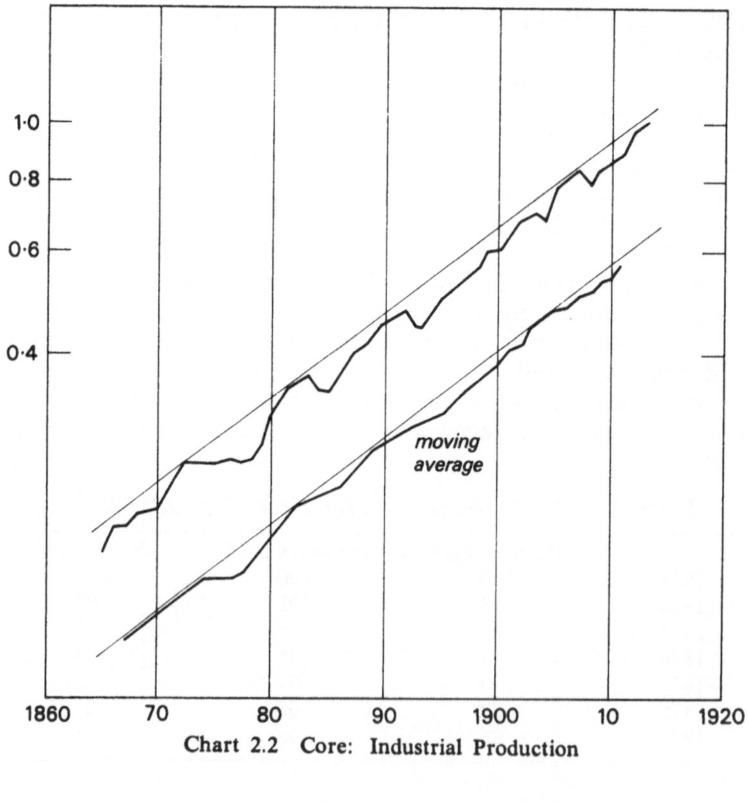

Chart 2.2 Core: Industrial Production

as it stood in 1913. European influences were still strong; output side-stepped, instead of falling. But recovery was long delayed; it took six years to achieve two years of normal growth from the peak. So by the year 1879 the gap between output and potential capacity had widened to 15 per cent. Such a wide gap would not appear again until after the depression of 1929.

THE EIGHTIES

2.06 The 1880s are crucial to our understanding of the behaviour of prices. We are familiar with the great 'American' depressions of the 1870s and the 1890s, so we can understand why prices fell in those decades. But why did prices also fall in the 1880s, being lower at the peak of 1890 than they were in 1883?

The eighties began well. Chart 2.1 shows the core peak of 1883 well on trend. That prices were lower than in 1873 is no surprise. Stocks of primary products will have been accumulating through the seventies, and the actual boom period – say the number of years lying within 5 per cent of the capacity line – was restricted.

One reason for the vigour of core prosperity in 1882–3 is that this is the last Juglar peak which all four countries have in common until after the First World War: this can be seen in Chart 1.1. It is also followed by widely differing experiences. For in the second half of the eighties Germany and the USA soared to ever-rising heights, while France and Britain were depressed. We must therefore study our countries separately.

2.07 In the United States the 1880s were a decade of great prosperity, displaying almost unbroken growth to 1892. Construction was still low in the first half, but was 'above the line' from 1886 to 1892. This helped to shorten the Juglar recession of 1883, and so effectively swamped the Kitchin crisis of 1887 that that event barely shows in the statistics of industrial production.

This was a classical Kuznets boom, incorporating railway building, immigration, residential building, import of capital and leaping production of iron and steel. The number of people in manufacturing increased by two-thirds in the ten years to 1890; those in services, including transportation, rose even faster: by three-quarters.[20] It was not a boom period for agriculture; its share of the labour force now fell below 50 per cent (from 51·3 to 42·7), absolute numbers rising by 12 per cent, which was less than during the preceding and succeeding decades (31 and 17 per cent). Still, the 12 per cent growth testifies to the continuing rounding out of the agricultural heritage at this time. Neither did the boom owe anything to exports, which increased over the ten years only by 3 per cent in value and 16 per cent in volume.[21] This is a classic case of a subcontinent growing rapidly by developing its own internal resources for its own use – much as the Soviet Union would be doing in the 1930s and the European Common Market in the 1960s, and as India and China and Brazil are now bracing themselves to do.

This boom began to lose its momentum after 1887, as construction slowed; but manufacturing continued to grow rapidly until 1892. The course of US industry does not help to explain why prices fell in the 1880s; we shall leave the USA aside until we come to study the 1890s.

2.08 The 1880s started badly for Germany, as for the USA, but the country gathered its forces and launched upon a boom which seems to have been almost unbroken until the outbreak of the First World War.

The big construction boom of the early seventies, financed partly by the French indemnity, collapsed in 1876 to unprecedented depths, from which the economy took a long time to emerge (see Chart 1.2). The number of miles of railway brought into operation tell part of the story:

1872–7	5,156 miles	1882–7	2,611
1877–82	2,688	1887–92	3,014

The figures testify that there was over-building in the middle seventies, which took a little time to digest. The towns were also flooded, with unfortunate results in unemployment. The annual increase of population in urban areas (more than 2,000 persons) ran as follows:

1871–5	468,000	1880–4	352,000
1875–80	412,000	1885–9	552,000

The movement to the towns was forced to slow down; overseas migration mounted in its place. The American statistics show the following average numbers of German immigrants:

1870–4	116,000	1880–4	184,000
1875–9	35,000	1885–9	105,000

The 1880s would see the last substantial flow of emigrants from Germany. Thereafter German industry would absorb most of the outflow from the countryside, as well as population growth.

Once industry got back on course, as it had done by 1882, it drove forward relentlessly. When one compares the industrial curves in Chart 1.1, Germany stands out for the mildness of its fluctuations. In the whole period from 1882 to 1913 there is no year in which production actually falls, and the average gap between actual output and potential capacity is much lower than for any other country. At first sight this reminds us that this particular index contains much interpolation, but the phenomenon is confirmed by Kuczynski's statistics of trade union unemployment, which are reproduced

Table 2.2 *Germany: Unemployment Percentages*[22]

	%		%		%
1889	0·2	1898	0·4	1907	1·6
1890	2·3	1899	1·2	1908	2·9
1891	3·9	1900	2·0	1909	2·8
1892	6·3	1901	6·7	1910	1·9
1893	2·8	1902	2·9	1911	1·9
1894	3·1	1903	2·7	1912	2·0
1895	2·8	1904	2·1	1913	2·9
1896	0·6	1905	1·6		
1897	1·2	1906	1·2		

in Table 2.2. These percentages, which average out at 2·4, are much lower than the comparable British figures, which average out at 4·4, and confirm that the economy was much less vulnerable to fluctuations than were France, the USA or the UK.

Foreign trade helps to explain the vigour of the economy, but if this were the whole story the German economy would have fluctuated as widely as the British. Clearly this economy, like the American, was driven by powerful forces of internal transformation, stemming from the same fact that, unlike the British, it still had a large agricultural sector, and considerable potential for applying both new agricultural and new industrial technology. Once they begin, backward economies can grow faster than the pioneers.

It is difficult to be sure how much foreign trade helped, because German trade statistics before 1906 are a booby trap. Germany's production of manufactures grew at a steady 4·2 per cent per annum from 1883 to 1913. Exports of manufactures (finished and semi-finished) have a turning point after 1900, rising thereafter because of the improving terms of trade of the periphery as well as heavy capital export. The German rate of growth of manufactured exports was 7·1 per cent per annum after 1900. Before that it seems that exports grew about as rapidly as manufacturing. Hoffmann's figures are 3·1 per cent per annum from 1883 to 1890 and 4·5 per cent per annum from 1890 to 1900. The earlier figure is too low. The incorporation of Bremen and most of Hamburg into the customs union in 1889 reduced Germany's recorded exports (because Germany's exports to the Hanse Towns for domestic consumption exceeded the Hanse Towns' exports to the outside world). The adjustment needed to make growth from 1883 to 1890 the same as for 1890 to 1900 (i.e. 4·5 per cent per annum) would be to reduce the recorded exports of 1883 by 9 per cent. Alternatively the growth rate for 1883 to 1888, which is biased downwards by another customs change in 1884, was 4·1 per cent per annum. Either path leads to the same conclusion: production and exports of manufactures were growing at about the same rate between 1883 and 1900. This was not export-led growth.

Manufacturing was, however, helped by import substitution, in the sense that imports of manufactures grew less rapidly than manufacturing, in marked contrast with Britain. According to Hoffmann's tables the volume of imports of finished and semi-finished manufactures grew at 3·8 per cent per annum from 1883 to 1890, then at 3·2 per cent per annum to 1900, and then at 2·8 per cent per annum to 1913. The figure from the 1880s is too high because of the change in the customs union. To correct for incorporation of the Hanse Towns we would have to increase recorded imports for 1883, and so reduce the growth rate (Hanse imports from the outside world exceeded Hanse exports of domestic produce to the rest of Germany). This correction merely reinforces the point that Germany was import substituting throughout the period up to the First World War. The principal areas of import substitution in the 1880s were the textile industry (Hoffmann's index of textile manufactures grows from its peak at 1884 to that of 1889 at an annual rate of 5·6 per cent, and thereafter to the peak of 1907 at 2·0 per cent per annum), and the iron and steel industry which almost doubled its production between 1879 and 1889.

Having once got on to course in the second half of the 1880s the German economy moves rigorously forward, and ceases to contribute to our understanding of the pulsations of the engine of growth.

2.09 In the second half of the 1880s the USA and Germany were thus very prosperous; Britain and France were not. France, to which we now turn our attention, experienced a great depression in the 1880s, exceeding in length even that of the USA in the 1870s, as Chart 1.1 shows.

Chart 1.2 shows that the behaviour of construction contributed greatly to the gloom, but the trouble is also manifested in manufacturing and mining. The average rate of growth of this latter index was 1·8 per cent per annum from 1869 to 1910, but the average rate from 1882 to 1890 (the peak for the core as a whole) was only 0·7 per cent per annum. The series for horsepower of steam engines employed in industry grows by 5·8 per cent per annum from 1883 to 1913; between 1883 and 1890 it grows only by 4·0 per cent per annum. But the most horrifying statistic is that pig iron output was lower in 1890 than at its peak of 1883. Given such conditions it is not surprising that the urban population, which increased by 1·9 million between 1872 and 1881, and by 1·7 million between 1891 and 1901, increased only by 1·2 million between 1881 and 1891; or that the labour force in industry and commerce, which had increased by 860,000 in the seventies increased only by 260,000 in the eighties.[23]

The standard explanation of these long familiar facts is that the industrial depression was caused by a severe agricultural depression which was occurring at the same time – a double agricultural depression, due in part to disease in the vineyards, and in part to the collapse of wheat prices. But this explanation will not hold water.

In the first place the agricultural depression had been going on for a very long time, but had not prevented France from having her biggest ever industrial boom, which peaked in 1882. Neither was the collapse of wheat prices preventing Germany or the USA from enjoying remarkable industrial booms at that very time.

The *phylloxera* had first attacked the vineyards in the 1860s. It spread steadily, and reached its worst at the end of the 1880s. Average output of wine per year ran as follows (in 000 hectolitres):

1865/9	58.8	1885/9	26·2
1870/4	52·1	1890/4	35·3
1875/9	46·1	1895/9	36·3
1880/4	34·2	1900/4	55·0

The epidemic lasted thirty-five years, being ended ultimately by the importation of resistant American varieties.

The effect of this attack was to turn France temporarily from a net exporter to a net importer of wine. This would depress the industrial economy because the overseas suppliers whose wine the urban community now bought (Spain was the largest supplier) were less likely to spend the money on buying the products of French industry. What is at fault is not the logic but the quantities. The *phylloxera* had already done most of its damage by the time of the great boom of 1881–3, which it had not prevented. The import surplus of wine rose from the average of 1881/3 to the average of 1889/90 by only 30 million francs (from 106 to 136 million). Arguably the import surplus would have risen even more if the agricultural depression had not caused an industrial depression, so this is not decisive proof. But in any case these orders of magnitude are too small to be relevant, especially since the balance of trade as a whole improved so strongly at this time (Table 2.3). One cannot deny that the *phylloxera* was an inhibiting influence, but its role in this drama is small.

When we come to the cereal farmers, the argument is a little more complex. France was by now a net importer of wheat, so we have to separate the domestic effects and the balance of payments effects of the fall in prices.

Table 2.3 *France: Balance of Trade, 1882 and 1890 (m. francs)*[24]

	1882	*1890*	*Increase*
Manufactures			
Exports	1,946	2,107	
Imports	950	893	
Net	+996	+1,214	+218
Primary products			
Exports	1,628	1,646	
Imports	3,872	3,544	
Net	−2,244	−1,898	+346
Balance of Trade	−1,248	−684	+564

The argument about the domestic effect is conducted in Keynesian terms. If farm prices fall, the farmers have less money to spend, but the urban community has correspondingly more money to spend; if they spend it, the net effect on aggregate demand is zero. But will they spend it? The propensity of French farmers to save is usually presumed to be higher than that of French workers, so the transfer should cause an increase in spending. On the other hand, it is also presumed that windfall gains tend to be saved rather than spent. One must also distinguish between short- and long-run effects. Maybe the urban community will ultimately spend its gains, but if it delays, total spending falls in the meantime; profits fall, investment declines, and the vicious spiral is set in motion. What does all this add up to? One cannot rule out *a priori* the possibility that the fall in agricultural prices depressed the demand for manufactures to some extent, but, given the vigorous boom of France earlier in the decade, and the vigorous booms of the USA and Germany in this same second half of the decade, low agricultural prices are not enough to explain an industrial depression so intensive that the output of pig iron was lower in 1890 than in 1883.

The balance of trade argument is also complex. Since France was now a net importer of wheat, the fall in prices increased domestic purchasing power. As Table 2.3 shows, there was a marked improvement in the balance of trade. But the Keynesian question arises again. Foreign countries now had less money with which to buy French goods; would this hurt French exports by more than it increased domestic spending?

This focuses attention on exports of manufactures, shown here, at constant 1899 prices, in Table 2.4. One can calculate that the rate of growth of exports of manufactures was low between the peak years 1882 and 1890; it averaged 1·4 per cent per annum, compared with 2·3 per cent per annum between 1890 and 1899, and the figure of 3·3 per cent per annum calculated by Maizels[25] for 1899 to 1913. If the 'normal' rate of growth of manufacturing was 2·0 per cent per annum, growth of exports by only 1·4 per cent would certainly exercise a downward drag on output.

Was the low growth rate of exports due to low purchasing power abroad? This may have been an element in the situation, but further examination of Table 2.4 suggests a different explanation. The two trouble spots were leather goods and fabrics, the latter comprising mainly silks and woollens, since the French export of cotton manufactures was small. Exports other than these two groups were doing well; their average annual increase was 3·1 per cent from 1882 to 1890, and 4·0 per cent from 1890 to 1899.

Table 2.4 *France: Exports of Manufactures at 1899 Prices (m. francs)*[26]

	1882	*1890*	*1899*
Metals	16·6	50·1	111·3
Chemicals	40·0	42·1	83·8
Dyestuffs	23·3	20·7	21·7
Paints	9·1	8·7	11·6
Chemical products	42·1	53·0	58·4
Pottery	33·5	51·7	65·3
Yarns	37·2	44·5	78·3
Fabrics	695·3	702·0	732·1
Clothing	135·8	168·5	142·1
Paper, books	31·0	43·4	56·4
Leather goods	238·7	241·3	216·8
Jewellery	143·0	172·7	207·2
Arms	2·9	8.9	15·7
Furniture	24·9	38·7	32·8
Musical instruments	8·3	7·4	10·8
Esparto products	16·9	15·2	18·3
Building materials	19·0	24·9	27·1
Miscellaneous	224·9	279·3	520·4
Total	1,742·5	1,973·1	2,410·1
Quantity index	72·3	81·9	100·0
Current values	1,946·0	2,106·5	2,410·1
Price index	111·7	106·8	100·0

The truth seems therefore rather to be that France was caught by its heavy specialisation in these commodities for which world trade was expanding rather slowly. As it moved away from leather and silk and woollens to iron and steel and machinery, the growth rate of its exports of manufactures exceeded the growth rate of production and pulled the latter up.

French exports may also have been handicapped by one other factor, namely the differential behaviour of French wages over the previous decade. The data are uncertain, but following Phelps Brown, the situation seems to have been as follows. The superboom of 1873 brought about an extraordinary increase in prices, as well as in wages, in Britain, Germany, and the United States, and was in all these three countries succeeded by a sharp cut in wages. The French experience was different. Still dislocated by the war with Prussia, and its internal political repercussions, France had no boom in 1873. French wages had been rising before 1873, and continued to rise thereafter, with only minor declines in the mid-seventies. In fact a new French construction boom was gathering momentum in the second half of the seventies, just as our other three countries were experiencing their deepest stagnation (Chart 1.2). There was therefore no collapse of French wages. Whereas between 1873 and 1882 German wages fell by 14 per cent, British wages by 5 per cent and US wages by 7 per cent (in dollars; in gold there was an increase of 6 per cent), French wages between thc same dates increased by 18 per cent. However, since French wages had not boomed in 1873, it is better to compare 1882 with some earlier date such as the boom date (for Britain and France) of 1866. Between these dates French money wages had risen by 32 per cent, German by 30 per cent and British by 11 per cent.

Our target is to find the effect of these changes in wages on French competitiveness and this is difficult to assess. Money cost per unit of output is affected by productivity as well as by money wages, but since French industrial productivity at this time was almost certainly rising less rapidly than British or German productivity, we may safely assume that the gap between the costs of output widened even more than the gap between money wages. This is supported by the changes in the price indexes for exports of manufactures: between 1866 and 1882 the British price index fell by 34 per cent, and the French by 24 per cent; indexes stretching back to 1866 are not available for Germany or the USA.[27] But this still does not answer our question, since Britain and France were exporting different commodities.

If these data are relevant it would follow that French exports were handicapped in the 1880s because of the extent of the increase of her wage level during the preceding decade. It then also becomes relevant that the growth rate of French money wages is reduced after 1882. Whilst, as we have just seen, French wages were growing faster than German or British up to 1882, they grew more slowly than either up to 1899, as we shall see in Chapter 4. French money cost of labour per unit of output fell very sharply in comparison with German or British cost over these two decades; the continual acceleration of French exports of manufactures from the 1880s to 1913 is not just an accident. In sum, the war with Germany put French industry out of line with what was happening to wage costs elsewhere, and the later 1880s became a painful period of catching up.

But before this readjustment started France, for other reasons, experienced a superboom peaking in 1882. The forces which produced this boom and then destroyed it are probably more important to an understanding of the deep depression which followed than anything that happened in foreign trade. The key to these events is to be found in the vagaries of government expenditure. This great depression was a self-inflicted wound.

To understand this we must go back to the Franco-Prussian War of 1870. The speed of mobilisation of the German army, compared to that of their own, made a great impression on French minds. Much of this difference was attributed to an insufficient railway network. Accordingly railway building was revived as soon as a new government came into office, and the length of track in operation increased from 15,630 kilometres in 1871 to 20,030 kilometres in 1876.

In December 1877 a new government was formed which included Charles de Freycinet as Minister of Public Works. Freycinet was an engineer, devoted to the proposition that one of the ways to develop the country was to improve its transportation system – not merely railways, but roads, rivers, canals, ports and harbours. He piloted through Parliament and gave his name to a transportation plan, designed to last ten years – much like what we would now call a 'Ten Year Development Plan', except that it was confined to the transportation sector.

Under the Freycinet Plan the state was to build an extra 16,000 kilometres of railways, at a cost of roughly 3,000 million francs. The other means of transport would absorb another 1,000 million francs, bringing the total cost of the Plan to about 4,000 million francs over ten years. The whole expenditure was to be financed by domestic borrowing.

The Freycinet Plan was received enthusiastically in the country. Parliament's main criticism, as is usual in these cases, was that the Plan was too modest. All the municipalities and other local authorities who felt themselves neglected manoeuvred to get their road or harbour or branch line added to the Plan.

The Plan got off to a good start, and is the main explanation of the super-boom which one can see in the French construction index in Chart 1.2. However, by 1881 it was running into financial difficulties, owing allegedly to the unwillingness of the market to absorb so much government stock. The first loan, of 450 million francs of redeemable 3 per cent stock, was raised in January 1878 without difficulty at 87. But the price of the second loan, of 1,000 million francs of the same in March 1881, was down to 83, although the general level of stock exchange prices was up. By the end of 1881 the government had issued a good deal of floating or short-term debt which it was anxious to extinguish by issuing a new long-term loan, but the prospects for such a loan seemed unfavourable.

The case against the Freycinet Plan was now championed by a powerful enemy, Léon Say, grandson of the famous Jean-Baptiste Say of Say's Law, and himself one of the leading economists of the day. Léon Say was Minister of Finance from 1875 to 1879, and again for a crucial six months in 1882. His general philosophy favoured keeping government expenditure low and financing its capital expenditure out of taxes and not by borrowing. He had gone along with the Freycinet Plan in 1878, when there was still much slack in the economy. Now at the end of 1881, out of office, he attacked the Plan vigorously in an article in the *Journal des Economistes.*[28] He explained that he had accepted a plan of 4,000 million francs because 400 million a year was within the country's savings capacity; indeed it was not very much more than the private railway companies (for whom the new expenditure would substitute) had already been investing. But conditions had changed. The Plan had grown to an inflated size; its cost had already reached 6,000 million, and seemed to be going still higher. Much of it was unproductive in his opinion; one ought to distinguish clearly between profitable and unprofitable improvements in transport. The financial burden could not be borne. The government's surplus on current account had shrunk since 1878, since Parliament had both reduced taxes and increased recurrent expenditure. Above all, the market was showing its unwillingness to digest so much government stock. The supply of saving was limited, and government could use so much only at the expense of reducing the amount left for private investment in productive enterprise.

Say returned to the Ministry of Finance immediately after publishing this article, and devoted the next few months to ensuring that government expenditure on the Plan would be cut drastically. In this he succeeded, even though the final vote – the issue was the budget for 1883 – was not taken until December 1882, five months after he had left office.

The Freycinet Plan was not without powerful friends; Freycinet himself was Prime Minister in the Cabinet in which Léon Say was the Finance Minister. What really persuaded Parliament was the onset of the Juglar crisis of 1882, commencing with the failure of the Union Générale bank in January of that year. This brought the whole stock exchange down, including redeemable 3 per cents, which by December 1882 were at 80.

Say advised that the state should abandon railway building almost completely, leaving it to the railway companies to find the money to build the system themselves, with the government merely guaranteeing their borrowings. This system was adopted in a series of agreements made with the railways in 1883.

The consequence of this episode was that French central government expenditure rose sharply between 1877 and 1883, and then contracted equally swiftly over the next few years. Table 2.5 shows that the net deficit rose from 294 million francs in 1877 to 801 million francs in 1882, and was back down to 210 million francs in 1890. Not all the increase was due to the Freycinet Plan; the 'extraordinary budget' of 1882 included 190 million francs for military expenditures in Indochina. Anyway the reduction of government expenditure was equal to about 2 per cent of the national income of France in 1890, and when allowance is made for the multiplier, such a large reduction in government expenditure is probably the major explanation of the depressed conditions of the second half of the 1880s.

To some extent the decline of government investment in railways was offset by additional investment by the companies, but not wholly so.

Table 2.5 *France: Central Government Expenditure (m. francs)*[29]

	Ordinary	*Extra*	*Deficit*
1877	2,764	261	294
1882	3,106	674	801
1890	3,122	205	291

Annual increase in railway mileage dropped from 1,170 km over 1877–84 to 760 km over 1884–90, with a low point of 370 km in 1889–90. The iron and steel industry was hit very hard. Imports (including rails) fell from 318 thousand tons in 1883 to 42 thousand tons in 1890, and exports rose from 10 thousand to 279 thousand tons between the same dates. Nevertheless, the total production of iron fell from 2,069 to 1,962 thousand tons, indicating a net reduction of domestic use (without allowing for stock changes) of about 650,000 tons. This is evidence of a drastic reduction in domestic investment. In fact, the rest of the economy held up quite well. Manufacturing and mining, excluding metals and metal working, declined by 5 per cent between the peak of 1882 and the trough of 1886, and then recovered by the peak of 1892 to 27 per cent above 1882. But metals and metal working declined 21 per cent to 1886, and was up in 1892 to only 2 per cent above the preceding peak. There is no doubt that the abrupt cut in construction was the major cause of this depression.

The story of the Freycinet Plan is worth narrating in detail because it illustrates so well the changes between nineteenth-century economic thought and that of our own times. Which government today would cut its expenditures because 3 per cent money was costing 80, or cut its expenditures because a financial crisis had heralded the onset of Juglar recession? Unfortunately, the story also illustrates how easy it is for a monetary ideologue to inflict misery upon millions of his fellow-countrymen, by following the light of simple moral codes.

2.10 The British great depression of 1883 shows up clearly in Chart 1.1. Industrial output fell by 10 per cent over three years, the greatest decline over these forty years. The wind was so cold that a Royal Commission was appointed to discover the causes of the depression. Needless to say, it did not!

The preceding boom had not been outstanding. It had been relatively short, since only the three years 1881 to 1883 were near capacity, and prices had not effected a full recovery from the disaster of the seventies. Moreover the peak, while high in relation to what would follow, was low in relation to the past. Industrial production had grown by 2·6 per cent per annum between the peaks of 1853 and 1873. The figure for 1873 to 1883 was down to 2·25 per cent per annum. This would be maintained to the peak of 1899, after which the rate would fall again, to 1·6 per cent up to the peak of 1913. Even by 1883 deceleration of the economy had already begun.

The second half of the eighties would be especially depressed. The growth rate between the peaks of 1883 and 1889 dropped to 1·7 per cent per annum. One can see how widespread this depression was by comparing the growth rates for each group of industries from the peak of 1883 to 1889, where they are down in every case except textiles, and from 1889 to 1899 where they revive again in every case except metals.[30]

	1873–83	*1883–9*	*1889–99*
Mining	2·5	1·3	1·9
Textiles	1·1	1·3	1·4
Metals	4·0	3·1	2·0
Food	1·0	0·8	2·0
Science	5·3	4·6	4·7
Other	1·1	0·9	3·9
Construction	2·5	−0·3	4·7
Total	2·3	1·7	2·6

What caused this slump? According to Brinley Thomas it is the counterpart of prosperity in the regions to which the British were emigrating or sending their capital, especially the United States, but also to some extent Australia and Argentina.

The facts about migration and export of capital are not in dispute. These phenomena are very marked by the Kuznets cycle, associated with alternating decades of prosperity in the United States. Here are the figures of British emigration and of the export of capital, on an average annual basis.[31]

	Migration (000)	*Export of capital (£m.)*
1870/4	206	73
1875/9	124	28
1880/4	262	56
1885/9	251	80
1890/4	202	64

The point at issue is whether resources went abroad in the eighties because they could not find employment at home, or whether the home market was depressed because of the emigration of labour and capital. The answer depends on whether entrepreneurs who wished to invest in British industry in the second half of the eighties were or were not experiencing shortages of capital or labour.

The answer seems clear in relation to capital. Nobody complained in Britain at this time of any shortage of investment funds. Manufacturing industry anyway largely financed itself, or at any rate did not depend on the sorts of savings which went into purchasing foreign bonds. But the heart of the matter lies in the financing of the building industry, since the very low level of construction was the biggest element in the slump. Here the last word has been said by Professor Habakkuk:

> This was a decade of low interest rates – consols were converted from 3 per cent to 2¾ per cent in 1888 – and funds were pushed abroad rather than pulled. The experience of the building societies does not suggest shortage of funds: at times during the eighties the directors of the Abbey Road Society were compelled to suspend the issue of shares because of the superabundance of money seeking investment.[32]

As for a shortage of labour, a preliminary test would be the unemployment rate, which should fall very low in 1889, but was instead at its now standard level for peaks: 2·1 per cent in 1889, compared with 0·9 in 1872, 2·3 in 1882 and 2·0 in 1899. If one averages with the years before and after the peak, then 1889 does slightly worse than its predecessors, since the average rates then appear as 1·2 in 1871/3, 2·8 in 1881/3, and 2·9 in 1888/90. This shows no sign of shortage of labour.

It is easy to exaggerate the effects of emigration on the size of the labour force. The increase in emigration (which is what matters for comparison) was not all that large; emigration was actually smaller in the second half of the eighties than in the first half, with its not negligible boom. And the difference between the annual emigration rates of 1885/9 and 1870/4, the time of the superboom, would only be 0·13 per cent of the population of 1885.

The labour force was growing at different rates in England and Wales, Scotland, and Ireland. The decennial rates of increase of the population aged 15 and over was as follows:

	England and Wales	*Scotland*	*Ireland*	*Great Britain*	*UK*
1861–71	12·3	8·6	−10·3	11·9	7·3
1871–81	13·8	11·4	−3·9	13·5	10·4
1881–91	14·1	9·5	−5·4	13·5	10·6

Ireland can be left out of the account at this point, since very little industrialisation was occurring there. The figures for Scotland are slightly suspect. Taking them as they are, they show the labour force decelerating in the eighties, although whether this was because of emigration or of decelerating natural increase we cannot say – just as we also cannot say whether emigration was due to a shortage of jobs or created a shortage of workers.

The most important figures are those for England and Wales, whose adult population exceeded that of Scotland in the ratio of seven to one. Here the picture is quite clear: emigration cannot have created a shortage of labour by comparison with the seventies since, despite emigration, the labour force was growing faster than ever in the eighties. The birth rate had already started to fall, so the total population was decelerating, but the adult population was still accelerating because of rising rates of natural increase some decades earlier. So the adult population grew faster in the eighties than in the seventies, in England and Wales, and taking Great Britain as a whole was at least growing equally fast. The proposition that emigration created a shortage of labour in the 1880s cannot stand.

Two other facts confirm this picture. If the labour force was growing, but not being offered employment in the factories, it would remain in the villages, and this would show up in a decline in the rate of growth of urbanisation. This is just what the figures show in Table 2.6. The slowdown

Table 2.6 *England and Wales: Percentage Annual Increase in Population*[33]

	Urban	*Rural*
1871–81	2·4	−0·4
1881–91	1·7	−0·3
1891–1901	1·8	−0·9
1901–11	1·2	+0·6

in the growth of urban areas between 1881 and 1891 is paralleled by a slowdown in the rate of exodus from rural areas, indicating that more people would have moved into the towns if the towns had been offering work. The table also offers a preview of a similar crisis between 1901 and 1911, when the growth rate of industrial production again slumped. On that occasion the rural population actually increased.

Now if the adult population was increasing normally, while housebuilding was depressed, this would show in the number of persons per house. These figures are given in Table 2.7. The first column is the number of persons aged 15 and over divided by the number of houses, while the numerator for the second column takes account of the changing proportion of children.

Table 2.7 *England and Wales: Number of Adult Persons per House*[34]

	Adults	*Adult equivalents*
1851	3·37	4·30
1861	3·29	4·20
1871	3·21	4·12
1881	3·16	4·07
1891	3·23	4·11
1901	3·28	4·06
1911	3·31	4·05

The first column of the table shows that the number of adult persons per house, which had been falling steadily, suddenly rose in the 1880s. However, that column is complicated by the fact that the proportion of children was falling sharply. When adjustment is made for this, housing improves in every decade except the 1880s.

The definition of houses was changed in 1901, so the figures for 1901 and 1911 are not strictly comparable with the earlier ones (houses used partly as shops were excluded). If one continues the trend of the second column, the number of adult equivalents per house in 1891 should not have exceeded 4·03, and this would mean that there was a shortage of nearly 2 per cent of houses. The number of houses built in one year averaged about 1·3 per cent of the stock. If one defines a boom as a period when output exceeds the average by 20 per cent, a 2 per cent shortage could carry a boom for eight years (by building 1·56 per cent of the stock in each year); and even a one per cent shortage could support a four-year boom.

Clearly, therefore, the country was ready for another housing boom in the 1880s, to follow the one that had ended in 1876. A new housing boom starting say in 1885 would have made sense, instead of which the new boom did not start for another ten years. Emigration cannot explain this since the population to be housed was there in Britain, not the United States. It was bottled up in the rural areas waiting for employment opportunities to open up in the towns.

Our contention therefore is that construction was at a low ebb because manufacturing was depressed, as opposed to the alternative theory that manufacturing was depressed because construction was low, following the migration overseas of the necessary resources of capital and persons.

The key to what was happening to manufacturing is in the unemployment statistics. In 1886, the worst year, unemployment averaged 10·2 per cent. Leading the list were the engineering, metal and shipbuilding unions, with 13·5 per cent unemployment. Following this cue, we get the following figures for pig iron, in million tons:

	Production	*Exports*	*Imports*	*Home use*
1882	8·6	4·4	0·2	4·4
1886	7·0	3·4	0·2	3·8

Exports have fallen by 1·0 million tons, and home use by 0·6 million tons. The fall in exports turns out to be mainly to other core partners: USA 0·40, Germany 0·17, France 0·15 million tons.

What we are witnessing is a turning point in British fortunes. Exports of iron and steel products reached a peak in 1882, and never regained this volume until 1906, some twenty-four years later. Up until 1882 Britain had supplied the rest of the core with a significant part of its requirements of iron and steel products, especially rails, but iron and steel production took off in Germany and the USA (but not France) in the 1880s, and British production was soon outdistanced. First these countries would wrest their own markets from the British; then they would wrest their neighbours' markets, Germany in Europe and the USA in Latin America; and finally in the decade before the war Germany, accompanied by Belgium, would defeat the British iron and steel industry on its home ground, and Britain would become the largest importer of iron and steel products in the world.

This decade also revealed another similar portent: the British export of cotton yarn reached a peak in 1884 (271 million lb) which it never regained. Cotton yarn had been the spearhead of the industrial revolution, since the new machines did even more for spinning than for weaving. So British yarn had reached into every corner of the world. Soon all the core countries were spinning yarn, and by 1870 their yarn imports from Britain were not large. But the periphery was also gaining strength, and from 1884 British exports of cotton yarn declined. India first regained her own market in the coarse counts, then set out to capture other British markets in the Far East. Meanwhile the British market for cotton fabrics continued to expand.

Table 2.8 *UK: Trade in Manufactures, at Constant Prices (£m.)*[35]

	Domestic exports	*Net imports*	*Net exports*
1882	229	44	185
1889	261	59	202
Growth rate per annum	1·9	4·2	1·3

The significant figure in Table 2.8 is the growth rate of net exports, which was at the low level of 1·3 per cent per annum. Whether the production of manufactures will grow at the same rate as domestic consumption depends on what is happening to exports minus imports. If net exports are growing more rapidly than domestic consumption the growth rate of production is raised; while a low rate of growth of net exports reduces the growth rate of production below that of domestic consumption.

The growth of UK production of manufactures was inhibited both by the high growth rate of imports and by the low growth rate of exports. UK net imports of manufactures (i.e. imports minus re-exports) had been growing rapidly for some time; having risen by 4·0 per cent per annum between 1873 and 1882, they now rose at 4·2 per cent per annum to 1889, and would rise again to 5·2 per cent in the 1890s to 1899, before falling back between 1899 and 1913 to the more appropriate level of 2·4 per cent per annum. The growth rate of exports of manufactures is more complicated; it is raised by capital export and reduced by improved terms of trade (which reduce the purchasing power of overseas buyers). It ran at 3·7 per cent from 1853 to 1872, at 2·2 per cent from 1872 to 1882, at 1·9 per cent from 1882 to 1889 (depressed by improved terms of trade) and at 0·4 per cent between 1889 and 1899 (further depressed by low capital export). Then the terms of trade turned against Britain, and capital exports boomed, so between 1899 and 1913 exports of manufactures rose sharply at 2·7 per cent per annum.

This steady strangling of the volume of exports of manufactures over the last quarter of the nineteenth century is of course why the whole of this period felt like one long great depression to an economy which had been propelled by exports over the preceding fifty years. Between 1889 and 1899 the growth rate of net exports would actually be negative, both in current and in constant prices, since the increase in imports would exceed the increase in exports in absolute value.

The low level of British exports was not due entirely to import substitution among her customers, or to the expansion of German exports, which was not negligible in the 1880s. World trade in manufactures itself decelerated sharply because of the terms of trade. The growth rate of the volume of this trade between 1882 and 1899 was only 2·5 per cent per annum, whereas from 1899 to 1913 it was up to 4·7 per cent per annum.[36] This wide swing is not mirrored in the trade in primary products whose volume grew over these two periods at constant rates (see Chart 7.1). The low growth rate of world trade in the downswing was not within the control of British manufacturers, and must be borne in mind in assessing their performance. All the same growth at only 1·0 per cent per annum when world trade in manufactures is growing by 2·5 per cent per annum is no cause for satisfaction.

The competition for restricted trade depressed the price level, and rendered the economy unprofitable. As we saw when studying the case of France, world prices fell very sharply after 1873, and so also did wages. It is clear that in the British case prices fell by more than costs. We can approach this subject by comparing what happened to money national income per occupied person with what happened to the average money wage in manufacturing.[37]

	National income (£m.)	*Occupied persons (m.)*	*Income per head (£)*	*Money wage (£)*	*Ratio of wage*
1873	82·9	14·09	82·9	49·7	0·60
1883	72·7	15·42	72·7	48·2	0·67
1889	80·4	16·42	80·4	50·3	0·63
1899	91·7	18·30	91·7	55·6	0·61
1913	107·1	20·84	107·1	63·0	0·59

Even if all these figures were absolutely correct they would not prove that the profitability of manufacturing had declined, since income per occupied person and output per person occupied in manufacturing are not the same, and since the relative cost of capital may also have changed. But the difference between 1873 and the 1880s is too large to be brushed aside. We can be sure that the profitability of the economy had declined in the 1880s, and that this was the main reason for the rather low domestic investment of that decade.

Some contemporaries were aware that the low profitability of the economy stemmed from the feeble growth of exports of manufactures, which had narrowed the gap between prices and wages, and they reported accordingly to the Royal Commission on the Depression in Trade and Industry. But what excited that Commission was the evidence of others that the depression was caused by the decline in the rate of production of gold, and that this was why prices were falling.

We shall postpone to our next chapter the question whether it was a shortage of gold that was causing prices to fall. That falling prices as such caused depression was arguable in the seventies, when all the core countries were depressed, more or less; it was not arguable in the eighties when Germany and the USA were booming. As we have just seen, favourable terms of trade were one element in depressing British manufacturing, resulting in depressed exports, but a general fall in prices, due to a shortage of gold, would not necessarily have altered the terms of trade.

The shortage of gold was more immediately relevant in another area, namely the struggle of the Bank of England to maintain an adequate gold reserve. We have seen that this may have been an element in restraining British recovery in the second half of the seventies; Hawtrey sees the same phenomenon in the second half of the eighties, when the Bank was continually shuffling Bank Rate up and down. This was a time of high capital export combined with low commodity exports (low both in volume and in price), and such times drain the balance of payments, especially as the USA was in effect using part of its borrowing to increase its gold reserve. The British were already developing that propensity to lend more than their balance of payments justified, which would manifest itself again in the ten years before the First World War,[38] in the second half of the 1920s, and again after the Second World War.

Professor Viner has suggested that the Bank was trying to work with too small a gold reserve.[39] From the 1880s onwards the British balance of payments usually deteriorated in a Juglar upswing (because prices of food and raw materials rose faster than prices of manufactures) and improved in the downswing. Therefore with each upward movement there was pressure on the gold stock, and the Bank tended to be forced into restrictive action. With a larger average stock of gold, the Bank could have more or less ignored the cyclical movements. Contemporaries pointed this out, and concluded that the Bank's main reason for holding so little gold was to protect its income by holding interest-bearing securities instead. The modern solution for central banks which do not wish to hold gold is to hold foreign exchange instead, in the form of balances at other central banks or short-term securities. But this was beneath the dignity of the Bank of England, which on the contrary expected British banks to be – as they soon became – depositories for foreigners' sterling balances. The income problem could also have been eased by a law requiring British commercial banks to keep balances in the Bank of England, thus providing the Bank with funds to reinvest. No law was passed, but from 1900 onwards the commercial banks were doing this of their own accord. The Bank's acute anxiety over its gold reserve eased in the nineties, returning only during a slight flurry in the boom of 1906–7. The world's gold supply accelerated, and foreigners increasingly left their balances in London instead of demanding gold. This new element of instability would not reveal its dangers until the crisis of 1929–31 and the devastation then caused by the movement of 'hot money' from one financial centre to another.

One cannot dismiss the possibility that British economic activity may have been inhibited between 1875 and 1880, and again between 1885 and 1890, by the Bank of England's constant juggling with Bank Rate. But this can hardly have been a major factor. Putting Bank Rate up from 2 to 4 per cent for six months had little effect on the cost of manufacturing or mining, and can hardly have affected decisions on how much to invest in the iron industry, which was then the most retarded. The raising of Bank Rate would postpone for a few months the issuing of foreign securities in London, to the embarrassment of countries at the periphery, and might therefore diminish industrial sales for some months, but the net effect on the volume of British industrial investment must have been small. It is clear that the British problems were more fundamental than a Kondratiev downswing in prices – they would be still worse when prices turned upward – or a shortage of gold in the Bank of England which ended in the 1890s. We shall come back to them in a later chapter.

THE NINETIES

2.11 For the reasons we have just examined, namely the weaknesses of France and Britain, the nineties opened badly. Our index for the core as a whole (Chart 2.1) gives 1890 as a prosperous year, but conditions were mixed. France was about to have two booming years, till 1892. The other three countries were already weakening. The USA would hold out until 1892, but Britain and Germany would turn down in 1891.

Similar confusion would reveal itself at the end of the decade. All four would experience some sort of pause in 1900. But whereas in Britain and France this would consist of a major setback from the boom of 1899, in Germany and the USA the setback would only be minor. Germany would indeed have had the most remarkable boom of all, not in the height of its peak – there was no peak – but in the long period of operation at full capacity, lasting five years, from 1895. In contrast the United States would still be in a long depression, marked by heavy unemployment.

The interest in this decade centres on the United States, which experienced prolonged depression, and we shall concentrate on this country.

2.12 In the United States this was a classic Kuznets great depression, like that of 1873. Underlying it was a big construction boom, which peaked in 1887 and then ran all the way down to 1898 (Chart 1.2). Railway investment peaked in 1887, immigration in 1888 and housing in 1889, this being the normal sequence.[40] That manufacturing continued to grow fairly vigorously until 1892 is a tribute to the momentum of industrial investment. The graph of manufacturing and mining is shown separately in Chart 2.1.

When the collapse came, it brought all the usual phenomena. There was panic on the stock exchange, six hundred banks collapsed, and scores of railway companies folded. Rumour again put the number of unemployed at 3 million, which was still implausible for a country with a factory population of only 4·4 million.[41]

As usual, too, contemporaries attributed the catastrophe entirely to financial factors, which, it so happens, were particularly interesting at this time when the country's dependence on gold would go through a crisis not again to be repeated until the 1960s.

This story goes back to the decision to cease coining silver in 1873, and to return to the gold standard in 1879. The general rejection of silver by so many countries had led to a fall in its price, at the expense of silver producers in the USA. Their demand for a return to bimetallism was joined by the farmers, who hoped for general reflation to stem the continual downward trend of agricultural prices. Bimetallism became the issue of the day.

A small amount of silver coinage was resumed in 1878, but without much effect on the price of silver. In 1890 Congress therefore passed the Sherman Silver Purchase Act, requiring the Treasury to buy 4·5 million ounces of silver every month. The price was not fixed, and after rising briefly, it continued to fall. Here the story becomes complex. The Treasury lost nearly half its stock of gold in 1890, and this created a minor panic. Opponents of the Silver Purchase Act attributed the loss to the fear that the Act was only the thin edge of a wedge, to be followed by the country leaving the gold standard altogether. This fear presumably caused a number of Americans and foreigners to transfer their assets into gold.

To understand the role of the foreigners one must bear in mind the fact that the United States had been running an adverse balance of payments throughout the eighties, and indeed for most of the nineteenth century up to this point. In 1889 British foreign lenders began to tighten their rein not because of anything happening in the United States, but because news from Australia and Argentina indicated that these two countries were overcommitted, and might be unable to meet their financial commitments. Foreign lending is highly subject to scares, and it may well be that the news of the Silver Purchase Act coming from America in 1890 also reduced confidence in American securities. At any rate it was said that some British owners of American railway securities registered in New York were selling them, and taking their money away in gold. Later in the year Argentina did default, nearly bringing down with it the famous London house of Baring Brothers. This firm was rescued by the Bank of England, to prevent a general financial panic, but the occasion further reduced London's appetite for foreign lending. According to Matthew Simon, money called for North America declined 65 per cent between 1890 and 1891.[42]

Given British unwillingness to lend, the adverse balance of payments set up a drain on gold which would have occurred with or without purchases of silver. The Silver Purchase Act was repealed in 1893, but the drain of gold continued until 1896. The issue whether to stay with gold inflamed US politics throughout this period. The gold party won the election of 1892 and again that of 1896. The political historians tell us that the election of 1896 settled the question finally, and that this is why the drain of gold then stopped, but gold drains are not stopped by ballot boxes.

Lying behind the gold controversy was the deficit in the balance of payments. The average annual net balance ran as follows:[43]

	$m.		$m.
1886/90	−209	1901/5	+146
1891/5	−78	1906/10	−47
1896/1900	+161		

The pattern is one of net borrowing in prosperous times, with net lending or repayments during recessions.

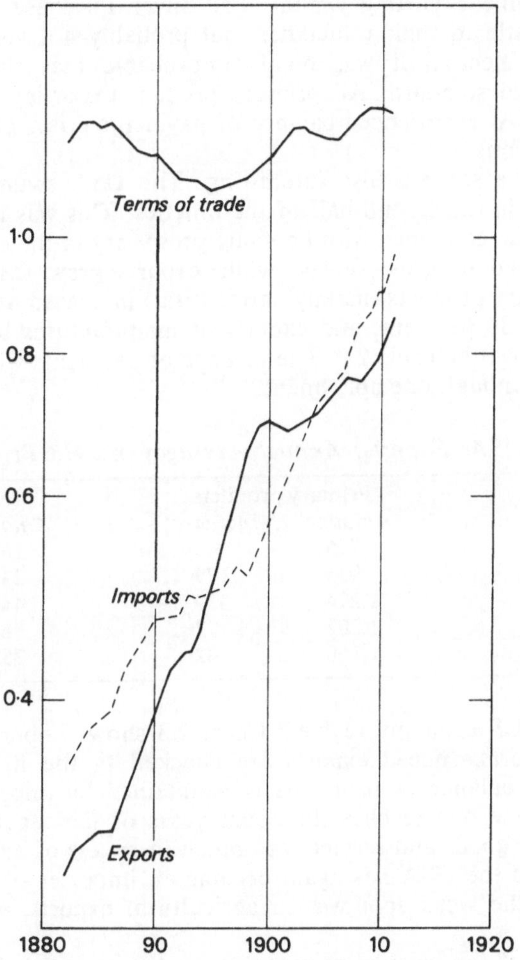

Chart 2.3 US Trade

It is interesting to see how this worked in the nineties, in relation to the behaviour of imports and exports. Chart 2.3 shows five-year moving averages of imports and exports, at constant 1913 prices, and also the terms of trade (export divided by import prices).[44] Imports and exports were both rising rapidly in the 1880s, but the import of goods and services was relatively large; and this, coupled with the deterioration of the terms of trade in the second half, is reflected in the large capital import of 1886–90.

In the first half of the nineties recession checked the rate of growth of imports, but the terms of trade were even worse, and capital inflow also diminished, so the country was forced to export gold; the average annual gold outflow[45] rose from $17m. over 1886/90 to $84m. over the six years 1891/6, after which came a small inflow, averaging $24m. to 1900. Exports continued their rapid growth. Given the behaviour of the terms of trade, the USA could have escaped exporting gold only if the British had been willing to continue exporting capital. The Silver Purchase Act may have contributed a little to their reluctance, but probably not very much, since after the 1892 election it was highly improbable that the USA would abandon the gold standard. All primary product exporting countries, and not only the USA, experienced balance of payments crises on the outbreak of major recessions.

The end of the story is also interesting. The USA swung into a large positive balance in the second half of the nineties. This was the outcome of recession at home, combined with booming prosperity in the other countries. Imports continued to grow slowly, while exports grew faster than ever; exports of primary products (mainly agricultural) increased over the average of five years by 36 per cent, and exports of manufactures by 84 per cent. The data are shown in Table 2.9. The balance of payments will always come right if there is enough unemployment!

Table 2.9 *USA: Exports; Annual Averages in 1913 Prices ($m.)*[46]

	Primary products		Manufactures	
	Amount	*Increase*	*Amount*	*Increase*
1886/90	756		167	
1891/5	935	179	239	72
1896/1900	1,274	339	440	201
1901/5	1,202	−72	568	128
1906/10	1,160	−42	752	184

After 1900 the US economy revived. Chart 2.3 shows imports again rising faster than exports. Indeed exports are checked in the first half of the decade, but the balance of payments is maintained by improved terms of trade. By the time one reaches the boom years of the second half of the 1900s imports of goods and services are much in excess of exports of goods and services, and the USA has again become an importer of capital. Table 2.9 shows that the weak spot was in agricultural exports, which declined after 1900.

The recovery of the balance of payments in the second half of the 1890s resulted from the prolongation of depression. This Kuznets great depression lasted a very long time, like that of 1929. After the great depression of 1872 manufacturing was back on its capacity line in ten years, in 1882; but after peaking in 1892 it took fourteen years to reach its next capacity peak in 1906. This is not simply a statistical artefact. Lebergott's estimates of the percentage of the labour force unemployed probably overestimates the unemployment of the first few years, having regard to the relative smallness of industrial numbers at this time, but they do show up the long delay in recovery:[47]

1892	3·0	1897	14·5	1902	3·7
1893	11·7	1898	12·4	1903	3·9
1894	18·4	1899	6·5	1904	5·4
1895	13·7	1900	5·0	1905	4·3
1896	14·4	1901	4·0	1906	1·7

The contrast with 1872 is fascinating. As we have pointed out earlier, that was a very deep slump, deeper than those of 1892 or 1906. But once recovery started, it proceeded rapidly. The growth rate of manufacturing and mining from the trough of 1876 to the peak of 1882 was 10·1 per cent per annum, whereas that from the trough of 1896 to the peak of 1906 was only 7·9 per cent per annum.

The time taken to begin recovery was not unduly long. The widespread American belief of the 1970s that depressions normally last only eighteen months is a myth fostered by the misconception that industry is typified by a Kitchin reference cycle. A three- to four-year turnabout is common for a Kuznets depression, although even a one-year turnaround is possible (UK, 1907); and the USA would have had a two-year turnaround in 1892 if the upturn of 1895 had not aborted.

Because of the relatively slow speed after the turnaround of 1896, US manufacturing did not regain its capacity line until 1906, by which time it was ready to swing back again into depression. This contrasts with the 1880s, where all twelve years from 1881 to 1892 are virtually up to capacity except for three (1884 to 1886). One should, however, note that growing along a capacity ceiling was not frequent in those days. The UK and France never experienced it during our period. Germany experienced it only from 1895 to 1899, and the United States only from 1887 to 1892, although the USA might have achieved it again from 1903 to 1906 but for a mini-recession in 1904. To grow along the ceiling has become more frequent since the Second World War, but it is a newly acquired accomplishment.

The slow US pace from 1896 was set by construction. Railway investment turned up in 1897, followed in the usual sequence by immigration and then residential building, but did not peak until 1906 (immigration 1907, housing 1909). We also know why railway investment was slow to revive: it was unprofitable. The Interstate Commerce Commission was publishing statistics of net operating revenues per mile of track (receipts less expenses) which are reproduced in Table 2.10.

Since the 1892 revenues of existing lines were not regained until 1899, it is not surprising that there was no rush to build more track until after the turn of the century. We do not imply that more would have been

Table 2.10 *USA: Railway Operating Profits per Mile ($)*[48]

1889	2,087	1896	2,072	1903	3,133
1890	2,300	1897	2,016	1904	2,998
1891	2,262	1898	2,325	1905	3,189
1892	2,404	1899	2,435	1906	3,584
1893	2,314	1900	2,729	1907	3,696
1894	1,946	1901	2,854		
1895	1,967	1902	3,048		

invested if the figures had not been published, although this is not ruled out.

Why would the great depression of 1872 be deep but 'short', while that of 1892 was 'shallow' but long? The mini-recession of 1896 could be part of the answer. Contemporaries attributed this to the fear of war with Britain over the Venezuelan boundary dispute, with which the year began, and to uncertainty whether the country would remain on the gold standard which climaxed in the Presidential election of that year; this was the year of William Jennings Bryan's declaration that the country should never again be 'crucified on a cross of gold'. But this cannot be the whole explanation of such a long recovery period.

Was the trouble due to monetary factors? We have seen that there was a large and continual drain of gold, lasting until 1896. This drain was ended by the recession, which restrained imports and expelled exports. Did causation also run the other way? Was the depression prolonged by the export of gold? The relationship between money and economic activity is difficult to pin down, and we reserve fuller discussion of this topic until our next chapter. There we will see, in Chart 3.6, that the US supply of money did indeed cease to grow between 1892 and 1897. The trouble lies in determining whether this happened because the demand for money was checked by the recession, or because the supply of money was checked by the outflow of gold. The discussion of that chapter suggests that the links between the supply of money and the supply of gold were loose – at any rate in the short run – since there was eight times as much money as there was gold, and (more importantly) the ratio between the two varied widely. Friedman and Schwartz do attribute the depth of the depression to the decision to remain on gold:

> It should perhaps be noted explicitly that we do not intend to suggest that the alternative involving abandonment of the gold standard was economically undesirable. On the contrary, our own view is that it might well have been highly preferable to the generally depressed conditions of the 1890s. We rule it out only because, as it turned out, it was politically unacceptable.[49]

They may be right. Countries which lived by exporting raw materials had a hard time maintaining fixed exchange rates through the cycle, since this subjected them to alternating periods of inflation and deflation.

However, the deflation was over by 1894, or at the latest by 1896, whereas the US economy continued to grow slowly until 1900, while others were booming.

Then was the USA held back by the fact that Britain, France and Germany were all booming at this time, a coincidence which does not occur at any other time in our period of forty years? This is a possible extension of Brinley Thomas's thesis that there was an 'Atlantic economy', although he himself has not stressed it. It is one thing to suggest that the British economy is depressed at times when its capital and labour are emigrating to the United States; but it is another to suggest that US growth is held up by prosperity in Western Europe. There was no shortage of labour, since the US labour force was under-employed in the second half of the nineties. And as for capital, US dependence on Europe was slight; the capital inflow of 1886/90 was only 1·8 per cent of gross national product, and that of 1906/10 was only 0·2 per cent. The proposition that the USA was depressed by prosperity elsewhere is not plausible.

Looking at home, we see that the main answer is that the recovery from 1894 was punctuated by three reverses, in 1895–6, in 1899–1900 and in 1903–4, before the final achievement of capacity in 1906. The intervening growth rates were as high as ever: 18 per cent in 1895, 10·1 per cent per annum from 1896 to 1899 and 8·9 per cent per annum from 1900 to 1903. But the economy was now more volatile than it had been in the preceding long Kuznets upswing from 1876 to 1892. We said in Chapter 1 that Kitchin cycles, though prominent in financial data, hardly showed in the data of industrial production. One should perhaps qualify this statement by distinguishing between before and after 1892, and by noting that though they hardly show – in the sense that production of manufactures does not fall (1899) or falls very little and briefly (1904) – they do add four or five years to the time required for attaining the full Kuznets peak.

If we had to explain entirely in domestic terms the dance of American manufacturing up the long upswing, we would attribute it to the increased volatility of construction, which can be seen in Chart 2.1. Why was construction more volatile? The suggestion is hazarded that, with the disappearance of the agricultural frontier, railway investment had lost the enthusiastic momentum of its earlier days. In the 1870s railway investment could recover quickly from a great depression because there was still half a continent to be peopled with farmers. In contrast, in 1900 the main railway network had already been built; the countryside had been settled, and the growth rate of agricultural output was falling sharply: the series runs: 1875/9 to 1885/9, 2·8 per cent per annum; 1885/9 to 1895/9, 2·4 per cent per annum; 1895/9 to 1905/9, 1·5 per cent per annum.[50] The labour force in agriculture, which had increased by 47 per cent between 1870 and 1890, would be virtually the same in 1910 as in 1900, and would already be declining. The average annual increase in miles of railroad dropped from 5,500 miles over 1872 to 1892 to 3,900 miles over 1892 to 1906. Henceforth, 'intensive' development would be required to take the place of 'extensive' development.

In this sense the economy was going through a 'structural change' in the second half of the 1890s. But one must beware of the more dramatic version of this change which is popular and authoritatively supported, namely the idea that the American economy had now matured. An economy which still has 40 per cent of its labour force in agriculture is not in any sense mature. All that had happened was that capital investment in railways to extend the agricultural frontier had ceased to be a pace-setter. Other pace-setters continued, and new ones (the new industries of the twentieth century) were emerging. The railways themselves had not yet made their last contribution, since although the geographical extension of the system slowed, its intensification continued. If we compare the five years to 1907 with the five years to 1892, miles of railway track added is almost the same in absolute terms (smaller relatively) but consumption of rails has doubled, intensive having succeeded to extensive development. The growth of the labour force as a whole has also slowed, but the numbers in manufacturing and mining were to rise even faster in the decade 1900–10 (44 per cent) than in the earlier prosperous decade 1880–90 (35 per cent). Structural change explains too much.

In fact only one of the three reverses in this upswing was wholly American, that of 1896, which was not shared by any of the three European partners. The recession of 1900 was the end of a major Juglar boom for these three countries, with a recession in world trade, and it would have been most surprising if this had not affected American data; the mildness of the reaction indicates strength rather than weakness in the American economy. The recession of 1903–4 was also international, showing in British and French production and in German construction (though not manufacturing), and can hardly be attributed to the unprofitability of the American railways, which had by now recovered (Table 2.10). It is only the recession of 1896 that can be blamed on the railways or on structural change. The story would then read somewhat as follows. The decline of the economy from 1892 was sharp but short. By 1895 manufacturing began to rise; but the economy was waiting for its accustomed lead from railway investment. Railway construction also rose significantly in 1895, but then relaxed again in 1896; so not until 1897 did the long upswing of manufacturing really commence in earnest. On this view, the culprit year is 1896, perhaps because of its rumours of impending war with Britain and its gold standard election; and perhaps because with the main railway network now built and geographical extension curtailed, the profits of the over-built railway system were still too low to inspire so soon a new railway investment programme.

THE UPSWING OF PRICES

2.13 The Kondratiev price downswing ended in 1895. Thereafter prices moved up all over the world until 1920. How did this affect the Juglar patterns that we have been studying?

The answer seems to be: not conspicuously. Since 1899 lies below the capacity line for the core as a whole in Chart 2.1, one can experiment with treating it as a turning point. The growth rates then run from core peak to core peak as follows:

1866–72	4·3	1882–90	3·2	1899–1906	4·3
1872–82	3·3	1890–9	3·1	1906–13	3·2

This is at first sight impressive. The growth rate is highest in two periods of rising prices, 1866–72 and 1899–1906, and decelerates steadily during the long price downswing.

But there are snags. One is the low growth rate from 1906 to 1913, when prices were rising vigorously. Another snag is that if one compares moving averages instead of single years[51] the middle growth rates are constant. When we take the central years of five-year moving averages peak core growth rates run as follows:

1867–73	3·8
1873–82	3·5
1882–90	3·5
1890–1905	3·5
1905–11	3·0

The moving averages have also eliminated all vestiges of peaks in 1899 or 1903, leaving simply a steady rate of growth from a trough in 1894. The year 1911 is not a legitimate moving average peak, because it includes four years before the true peak of 1913, instead of two before and two after, which would yield a higher average. One can speculate as to what the moving average would show if war had not erupted in 1914. The answer is that even a very favourable assumption still shows a decline in the growth rate. (For example, if 1914 and 1915 stand in the same relation to 1913 as 1900 and 1901 stand in relation to 1899, then the moving average growth rate from 1905 to 1913 is still only 3·3 per cent per annum.)

Anyway, to answer the question how growth rates were affected by Kondratiev price upswing and downswing it is not enough to look at the combined core, because this is composed of discordant individual patterns. If the industrial rate of growth was strongly affected by what was happening to the price level, all four countries should display the same upward or downward trends; but they do not. The year 1899 looks like a turning point for the core only because in that year the American depression more than offset the British, French and German booms. (A similar depression in 1873–6, we may remember, did not bring core production down because the USA's proportion of the core was then much smaller.) If one were to exclude the USA, 1899 would cease to be below the line, and our impression would be reversed. For now the British boom of 1899 and serious retardation thereafter would give us a decelerating core from 1899 to 1913. Omitting both Britain and the USA, one is left with a rapidly expanding Germany unchanged in course, and France now trending upwards. In short, taking 1895 to 1913 as a whole, the experience of these four countries is as varied as it was before prices took their upward turn.

It is now clear why simple study of the core as a whole would have been misleading, and why each country has been examined in turn before examining their sum. The shape of the sum turns out to be accidental; it has no design to which the parts conform. It tells us what happened in history at this particular time, but yields no clue to how the sum had behaved earlier, or might behave in the future.

So much for causes; effects are a different matter. The demand for food and raw materials in the world market depends on the sum of core demands, whatever the causes may have been. In denying that the Kondratiev upswing of prices caused faster industrial growth of the core we are not also denying that faster growth of the core up to 1907 may have contributed to causing the Kondratiev upswing. Neither do we deny that changes in the terms of trade, which were associated with the upswing, may have affected the rate of growth of countries at the periphery. These are separate questions, to which we return in later chapters.

2.14 Our review of Juglar progress to 1913 can now be brief, since it follows the same pattern.

The period includes three peaks: those of 1899, 1906–7 and 1912–13, and one great depression each for France, Britain and the United States.

The US boom of 1906–7 simply repeats its predecessors. Railways are still in the vanguard, although extensive has now given way to intensive development. Immigration is larger than ever absolutely; much larger relatively to population than in 1887/92, and matching relatively even the huge influx of 1880/4. Housebuilding is also at an unprecedented peak. The economy again switches to importing capital, which it will not find itself doing again for the next half century.

All this is followed as usual by a precipitous decline in manufacturing, panic on the stock exchange, widespread failure of banks and high unemployment rates. The inflow of immigrants drops from 11·6 per thousand over the six years to the boom of 1907 to 10·0 per thousand over the six years to 1913, a smaller than average Kuznets decline; but the chief source has now moved to Eastern and Southern Europe, with its overflowing reservoirs of population and greater dependence on push factors. This depression is not as deep as those following 1873 or 1893, but promises to be recalcitrant, if the low level of manufacturing indicated by Chart 2.1 is to be believed. Neither the Kitchin flurry of 1910 nor the worldwide Juglar boom of 1913 brings the economy near full capacity. But we cannot complete the story, since endogenous development is interrupted by the First World War. Whether this would have been a great great depression, like those of 1872 and 1929, or only a moderately great depression like that of 1892 we shall never know.

2.15 France picked itself up in 1890, from the shambles of Léon Say's depression, and experienced a decade of great prosperity; all three European core members contrasted sharply with the USA in this respect in the nineties. A small French setback in 1892 was followed by a vigorous building boom, terminating in 1899. The sharp decline of building then produced what we have to call a great depression, since it is significantly worse than that of 1892, though not nearly as bad as that of 1882.

Why did France have these precipitous declines in building which show so dramatically in Chart 1.2? That of 1870 is obviously due to the Franco-Prussian War, but those which followed may perhaps be attributed to the fact that French population was by now virtually constant. If population is increasing, some building must go on even in the depths of a depression, whereas a constant population presumably crowds all its activity into spasms of building only in prosperous times.

Nevertheless, the average rate of growth was good, contrary to popular belief. Manufacturing grew constantly from peak to peak (1892–1899–1909) at 2·0 per cent per annum. Considered as growth per head of population (1·8) this was not as good as Germany (2·9) but much better than Britain (1·1). The iron and steel industry, still very backward in 1890, now set the pace. Pig iron output grew constantly from peak to peak (1892–1899–1909) at 3·3 per cent per annum. Exports of manufactures were also helpful, growing by our calculations[52] from 1890 to 1899 at 2·3 per cent per annum, and at 3·2 per cent per annum from 1899 to 1913, by Maizels's calculations.[53] The great burst of iron and steel production between 1909 and 1913, which underlay the superboom of that period (France skipped the Juglar recession of 1907) received some stimulus from armament expenditure, including naval construction. The share of the war departments in the expenditures of the central government rose from 29 per cent in 1909 to 36 per cent in 1913.

2.16 The trend of British experience runs in the opposite direction: towards increasing gloom. The Kondratiev upswing starts well. The long delayed building boom – nearly twenty years had passed without one – took off in the mid-nineties, carrying all other forms of economic activity along with it; and, as Brinley Thomas would say, substituting or making up for reduced emigration and capital export.

What is more, construction did not slump sharply in 1900 or pay much regard to the Boer War; it did not edge out until 1906. So the Juglar recession of manufacturing from 1900 onwards was well-behaved. As in 1873–8 output did not actually fall; it merely sidestepped, in marked contrast with 1883, or 1891 or 1907. Lomax's index shows even less recession than ours (see Appendix I). Moreover the trough came fairly soon, and the economy moved upwards to the Juglar boom of 1907.

The Juglar of 1907 was sensitive to the renewed decline of building. Output collapsed so sharply in 1908 that what follows has to rank as a mini-great-depression, of the same order as the French mini-great-depression of 1900. Yet the economy recovered very rapidly, reaching a new boom in 1913, which would be on trend if a new capacity line were to be traced touching the peaks of 1899, 1907 and 1913.

Such a capacity line, however, would be false because we know that the economy was not at this time running along potential capacity. First, we have the evidence of the unemployment figures, which ran as follows:

1899	2·0 per cent	1907	3·7
1900	2·5	1908	7·8
1901	3·3	1909	7·7
1902	4·0	1910	4·7
1903	4·7	1911	3·0
1904	6·0	1912	3·2
1905	5·0	1913	2·1
1906	3·6		

Then there was an outburst of emigration. This had peaked its five-year average in 1880/4 at 262,000; now it peaked again in 1909/13 at 416,000. Moreover, many more of these new emigrants were now leaving the towns.[54] Up to 1901 the rural population of England and Wales had lost an average 400,000 persons per decade, while the towns gained 3,270,000. Now between 1901 and 1911 the rural areas actually gained 440,000 persons, while the towns gained only 3,100,000. The reason that the unemployment percentage was down to 2·1 in 1913 was not that the boom was good, but that so many people had ceased looking for jobs in British towns.

What we have here is another stage in a retardation of British industrial growth which had begun in 1873. The phenomenon is as complex as it is interesting and we shall come back to it.

2.17 Taking the core as a whole, the boom of 1906–7 had to be outstanding, partly because American production was by now so large in relation to the whole, and partly because it was a good time for all our countries except Britain. The immediately succeeding years would also have to be depressed because both the USA and the UK would be descending in their building cycles.

The shape of core depressions was largely determined in our period by who partnered whom. American great depressions were regular, in the sense that every other Juglar depression was a great depression: 1872, 1892, 1906. More strictly, since the USA did not experience Juglar depression in 1899, one should say that an American great depression coincided with every other British Juglar. French great depressions were also on alternate Juglars: 1882, 1899. But Britain went her own way: from 1882 to 1907 constitutes not two Juglars but three. Hence, contrary to popular theory, the UK fluctuation was adverse to the American in the eighties and nineties, but it accorded with the American in 1907 and also in 1873 if that is counted as a great depression for Britain.

If we skip to the great postwar depression of 1929, its severity stemmed partly from the coincidence of great depressions in Germany and the USA at that time, with the French also forcing their economy down by refusing to devalue their currency. The nearest parallel to this coincidence in our period was the second half of the 1870s when residential construction was at a standstill simultaneously in the USA, Germany and Britain, and this is no doubt why, looking at the core as a whole, this is the worst group of four years. The partnership of Britain and France in the second half of the 1880s was offset by German and US prosperity; and German, French and British prosperity held up the second half of the nineties, against the American whirlpool.

How did this kaleidoscope of partnerships react on prices? To this we shall now turn.

Chapter 3

The Kondratiev Price Swing

SYNOPSIS: 3.00 This chapter examines each of the five theories advanced to explain the Kondratiev price fluctuation.

3.01 The investment ratio: there is no hard evidence that the investment ratio was higher during the upswing of prices than during the downswing.

(3.02 A technical interlude explains the statistical analysis that follows.)

3.03 Industrial production: the index of core industrial production shows no acceleration during the upswing of prices.

3.04 Agricultural production: this result is positive. The turnaround of prices can be explained by a decline in the rate of growth of supplies of wheat, wool and cotton, with the prices of substitutes acting in sympathy.

3.05 The stock of gold: this result also is positive, yielding a rival explanation of the turnaround of prices.

3.06 The wage–price spiral: this yields a positive answer in the 1870s, otherwise a negative answer. Contrary to expectation, after 1883 the secular rate of growth of money wages was the same in downswing and upswing.

3.07 If changes in agricultural supplies were the main explanation of the turnaround in prices, then prices fell too much in the later 1870s, rose too slowly in the first half of the 1900s, and rose too much thereafter. This is attributable to slowness of reaction at turning-points, followed by over-reaction.

3.08 If relevant, the stock of gold would operate through changes in the stock of money. The links between the stock of gold and the stock of money were loose; other factors caused the stock of money and the stock of gold to rise at different rates with varying margins of difference. Both in the UK and the USA the velocity of circulation contributes more than the stock of money to explaining the turnaround in prices.

3.09 The proximate cause of the Kondratiev fluctuation in prices seems to have been changes in the growth rate of agricultural supplies. There were associated changes in the demand for and supply of money. The changes in gold supply were accessory rather than determinant.

3.00 Prices fell sharply from 1873 to the mid-1890s, then rose again sharply to 1913. Timing and rates of change are not exactly the same for all price series, but the general direction is universal. For example, in foodstuffs the price of meat held up better than the price of cereals. Prices of raw materials fell faster in the 1870s than in the 1880s, while the prices of food fell more in the 1880s than in the 1870s. Money wages fell sharply in the 1870s, but then resumed their upward drift. Countries also had different experiences, as can be seen in Table 3.1. Translated into gold (the US currency was below par in 1873), the British cost of living fell by more than that of any other country, because of the absence of tariffs. The German cost of living fell least after 1882, and rose fastest after 1899, partly because the tariff maintained the prices of cereals, and partly because German money wages rose fastest, pushing up the prices of services and of all those industries (such as construction) where productivity was still growing relatively slowly. In this chapter we shall be analysing the general influences on prices, but we must not forget that each particular price was also subject to special influences. There were even some prices that were lower in 1913 than in 1900, notably silk, sugar, cocoa, copper, coal and pig iron, not to mention some other manufactures.

Table 3.1 *The Cost of Living (1890/1900 = 100)*[1]

	1873	*1882*	*1890*	*1895*	*1900*	*1913*
France	110	111	102	99	94	111
Germany	118	101	100	98	104	127
UK	141	118	103	96	105	118
USA	143[a]	118	105	97	97	114

[a] 125 at gold parity.

Five sets of influences have been offered as candidates for explaining the Kondratiev swing. First, changes in the investment ratio. Secondly, changes in the growth rate of industrial production. Thirdly, changes in the growth rate of agricultural production. Fourthly, changes in the growth rate of gold production. And fifthly, rapid unionisation after 1900. These five are not mutually exclusive.

THE INVESTMENT RATIO

3.01 The first explanation postulates that an increase in investment opportunities will raise prices, because the propensity to invest will rise faster than the propensity to save. The difference can be made up by an expansion of credit from the banks or other financial intermediaries, or from suppliers' credits. This implies that the supply of money is a function of the demand for money, which could not be the case if gold were the only form of money, or banknotes issued by a government. So this explanation is associated with pointing out the fuzziness of the definition of money. Alternatively the explanation works if there is a change in the velocity of circulation of money – that is, if people do more business with the same amount of money. The most common way to do this is to extend each other more credit, and this leads us back to the fuzziness in defining money.

As we have seen, Schumpeter believed that prices turned around at the end of the century because of a new spurt of investment in new technology, including steel, electricity, automobiles and chemicals. If this is so, it should show in an investment ratio rising around that time. The following figures summarise the available information, for peak years. They show gross fixed investment (including foreign investment) as a percentage of gross national product (net investment and product with inventories in the German case). There are no data for France.[2]

	1889/90	*1899/1900*	*1906/7*	*1912/13*
UK	11·9	11·5	13·4	13·9
Germany	18·3	19·5	19·6	18·3
USA	20·0	19·8	20·5	18·3
Total	17·3	17·4	18·8	17·4

The figures are not very reliable and must be interpreted with caution. Surprisingly the case which looks like confirming the prediction is the British, where the high level of investment in the two later peaks is due not to domestic investment in new technology, but to foreign investment. However, the cause is not germane, since the effects on prices would be the same whatever the cause. The US evidence runs the other way: the investment ratio is about the same in 1906/7 as in 1889/90, and is even lower in 1912/13. On the other hand, as suggested in Appendix II, the US ratio may be somewhat high for the first two peaks. If we take one percentage point off the first two totals to adjust for this, we do get an increase in capital formation after 1900.

One element of the result is not in dispute, namely the lower level of investment in 1912/13 than in 1906/7 (except for Britain where foreign investment had mounted). This conforms with our curve of core industrial production (Chart 2.2). It also conforms with the behaviour of prices, which rose much faster between 1900 and 1907 than between 1907 and 1913. Here are the growth rates for wholesale prices, in per cent per annum.

	1900–7	*1907–13*
USA	2·1	1·2
France	1·4	1·0
Germany	1·1	0·5
UK	0·9	1·0
UK (ex-freights)	1·5	0·7

The exception is the UK, which ceases to be an exception when the index is adjusted by subtracting freights.[3]

However, wholesale prices did not fall between 1907 and 1913; they merely rose less rapidly. Why did they continue to rise? Our investment data do not answer this question. Neither do they really explain why prices were rising so much between 1900 and 1907. The unweighted average increase for the four countries is 11 per cent, which seems rather a large increase to attribute to even a two percentage point increase in the investment ratio.

In sum, a relatively high investment performance by the core (including its foreign investment) may have contributed towards accelerating prices to 1907, and a relatively low investment performance towards the deceleration of prices to 1913; but we have yet to find the fundamental causes of the upswing.

TECHNICAL INTERLUDE

3.02 We are still left with four potential explanations of the Kondratiev price swing: namely, the growth rates of industry, agriculture, and gold production, or a wage spiral. To elucidate their respective contributions we shall resort to some regression analysis, so we must pause to explain our procedure.

We have taken four commodities traded in international commodity markets, namely wheat, cotton, wool and coffee.[4] In three of these cases, wheat, cotton and wool, but not in coffee, the price has the characteristic Kondratiev swing. Leaving aside questions of causality, we wish to discover whether the same swing is found in core industrial production (serving as a proxy for demand), in world production of the particular commodity and in the world supply of monetary gold.[5]

We have first put all our indexes into common logarithms, and then reduced them to five-year moving averages. We are interested not in year-by-year movements but in the secular movement over forty years, which comes out more clearly when the annual fluctuations are removed.

At this stage our question can be answered by simple inspection; by plotting the price series in the same graph with any of the other three series we can see whether the price series and the non-price series share the same V-shaped swing. The next stage of sophistication is to run a time trend through the non-price series, and see how its deviations from this trend match the price series. The third stage is to regress the price against any one independent variable and time. This is what we have done in each case with our first three regression equations.

We could stop the exercise at this point, but we have in fact gone on to compute the results of combining the independent variables in various ways, to see how much a combination adds to the closeness of fit of the original result. We report all these results in Tables 3.2 to 3.5, but the only result we actually use in our analysis is that which is obtained by combining demand and supply. When all the variables are in we have a regression equation of the form

$$\text{Log } P = a + b \log D + c \log S + d \log G + rt$$

where P is an index of the commodity's price, D is the index of core industrial production, S is an index of world production of the same commodity, G is the world's stock of monetary gold and t is a time trend. The reader should resist any temptation to regard this as a model of factors determining the price of a commodity. Its only potential value is that it shows how little difference is made to the fit by using three independent variables instead of two.

The basic problem can be outlined by considering the limitations of the regression which includes demand and supply. In the first place, since we are working with five-year moving averages we get very high significance coefficients, much higher than if we left in the annual fluctuations. We also impose on ourselves an increased auto-correlation of residuals, since an error in any one year is automatically spread over the preceding four years

Table 3.2 *Regression Results for Price of Wheat, 1866–1913*[a]

Equation	*Constant*	D[b]	S[c]	G[d]	*r*	R^2	SEE
(1)	2·77	1·43			−0·027	0·607	0·059
	(1·23)[e]	(1·89)			(2·34)		
(2)	0·001		−2·83		0·016	0·794	0·043
	(15·0)		(6.62)		(4·90)		
(3)	0·239			1·65	−0·022	0·925	0·026
	(6·95)			(13·8)	(17·9)		
(4)	0·927	1·16	−2.97			0·830	0·039
	(36·9)	(6·17)	(8.18)				
(5)	0·794	1·54	−2·86		−0·006	0·833	0·039
	(4·82)	(3·08)	(7·36)		(0·82)		
(6)	0·676	−1·39		1·57		0·859	0·035
	(29·1)	(12·3)		(9·45)			
(7)	0·055	0·66		1·62	−0·031	0·932	0·025
	(0·57)	(2·03)		(13·8)	(6·50)		
(8)	0·808		−1·77	0·83		0·879	0·033
	(40·4)		(13·5)	(8·33)			
(9)	0·024		0·71	1·94	−0·030	0·929	0·026
	(0·16)		(1·49)	(8·70)	(5·30)		
(10)	0·775	−0·35	−1·35	1·04		0·881	0·033
	(18·1)	(0·88)	(2·68)	(4·12)			
(11)	−0·050	0·55	0·44	1·80	−0·035	0·933	0·025
	(0·33)	(1·60)	(0·89)	(7·63)	(5·51)		

[a] Number of observations = 44.
[b] D = index of industrial production.
[c] S = supply of the commodity.
[d] G = world's monetary stock of gold.
[e] Figures in parentheses are *t* values.

Table 3.3 *Regression Results for Price of Cotton, 1866–1913*[a]

Equation	*Constant*	D[b]	S	G	*r*	R^2	SEE
(1)	−0·811	4·61			−0·073	0·430	0·092
	(2·32)	(3·93)			(4·17)		
(2)	0·863		−3·67		0·050	0·434	0·092
	(10·6)		(3·98)		(3·66)		
(3)	−0·192			2·69	−0·031	0·775	0·058
	(2·51)			(10·1)	(11·3)		
(4)	−0·675	5·87	−6·20			0·854	0·046
	(6·84)	(13·0)	(13·7)				
(5)	−0·001	7·09	−5·62		−0·027	0·881	0·042
	(6·64)	(12·3)	(12·3)		(3·01)		
(6)	0·435	−1·81		2·34		0·603	0·076
	(8·68)	(7·44)		(6·55)			
(7)	−0·001	3·42		2·47	−0·080	0·890	0·041
	(7·29)	(6·47)		(12·9)	(10·2)		
(8)	0·108		−1·68	2·11		0·751	0·061
	(1·86)		(10·6)	(9·08)			
(9)	−0·164		−0·174	2·64	−0·028	0·775	0·058
	(1·16)		(0·235)	(7·79)	(2·08)		
(10)	−0·522	4·31	−5·16	0·80		0·883	0·042
	(5·14)	(6·74)	(9·79)	(3·16)			
(11)	−0·001	5·31	−3·18	1·47	−0·051	0·959	0·025
	(12·0)	(13·2)	(8·09)	(8·59)	(8·47)		

[a] Number of observations = 44.
[b] See notes to Table 3.2.

Table 3.4 *Regression Results for Price of Wool, 1871–1913*[a]

Equation	*Constant*	D[b]	S	G	*r*	R^2	SEE
(1)	−0·052	2·01			−0·032	0·182	0·064
	(0·20)	(2·27)			(2·38)		
(2)	0·825		−1·94		0·011	0·820	0·030
	(31·2)		(12·3)		(10·0)		
(3)	0·034			1·95	−0·022	0·854	0·027
	(0·90)			(13·9)	(14·5)		
(4)	0·605	0·69	−1·81			0·811	0·031
	(29·9)	(9·72)	(12·02)				
(5)	0·794	0·10	−1·92		0·010	0·820	0·030
	(5·49)	(0·22)	(11·2)		(1·32)		
(6)	0·467	−1·23		1·64		0·645	0·042
	(15·8)	(8·09)		(7·75)			
(7)	−0·547	2·00		1·95	−0·052	0·969	0·013
	(10·2)	(11·5)		(29·9)	(19·2)		
(8)	0·552		−1·41	0·75		0·914	0·021
	(37·8)		(19·6)	(15·8)			
(9)	0·381		−1·00	1·18	−0·008	0·930	0·019
	(6·12)		(6·15)	(7·39)	(1·32)		
(10)	0·546	−0·10	−1·33	0·84		0·916	0·021
	(33·3)	(0·80)	(10·6)	(6·57)			
(11)	−2·94	1·61	−0·40	1·64	−0·041	0·977	0·011
	(3·30)	(8·30)	(3·33)	(15·1)	(9·47)		

[a] Number of observations = 39.
[b] See notes to Table 3.2.

Table 3.5 *Regression Results for Price of Coffee, 1871–1913*[a]

Equation	*Constant*	D[b]	S	G	*r*	R^2	SEE
(1)	0·001	−2·24			0·027	0·394	0·111
	(2·64)	(1·45)			(1·13)		
(2)	0·001		−2·82		0·024	0·764	0·069
	(18·2)		(7·87)		(5·88)		
(3)	0·981			−0·99	0·032	0·408	0·110
	(5·46)			(1·74)	(0·52)		
(4)	0·573	1·43	−2·60			0·719	0·075
	(8·84)	(4·83)	(6·67)				
(5)	0·001	−1·31	−2·76		0·043	0·776	0·068
	(4·57)	(1·37)	(7·73)		(2·98)		
(6)	0·898	0·05		−0·77		0·404	0·110
	(11·6)	(0·12)		(1·39)			
(7)	0·001	−2·23		−0·99	0·037	0·443	0·108
	(3·12)	(1·49)		(1·78)	(1·57)		
(8)	0·702		−1·43	0·72		0·578	0·093
	(8·56)		(3·85)	(1·85)			
(9)	0·001		−2·74	−0·50	0·029	0.776	0·068
	(10·7)		(7·58)	(1·38)	(5·57)		
(10)	0·592	1·56	−2·55	−0·24		0·722	0·076
	(8·20)	(4·27)	(6·33)	(0·62)			
(11)	0·001	−1·34	−2·67	−0·51	0·048	0·789	0·067
	(4·85)	(1·42)	(7·45)	(1·43)	(3·26)		

[a] Number of observations = 39.
[b] See notes to Table 3.2.

and the succeeding four years. This shows up in very low Durbin–Watson statistics. If we were interested in the year-by-year movement we would not go into moving averages, and would be using not Ordinary Least Squares but some more powerful technique, such as the Cochrane–Orcutt iterative procedure. But our interest is secular and not cyclical. In the second place, we suffer from multi-collinearity, and probably also from incomplete specification, both of which show in the coefficients of the independent variables changing significantly as the number of variables is changed. Finally, these coefficients are not to be thought of as elasticities. Price is a function of demand and supply, but over a period of forty years supply is also a function of price. If we were seeking to determine the elasticity of demand for any of our commodities we should have to proceed quite differently. So we must reiterate that our sole object in putting demand and supply together is to see how much the closeness of fit is improved over the result when they are considered separately. For this all we need is a combination of visual inspection and the R^2s.

The results reported in Tables 3.2 to 3.5 are for actual prices in gold, though we have also done the work using as deflators an index of the prices of manufactures[6] and alternatively the GDP deflator.[7] If one were seeking to estimate elasticities one would have to work with deflated prices, but this is not our objective. We wish to see whether it is possible to separate the effects of supply and demand and of gold on prices, and for this purpose we need actual prices with and without gold. As expected, in cotton and wool prices deflated by prices of manufactures gave better results than either GDP deflated or undeflated prices (but not in wheat or coffee, which have special problems). Surprisingly, the best results were obtained with undeflated prices and the index of the world's monetary stock of gold. The regression coefficients are given here for equations representing demand and supply and a trend, taking 1871 to 1913 for all four commodities:[8]

	Price deflated by		*Undeflated price*	
	Manufactures	*GDP*	*ex-gold*	*with gold*
Cotton	0·89	0·86	0·82	0·93
Wool	0·85	0·80	0·81	0·98
Wheat	0·42	0·74	0·78	0·95
Coffee	0·55	0·70	0·72	—

The introduction of gold perverts the coffee regressions by giving the wrong signs.

The reader is thus warned that the coefficients of the independent variables in Tables 3.2 to 3.5 are not the coefficients corresponding to a stable price level. The terms of trade coefficients are reported in a note below.[9]

Note finally that we have used not actual prices but prices minus freights.[10] This is done by subtracting 10 per cent of the index of shipping freights from the commodity price index. The purpose of this is to bring to the fore demand, supply and monetary explanations, by excluding that part of price changes which was due only to the fall in freights. This seems worth doing, even though it adds another source of error.

We may now resume our analysis, starting with the effect of industrial production.

INDUSTRIAL PRODUCTION

3.03 The second explanation of the Kondratiev upswing postulates that changes in the rate of growth of industrial production will produce corresponding changes in the price level. For example, acceleration of industrial growth will put a strain on agricultural supplies and drive up agricultural prices. In the original version of the Quantity Theory of Money, a rise in agricultural prices would have to be matched by a fall in industrial prices since the supply of money and the velocity of circulation of money are assumed to be constant. However, this model of the Quantity Theory assumes downward flexibility of money wages, which may not be so. Indeed money wages may be linked positively to agricultural prices, in which case money wages will rise as agricultural prices rise, and we shall have an upward spiral process instead of a downward movement cancelling an upward movement. Here again we meet the same implications as when we considered the effects of a changing investment ratio on prices: the mechanism assumes that the supply of money, or the velocity of circulation of money, will respond to changes in the demand for money.

If industrial production is the explanation of the upturn of prices, we should find that industrial production of the core as a whole was growing faster after 1899 than it was growing before. To study this problem was our main reason for constructing the combined index number shown in Chart 2.3.

This index is not presented with a high degree of confidence. Appendices I and II show the extent to which guesswork and interpolation enter into the construction of the individual country indexes. The correct weighting also raises problems because of great differences in value added per man (so that weighting by value added gives different results from weighting by numbers employed) and also in the domestic prices of manufactures (so that weighting by money income and by real purchasing power give different results).

Taking it as it comes, one can see merely by inspection of this index of the combined core industrial production (Chart 2.3) that it is not going to be of much help in explaining the Kondratiev price swing. The moving averages give a good picture of Juglar behaviour, showing up especially the depressions of the 1870s and the 1890s; and since prices follow a Juglar pattern, one cannot fully explain prices without taking industrial production into account. At the same time the curve shows that the rate of growth was roughly the same from one peak to the next; it is not going to be able to explain why prices were so much higher in 1913 than in 1900 – not to speak of 1907.

This is borne out by the regression analysis. Equation 1 of Tables 3.2 to 3.5 reports the results when using only industrial production and a time trend as independent variables. Only cotton yields a respectable R^2 (0·43). The result is low for wool (0·18), not significant for wheat, and has the wrong sign for coffee. Chart 3.1 reproduces the best of these fits, that for cotton. The defects stand out clearly. The peaks of demand (1873, 1883, 1891 and 1906) lie virtually on a straight line. Demand cannot explain why the price of cotton was so high at the beginning and the end of our period.

Chart 3.1 confirms the conclusion yielded by examining the investment ratio: 1907 was a bigger peak than either 1899 or 1913. But it also shows why this information does not get us far. We want to know why prices were higher in the 1900s than in the 1880s, and why they sank in the second half of the 1880s and rose in the second half of the 1900s. Our investment data for the end of the eighties are very uncertain, and the industrial index offers no reason for prices to be higher in the later period.

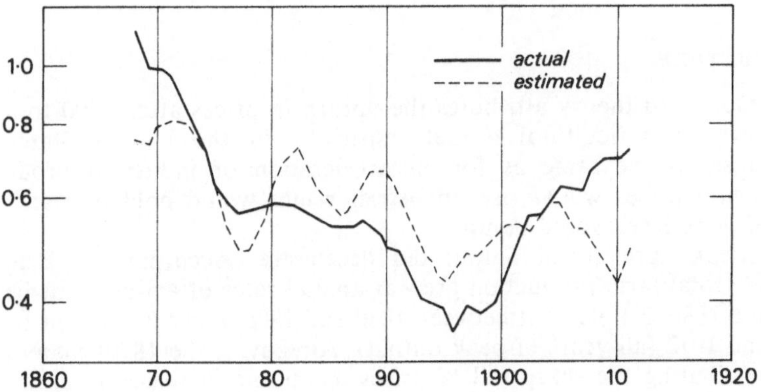

Chart 3.1 Price of Cotton: Equation 1 (Influence of Demand Only)

Does the index not err in presenting a constant rate of growth from 1873 to 1906? The individual indexes for France, Germany and the USA show constant growth between those dates, while the British index shows retardation. Should the sum of these four not show retardation? The answer is an intriguing mathematical point. If one has a number of time series, each with a constant but different rate of growth (i.e. each making a straight line on semi-logarithmic paper), the result of adding them together is a new combined series with a steadily increasing rate of growth (i.e. making a curve on semi-logarithmic paper). This is because the fastest growing series is of small weight at the beginning but of large weight at the end. The growth rate of the new combined series approaches asymptotically the growth rate of its fastest component. Hence a straight line joining the two ends of the combined series on semi-logarithmic paper will have a gap between itself and the series, which will be greatest in the middle of the series. We have calculated how big this gap should be, assuming the four countries to be growing at the rates indicated by the capacity lines in Chart 1.1, and using the weights of Appendix II. The answer is a gap of about 2·8 per cent in the early 1890s. So, if all our four countries had grown at constant rates, the combined growth rate would have been higher in the second half of the period. Instead, the convexity of British growth has offset the concavity of combining the other three, to yield constant growth for the four taken together.

For the purpose of this exercise, the greatest weakness in our combined index of industrial production lies in the uncertainty as to the relative levels of German industrial production in the 1870s and 1880s. If Hoffmann is right, the German economy slowed down even more remarkably than the British between 1873 and 1883. This retardation in the 1880s would then help to explain why prices were so much lower in the 1880s than in the 1870s. We have therefore wrestled hard with this problem, and indicate in Appendix II why Hoffmann's version seems unacceptable.

To conclude, therefore, industrial production must be kept in the analysis to explain the Juglar movement in prices, but we must look elsewhere for explanations of the Kondratiev.

AGRICULTURE

3.04 Our third theory attributes the upturn in prices after 1900 to a slowing down of agricultural output, especially in the United States. The mechanism is the same as for an acceleration of industrial production: agricultural prices would rise, industrial wages would hold or rise, so the general price level would be up.

American agricultural output did decelerate. According to Bean and Strauss[11] total farm production grew at annual rates of 4·5 per cent between 1870 and 1880, 2·4 per cent between 1880 and 1898, and 1·3 per cent between 1898 and 1912 (all years of peak output). Already in the 1870s many people were attributing the sharp fall of prices to the big increases in agricultural output, following the ending of the Civil War, the enormous railway building of the second half of the 1860s, and the large influx of immigrants. Observers were slower to pick up the connection between rising prices and American agricultural output after 1900.

More importantly, American exports to the rest of the world decelerated even more than American production. Exports of wheat from the USA declined absolutely; here are the figures in millions of bushels per annum:

1866/72	36	1890/9	171
1872/83	112	1899/1907	161
1883/90	117	1907/13	117

Cotton exports continued to grow absolutely, but at a declining rate:

1868/72 to 1878/82	6·4	per cent per annum
1878/82 to 1888/92	2·8	
1888/92 to 1898/1902	2·9	
1898/1902 to 1908/12	2·2	

The arrival of the boll weevil in 1892 will have contributed to this decline.

However, American deceleration was not the only adverse influence. The important commodity wool was also affected by a prolonged drought in Australia, extending from 1895 to 1903. In the course of this the number of sheep in Australia was halved (from about 110 million in 1892 to about 54 million in 1903).

Now changes in the prices of wheat, wool and cotton would communicate themselves to most other agricultural commodities. A commodity could be a substitute on the side of demand, especially if it were one of the numerous foodstuffs which constitute the bulk of agricultural output, or it could be a substitute on the side of supply, in the sense that it was using resources otherwise suitable for producing foodstuffs, or cotton or wool. So one does not have to study the demand and supply of each commodity separately. If one can explain why important food and fibre prices altered, most other agricultural commodities fall into line. And if one can explain agricultural prices in general, the jump to industrial prices does not involve too large a gap.

Regression analysis shows that supply by itself is an excellent explanation of the Kondratiev price swing in our four commodities. Equation 2 uses only supply and a time trend. The R^2s are 0·82 for wool, 0·79 for wheat and 0·76 for coffee. The coffee result, reproduced in Chart 3.2, is the most remarkable. The price of coffee did not behave like most other prices, sliding down to the mid-nineties and up again. Instead it did a double dance, and the ability of our procedures to reproduce this from two series (supply and trend) which move steadily upward is very comforting indeed, having regard to the uncertainties which surround us.

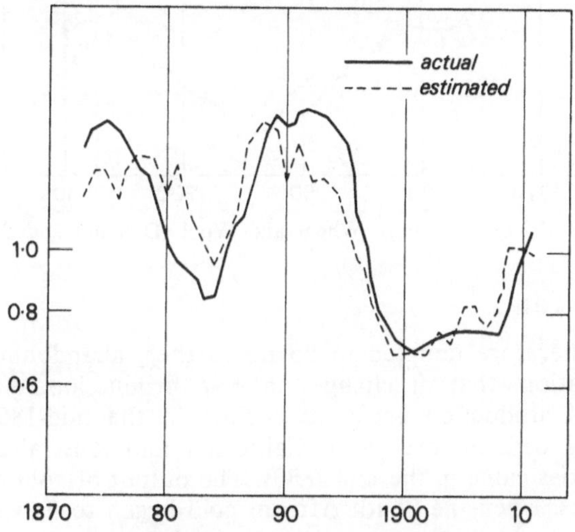

Chart 3.2 Price of Coffee (Supply Only)

Demand and supply should do even better than supply alone, and this is clearly the case in cotton, where the R^2 for supply is low (0·43) but that for supply and demand (Equation 4) is satisfactory (0·85). Demand slightly improves the fit for wheat; but in both wool and coffee, supply prefers the partnership of a simple trend (Equation 2) to that of our index of industrial production (Equation 4).

We reproduce in Chart 3.3 the results of matching demand and supply in wheat, cotton and wool (Equation 4), which yield R^2s of 0·83, 0·85 and 0·81 respectively, and large *t* ratios. It is quite clear that changes in supply explain most of the downswing in the early 1870s and most of the turnaround in prices after 1895.

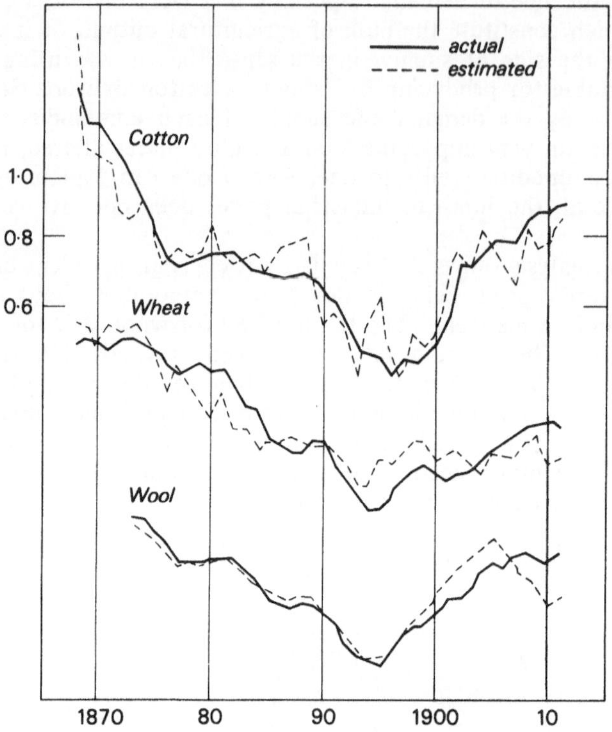

Chart 3.3 Prices of Cotton, Wheat and Wool (Demand and Supply)

GOLD PRODUCTION

3.05 We are therefore tempted to go no further, abandoning the fourth possible explanation, that of changes in gold production. As we saw in Chapter 2, gold production began to decline in the mid-1850s from the peaks associated with discoveries in California and Australia. The South African discoveries came in the mid-1880s. The output of gold declined until the early nineties, when the South African gold began to flow in significant quantities.

But gold cannot be abandoned as an explanation, since the regression analysis shows that gold by itself (Equation 3) does even better than supply by itself (Equation 2). For wheat we get R^2s of 0·92 and 0·79; for cotton 0·77 and 0·43; and for wool 0·85 and 0·82.

Coffee is the only case where supply yields a much better fit than the stock of monetary gold – presumably because its price rose sharply at the end of the 1880s when most other prices were falling. We part company with it here, since it does not help to illuminate the effects of gold.

That the stock of monetary gold gives a good fit is no surprise. Kitchin showed, in the memorandum which assembled the gold stock data, that his series correlated very strongly with British wholesale prices, up to 1913. When the general price level is moving downward, and is expected to continue to fall, the current price of a commodity will fall below what current consumption and supply would otherwise justify, and vice versa. This will result in its price correlating better with the general price level than with its own supply and demand data, if demand is measured not in money but by some real index such as industrial production. We know that the price of each of our commodities fell and then rose not only because of changes in its own supplies but also because the general price level also added cumulatively to the fall and to the subsequent rise. The effect was very substantial. British money income (GDP) per head fell 13 per cent between 1873 and 1883 (two peaks), and thereafter rose to 1913 at a rate which averaged 1·3 per cent per annum. The cumulative forces were certainly powerful.

3.06 We must spend a moment with money wages, since they are normally expected to play an important role in the cumulative process.

It is generally assumed that in our period money wages must have spiralled after 1900, as prices went up. As we have already noted, trade union numbers exploded at this time. Between 1900 and 1913 membership of unions soared from 2·0 to 4·1 million in Britain, from 0·1 to 1·0 million in France, from 0·9 to 3·0 million in Germany, and from 0·8 to 2·7 million in the USA. This was a period of fierce industrial struggles as workers tried, unsuccessfully, to keep real wages rising as fast as before 1899. We shall examine this more closely in our next chapter.

In fact, except in the USA, money wages rose no faster after 1899 than before. Annual growth rates of money wages, from peak to peak, ran as follows: [12]

	1883–99	*1899–1913*
France	0·8	0·9
UK	0·9	0·9
Germany	2·0	2·1
USA	0·7	2·4

These remarkable figures testify that in the European members of the core, money wages grew at steady rates from 1883 to 1913. The changed direction of the cost of living made no difference. Neither did the great burst of unionisation and strike activity which opened the twentieth century.

The USA was the exception; there wages shot up sharply after 1899. But the reason for this was that 1899 was not a peak year for the USA, and one must count from peak to peak. The American peaks are 1891, 1907 and 1913. Wholesale prices rose faster after 1907 (1·2 per cent per annum) than before (0·9 per cent per annum), but money wages rose at a constant rate from 1891 to 1907 to 1913 (1·4 per cent per annum). Wages did not accelerate as prices accelerated.

If money wages grew secularly at the same rate whether prices were rising or falling, regression analysis will show that their effect on prices was zero; they were not an element in the cumulative forces.

However, the situation was different before 1883. The very large increase in money wages to 1873 was followed by a very large fall – the last large fall in wages for fifty years until 1921. Between 1873 and 1883 German money wages fell by 16 per cent and the British by 3 per cent. US money wages rose by 10 per cent in gold (they fell by 3 per cent in US dollars); and French money wages rose by 19 per cent (they had not boomed to 1873). In total this amounts to a substantial deflation of the price level in the 1870s. On comparing actual prices with estimates calculated from demand and supply one should expect prices to seem to be too high in the early 1870s or too low in the early 1880s or both.

3.07 We tackle this by studying the residuals obtained by subtracting the estimated price (afforded by the regression equation) from the actual price of each year. This is shown in Chart 3.4 for Equation 5 (which uses demand, supply and a trend) except that for wool we chart Equation 2 (supply and a trend only) because the coefficient for demand is not significant.

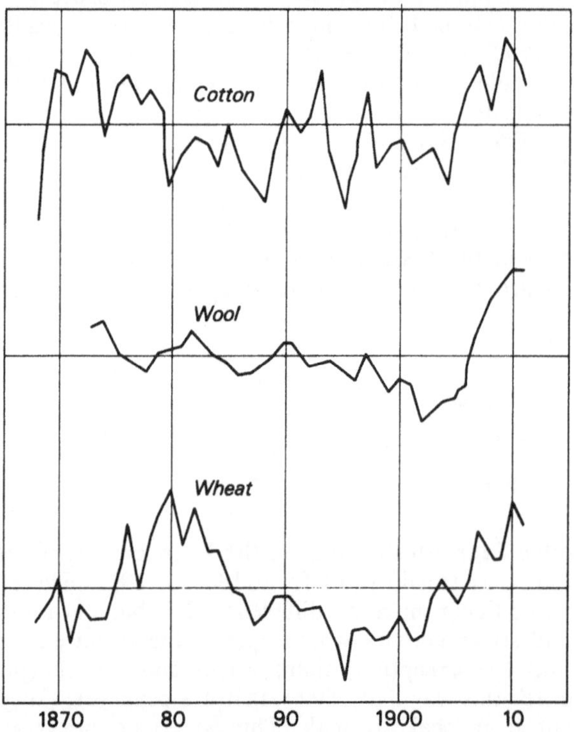

Chart 3.4 Residuals (Demand–Supply)

Both cotton and wool show the expected behaviour in the 1870s and 1880s; the actual price is first too high and then too low. Wheat does not. But all three also show expected behaviour after 1900; here the price begins too low and rises too high.

Wheat was expected to show a more pronounced divergence after 1900 than the other two series, but does not do so. The actual price was expected to be rising much faster than current consumption and supply would yield.

We have seen that US wheat exports were declining absolutely. To make up the deficit the world had to turn to expansion of wheat production in Canada, Argentina, Australia, Russia and Central Europe. Costs were higher in those countries because they were less mechanised; moreover transportation costs to Europe were higher from Argentina or Australia than from the USA. So even if volume sold had been the same, the price would have been higher. This is one of the defects of our model; it assumes that price is determined by the demand and supply of the moment, and ignores the extent to which in the long run price is determined by cost because supply is determined by cost.

This divergence turns out to be unimportant, since wheat prices are no more out of phase after 1900 than the prices of wool and cotton. Much more important is the divergence in the 1870s, when wheat prices are holding out against the rapid downward rush of other prices. The price of wheat (ex-freights) actually rose to a new peak in 1877, and remained high until 1882. Europe suffered a series of bad harvests in the second half of the seventies, which produced fear of famine, and prices rose much higher than the actual harvest deficits merited.[13] Also, it is conceivable that the price of wheat in gold went up with the dollar as revaluation proceeded back to par in 1879. This implies that the price of wheat was more subject to internal US conditions than the price of cotton, which is plausible, since exports were more important to cotton. Finally, the data for wheat production between 1865 and 1875 are highly uncertain, and our estimates may be too high.

We have isolated our problems. Price is too high then too low in the downturn; too low then too high in the upturn. Also over the whole period the stock of gold gives a better fit than the supply of the individual commodity.

To study this we go to the residuals obtained from Equation 2 (supply with a trend) and Equation 3 (gold stock and a trend). These are graphed in Chart 3.5.

It is immediately clear that gold gives a significantly better fit only after 1900. Before then it has much the same pattern as supply. This means that in the second half of the 1870s cotton and wool were underpriced having regard both to available supplies and to the stock of gold. The whole wage–price level had been lowered. (This does not show in wheat, which was overpriced for reasons of its own.)

The picture is different after 1900. Now prices were about right having regard to the gold stock or the general price level for which it is perhaps a proxy. But the public had become so accustomed to low and falling prices for wheat, cotton and wool that it took several years to grasp that supply conditions had changed. It is possible that large stocks still overhung the market, from the weakness of the mid-nineties. The combination of an American recession with a European boom may also have been confusing. Then the penny dropped, and prices swung too far in the opposite direction. By the very end of the period there were already signs of a correction. Prices caught up by accelerating rapidly to 1907, but, as already noted, wholesale prices rose less rapidly after 1907 than before, and the growth rate of money wages also slackened (except in Germany). This slackening

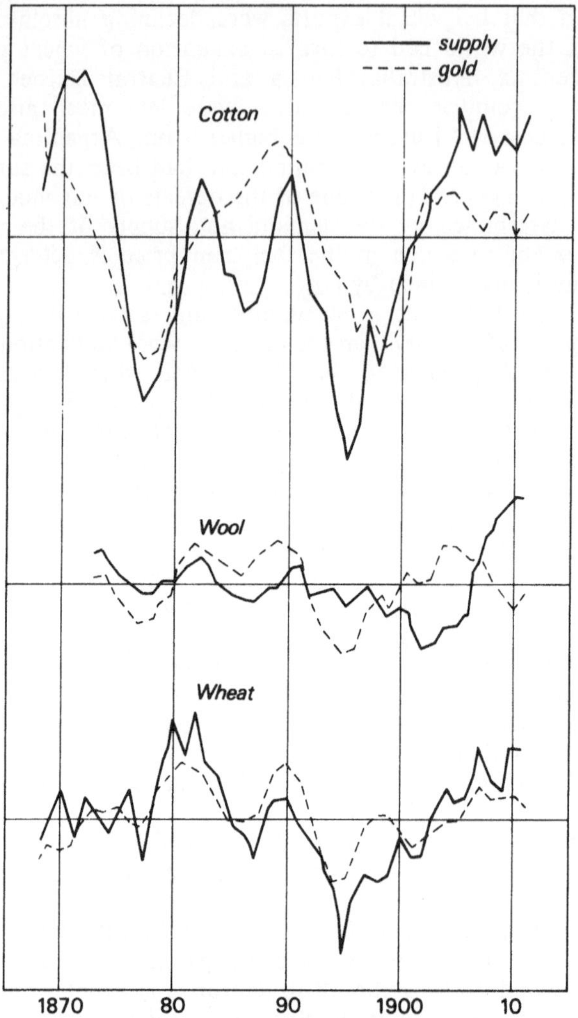

Chart 3.5 Residuals (Supply, Gold)

of the rise in prices corresponds with the slackened growth of industry and the lower investment ratios of the core as a whole. What would have happened after 1913, but for the war, we cannot know.

Our data are not adequate for analysing in this detail the transition from the sixties to the seventies. The role of the supply of agricultural products is therefore not so well established at this turnaround, although the inflow of American wheat and cotton was the most popular explanation in Europe at the time. In fact, except for cotton, the agricultural terms of trade were well maintained in the seventies; their slide began in 1883. The spectacular event of the seventies was the extraordinary explosion and collapse of money wages in Britain, Germany and the USA, to and after 1873. This was an exceptional event. During most of the nineteenth century, continuing to

1913, money wages went up only a little in each Juglar upswing, and came down even less in the Juglar downswing, and it was this relative stability of money wages which underpinned the general price level. The explosion and slippage of money wages just before and after 1873 destabilised the price level with respect to changes in the level of industrial activity (or perhaps of capital formation, since the cause was the wide swing in construction). Prices rose too high in the upswing and fell too low when production fell. By too high and too low we mean that because money wages changed, prices changed by more than can be explained by the physical facts of demand and supply of commodities, assuming constant money wages and an elastic money supply. Chart 3.5 offers some slight evidence that prices rose excessively in the boom of the early 1870s (actual prices were closer to gold than to the price suggested by current agricultural supply).

Hence it is not possible to say how much of the fall of prices in the 1870s was due to agricultural supplies and how much to the collapse of the price level. At first, until about 1876, agricultural prices fell faster than industrial prices; but prices of manufactures continued their downward slide to about 1879, which was also the turning point for money wages. The demand and supply situation contributed to bringing down agricultural prices in the 1870s but demand and supply were clearly supplemented, if not surpassed, by the collapse of money wages. After 1883 money wages moved up almost continuously, and the burden of explanation has to rest mainly with agricultural supplies.

But this is not the entire explanation. Apart from falling too much in the 1870s, from the standpoint of the effect of agricultural supplies, prices were also too slow to rise at the end of the 1890s, and rose too fast in the second half of the 1900s. Were these discrepancies due to changes in the stock of monetary gold?

THE SUPPLY OF MONEY

3.08 A monetary explanation may seek to supplement an agricultural explanation of the turnaround of prices after 1895, but cannot displace it. The turnaround in agricultural supplies happened, and must have had some corresponding influence on agricultural prices. The change in the terms of trade in favour of agriculture is just what we would expect from it. However, this does not rule out a simultaneous but independent monetary contribution. An increase in prices that derived solely from an increase in the quantity of money might alter the terms of trade in this way for one or other of two reasons. If the elasticity of supply of manufactures was large but the elasticity of supply of agricultural commodities was small, agricultural prices might rise faster than the prices of manufactures. This would show up in an acceleration of both types of output, with greater acceleration in manufactures, so the circumstances of 1895 to 1913 do not fit this case. An alternative possibility would be greater flexibility of agricultural prices, in comparison with 'administered' prices of manufactures. This flexibility, combined with rising price expectations and the ease of stock piling some agricultural commodities, could send agricultural prices rising quite high in relation to prices of manufactures. This divergence could not continue indefinitely, since the basic demand and supply factors would ultimately reassert themselves, but the situation could continue over many years. We cannot therefore rule out the possibility that an independent monetary inflation contributed towards moving the terms of trade in favour of agriculture.

We have been using the stock of monetary gold to reflect monetary considerations, but from the stock of gold to the stock of money is quite a jump, and from money to prices involves another barrier, the velocity of circulation of money.

In 1770 the money of our four core countries was essentially metallic, and changes in the output of gold and silver showed at once in changes in the quantity of money. Two hundred years later, in 1970, changes in the output of gold and silver had no effect on the quantity of money. Our period, 1870 to 1913, was a transition period, during which other forms of money, most notably bank deposits, were rapidly displacing the precious metals. It was not important that the stock of gold was now only a small fraction of the stock of money – in 1913 only 12 per cent in the USA and 14 per cent in Britain. What matters is that the ratio between the stock of gold and the stock of money was changing all the time. It is therefore rash to assume that changes in the stock of monetary gold in this period were exactly reflected in changes in the stock of money.

The evidence is clear for the United Kingdom. According to the data presented by Sheppard,[14] the stock of money[15] rose at a more or less constant rate no matter what was happening to the stock of monetary gold.[16] It grew at 2·7 per cent per annum from 1883 to 1899, by 0·8 per cent per annum from 1899 to 1905, and by 2·8 per cent per annum from

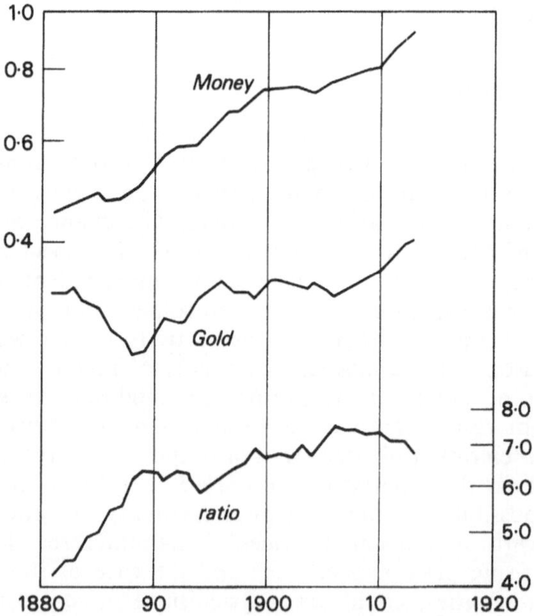

Chart 3.6 UK: Stocks of Money and Gold

1905 to 1913, thus growing least when prices were rising most rapidly (1900 to 1907). Over this period the ratio of money to gold doubled; it rose very rapidly when the country was losing gold, as in the eighties, and fell steadily after 1907, when the country was gaining gold swiftly. One cannot use changes in the quantity of money in the UK to explain the UK price level. All this can be seen in Chart 3.6.

If the quantity of money and output grew at more or less constant rates over the long period, how was the swing in prices sustained, in monetary terms? The answer is: by changes in the velocity of circulation,[17] which fell sharply during the downswing of prices, and rose sharply during the upswing (see Chart 3.7). So not only was the quantity of money not determined by the quantity of gold, but the quantity of trade was not determined by the quantity of money.

Chart 3.7 Income Velocity of Circulation

The American story is both similar and different.[18] The difference lies in the closer relationship between the behaviour of prices and the stock of money. The similarity lies in the equally poor relationship between the stock of money and the stock of gold.

The poor relationship between money and gold is obvious in Chart 3.8, from the curve showing the ratio between these two. The USA was rebuilding its stock of gold in the 1880s, following its return to the gold standard in 1879. Gold increased faster than money up to 1888; thereafter gold was retained with difficulty to 1890, and then drained out to 1896. But the stock of money continued to increase until 1892; thereafter, in face of a great depression, it was held more or less constant despite the depletion of the stock of gold. Not until after 1898 is there a smooth correspondence between the stock of gold and the stock of money. But from 1898 to 1913 money now rises faster than gold. The difference is 1·6 per cent per annum (gold 6·0, money 7·6). If the increase in the GNP deflator[19] over this period (at 1·9 per cent per annum) was due to the increase in the quantity of money, then we can say that prices would have been nearly constant if money had risen at the same rate as gold; the chief culprit was not gold but the divergence of money from gold. In the USA as in the UK, the ratio of the stock of gold to the stock of money was by now so small, and the connection so loose, that changes in the quantity of gold can no longer be expected to be the sole explanation of changes in the quantity of money.

Now for the relationship between money and prices. In the case of the UK, as we have seen, this was not close, because of wide variations in the

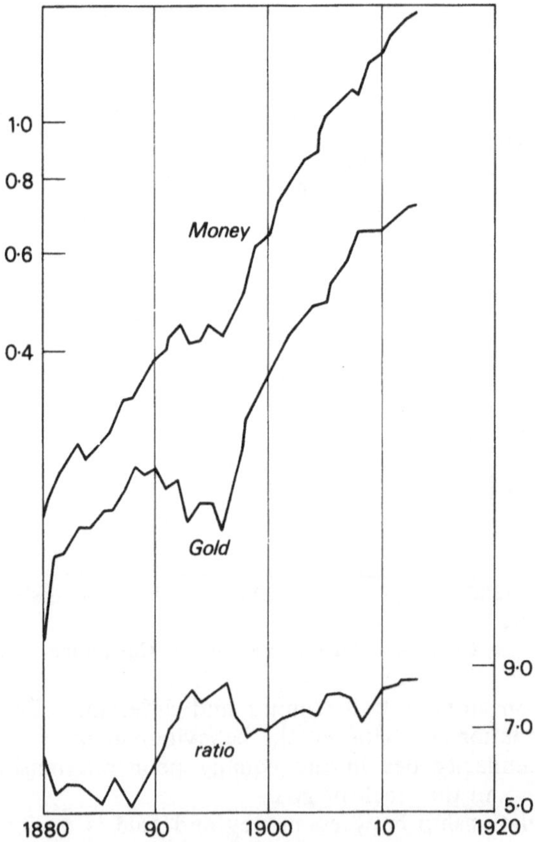

Chart 3.8 USA: Stocks of Money and Gold

velocity of circulation. In the case of the USA the relationship was much closer. Friedman and Schwartz state the position as follows:

> The stock of money grew both from 1879 to 1897 and from 1897 to 1914. But the rate of growth during the earlier period, though large by present-day standards and much larger than during the greenback period, was decidedly smaller than during the later period. It averaged about 6 per cent per year from 1879 to 1897, about 7½ per cent from 1897 to 1914. The different rates of monetary growth were associated with a corresponding difference in the behaviour of prices. Prices fell at the rate of over 1 per cent a year from 1879 to 1897, and rose at the rate of over 2 per cent a year from 1897 to 1914.[20]

The dating is crucial. As can be seen in Chart 3.8, if one took instead 1884, 1892, 1904 and 1913 one would find that the stock of money grew secularly at an almost constant rate. These intervals yield 2·6, 2·5 and 2·6 per cent per annum, despite the turnaround in prices (the GNP deflator) whose intervals for the same dates would be −1·3, 0·6 and 4·4. We choose instead peak dates of production: 1882, 1892 and 1906 (see Chart 1.1).

To analyse what is happening we must take all four elements in the quantity of money equation – production, prices, money and the velocity of circulation. Industrial production grew at the same rates between 1882 and 1892 and between 1892 and 1906 (by 5·0 per cent per annum), but we have to work with real national income, which apparently grew by 3·7 per cent per annum in the first period and by 4·3 per cent per annum in the second.[21] (This difference is improbable, but as our footnote explains it does not matter.) The GNP deflator fell at 2·0 per cent and then rose at 0·8 per cent per annum. The quantity of money rose at 5·6 and then at 6·5 per cent per annum. And the velocity of circulation fell at 4·0 and then at 1·4 per cent per annum. When we put these percentage growth rates per annum together we get the following:

	Money stock	*Velocity*	*Real GNP*	*Price*
1882/92	5·6	−4·0	3·7	−2·0
1892–1906	6·5	−1·4	4·3	+0·8
Difference	0·9	2·6	0·7	2·8

Since the elements we are using are those of the quantity equation identity, the sum of the differences of the first two columns is equal to the sum of the differences of the second two columns. To paraphrase, the growth rate of money income rose by 3·5 percentage points per annum; to this money contributed only one-quarter, while the change in the velocity of circulation contributed three-quarters.

Now the quantity equation does not indicate causation. We may have one, two or three exogenous variables; or any number of mutually determining variables, from one to four. For example we may postulate that prices were determined on the world market, and that the growth of production was also an independent variable. Then if the action was coming from the growth of the stock of money, the velocity of circulation was being forced to accommodate to it. But maybe the action was coming from the velocity of circulation. The US economy was monetising rapidly in the last quarter of the nineteenth century. Farm households produced less for subsistence, and bought in more. The banking habit was growing rapidly as the country urbanised. But whereas bank deposits grew 4·4 times as fast as money income between 1882 and 1892, they grew only 1·3 times as fast between 1892 and 1906. If output, prices and the velocity of circulation all changed exogenously, then the dependent variable was the quantity of money. But one could work the analysis any way, starting for example with an exogenous supply of money, and ending with endogenous prices, as the monetarists prefer to do.

We make the following suggestion concerning the behaviour of the velocity of circulation in mild inflations. If the inflation derives from increased spending on the part of the public, the supply of money lags, and the velocity of circulation increases. This is familiar from cyclical experience. But if the inflation derives from an increase in the quantity of money, the velocity of circulation falls. The public takes some time to realise that there has been a permanent turnaround in the trend of prices. Its first reaction to rising prices and to having more money is to build up its cash balances. This does not hold if prices are rising very fast, since a rapid increase in prices erodes public confidence in money; even so the relative stability of the velocity of circulation even when prices are rising very fast indeed has been noted by Cagan as a normal prelude to hyperinflations.[22]

Faced with the situation that money supply contributed 0·9 and a rise in the velocity of circulation 2·6, we may hazard that this was a demand-induced inflation, and not an inflation originating primarily in an increase in the supply of money. Prices rose because the supply of agricultural products was decelerating, and the supply of money had to grow faster than the supply of gold in order to support the level of money income. We cannot deduce this from the equations, but it seems more plausible than the alternative hypotheses.[23]

The banks were able to meet the demand for money not because their reserves were growing rapidly – on the contrary the growth rate from 1892 to 1906 was only 4·0 per cent per annum – but because it was safe to increase the ratio of deposits to reserves, which rose from 5·9 to 8·9; and this it was safe to do because the public's demand for deposits was rising so rapidly, namely at 7·1 per cent per annum or 1·4 times as fast as money income. The stock of gold held by the Treasury could potentially have played a role, via the banks' holding of cash, but cash grew relatively slowly, and the ratio of bank to public holdings of cash was about the same in 1906 as in 1892.

Since our countries were on the gold standard, what was happening to the world's monetary stock of gold becomes relevant not as a cause but as an accessory. If the world's gold stock had been constant after 1900 when agricultural deficits were pushing up prices, and bankers creating more credit, some leading countries (European countries importing agricultural products, rather than the USA) might have run short of gold, if they had difficulty in exporting enough manufactures, and would then have had to halt the process. In the same way the fact that the flood of wheat, cotton and wool was reducing the price level in the 1870s and 1880s made it easier for Western European monetary systems to live with a declining rate of growth of gold stocks (but more difficult for the USA and other exporters of agricultural products to live with the gold standard).

Schumpeter took his argument to its ultimate conclusion. For him the changes in gold production did not initiate the Kondratiev swing in prices; it was the swing in prices that stimulated the changes in gold production. It is both true and important that a declining price level increases the profitability of mining gold, and so expands the output of existing mines, whereas a rising price level reduces the output of the mines. However, the big changes in gold production were due to new discoveries rather than to changes in the output of existing mines. More people look for gold when mining is more profitable because of falling prices than look when mining is less profitable because of rising prices. But looking is not the same as finding. The finding of new large and rich deposits of gold, like those of California, Australia and South Africa, includes such a large random element that one must not incorporate it mechanically into a self-generating theory of prices. We accept neither that changes in gold supply caused the changes in prices nor that changes in prices caused the changes in gold supply. History is full of fortuitous coincidences, and this was such an occasion.

3.09 In sum, we find as follows. First, the original cause of the Kondratiev swing lies in changes in the rate of flow of agricultural output. Secondly, these changes had cumulative effects on the price level, which fell fairly sharply in the seventies, was slow to rise at the turn of the century, and then rose faster than the agricultural quantities required. Thirdly, the unusual rise followed by collapse of money wages in the seventies added to the instability of the price system. Fourthly, these cumulative changes were reflected in changes in the velocity of circulation, and to a lesser extent in changes in the quantity of bank credit. Fifthly, the changes in the quantity of bank credit were facilitated by changes in the rate of flow of gold production, which were themselves an accessory to the turnaround of prices rather than its cause.

Chapter 4

The Check to Real Wages

SYNOPSIS: 4.00 A pronounced feature of the upswing of prices was that real wages in manufacturing rose much more slowly after 1899 than before (actually declining in Britain and France). This chapter investigates the three possible explanations: decelerating productivity, a shift to profits, or adverse terms of trade.

4.01 The rate of growth of industrial productivity declined slightly in Great Britain, but not elsewhere.

4.02 Statistics on the relative shares of wages and profits in manufacturing industry are either non-existent or inadequate. 4.03 Statistics on relative shares in national income as a whole are less sparse, but not reliable. 4.04 After much manipulation, stock exchange data suggest that the rate of return on new investment was not higher in 1913 than in 1899, except perhaps in France. 4.05 Definite conclusions are not possible, but it seems unlikely that the deceleration of real wages can be attributed to any large extent to a shift to profits.

4.06 The Kondratiev turnaround in the terms of trade between industry and agriculture is therefore the main explanation. 4.07 Money wages rose at the same rate during the upswing as during the downswing; this is why real wages rose especially fast before 1899, and especially slowly thereafter. 4.08 Money wages rose at different rates in the four countries, but these differences were offset by differences in the growth rates of productivity. So money cost of labour per unit of output rose at roughly the same rate in each country. 4.09 Each country had its own rates of change of productivity, money wages and the terms of trade, but these were inter-related by the competitive constraint that money labour cost per unit of output must rise at roughly the same rate in all four.

4.00 We have said that the upswing of prices did not affect the rate of growth of industrial production in our core countries. It did however check the rate of growth of real wages in all these countries, and this we must now explore.

Phelps Brown's figures for money wages in manufacturing, and the cost of living, yield the following growth rates for real wages:[1]

	1883–99 (% *p.a.*)	*1899–1913* (% *p.a.*)
UK	2·0	−0·3
France	1·6	−0·1
Germany	1·9	0·5
USA	1·8	1·1

The common feature was the change in the terms of trade between industry and agriculture, associated with the Kondratiev swing in prices. But since the experience of the four countries differed so markedly, other features were also clearly at work. Thus British and French real wages actually fell, while German and American wages continued to rise, but at reduced rates. In both Britain and France real wages had been rising faster than productivity before 1900, so it is not surprising that they experienced the greater check when prices turned around.

A check to real wages may come about in one of three ways. First, there may be a decline in the rate of growth of productivity. Secondly, the growth rate of productivity may be constant, but the share of wages in the product relative to profits may be falling, either because the physical amount of capital per unit of output is rising, because the cost of producing capital is rising relative to the price of output, or because the rate of return to capital is rising. And thirdly, the growth rate of productivity may be constant, and the relative share of labour may be constant, but the terms of trade may be moving against industry in favour of agriculture. Here we have the important distinction between the industrial worker's product-wage (the wage measured in terms of his own product) and his real wage (the purchasing power of the money wage in terms of the things he buys). We know that the terms of trade moved against industry. We want to find out whether there was also a change in the growth rate of the product-wage. Information on these topics is meagre, so this chapter is highly speculative.

PRODUCTIVITY

4.01 Let us begin with productivity. Can the check to real wages be attributed to a decline in the rate of growth of productivity?

In our first case, the United Kingdom, we shall confine ourselves to manufacturing. The figures for construction are too frail to be worth bringing into this account (this applies as much or even more to the other core countries), and there is nothing mysterious about mining. Productivity in coal mining increased in the USA up to the war, but in all the countries of Western Europe it was declining. The British figures of coal output per head show an annual rate of decline of 0·2 per cent from 1883 to 1899 and 0·7 per cent thereafter, resulting from both shorter hours and less productive seams.

For numbers in manufacturing we have only decennial census figures, which have to be rearranged to separate salespeople from producers (e.g. workers in chemical factories from workers in drugstores). This rearrangement has been done in Appendix I. If we assume that the growth rate of the population in manufacturing was the same between peaks as between censuses – a not implausible assumption, since the censuses include the unemployed – then we get the following growth rates for manufacturing:

	Output	*Persons*	*Product per person*
1883–99	2·20	1·05	1·15
1899–1913	1·80	0·90	0·90

The reduction in the growth rate of output per person is not wholly explained by a fall in hours per week. Much of the fall in hours, such as it was, occurred before 1899. To explain the whole reduction, which comes to 3·6 per cent over fourteen years, one would have to assume a rather larger fall in hours – say 7 per cent – because output does not fall proportionately. This is larger than the evidence justifies.[2]

Firm positions cannot be taken, since we are certain neither of numbers engaged nor of hours worked. The whole difference in the growth rate of productivity disappears if we raise the 1899 population by one per cent (assuming that the slump was followed by slower growth to 1901), reduce the 1913 population by one per cent (for more unemployment then than in 1899) and allow 2 per cent for reduction due to shorter work week.

But the decline of the rate of growth of productivity is supported by other evidence. G. T. Jones demonstrated a long time ago[3] that productivity had levelled out in the cotton industry in the 1880s; and his conclusion that productivity in pig iron was also static has been reinforced by McCloskey who, somewhat to his embarrassment, found it to be falling.[4] To be sure, productivity was rising fast in some other industries, but cotton and pig iron weigh heavily in the total.

Was the deceleration of productivity due to a decline in the rate of growth of capital per man, or was it in the 'residual', that is to say due to an exhaustion of the fruits of technology? There are no separate figures for capital in manufacturing. Feinstein's figures are for gross domestic product and net capital stock as a whole. We have adjusted by subtracting figures relating to agriculture, domestic service, government and ownership of dwellings. We can then make the following comparisons for what is roughly 'industry and trade':

	1883–99	*1899–1913*
Growth of output per person	0·9	0·9
Growth of capital per person	0·3	0·2
Capital–output ratio (1899, 1913)	2·2	2·1

In this series there is no decline in the rate of growth of productivity. Capital per head is growing very slowly (Britain is exporting a large proportion of her savings) – slightly more slowly after 1899. Whence it follows that output is growing slightly faster than capital, and that the 'residual' is rising slightly. This result is somewhat doubtful, since an increasing residual is hard to square with what we know about declining productivity in individual industries, as well as in manufacturing as a whole.[5]

In assessing manufacturing productivity in France we run straight into a major difficulty: the statistics of employment. If we use the population census figures, and make the same assumption as for the British, that the growth rate is the same from peak to peak as from census to census, we get the following growth rates for manufacturing and mining (without building):

	Output	*Persons*	*Output per person*
1882–92	1·7	0·3	1·4
1892–9	2·2	2·9	–0·7
1899–1909	1·9	0·6	1·3

Clearly the growth rate of the number of persons from 1892 to 1899 cannot be right. Two things are wrong. One is that the classification of persons as between industry and commerce changed in 1896. Toutain[6] offers figures which correct for this, but since industry and commerce grew in the same proportion between 1881 and 1911, we can use their sum as our series for employment in manufacturing, thereby evading inconsistencies in the distribution between these two in the intervening years. The other problem is much more serious. The census authorities also redefined the active population in 1896 in a way that increased the total by about 15 per cent. To adjust for this is a much more hazardous undertaking. Making the adjustments described in our footnote, we get a new population series, with the following results for growth rates of manufacturing (including mining).

	Output	*Persons*	*Output per person*
1882–92	1·7	0·4	1·3
1892–9	2·2	0·8	1·4
1899–1909	1·9	0·8	1·1

The somewhat slower growth of productivity after 1899 would be reversed if we went on to 1912. But the jump of output between 1909 and 1912 (see Chart 1.1) is so large that it must partly be due to an overweighting of iron and steel in the production index. Making the best of numerous defects, we would settle for the proposition that French productivity per man rose at about the same speed after 1899 as it had risen between 1892 and 1899, say at about 1·3 per cent per annum. So the declining real wage must, in France, seek some other explanation than declining productivity.

The German case also is frustrated by inadequate labour statistics. The basic data are from the occupational censuses of 1875, 1882, 1895 and 1907, and the first of these is not reliable. Hoffmann has interpolated annual data for each industrial group, using his knowledge of output and employment, but the results are strange. Thus starting from 1873, his annual growth rates for numbers in manufacturing run from peak to peak as follows: 0·9, 2·8, 2·0, 1·6 and 1·4; an implausible result for a country where the decennial growth rates for the urban population are 2·5, 2·4, 2·7 and 2·6.

We have taken Hoffmann's populations for the census years, and have interpolated, using our hardy assumption that the number of workers grows at the same rate between peaks as between censuses. This assumption yields the following annual growth rates for manufacturing:

	Output	Persons	Output per person
1883–90	4·2	2·0	2·2
1890–9	4·3	2·1	2·2
1899–1912	4·1	2·0	2·1

Here again one should assume for practical purposes that there is little if any change in the growth rate of productivity beyond such as may result from shorter hours. The change in the rate of growth of real wages must originate in the terms of trade or the share of wages or both.

The American case differs from the others in that real wages were rising as fast as ever up to the peak of 1906. The setback thereafter was due to the coincidence of industrial depression with a sharp rise in agricultural prices – not unlike the situation in the early 1970s. Therefore in seeking long swings, we have to look further back in time, comparing the peaks of 1872, 1882, 1892 and 1906, where possible.

John W. Kendrick has written the authoritative book on American productivity.[7] Unfortunately his annual series start only in 1889, and therefore include only one of our periods, 1892 to 1906. To be able to make comparisons with peaks before 1892 we shall have to resort *faute de mieux* to our usual assumption that the labour force grew between peaks at the same rate as between census years. This assumption yields the following annual growth rates for manufacturing and mining together:

	Output	Persons	Output per person
1872–82	5·1	3·1	2·0
1882–92	5·0	3·1	1·9
1892–1906	5·2	3·35	1·85

The growth rate of productivity per person was presumably constant, except for some small reflection of shorter hours. The long depression at the end of the century started the theory that the country had run out of technological opportunities, but this was not so. The great depression was a repetitive phenomenon. And statistics of decade averages of output hide what is really happening.

DISTRIBUTIVE SHARES

4.02 The conclusion so far is that, except for Great Britain, changes in the growth rate of productivity explain little or no part of the change in the rate of growth of real wages; and even in Britain this could not be the major factor. Let us now consider the division of the product; was there a shift to profits after 1899?

Nowadays the Census of Manufactures would yield a direct answer to this question, but the only pre-1913 censuses which asked about profits were those of the United States. According to these censuses the share of gross profits in value added in manufacturing[8] moved in the United States from 42 per cent in 1889 to 50 per cent in 1899 and 49 per cent in 1904 and 1909. These dates come at different stages of the business cycle; 1889 and

1904 were reasonably prosperous, whereas 1899 and 1909 were well below trend; so it is hard to interpret their meaning. The same comment applies to Kendrick's estimate of the capital–output ratio in manufacturing, at constant prices, the index of which (on 1929 base) rises from 96 in 1889 to 107 in 1899 and 125 in 1909. The share of heavy industry in American manufacturing was undoubtedly larger after 1889 than before, but some part of the increase in the ratio must be due to comparing a prosperous 1889 with a relatively depressed 1899 and 1909. For the economy as a whole Kendrick gets the opposite result; his capital–output ratio falls from 1889 to 1899 and falls again to 1909. However, we cannot tell what to make of this since, as we have suggested in Appendix II, Kuznets's figures underestimate the amount of capital in the 1880s and earlier.

Where census data are absent it is possible to manufacture one's own profit share ratios from statistics of varying relevance. This is done, for purposes of illustration only, in Table 4.1, for Great Britain in 1883, 1899 and 1913, years of peak production. We have index numbers for prices of manufactures, capital, labour and materials, and we know roughly what the shares of the cost elements were.[9] Here the price of manufactures comes from export statistics, which are not necessarily representative of industrial production for the home market. The price of raw materials is from the Sauerbeck–Statist index, and it is assumed that use of materials per unit of output diminishes by 0·5 per cent per annum. The capital–output ratio is assumed to be constant; and the price of capital

Table 4.1 *UK: Hypothetical Cost of Manufacturing*

	Base	1899 on 1883		1913 on 1899	
	Ratios	*Price*	*Cost*	*Price*	*Cost*
Capital	290	0·995	289	1·100	341
Labour	360	0·964	347	1·004	374
Materials	350	0·912	295	1·300	384
Total cost	1,000		931		1,099
Price of manufactures	1,000		884		1,250
Profit	—		−47		+151

goods combines, with equal weights, Feinstein's indexes for 'plant and machinery' and for 'other building'. The money cost of labour is found by dividing the money wage index by the productivity index.

The results of Table 4.1 illustrate why, although we have made similar tables for all the core countries, we do not publish them here, and do not rely on them. The result for 1913 relative to 1899 – an increase in the profitability of manufacturing – is implausible but possible; but the result for 1899 on 1883 – a decline in the profitability of manufacturing if the capital–output ratio is held constant – is quite implausible, to the point almost of impossibility. Artefacts of this kind are highly sensitive to one's choice of indexes, and the results of multiplying large aggregates together and subtracting the results are bound to be somewhat arbitrary.

4.03 If the scene is shifted from manufacturing alone to the whole economy, more material comes in sight on income distribution, for we then have two national income series on an annual basis, Feinstein's for the United Kingdom and Hoffmann's for Germany.

Feinstein's figures show the share of profits constant in the United Kingdom (apart from cyclical fluctuations) from the second half of the 1880s down to the First World War. However, his capital–output ratio changes, so this constancy obtains because after 1899 a rise in the capital–output ratio is offset by a fall in the rate of return to capital. Feinstein's figures for profits include the labour income of the self-employed as well as their profits, so they are vulnerable to changes in the proportion of self-employment. They also include income from agriculture, domestic service, government and ownership of dwellings. If one subtracts these items from both income and capital, the ratio of profits to income in the 'business sector' declines between 1899 and 1913 from 40 to 38 per cent. The rate of return on net capital (including stocks) at current replacement cost also falls, from 16·0 to 14·8 per cent. We shall come back to this later.

Hoffmann gives figures for Germany from which one can calculate the share of profits in a sector grouped broadly as 'industry and trade', but these figures are not from tax returns or other independent sources. Profits are calculated by taking the capital stock from a regional sample, multiplying by a price index for capital, and multiplying the result by an assumed rate of return, which he holds constant. Since his price of capital goods is rising sharply, his share of profits is also rising sharply.[10] The ratio of assumption to measured data is so large that we cannot rely on the result. Besides, he has assumed the very thing we are seeking to discover, namely whether the rate of return to capital was constant or not.

A number of writers have estimated the share of profits in the USA at various dates up to 1914. Lebergott has reviewed this literature in detail, and concludes, with reason, that these estimates cannot yield a reliable picture of the secular trend.[11]

4.04 We turn now to material of a very different sort – corporation profits, as reflected in data on earnings, dividends and prices on the stock exchange. It has to be processed, but is then very suggestive.

The most comprehensive stock exchange series are those for the United States, as reported and analysed in Alfred Cowles's excellent volume.[12] One of his series reports annual earnings per share, for a number of companies, stretching back to 1872. This series rises rather fast, because of the reinvestment of retained earnings; to arrive at the rate of return to capital we must first reduce the earnings per share proportionately as reserves were built up. This is easily done since another series gives dividends per share for the same sample. By cumulating the difference year by year we get an index showing how one share would grow if retained earnings were used in each year to purchase additional share fractions; the answer is that the purchaser of one share in 1872 would by 1913 have owned 3·4 shares. When we divide earnings per share by this index of accumulated shareholding, we get earnings per share adjusted for reinvested reserves.

This adjusted earnings index has to be compared with changes in the price of capital goods, so as to get at changes in the rate of return to new investment. Kuznets has given us figures for capital formation by business in current and 1929 prices; these yield an index of the price of capital goods.[13]

Kuznets's figures are five-year moving averages, so our adjusted earnings per share must also be in five-year moving averages.

When we compare these two series – adjusted earnings per share and the price of capital goods – it is at once clear that earnings per share are falling too rapidly. The reason for this is that retained earnings are overstated, presumably because firms were not writing off enough in depreciation. Cowles made the same point, and offered various reasons, some more plausible than others.[14] We have made the following rough adjustment. Assume that the rate of return to investment in new capital was the same in the early 1880s and the early 1890s, as represented by 1879/82 and 1891/5, which are the moving average peaks. This means that the two series should fall by the same percentage over these two dates. We achieve this by altering the growth rate of the earnings series. This has been growing on the average by 3·0 per cent per annum; we make it grow instead on average by 2·3 per cent per annum (i.e. we divide it by a series which grows each year by almost 0·7 per cent per annum).

The result is shown in Chart 4.1, which is semi-logarithmic. Points where the two series come together yield the same rate of return to new investment; points where earnings lie above capital are more profitable, and points where earnings lie below capital are less profitable. The graph indicates that if the first half of the eighties and the first half of the nineties were equally profitable, then the period from 1900 to 1907 was even more profitable. The graph also confirms the evidence of the statistics of industrial production that 1908 saw the onset of another Kuznets great depression. However, its portrayal of a great depression in the second half of the 1880s is anomalous; examination of stock exchange prices suggests that the earnings of the Cowles sample were unrepresentatively low;[15] and comparison of Kuznets's price of capital goods index with that of Feinstein for Great Britain (also in Chart 4.1) suggests that the price of capital goods may have fallen faster in the second half of the 1880s than Kuznets's figures show. The existence of such anomalies dampens our enthusiasm for the method, which might otherwise be fired by an apparently clear demonstration of a boom in profits in the first years of the new century.

When we turn to Great Britain there are no series on company earnings, so we must use instead the data on the price of industrial shares.[16] To translate from share prices to earnings per share we need to adjust for changes in the price–earnings ratio. We have no data on this ratio, but we can isolate one of its more important secular elements, namely changes in the long-term rate of interest. So we divide the index of share prices by an index of the price of bonds (mostly government issues) which is also given in the same publication. The result approximates to an index of expected profits per share; 'expected', since share prices reflect the future as well as the past. This procedure somewhat exaggerates the effect of a change in the long-term rate of interest. A doubling of that rate of interest will halve the price of perpetual and riskless bonds, and will also reduce the price of

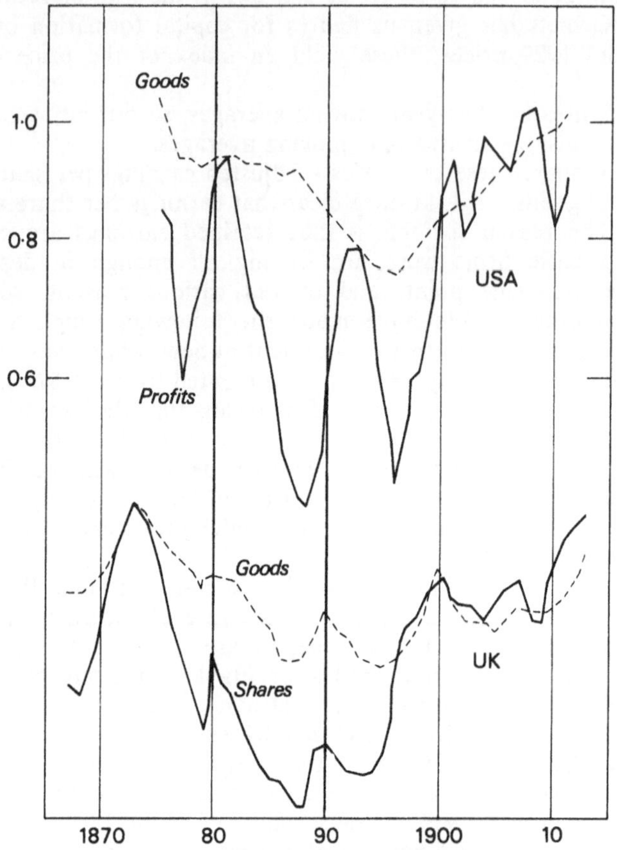

Chart 4.1 Profitability and Capital Goods

shares, but not by as much as one half. As a result our 'expected profit' curve is too low in the 1880s and 1890s relatively to the 1870s and 1900s. This affects adversely comparisons between distant but not between adjacent dates.

When this expected profit series is compared with the price of capital goods,[17] we find the same phenomenon as in the American case, namely that adjustment has to be made for reinvestment of retained profits. We handle this by assuming that business was equally profitable over 1872/4 and 1898/1900, whence it follows that shares grew by reinvestment at an average annual rate of 0·44 per cent per annum. This is much smaller than the American reinvestment rate of 2·3 per cent per annum (reinvestment of profits was much higher in the USA than in Britain, France or Germany), and the difference is so large that the rate of return to capital must also have been higher.

Chart 4.1 shows that if one assumes that the rate of return to new investment was the same in 1872/4 and 1898/1900, then the 1880s and first half of the 1890s were very unprofitable; and investment is again very profitable from the turn of the century onwards. Here we must remember the warning that our procedure exaggerates the trough. However, the gap is so large that it would still be there even if we had not divided the share index by the bond index. There is no real doubt that the 1880s and early 1890s were abnormally depressed, although some British historians have persuaded themselves that this was not so.[18]

The anomaly in this chart is the widening gap between the two curves after 1907. Most of our statistics of large aggregates show this to have been a difficult time; construction and domestic investment were down, and unemployment and emigration were up; and although the exports of goods and services were well maintained (rising in current prices at 3·4 per cent per annum over 1907 to 1913), these barely kept manufacturing production on trend. As Feinstein's data suggests, it was a time of falling rather than rising rates of return to investment. Why then the rising gap between our two curves?

The answer seems to lie with the stock exchange. Our curve for profit expectations is derived by dividing a share index by a bond index. Inspection of the share index reveals only normal cyclical movements, without suggestion of secularly increasing profitability; the upturn in our curve comes from a pronounced decline in the bond index. What can have caused a widening of the gap between share and bond prices?

We have already given one possible answer: rising interest rates depress bond prices proportionately more than share prices. However, to cover the field we must also consider two other possible contributors.

One possibility would be the big increase in the relative supply of bonds caused by the spurt in foreign investment at this time. The volume was so great that it began to make a claim on the domestic product. Ever since about 1890 Britain had been exporting less capital than the income coming in as interest and dividends on previous lending. The surplus averaged £44 million over 1891/9, and £39 million over 1900/7. Now there was a turn-around to −£3 million over 1908/13. It is true that gross domestic capital formation was much reduced in this latest period, from 10·2 per cent to 6·5 per cent of gross national product, but the addition of foreign investment now brought total gross investment up from 13·9 to 15·3 per cent of GNP. This increase in the total demand for savings could be expected to have some effect on the price of bonds, especially if profits (and therefore savings) were not particularly buoyant; but why should it not equally affect the price of shares? The larger foreign investment did indeed increase the supply of bonds more than the supply of shares, but one would have expected that by 1913 these two types of paper would have become highly substitutable at the margin.

A better answer is one familiar in our own day: share prices should rise relatively to bonds if the public believes that the general price level (and therefore profit per share) is set to rise indefinitely. The rate of interest rises, but share prices should fall less than bond prices. What we have probably tracked down is that by 1913 the financial public had realised that prices were now in a secular upswing, and had been rising ever since the Kondratiev turning point of 1895. When we add to the rise in the rate of interest the fact that the cause of that rise was expectations of rising prices, we have an adequate combination of reasons for the widening gap between bond and share prices.

Germany can be treated more briefly since the procedure is exactly the same as for Britain. Donner's index of industrial shares is divided by the reciprocal of his rate of interest on 'first class paper'[19] and the result is compared with a Hoffmann index of the price of capital goods.[20] Here we assume that reinvestment of earnings is at a rate of 0·5 per cent per annum, and then find as in Chart 4.2 that this makes the rate of return on new investment at the Juglar peaks remarkably constant from 1880 onwards. We also find remarkable confirmation from the stock exchange of two features that stand out in the statistics of industrial production for Germany, in contrast with those of the other three core members: first, that there was no Kuznets great depression after 1880; and secondly, that the fluctuation from peak to trough within the Juglar cycle was rather small, a feature which also emerges in the unemployment statistics (see section 2.08). The reader must bear in mind that the German and American series in Charts 4.1 and 4.2 are five-year moving averages, while the British and French series are annual data; but the conclusion still remains: the

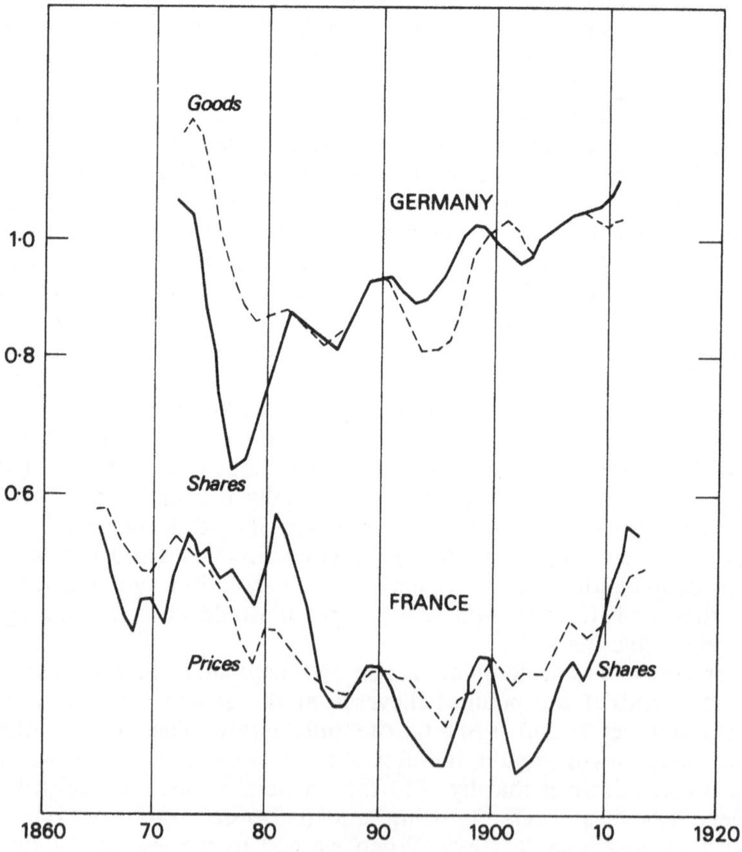

Chart 4.2 Profitability and Prices

German economy was the most stable. At the same time Chart 4.2 throws doubt on Hoffmann's price of capital goods, which seems to be relatively too high in the 1870s and much too low in the middle 1890s, especially when we remember that our having divided the share index by the bond index already exaggerates the real difference in profits per share as between 1873 and 1882 or 1890.

In the case of France we are able to divide an index of share prices by an index of bond prices;[21] but unfortunately we have no index for the price of capital goods. What we show instead in Chart 4.2 is an index of the domestic prices of manufactures.[22] The result is astonishing, because the two series move so closely together, indicating almost equally profitable peaks at 1873, 1890, 1899 and 1907, and superbooms at 1881 and 1912. If we take this seriously it follows that there was no net reinvestment of company profits, presumably because reserves tended to be wiped out in the deep Juglar slumps to which the economy was prone. But we must eschew conclusions, not only for lack of capital goods prices, but also because our procedure has presumably exaggerated the trough in profits in the 1880s.

4.05 Can we now reach any conclusion about the share of profits after 1899? The German case seems to be the easiest: there was no change in the rate of return to capital. In Chart 4.2 the gap between share prices and the price of capital goods widens after 1907, but share prices are on trend, and the downward movement of the price of capital goods is probably a statistical aberration.

Even if the rate of return to new investment was constant there could still be a shift to profits if the capital–output ratio rose, or if the price of capital rose relatively to the value-added price of output. These ratios we are not in a position to check. In Germany, Britain and the USA the price of capital rose by less than the GDP deflator, but that deflator includes agricultural prices. What we need is a deflator for manufactures, and this we do not have. We have already referred to estimates of the capital–output ratio in manufacturing; such as they are they do not meet our requirements. We must therefore confine ourselves to conclusions about the rate of return to capital.

After Germany France is the easiest case to account for. The rate of return to new investment recovers after the great depression of the 1880s, and is then constant at peaks until 1907, after which it shoots up to 1912. The year 1908 is a turning point for real (cost of living) wages which have been rising slowly and then turn sharply downwards. It is probable that the superboom in metals and construction which immediately preceded the war was accompanied by a shift to profits.

The British case is now only slightly less certain. That there was a remarkable revival of profits at the end of the century, associated with the superboom in construction, cannot really be disputed. Thereafter the rate of return to capital stayed constant or fell, and if we are comparing 1913 with 1899, a shift to profits cannot be part of an explanation of a fall in real wages.

The statistical evidence for the United States is mixed. But contemporaries felt strongly that there was a shift to profits after 1900, and that feeling is supported by the Census of Manufactures (1904 compared with 1899), and by the data on corporation earnings. The data on domestic savings may also testify in favour of a shift. The domestic savings ratio (gross investment minus capital import, divided by gross national product) can be calculated from Kuznets's five-year moving averages. The highest averages which include the peak years of 1892 and 1906 are those for 1890/4 and 1902/6, and are respectively 23·3 and 23·2 per cent, but as indicated the earlier figure may be too high. Many of those contemporaries who believed that there had been a shift to profits attributed the change to heavy immigration, which kept wages down. But the change in the immigration ratio since the last Kuznets boom was small. The ratio of immigrants to population averaged 9·8 per thousand over 1880/9 and 10·3 per thousand over 1900/7. The verdict has to be 'not proven'. Profits were indeed higher in 1906 than in 1899, but 1899, though a boom year in Europe, was not a boom year in the USA. In making US comparisons one must always be careful to note the different phases of the Kuznets fluctuations because in the short run investment rises faster than savings.

In any case the high profitability of Chart 4.1 stops in 1907; a great depression follows, and by 1913, which is the terminal year of our comparison, profits are on the low side. To explain low real wages in 1913 we must look elsewhere than to the share of profits.

In sum, the only country which may have had a shift towards profits between 1899 and 1913 is France, and there only after 1907. This is remarkable because the period was one of rising prices. If inflation raised the profit share, this was all accomplished in Britain between 1895 and 1899 and in the USA by 1906. Perhaps the explanation lies in the origins of the inflation which, we have suggested, were not monetary but structural (relative agricultural stagnation). It was thus in the industrial sector a cost-push rather than a demand inflation. Profits tend to rise in a demand inflation because costs lag behind prices; but profits may well fall in a structural inflation because prices lag behind costs. These shifts to profits which we seem to have identified (in Britain and the USA over the Juglar of 1899–1907, in France 1910–12) stemmed from increases in capital–investment ratios, and are normal in any situation where investment is rising faster than savings – irrespective of whether the general trend of prices is upwards or downwards.

THE COST OF LIVING

4.06 In sum we find that, in a comparison of real wages in the terminal years 1899 and 1913, there may have been a shift towards profits in France, and a decline in the growth rate of productivity in Britain. This helps to explain why the rate of growth of real wages declined by more in these two countries than in Germany or the USA. But the differences between real wage behaviour in our four countries are so large that these are only minor elements of the explanation; the major elements must lie in different growth rates of the cost of living and of money wages.

The differences in the behaviour of the cost of living were quite marked.

The annual percentage rates of growth, using Phelps-Brown's data, were as follows:

	1883–99	*1899–1913*
UK	−1·1	+1·3
USA	−1·2	+1·3
France	−0·9	+1·0
Germany	+0·1	+1·7

The cost of living both fell more before 1899 and rose more after 1899 in Britain and the USA than in France, because French agriculture was protected while British and American agriculture were not. It is also not surprising that the rates of change in Britain and the United States were about the same. The German case is more complex. German agriculture seems to have been the most heavily protected; Hoffmann's index of the price of imported food falls 18 per cent between 1883 and 1899, whereas his index of retail food prices rises 2 per cent. Presumably the 'social contract' called for food prices to be maintained at the cost of a faster increase of money wages than obtained elsewhere. This faster increase of money wages seeps into all other prices – construction, house rent, transport and other services – so that the German GDP deflator also rises between 1883 and 1899, in contrast with sharp declines elsewhere. One might expect that, as in France, the same factors that braked the downward movement of prices in the Kondratiev downswing would also brake the upward movement of prices in the upswing. Retail food prices did rise by less than the prices of imported food, between 1899 and 1913; and the German deflator did rise somewhat less rapidly than the British or the American, but the fastest rising money wage continued to produce the fastest rising working-class cost of living. That the country could still hold its own in industrial competition was due to the fact that having the fastest rising money wages and cost of living was offset by having also the fastest rising productivity.

MONEY WAGES

4.07 Real wages rose faster than productivity in Britain and France between 1883 and 1899, and rose more slowly than productivity after 1899 in all four countries. It is normal for real wages to rise less than productivity in manufacturing because the industrial workers have to share some of the productivity gains with workers in other sectors whose productivity grows more slowly, but the size of the gap was abnormal.

Why did this change take place? The answer turns out to be simple and astonishing: because there was no secular connection between movements in money wages and the cost of living. Astonishingly, money wages rose at a constant rate irrespective of what was happening to the cost of living. Here are the average annual percentage increases of money wages:

	1883–99	*1899–1913*
UK	+0·9	+0·9
USA	+0·7	+2·3
France	+0·8	+0·9
Germany	+2·0	+2·2

The maverick is the USA, and this only because 1899 is not a peak date for the USA, as it is for the other three. If we take the USA's own peak dates for money wages, 1884, 1891, 1906 and 1913, the inter-peak growth rate of money wages from 1884 to 1913 was almost constant (1·3, 1·4, 1·4), although the growth rates of the cost of living between the same dates varied widely (−1·2, 0·2, 0·8).

Of course the choice of dates is fundamental. Over this period one can usually find deceleration in a statistical series by moving from peak to trough to peak, and specifically by choosing the year 1895 as turning point. This is the trap into which students of this period fall most often. We have tried consistently to avoid it by measuring only from peak to peak. When this rule is followed it is clear that the secular movement of money wages did not correspond with the secular movement of the cost of living.

There was close correspondence within the Juglar cycle. Immediately following the peak year money wages either fell, as in the USA, or stagnated as in the other three. Money wages had fallen drastically in three of these countries after the peak of 1873 (the French exception was explained in section 2.09) but a large absolute fall of money wages was unusual behaviour for the countries of Western Europe, and except for very minor movements in Germany, would not again be repeated until the huge price deflations of 1920 and 1930. US money wages continued to go up and down all through our period.

The upward movement would begin in all four countries as industry revived, and would accompany the rising cost of living until the next Juglar peak, when the movement would again be halted. It is thus possible to say, as is commonly said, that the upward movement in money wages was occasioned by the upward movement of the cost of living; but while this may have been true within the Juglar cycle, it was, as we have seen, not true secularly over the period 1883 to 1913.

This should not surprise us as much as it does. Adam Smith had already remarked in 1776 on the lack of connection between money wages and the cost of living:

> The wages of labour do not in Great Britain fluctuate with the price of provisions. These vary everywhere from year to year, frequently from month to month. But in many places the money price of labour remains uniformly the same sometimes for half a century together.[23]

That tradition of long secular stability of money wages continued in Britain until the outbreak of the Napoleonic wars, and was then resumed again in the 1820s, lasting another three decades until the outbreak of the Crimean War. This can be seen in Chart 4.3. One can also see from that chart[24] the great fall in real wages at the end of the eighteenth century, indicating the failure of money wages to rise at that time as fast as the cost of living. Another feature of the chart, to be noted in passing, is how little real wages rose over the seventy years between 1790 and 1860, despite the high productivity of the industrial and agricultural revolutions. The rise from 1781/9 to 1821/9 averages only 0·35 per cent per annum, and from 1821/9 to 1856/64 only 0·4 per cent per annum. This phenomenon is

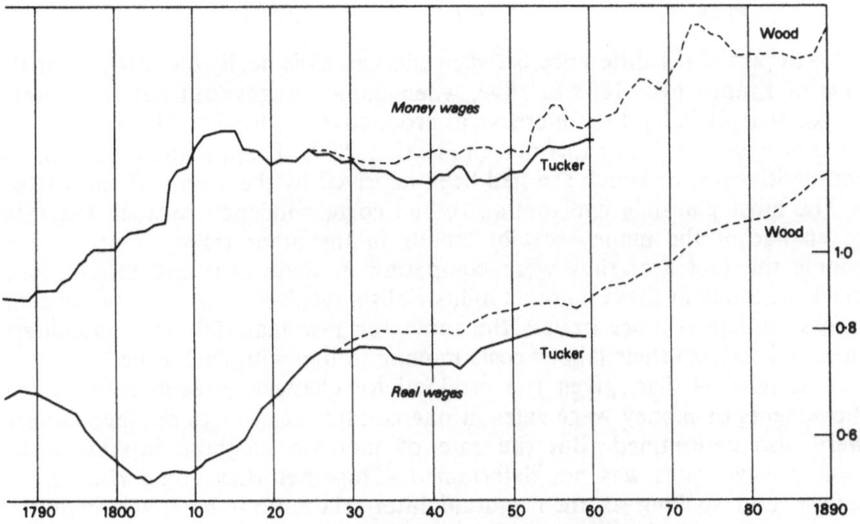

Chart 4.3 Urban Wage Rates, 1785–1890

evidence for the theory that in the early stages of capitalist development the existence of an 'unlimited supply of labour' keeps real wages low, in favour of profits and accumulation.[25]

Thus the general expectation that real wages will rise by a substantial amount in every decade did not emerge in Britain until the last quarter of the nineteenth century, nearly a century after the commencement of the industrial revolution.

4.08 Given that by the time our period opens money wages had acquired the habit of rising with the Juglar upswing of the cost of living, what determined the amount of this rise, and whether it would exceed or fall short of the rise in prices?

The clue to the answer lies in labour productivity. Again astonishingly, it turns out that although productivity increased at different rates in the core countries, the increase in money cost of labour per unit of output (money wages divided by productivity) was roughly the same among close competitors. Here are the figures of annual percentage increases of money cost of labour per unit of output:

	1883–99	*1899–1913*
UK	−0·25	+0·03
Germany	−0·2	+0·1
France	−0·6	−0·2 (1899–1909)
	1882–92	*1892–1906*
USA	−0·1	−0·04

In each period the difference between the figures is negligible, except for the case of France over 1883 to 1899, when money wages (but not real wages) lagged sharply behind the increase in productivity. This French exception we have already met and explained (in section 2.09); France was regaining the competitiveness of which she had been deprived by the events of the 1870s.

The most plausible explanation of the correspondence between the rates of change of the money cost of labour in the other three countries is of course the fact that they were competing in their own and international markets. Since in these markets industrialists received more or less the same prices, and paid more or less the same for raw materials and machinery, they had to keep their labour costs moving in line with each other.

This tells us that, given the productivity changes in each country, the movements of money wage rates in one country relative to another country were also determined. But the rate of increase of these interconnected money wage rates was not determined – together they could rise fast or slowly, and so long as their mutual inter-relationship held, the condition that money costs should all rise in the same proportion would be fulfilled.

What then determined the secular rate of rise of money wages? The most popular answer, the cost of living, we have already had to reject, since money wages rose at a constant secular rate whether the cost of living was falling or rising. A second candidate would be the terms of trade. If money wages were rising very fast, while food and raw material prices held steady, real wages would rise very fast, and industry would soon be bankrupt unless the prices of manufactures rose very fast in relation to food and raw materials. This could not happen. The terms of trade were determined by demand and supply measured in physical units. A rise in the price of manufactures would have generated a corresponding change in the prices of food and raw materials. Hence the terms of trade were not a constraint on prices or wages. This brings us to the third candidate: the supply of money. But we have already seen, in Chapter 3, that this was highly elastic, and have rejected its claim to have caused the Kondratiev downswing and upswing of prices. In truth, we do not believe that the economic system contained within itself any very firm constraint on the rate of increase of money wages and prices. Such a constraint existed earlier in the nineteenth century when the precious metals were the largest element in the money supply, but by our time gold was less than 15 per cent of the money supply, and its relationship to the supply of bank money was elastic. That the economic system of the 1970s does not contain within itself a firm constraint on the rate of increase of wages and prices is obvious to all; our suggestion is only that the transition to this rudderless state had already taken place by the last quarter of the nineteenth century.

We offer the following mechanism, at least for Western Europe. The leader was Germany, the country whose exports were growing most rapidly all over the world, with highly competitive prices and other conditions of sale. All would-be competitors, especially France and Britain, had to try to meet German prices, and therefore could concede only that level of increase of money wages which, given their productivity, would keep their money labour cost in line with the German money labour cost.

So what determined the rate of change of money wages in Germany? Habit. Money wages rose faster in Germany than anywhere else, and a 2 per cent per annum increase must have seemed extraordinary to the world of labour of those days. It did not, in fact, produce an extraordinary rise in real wages, because the cost of living also rose fastest in Germany, partly as a result and partly because of agricultural protection; over 1883 to 1899 real wages actually rose fastest in Britain. German workers and managements, we suggest, got into the habit of settling for around a 20 per cent increase in wages per decade, and kept to this rate irrespective of productivity or the cost of living. That settled, the movement of money wages in other countries fell into line.

Our world today is very different because, although international competition is even fiercer (for tariff barriers are much lower), there is no gold standard to keep domestic prices in line with each other. Money wages have no longer to be in step because changes in the foreign exchange value of the currency can be used in an effort to cut the link between domestic and foreign prices. This effort meets with only partial success, since a change in the foreign exchange rate itself sets in motion forces which alter domestic prices. It is more than ever necessary to be competitive, but this result is no longer achieved with the smoothness with which the money costs of labour were kept in line in these years before the First World War.

4.09 If this analysis is correct, the basic answer to the question why real wages decelerated after 1899 is the turnaround in the terms of trade. The fact that money wages did not keep up with the cost of living merely restates the problem. If money wages of the group of countries as a whole had risen faster, the cost of living would have risen faster. There are of course lags in such relationships, but in international commodity markets changes in prices respond quickly to changes in monetary demand. If money wages in any one country had risen faster, while others continued their pace, that country would have ceased to be competitive (*ceteris paribus*, including its own productivity) and rising bankruptcy rates would have put a brake on money wages. Here the time lags are greater, as the British case demonstrates, but the mechanism still works.

As one looks over this long period from 1883 to 1913 one cannot but marvel at the dependence of the standard of living of workers and capitalists alike (small distributional shifts explained little) on such a simple force as the demand and supply of agricultural commodities, and the resulting terms of trade between industry and agriculture; permitting a long spell in which the urban standard of living rises faster than productivity, which gives way to another long spell in which the standard of living rises more slowly than productivity. One tends to assume that leading and powerful capitalist countries have a sovereign independence which enables them to control their own economic destinies; but this is not what the record shows.

Chapter 5

The British Climacteric

SYNOPSIS: 5.00 The rate of growth of industrial production declined continually in Britain from 1873 onwards. 5.01 This deceleration was only partly offset by the growth of services; it was fully offset after 1899 (but not before) by the growth of income from abroad. This Chapter explores the deceleration of industry.

5.02 Population cannot explain the change since the growth rate of the industrial population was increasing up to 1901, and did not then decline. The main problem was a declining rate of growth of productivity. 5.03 This decline was associated with a very low ratio of domestic investment, due partly to weaknesses in foreign trade, partly to exhaustion of the technological opportunities of the original industrial revolution, and partly to lag in adopting new industries.

5.04 In foreign trade exports grew slowly and imports of manufactures grew rapidly. Britain lost out in competition with Germany and the USA. 5.05 German competition was based on lower wages, faster rising productivity and greater energy in selling. 5.06 American competition was based on higher capital intensity which the British could not match, not because of differing relative prices of capital and labour (as is alleged) but because British workers produced less than American workers with the same machines. 5.07 The British also lagged in adopting new industries and new technologies.

5.08 The textbook remedies were all out of reach, being incompatible with Britain's free trade ideology, educational patterns, worker attitudes, and self-chosen role as guardian of the gold standard.

5.00 The growth rate of British industrial production fell after 1873, and declined to 1913. This is now generally accepted. The revision of Hoffmann's index of industrial production, which we report in Appendix I, has raised the rate of growth, but has left the deceleration. Taking only manufacturing and mining, and excluding the much more doubtful figures for construction, the growth rates now run as follows, counting from peak to peak:

1853–73	2·7
1873–83	2·2
1883–99	2·1
1899–1913	2·0

Our task is to explain this deceleration.

GROWTH RATES

5.01 First, was this deceleration of industry offset by acceleration in the rest of the economy? There was indeed considerable expansion of the service trades at this time, especially of shipping and of financial services, which brought in a large income. This can be seen in our calculation of real Gross Domestic Product from 1853 to 1913, which is also reported in Appendix I. Service income accelerated its growth rate from 1·6 per cent per annum between 1853 and 1873 to 2·2 per cent per annum between 1873 and 1913. But this was not enough to offset the deceleration of industry and agriculture, so the growth rate of total GDP also decelerated, as follows:

1853–73	1·95
1873–83	1·90
1883–99	1·85
1899–1913	1·70

Neither was this compensated by income from abroad. Indeed GNP declined faster than GDP between 1873 and 1899. Only between 1899 and 1913 was the rise in income from abroad enough to offset the deceleration of domestic output. The annual percentage growth rates of real GNP were as follows:

1853–73	2·1
1873–83	2·0
1883–99	1·9
1899–1913	1·9

5.02 The next question is whether these growth rate changes merely reflect changes in the rate of growth of population. The answer is that this question is relevant for the last sub-period, 1899 to 1913, but not for earlier periods, since before 1899 the growth rate of the occupied population was rising all the time. The census figures are tricky, for reasons reported in Appendix I, where we have tried to put them on a comparable basis. One of the necessary adjustments is to reduce all occupied population figures for 1871 and before by at least 4 per cent, because these earlier censuses included retired persons, and the later censuses did not. With these adjustments, the figures between corresponding dates ran as follows, for the average annual growth rate of the occupied population of the United Kingdom:

1851–71	0·7
1871–81	0·9
1881–1901	1·1
1901–11	0·9

The occupied population of the UK was rising faster after 1871 than before, so population change cannot explain the deceleration of output, at any rate before 1901.

This acceleration of population growth is compounded of two different factors. One is that the population of Ireland was declining absolutely all this time, but declined faster before 1871 than it did thereafter. The other factor is the simultaneous slight acceleration of the population of Great Britain (England, Wales and Scotland). Shown separately, the occupied populations grew as follows:

	Great Britain	*Ireland*
1851–71	1·20	−1·10
1871–1901	1·25	−0·55
1901–11	1·10	−0·75

The occupied population of Great Britain was accelerating in the last quarter of the nineteenth century because the birth rate had increased in the middle of the century. The decline in the birth rate did not begin until the end of the 1870s, and this was not transmitted to the occupied population for another fifteen years. The following figures (per thousand of population) illustrate the determinants of the rate of natural increase in England and Wales, over intervals of thirty years:

Averages	*Birth rate*	*Death rate*	*Natural increase*
1845/9	32·6	23·3	9·3
1875/9	35·6	21·2	14·4
1905/9	26·7	15·1	11·6

This establishes so far that population change cannot explain the deceleration of output as a whole between 1870 and 1900. But our main concern is with industrial production and the industrial population.

It is not easy to establish what happened to the industrial population. As was explained in the last chapter, census figures have to be arranged to distinguish between industrial workers and workers in distribution; and we do not know how many 'general labourers' should be assigned to manufacturing. Working with the figures in Appendix I we get the following annual rates of growth of persons occupied in manufacturing (separately) and in mining and manufacturing (together):

	Manufacturing	*Manufacturing and mining*
1851–71	0·6	0·65
1871–81	0·8	0·95
1881–1901	1·05	1·20
1901–11	0·9	1·20

The mining industry was growing rapidly, so the population in industry as a whole was accelerating to 1901 while industrial output decelerated all the time. A major element in this declining productivity was the declining productivity of mining after the mid-1880s, a phenomenon which was general in Western Europe. If we separate out manufacturing and mining, and assume that the growth of the occupied population between peaks in production was the same as between census dates, we get the following annual rates of growth of productivity per person:

	Manufacturing	*Mining*
1853–73	1·85	3·0
1873–99	1·15	0·05
1899–1913	0·90	−0·7

While the decline in mining productivity was the more spectacular, there was also a constant decline of the rate of growth of productivity in manufacturing.[1]

We may yet evade the issue: can this decline have been due merely to shorter working hours? Definitely not. The standard working week was still 55 hours in 1913, and many observers doubt that the decline from 65 hours had affected output adversely, except in mining. In any case the orders of magnitude are too dissimilar. The growth rate of productivity fell from 1·85 before 1873 to an average of 1·1 up to 1913. To explain this fall over forty years by a reduction of hours would require hours to have fallen by more than 27 per cent (since output would fall by less than hours). So the question remains: why did the growth rate of productivity decline?

INVESTMENT

5.03 It has often been remarked that to seek the causes of social change is like peeling an onion. Each answer is the occasion for a new question: if *b* caused *a*, then what caused *b*? The problem in hand is no exception. Wherever we begin, we shall have to shift continually as each answer opens up new questions.

Let us begin with investment. Low investment ratios are both a cause and a symptom of malaise. The effects are easy to discern; the causes are more complex.

The British ratio of domestic investment was low throughout our forty years. According to Feinstein's figures, the stock of real capital increased between 1873 and 1913 at an average annual rate of only 1·4 per cent per annum, which is rather low for a country whose occupied population was growing by 1·0 per cent per annum, and is probably an underestimate. The biggest investment boom during this period occurred at the end of the century, peaking in real terms in 1903. The average ratio of gross domestic investment to gross domestic product over 1899 to 1904 was 11·2 (including houses; 9·1 excluding houses). These are very low proportions, but they are the best in four decades, according to Feinstein's count.

While domestic investment lagged, foreign investment mounted. At its peak in the eight years just before the outbreak of the war (1906/13) foreign investment averaged 8·4 per cent of net national product. Even if we write up net domestic investment to say 5 per cent, the contrast is striking.[2]

Why did the British invest so much abroad and so little at home? One view is that overseas investment was very profitable, so the home market was starved of capital. The other view is that the home market had an excess of capital, for lack of investment opportunities, so capital was pushed overseas. There is no evidence that entrepreneurs experienced a shortage of capital in the home market. We have already referred to this topic in analysing the depression of the 1880s, noting that interest rates were falling, and borrowers scarce. Neither was foreign investment all that profitable. Most of it was on fixed interest terms. One could lend to the British government at 3 per cent or to a fairly reputable foreign government at 5 per cent (less reputable ones or doubtful railways at perhaps 8 per cent). Investment in mortgages at home might bring 5 per cent; in commerce and industry perhaps 8 to 10 per cent. Industry's need for capital was small, in comparison with housing, public works and public utilities. At the peak of 1903 according to Feinstein, 'plant, machinery, vehicles and ships' absorbed only 30 per cent of net capital formation, equal to only 2·0 per cent of net national product. Industry also largely financed itself. It is very difficult to believe that if entrepreneurs had wished to invest more in industry they would have been inhibited by lack of capital. And if industrial investment had been profitable, it is highly likely that associated investment in infrastructure, housing and so on would have been forthcoming. Some of this would have been at the expense of foreign investment, but not all; for faster domestic growth would also bring larger profits and greater savings. This is the consensus of students of this subject, although it is difficult to quantify.

The shortfall of domestic investment contributed to a low rate of growth both directly and indirectly. This distinction is meant to separate the functions of capital as a factor of production, and of capital as a bearer of new technology. The distinction is difficult to sustain because the move from less to more capital almost always involves some change of technology. Yet it is a distinction which the econometricians have decided to pursue, and on which they will for some time be continuing to break their heads.[3] For our purposes it suffices to note that in so far as each generation of machines is more productive than its predecessor, a country with a high investment ratio will, other things being equal, have higher productivity than a country with a low investment ratio, because a greater proportion of its machines will be of the latest designs. So what we are saying is that British productivity was diminished not merely by the small amount of capital, but also by the extent to which its capital was out of date; and both these resulted from the low investment ratio.

There is another connection between a low investment ratio and low productivity. Here the distinction is between new investment which replaces old capital by new capital, and new investment which expands employment in an industry, or transfers workers to industry from other sectors. A new machine should replace an existing machine if the average cost of using the new is less than the marginal cost of using the old; whereas if one is expanding employment in the industry the new machine will be installed so long as its average cost per unit of output is less than the average cost of duplicating the old machine. Moreover, in considering replacement, the issue is more than a comparison of prime cost of the old with average cost of the new, since the cost of adopting the new may be more than simply the average cost of the new equipment. Suppose, for example, that an innovation on the railways requires use of a wider track. To use it on an existing railway system requires that existing tracks be replaced by new ones, tunnels be widened, new and wider bridges be built, and station platforms be relocated. Hence it is cheaper to adopt the new system in a new country than it is in an old country with an existing railway system. This is one of the disadvantages of having been first which the British frequently assert, especially in relation to the layout of their railways, mines, ironworks and roads. The new country has the advantage of not having to begin by tearing down the structures of an old system before adopting a new one.

One consequence of this is that an economy whose industrial population is constant will have more incentive to invest abroad and less to invest at home than an economy whose population is growing rapidly. Given the same investment ratio, the latter country may have less capital per head in industry, but may nevertheless have the same or higher productivity because a larger proportion of its capital will be of the latest designs. The former country will have invested more of its capital in other countries. Now the British industrial population was bound to grow more slowly than the German, since already by 1871 it had reached 35 per cent of the occupied population, and this alone would constrain productivity. However, we must not take this argument too far. Since the Second World War many developed countries with industrial populations growing less rapidly than the pre-1913 British have been investing heavily in increasing capital per head.

Why was the domestic investment ratio so low? Because new investment was not sufficiently profitable. We saw in Chapter 2, looking at the ratio of wages to income, and again in Chapter 4, looking at share prices, that the economy was relatively unprofitable in the eighties and the first half of the nineties. It was being squeezed by a combination of relatively stagnant world trade in manufactures and rising competition, which had brought down prices to levels incompatible with current money wages and productivity.

The ultimate cause was exhaustion of the innovations which had propelled the industrial economy in the century up to 1880. By this time the British railway system was largely completed, though France, Germany and the USA would continue to invest in expanding their systems for much longer. Railways were such a large user of capital goods that the system had to find some substitute propellant if it was to maintain its growth momentum. The old technologies in the basic industries, especially iron and cotton, were also reaching exhaustion, and although the United States was developing new highly capital-intensive methods, yielding twice as much output per head, the British were slow to move in this direction. They were also slow in developing the new science-based commodities, leadership in which had passed to Germany and the United States. Given the inevitable passing of British domination of world trade in textiles and iron, the economy needed a higher input of new technology if it was to maintain a reasonable share of world trade at prices compatible with its now constantly increasing money wages. These two checks – the exhaustion of the old technology and the challenge in foreign markets – were not necessarily connected, since either could have occurred without the other. But in fact they happened together, and one check reinforced the other. The internal and the external were linked because the solution to both was a shift to pioneering new technologies and commodities; or at the very least to adopting with minimal delay the discoveries and inventions of other countries. If Britain had been pioneering new commodities in her domestic market, she would also have been leading in world trade; or if she had led in world trade, the external demand would have buoyed up domestic investment. So whether one starts with the internal or the external situation, the road will lead back to innovation. Given the importance of foreign trade in the period up to 1880, we will start there.

FOREIGN TRADE

5.04 As other countries industrialised, Britain's proportionate share of world trade in manufactures diminished. There are estimates of the British ratio at various dates,[4] but this ratio does not matter. What mattered to Britain was that its foreign trade should grow fast enough to support domestic needs, including full employment, and this did not happen.

The growth rate of British exports of manufactures in constant prices[5] decelerated very sharply after 1873. Between 1853 and 1873 it was 3·3 per cent per annum; from 1873 to 1899 it was 1·6 per cent per annum. After 1899 the growth rate revived (2·7 per cent per annum to 1913), but the dark side of this revival was the extent to which it was due to a combination of adverse terms of trade and extraordinarily heavy capital export.

In any case what mattered was not exports as such, but exports minus imports. The growth rate of imports was coming into equilibrium; having been 6·6 per cent per annum between 1853 and 1873, it fell to 4·5 per cent per annum from 1873 to 1899, and fell again to 2·3 per cent per annum between 1899 and 1913. But in the period 1873–99 the combination of 1·6 per cent growth of exports and 4·5 per cent growth of imports subjected British manufacturing to a terrible beating, for which the term 'the Great Depression of 1873 to 1896' does not seem to be inappropriate. Here are the figures for exports and imports of manufactures at constant prices (£m.).

	1853	*1873*	*1899*	*1913*
Exports	92·7	179·2	272·5	396·7
Imports	8·5	30·9	97·6	135·1
Net exports	84·2	158·3	174·9	261·6

The figures bring out the painful fact that the volume of net exports grew only at 0·4 per cent per annum between 1873 and 1899. However, the figures look even worse in current prices, falling from £178·3m. to £118·5m.

The fall in the growth rate of net exports of manufactures will have damped industrial production. We can estimate the effects by experimenting with different growth rates for foreign trade. Table 5.1 shows actual trade, production and domestic use of manufactures in 1873 and 1913, at 1913 prices. In column 3 we have the actual annual percentage rates of growth. In column 4 we assume that the growth rate of imports had instead been 2·5 per cent per annum, and the growth rate of exports 2·8 per cent per annum, which is considerably lower than the growth rate of world trade in manufactures as a whole (about 3·5). This leaves two unknowns, the growth

Table 5.1 *UK: Balance Sheet of Manufactures*[6]

	Actual			Hypothetical	
	1873 *(£m.)*	*1913* *(£m.)*	*Growth rates*	*Growth rates*	*1913* *(£m.)*
Imports	31	135	4·8	2·5	83
Exports	179	397	2·0	2·8	536
Production	342	767	2·1	2·8[a]	1,013[a]
Domestic use	194	505	2·4	2·7	560

[a] Residual.

rates of production and of domestic use. If we assume that as a result of greater prosperity the growth rate of domestic use rises to 2·7 per cent, it follows residually that the growth rate of production rises from 2·1 to 2·8 per cent per annum (say 1·2 for labour force and 1·6 for productivity).

A higher growth rate of British exports of manufactures would not necessarily have been at the expense of competitors in other industrial countries. A faster growth rate for Britain would have meant greater imports of food and raw materials. The less developed countries would have produced more, and world trade as a whole, both primary and secondary, would have been larger. Possibly the terms of trade would not then have moved so much against primary products up to 1900, but the extra burden could have been borne, with the higher growth rate of production.[7]

Four factors contributed to Britain's trade difficulties in this period.

In the first place the volume of exports to some extent reflected foreign lending. As we saw in Chapter 2, this varied considerably, being high in 1873, low in 1899 and extraordinarily high in 1913 (10 per cent of net national product). In so far as extraordinary foreign lending reflected a shortage of domestic investment opportunities, the high growth rate of exports associated therewith was a symptom of trouble rather than a cause of prosperity.

Secondly, the volume of exports of manufactures varied inversely with the terms of trade in a ratio of almost one to one. This was true both for world trade as a whole, and for British trade. It shows itself in the statistics of world trade in the form of the constant proportion assumed by manufactures in world trade between 1880 and 1929. This is a curious phenomenon which has not reappeared since the Second World War. We have discussed it elsewhere.[8]

The upshot was that the growth rate of the volume of British exports of manufactures decelerated sharply during the Kondratiev downswing of prices, and accelerated sharply thereafter. From the standpoint of the economy as a whole this downswing had one advantage. The industrial workers especially experienced a rapid rate of growth of real wages, well in excess of the growth rate of their physical productivity. But industry was depressed all the same by low prices and slow income growth, and industrial investment was accordingly restrained.

All this should have come to an end with the price upswing after 1900. The terms of trade improved, and exports and net exports leaped upwards at 2·7 and 2·9 per cent per annum respectively. Manufacturing became markedly more profitable, but the growth rates of manufacturing (output and persons) again declined.

This is a puzzle. Perhaps the solution lies in the nature of the boom, which was for the traditional commodities bought by the less developed countries of the day, who were the ones benefiting from the terms of trade – especially cotton, pig iron and coal – and not a boom for the modern commodities with a long-term future in international trade – such as automobiles and electrical machinery. At the same time that British exports of pig iron were swelling to the poorer countries, Britain was herself becoming the world's largest importer of steel. As we have just suggested, large exports resulting from large foreign investment are probably more a symptom of domestic unease than an occasion for domestic investment. In this case domestic investment in manufacturing was presumably restrained by Britain's backwardness in the new commodities, which is our next point.

The two preceding influences on the level of British exports, namely capital export and the terms of trade, were fluctuating and temporary factors. Now we come to two more influences of a more permanent character. These two are related, namely the rise of competitors, and the changing commodity composition of trade, from old to new commodities. We shall begin with the competition.

5.05 In 1850 Britain was the main source of the world's supply of the commodities of the industrial revolution – cotton textiles, coal, pig iron, railway materials and steam engines. Obviously this could not last. As other countries industrialised, the British situation would be eroded in three ways. First, these other countries would make these products for themselves. Secondly, the most successful industrialisers would begin to compete with Britain in third markets. And thirdly, the British market itself would be invaded. Britain could escape this trap only in two ways: by reducing its propensity to import, and by moving out of the older commodities into new ones. Her failure at both strategies was the major cause of her troubles.

France, Germany and the United States were in the first stage of evolution in the middle and third quarters of the nineteenth century. By 1870 they had freed themselves from dependence on British cottons, and had nearly escaped dependence on British coal. They still used a lot of British iron, but this situation too would change in the 1880s. By then, too, other countries would have discovered import substitution, including Belgium, Russia, India (yarn), Brazil, Canada and others.

Germany entered into the second and third stages in the 1880s, competing in third markets, and invading the British market itself. The USA joined the competition after 1895.

The geographical pattern of German competition is interesting. The industrialising less developed countries (LDCs) of our day are frequently advised to form regional customs unions and concentrate on selling manufactures to each other. Germany did begin by securing the local base. The *Zollverein*, established in 1834 and constantly extended, provided the regional framework for the stage of import substitution. But as soon as the industrial base was established, the Germans launched their trade drive everywhere. An early phase, in the 1880s, was to use Britain's own wholesale exporting firms and their markets overseas, by selling to these firms for re-export. The British were shocked to find that re-exports had jumped from 2·2 per cent of their total exports of manufactures in 1873 to 4·0 per cent in 1882. The British domestic market itself was also feeling the blast in the 1880s, and by 1899 was taking 19 per cent of Germany's exports of manufactures. Simultaneously Germany sought and gained footholds in all the other European markets, and shortly afterwards German trade spokesmen were roaming the world.

Maizels has divided the world into industrial countries, semi-industrial countries, and the rest. Table 5.2 compares the performance of Germany and the United Kingdom in these markets. It will be observed that by 1913 Germany was exporting more manufactures than the UK both to industrial countries and to the rest of the world.

Table 5.2 *Germany and UK: Exports of Manufactures, 1913 ($m.)*[9]

To	*From Germany*	*From UK*
Industrial	925	624
Semi-industrial	218	810
Rest	583	526
Total	1,726	1,960

The German total had nearly caught up with the British total (having been somewhat less than half thirty years earlier), and the British position was maintained only in the semi-industrial countries. Most of these were satellites of the British economy in one sense or another, and their adherence to British goods derived from imperial relations, imperial preference or dependence on the British market or on British overseas lending, in which the borrowers frequently had British connections. Maizels's 'semi-industrial' group includes Australia, New Zealand, South Africa, India, Argentina, Brazil, Chile, Colombia, Mexico and Turkey. Britain did not impose discriminatory practices upon her 'non-self-governing' colonies, but the self-governing Dominions themselves imposed discrimination in favour of British goods (Canada in 1897, South Africa and New Zealand in 1903 and Australia in 1907) in the hope of inducing reciprocity. Even this tariff discrimination was of little significance. Dependence on the British market, dependence on British lending, and business connections were the major forces supporting loyalty to British goods, bolstered in the British territories by sentiment, and by the official policy of buying only British goods for the public sector.

What accounts for the tremendous German achievement? The causes may be grouped into three: competitive prices, sales energy and leadership in new commodities.

Germany began with a price advantage over the UK, which it maintained throughout this period. The price advantage was due to the fact that whereas in 1883 German product per head was about 70 per cent of the British, the German money wage was only about 60 per cent of the British. Money wages grew much faster in Germany than in Britain, but productivity grew much faster too, and as we saw in the preceding chapter, money labour cost per unit of output changed at the same rate. So a gap remained; in 1913 productivity was perhaps 6 per cent lower in Germany, but wages were 14 per cent lower. As can be seen in Table 5.3, prices of manufactures exported fell less and rose more in Britain than in Germany. The figures are not entirely trustworthy, but the general impression they convey is right; prices were falling faster elsewhere than in Britain.

Table 5.3 *Prices of Manufactured Exports*[10]

	1883	*1899*	*1913*
UK	113	100	125
Germany	126	100	108
France	110	100	112
USA	127	100	112

Added to this price advantage was a tremendous sales effort. The world was flooded with German salesmen. All kinds of sales organisation were tried: wholesale export houses, manufacturers' representatives selling directly to the foreign buyer, manufacturers' export co-operatives, sales through foreign commission agents, and so on. Numerous consulates were opened at strategic points, and consuls were expected to promote sales of German goods, a decision which shocked British conceptions of diplomatic behaviour. Trade credits were liberalised. The British were masters of the three months trade bill and of the long-term bond; the Germans developed intermediate credits of a year or more, which better suited the kinds of capital goods that they were selling. The British were astonished by the vigour and inventiveness of the German effort, and poured out articles, pamphlets and books on the subject from the mid-1880s onwards. Some of the literature was the occasion for self-flagellation. It was said that German salesmen abroad learnt the native languages and carried catalogues in the native languages, in contrast with British salesmen; that German manufacturers would design to the customer's specifications or (alternatively and in contradiction) derived success from concentrating exclusively on standardised mass-produced commodities. The literature also accused the Germans of every kind of chicanery, including piracy of trademarks. But of course one does not build up a huge trade over thirty years by gimmicks and chicanery.[11]

This kind of successful trade drive is more familiar to us than it was to the late Victorians. The Germans were followed by the Americans, starting in the nineties. Then came the Japanese, especially after 1929 and again after 1960. And now it is Brazil.

American exports of manufactures were growing respectably but not spectacularly in the 1880s. Lipsey's figures in constant prices yield a growth rate for finished manufactures of 3·9 per cent per annum between the two peaks of 1883 and 1891. Then comes an explosion. The growth rate rises to 11·7 per cent per annum between 1891 and 1899 helped, as we have suggested before, by a deflated economy. From 1899 to 1913 the rate is 6·5 per cent per annum, which is no mean achievement. The commodities leading this explosion are machinery and iron and steel products. In 1913 the share of metals, engineering and chemicals is, according to Maizels, 70 per cent of US exports of manufactures compared with 41 per cent of British exports of manufactures. The US also, like Germany, was looking to wealthier markets. It sent 62 per cent of its exports of manufactures to Canada and Western Europe, whereas the British sent only 29 per cent to North America and Western Europe.

The two factors we have so far mentioned, low prices and highly concentrated sales effort, are characteristic of all sales drives. But one must go behind these and ask what causes a country to set out on this road. Such highly unbalanced growth may originate in one or other of three cases. First, the country may be deficient in natural resources, and thus have an inescapably large propensity to import food and raw materials. This was the case of Japan. Secondly, the country may have the natural resources, but be failing to develop them, leaving its farmers and service workers with incomes too low to absorb the surplus of manufactures. This is the case of Brazil. Thirdly, the country may, through its leadership in technological skills, have a comparative advantage in industry which produces a large foreign demand for what it offers. Here Britain was the pioneer before 1880, after which date its mantle was inherited by Germany and the United States.

The entrepreneurial drive to invest in manufacturing is a crucial element. It is compounded partly of those price relations which determine the profitability of investment, partly of the degree of help or hindrance offered by the government, and partly of the dynamism of the entrepreneurial class itself. Germany and the USA had all three: wages low in relation to productivity, governments which accounted industrialisation and foreign trade among their top priorities, and businessmen with unlimited confidence.

PRODUCTIVITY

5.06 When we talk about productivity we must distinguish between the old industries of the industrial revolution, including coal, pig iron, textiles and steam power, and the new industries which grew up after 1880, especially electricity, steel, organic chemicals and the internal combustion engine.

British productivity was much higher than German productivity in the old industries around 1880. Therefore it was easy for German productivity to keep rising. In Britain, however, the old technology had been extended about as far as it could. In the cotton textile industry, and again in the utilisation of coke for making pig iron, productivity moved on to a plateau in the 1880s. Even so, German productivity was still lagging, and had not fully caught up with the British even in 1913.

For British productivity to have increased considerably the British would have had to convert to American methods. This involved using about twice as much horsepower per head, and getting about twice as much product per head. The data relating to comparative productivity are set out in Appendix II; relying mainly on Flux's and Rostas's census comparisons, we put American productivity at 1·9 times the British in 1913.[12] Rostas also offers figures of horsepower per worker, which are 1·4 for Britain in 1907 and 2·9 for the USA in 1909, and it is generally assumed that capital per head was in the same ratio.[13]

Why did the British not adopt American methods? The favourite answer of some economists is: because wages were lower in the UK. But this will not work. UK wages according to Phelps Brown were 52 per cent of the American in 1913. If twice as much capital per head produced twice as much output, the American technology would have been more profitable in Britain at any (positive) levels of wages. The error springs from making the wrong comparisons.

Let us assume that the cost of a unit of capital is the same in both countries, that the Americans use twice as much capital per head, that the American wage is twice the British, and that the American technology yields twice the British output per head. If

w = US wage for one day's work
k = daily cost (including interest and amortisation) of hiring the capital used with one man in the USA
P = cost of one half day's output in the USA, considered to be one unit of output

then the cost of producing one unit of output in the USA is

$$0{\cdot}5w + 0{\cdot}5k = P$$

and the cost of producing one unit of output in the UK with British technology is

$$0{\cdot}5w + 0{\cdot}5k = P$$

Cost per unit is the same, so Britain and the USA can compete in the same international market despite their different wages and technologies.

Two propositions which are sometimes deduced from this equality are both false. It is not true to say that because money cost per unit of output is the same, therefore real cost must be the same, the difference in factor proportions being exactly offset by difference in factor prices. Real costs are not the same: one man plus one capital will produce in the USA as much as two men plus one capital in the UK (i.e. two units of output).

Neither is it true to say that the equality of money cost proves that the UK is using the right combination of factors. To find out whether the UK is using the right technology one must compare not Britain using one technology and the USA using another, but the cost in Britain at British factor prices for both technologies. One will then find that when using British technology the British cost per unit is

$$0{\cdot}5w + 0{\cdot}5k$$

but when using US technology at British wages (with twice the output and twice the capital), the British cost per unit would be

$$0{\cdot}5\ (0{\cdot}5w + k) = 0{\cdot}25w + 0{\cdot}5k$$

So the American technology would have been cheaper in Britain too. In fact on the assumptions so far made the American technology would be cheaper in Britain at any wage exceeding zero.

The real reason why it did not pay the British entrepreneur to adopt American techniques was that they yielded less in Britain than in America. Whereas twice the capital per head yielded twice the product in the United States, it yielded much less than twice the product in Britain. Given the wage levels and capital costs, the comparative yields determined which technology would be cheaper in Britain. We can calculate the turning point as follows. British cost is the same when the British technology yields the same cost at British wages as the American technology, that is when

$$\frac{0{\cdot}5w + k}{n} = 0{\cdot}5w + 0{\cdot}5k$$

where n is output per man per day. The solution to this equation depends on the ratio of w to k. Assuming that in the USA wages are 55 per cent of output and capital costs are 45 per cent of output, it follows that

$$w = 1{\cdot}\dot{2}k$$

whence it follows that

$$n = \frac{1{\cdot}6\dot{1}k}{1{\cdot}1\dot{1}k}$$

$$\therefore n = 1{\cdot}45$$

Since the American output per man was two units, the American technology would pay only if the British got from it 72·5 per cent as good a result as the Americans got from it.

If the British were not doing as well as this, they needed a lower wage for the American technology to yield the same cost in Britain as in the USA. Suppose that n is only 1·3. Then we have the same money cost when

$$0{\cdot}5w + 0{\cdot}5k = \frac{xw + k}{1{\cdot}3}$$

$$\therefore x = 0{\cdot}3636$$

The British wage would have to be 36 per cent of the US wage for the American technology to yield the same cost there as in the USA, but at this lower wage the British technology would be cheaper in Britain, and could undersell the American technology both in Britain and in the USA.

The moral of this little exercise is to eschew all econometric calculations in this field which begin with some version of 'let us assume that the two countries have the same technology', in which case all differences in factor combinations have to be explained by relative factor prices. Two countries do not have the same technology when the same combination of inputs yields more output in one than in the other.

As we have seen before, British entrepreneurs were under heavy pressure in the last quarter of the century, since the economy had turned unprofitable. American methods were fairly widely known. If entrepreneurs had expected them to yield the same output in Britain as in the USA, they would most probably have adopted them.

There is no dispute that the difference between British and American productivity from the same inputs was substantial. The best statistical work on this derives from Rostas's comparisons of the two censuses of manufactures in the mid-1930s. We find for example that in boots and shoes, where British and American factories were using almost exactly the same machinery, American output per manhour exceeded the British by about 80 per cent Many companies have factories in both Britain and the United States, using exactly the same machinery Their consensus is that the yield per man is much higher in the United States.

The causes of these differences are also well known. The American pace is faster. The work is organised to produce a faster flow-through. There is greater standardisation, to secure the economies of repetition. Factory discipline is tighter. Work study plays a larger role in setting production norms. In fact, starting from about the 1880s the Americans set out to study the economising of labour in factory operations; their factory is a more 'scientific' place than the British factory.

In contrast Phelps Brown believes that there was actually a slackening of the pace of British factory workers from the 1890s onwards, which he attributes to the rise of trade unionism and the increasing resentment of the working class against the factory system.[14] This cannot be proved, but is not without plausibility.

How did American entrepreneurs get away with increasing the pace? The explanation lies perhaps as far back as the beginning of the nineteenth century, when America led in inventing what would later become the basis of the assembly line, namely the standardisation and bulk production of interchangeable parts – beginning with guns and clocks and moving into engineering. Already in the thirties and forties visitors to America were reporting the working man's fascination with useful gadgets. At any rate he was already accustomed to taking pride in the quantity of his output, whereas the British tradition, descending from the guilds, was rather one of pride in craftsmanship and in the quality of the result. This British suspicion of quantity was more than a little reinforced by the British worker's experience of the effects of innovation on employment, which differed in significant degree from that of the American worker. For while in Britain the new technology had expanded employment in cotton and in iron, it had also played havoc with employment for handloom weavers in wool, as it would also do to the domestic clothing and footwear industries. The American experience was different. In the first half of the nineteenth century the economy was import-substituting. New inventions cut costs, and by reducing imports created more employment at home; the machine was a friend to employment rather than an enemy.

As the century proceeded these explanations became less and less relevant to the contemporary situation. At least from the 1870s onwards American workers were subjected to severe and long bouts of unemployment, by which time import substitution had also ended. Why did they not learn to fear innovation as much as the British workers? Some certainly did, but their fear could not be so easily translated into action. For one thing, there was always that long line of immigrants looking for jobs. The worker had to adjust, or get out. Again the British unions put high on their agenda protection of workers from dismissal without due cause, and would certainly not have permitted the dismissal of workers for falling behind production targets set by time and motion study. But trade unions hardly existed in the USA in the decades when those practices were spreading. And by the time trade unions achieved power in the USA they were so concerned about wages that many maintained their own work-study experts to help the less efficient firms whose methods were restricting their ability to pay high wages. It was inconceivable that a British trade union would specialise in showing the employers how to speed up output.

More surprising, perhaps, is the alleged contrast between the attitudes of British and German or other continental workers. In our day Europeans speak of 'the British disease', by which they mean a combination of a continual tendency to go on strike and a relatively slow work pace. Forty years ago the conventional wisdom was that the German workers' movement, with a high proportion of Marxist leaders, was more militant than the British workers' movement, yet today the British workers seem much more alienated than the German workers. Much has happened over that forty-year interval, including the liquidation of the German Marxist leaders under Hitler and after. But looking back one can also see reasons why the British workers should be more alienated than the German, even before the First World War. One reason is that they suffered more from unemployment. From 1870 onwards the British economy moved from one deep slump to the next, punctuated only by brief booms, while the German evidence is of long periods of near full employment, penetrated by short recessions. The German economy also expanded fast enough to absorb all who wanted industrial jobs, whereas the British economy was expanding so slowly that British people had to emigrate right up to 1913. Moreover, until the triumph of Keynesianism in the 1930s, British leaders, including the economists, took it for granted that the British economy could not be expected to maintain full employment. The workers' natural reaction to this was alienation from the system, and unwillingness to co-operate in any measures which might reduce the demand for labour, coupled with the conviction that the nation's leaders were an enemy, in whom no confidence should be reposed. This 'enemy' also showed itself more callous than its German counterpart, since social insurance was introduced in Germany as early as 1885, and did not find its way across the Channel for another quarter of a century. It is true that Bismarck introduced social insurance not out of the kindness of his heart, but to buy working-class political support against his political enemies. He may have judged correctly. At any rate, the British workers had better reason to be alienated from industrial capitalism than the German workers.

Given the lower work pace of the British workers it is easy to see that the main reason why the British employers did not adopt the American technology was that it was not as productive for them as it was for American employers. No moral judgement is implied in this. Men who have to work at a fast pace set by their employers are not necessarily better off than other men who set their own pace, even if they are paid twice as much (actually only 33 per cent more in real terms, since the US cost of living was 50 per cent higher: the rest accrued to urban landlords in higher rents, to employers in higher profits, and to the non-industrial sectors of the economy in improved terms of trade). However, the matter is not quite so simple. A slow growth rate of productivity did not matter so much before 1900, because the terms of trade were moving in favour of industry. After 1900 the terms of trade were moving against industry, but the unions had by then become accustomed to an annual rate of growth of real wages which was simply not compatible with their attitude to work and machinery. Thus began that gap between reach and grasp which was to plague British industry in the 1920s, and again in the 1970s.

Given that the American methods were not profitable in Great Britain, the British were also deprived of some techniques which were a part thereof, especially mass production of the cheaper ranges of commodities. Examples of this are to be found in greater concentration on fabrication from steel than on mass production of steel; in specialisation on the finer counts of cotton yarn rather than the coarser counts, for which the more productive ring spindles would have been more appropriate,[15] and in a movement away from the cheaper to the more expensive kinds of textile fabrics. Frustrated in price competition, the British tried, correctly, to build up a reputation for quality and for production to the customer's special design. The reputation for quality was especially relevant not only to textiles, but also in such other fields as shipbuilding, electric cables, steam turbines, bicycles, railway equipment or textile machinery – not all British trades were on the decline.[16] To the extent that the British were upgrading the quality of their product, the index of industrial production, based largely on raw material inputs, understates the growth of British production; and the low volume with high prices revealed by the trade statistics is partly justified. This is not of course the whole answer, since if it were the relative unprofitability of the period 1873 to 1899 would not have occurred, and the average unemployment level would not have been so high.

INNOVATION

5.07 Earlier we named three factors in Germany's success: competitive prices, sales energy and leadership in new commodities. Now we come to the third.

The less developed countries of our day have all learned to enter world trade via the cotton and clothing industries. Germany too began there, but she did not stay there long. By 1913 Germany's exports were much more

Table 5.4 *Germany and UK: Exports of Manufactures, 1913 ($m.)*[17]

	From Germany	*From UK*
Metals and engineering	695	680
Chemicals	239	119
Textiles and clothing	324	950
Other	468	211
Total	1,726	1,960

advanced than those of the UK. The only one of Maizels's four groups in which the UK exported more than Germany was textiles and clothing; this emerges in Table 5.4.

In the century before 1880 most of the important inventions of the industrial revolution (with the notable exceptions of the cotton gin, some machine tools, the sewing machine and the idea of interchangeable parts) originated in Great Britain. More important, all inventions, wherever they originated, were quickly followed up. After 1880 a very large proportion of the new inventions originated elsewhere. More important, whether they originated in Britain or elsewhere, the British economy lagged in exploiting them. Perhaps the most spectacular case is that of steel whose major innovations (the Bessemer converter, the Siemens' open hearth, and the Gilchrist–Thomas process) were all British; whereas the British were rapidly outdistanced in steel production by both Germany and the USA.

Controversy has raged over whether the British lag in adopting new processes and pioneering new commodities after 1880 was due to entrepreneurial failure or to objective economic circumstances.[18] There is no evidence that British businessmen were any less enterprising after 1880 than their forefathers. There is a general expectation that the third generation will be less enterprising than the first, but there is no evidence that the older firms were ossifying.[19] Indeed in the older industries, where the older firms were – especially cotton, pig iron, steam engines – productivity per unit of input seems to have been as high as anywhere else. Moreover it would not have mattered if the third generation was weak, since new men could have entered industry, just as in the first generation. British industry was less monopolised than any other, and the costs of starting in business were still relatively low.

Yet something was lacking. Britain's competitive weakness was not in the old industries but in the new. These new industries were characterised by a higher scientific level than the old – one exception being the bicycle industry, which tests the rule because Britain was in the forefront of this new trade. But whereas any intelligent and observant person with a stroke of genius could invent the steam engine or the flying shuttle, or the hot blast, innovation after 1880 for the most part needed something more than genius. It required scientific knowledge to develop electrical machinery, organic chemicals or workable internal combustion engines.

To put the matter differently, academic science contributed next to nothing to the industrial revolution, and did not become entwined with industrial progress until after 1880. Between academic science and industry lay a big gulf which had to be bridged. The Germans bridged it in the last quarter of the nineteenth century, but the British failed to do so.

Once the nature of the problem became clear to all, as it did shortly before the onset of the Great War, science and industry blamed each other for the gap. Industry blamed the universities for concentrating on the humanities and neglecting science. The universities retorted that industry would not hire their science graduates, or, if hiring them, misused them in junior and non-scientific positions.[20]

It also became clear that the gap existed not only at the managerial level, but also at the intermediate level of foremen, supervisors and technicians.

Britain lagged far behind Germany in the provision of technical schools. Even more important, perhaps, was the general backwardness of British mass education compared with the American. The big deficiency was in secondary education, which the British reserved for a handful, with the result that the intermediate industrial class was better educated in Germany or the USA than in Britain. This class, being on the shop floor, plays an important role in improving production techniques.

The weakness at the intermediate level probably relates to another puzzle. If British entrepreneurs were not ripe for new scientific commodities, why did German and American entrepreneurs not come to Britain and start the new industries? Exchange of entrepreneurs was an old story. British entrepreneurs had played a hand in starting industries in France and Germany, and French entrepreneurs were to be found throughout the continent.[21] Some foreign entrepreneurs did come, specialising in alkali chemistry and electrical machinery, but their effect was limited. Perhaps they too were inhibited by the restricted education of the intermediate class.

It was not necessary for British entrepreneurs to be scientists; what mattered was that they should be receptive to science, and understand how to use scientists. There is no doubt that British ideology was at this time hostile to science, and even more so to industrial science. This was the great age of the public school (an offshoot of the railway, without which parents could not have moved so many children so many times a year) which, being based on the proposition that the English were the modern descendants of Periclean Athens, found little virtue outside the classics and religion. At this time too, the public service grew enormously, attracting the best brains into Parliament, the home civil service, the Indian civil service and the diplomatic service. Of course there were plenty of brains in the classes from which industrialists had typically been recruited. What gentlemen's sons thought or did is not relevant to us since industrialists had never been gentlemen's sons. What does matter is that the non-gentlemen's sons were going (as they always had) through a school system which held applied science and technology in contempt. This had not mattered in 1830, but it was crucial to industry in 1900, when industry was in need of an increasingly scientific base.

Consequently organic chemicals became a German industry; the motor car was pioneered in France and mass-produced in the United States; Britain lagged in the use of electricity, depended on foreign firms established there, and took only a small share of the export market. The telephone, the typewriter, the cash register and the diesel engine were all exploited by others. When after 1900 the economy was profitable, capital was exported instead of being invested at home. Most tragic was the failure in steel. Temin has rightly emphasised that Britain could not have expected to make more steel than Germany, let alone the United States.[22] But there was no need for her to become the world's largest importer of steel, incapable of meeting Belgian and German prices. An important element in Germany's success was the achievement of heat economies which were surely within the British grasp.

5.08 One can of course dismiss the entire controversy by reducing it to a matter of relative prices and profitability. On this view it was lack of profitability that held up investment. If the gap between wages and prices had been adequate, some entrepreneurs (British and foreign) would have been in the forefront with the new technologies and others would have followed rapidly.

We have seen that the economy was definitely unprofitable in the 1880s and 1890s, and although unprofitability gives some stimulus to the adoption of cost-reducing technologies it is not surprising that domestic investment slowed at that time. However, profitability revived in the second half of the nineties, and was duly accompanied by high investment. What happened between 1900 and 1913 remains uncertain. Exports were booming, but domestic investment declined to its lowest level. Profitability seems to have been reduced, but not by so much as to explain the phenomenal decline of domestic investment. The best conclusion seems to be that the old export industries which were leading this boom were profitable (cotton, iron, steam engines, railway equipment, coal, shipbuilding), but that the new industries were still not sufficiently attractive, given the scientific and technological environment of British industry.

It is then a matter of choice whether one blames prices or the environment. Given the price level, the environment was the source of the trouble. Given the environment, the problem lay in relative prices.

Let us follow the argument through. We shall assume that the environmental deficiencies could have been overcome if the system had been sufficiently profitable, since congenial entrepreneurs would have emerged from somewhere, internal or external. We are saying then that Britain's competitive power would not have declined if Britain's money costs had fallen faster or risen more slowly than German and American costs. The standard solutions for this problem, if there was a problem, would be either a lower level of wages and other incomes, or a devaluation of the pound.

It is first necessary to establish that there was a problem. If devaluation is a remedy only for a shortage of foreign exchange, then there was no problem requiring devaluation, since foreign exchange was abundant. Keynes has, however, taught us not to fall into this trap. The balance of payments can always be brought into equilibrium by varying the level of employment. If there was a case for devaluation, it would be not in order to earn more foreign exchange, but in order to have a higher level of employment.

Did the British economy need a higher level of employment? This question divides into two: a higher level of employment as a whole, or a higher level of employment in manufacturing industry? Britain needed a higher level of employment as a whole. Part of the evidence for this is her relatively high unemployment rates compared with those of Germany (see Table 2.2 and accompanying text). Looking again at Chart 2.1 it is hardly an exaggeration to describe the British picture for 1883 onwards as one of continuing gloom, punctuated occasionally by spurts of prosperity. Another part of the evidence is the continued need for the English to emigrate, long after emigration from France and Germany had dried up. Indeed, more people than ever were emigrating just before the First World War, and more than ever remaining in rural areas for lack of job opportunities in the towns (see section 2.16). We saw at the beginning of this chapter that the expansion of service industries was not enough to compensate for decelerating income from industry; now we also note that it was not enough to meet the employment needs of the still high rate of natural increase of the population.

If the British had a surplus of foreign exchange, this surplus was due partly to the same factor that produced unemployment, namely the fact that the British had been investing their capital abroad instead of at home. More employment at home might have resulted in a smaller surplus of interest and dividend income from abroad, but one cannot even be sure of this. Lower British prices would both have cut imports and have increased exports, thereby increasing the surplus on visible trade. Total profits and savings would have risen with employment, so home investment would not have been entirely at the expense of foreign investment. Even if it were, one could adopt the moral conclusion that income from employment at home was better than income from dividends abroad, earned at the expense of creating unemployment at home.

Besides, some of the non-manufacturing employment at home would prove to be a poor long-run investment. In particular, Britain built up huge foreign exchange receipts from shipping and from exporting coal. In shipping she was building a near monopoly of world trade, much like her earlier monopolies of cotton textiles and pig iron – with much the same fate in store. British shipping was a headache industry from 1920 onwards. Similarly the coal mining industry grew swiftly. Employment in coal increased at 3·0 per cent per annum, while productivity and the relative price of coal both declined sharply. This was an untenable situation, marked by an ever increasing momentum of strikes and bitter industrial conflict. This industry too was an albatross from 1920 onwards. More steel, electricity or chemicals would have been much sounder bets. This is all hindsight, but is nevertheless true.

If it is agreed that British prices were too high, and if the obstacles to reducing real costs could not be overcome (exhaustion of the old technology, worker resistance to the higher work norms needed to support greater capital intensity, lack of sympathy for industrial science) then the standard solutions would be (a) lower wage income levels or (b) devaluation of the pound.

We have seen that between 1883 and 1899 money wage costs per unit of output (wages divided by productivity) declined by about the same amount in Britain and in Germany (by much less than in France). Since German costs were lower than the British in 1883, the Germans had leeway in which to reduce their prices relative to British prices, as they did. British money wages were not in fact rising very fast: the rate of increase was 0·9 per cent per annum, in comparison with Germany's 2·0 per cent. This was faster than in the first half of the nineteenth century, but conditions had changed. The trade union movement became very militant at the end of the 1880s, and a lower rate of growth of money wages was not feasible. Why was labour so militant at this particular time? Here we have an interesting vicious circle. Labour was restless not because of the wage situation –

thanks to falling import prices real wages were now rising quite fast by contemporary standards (and nearly twice as fast as productivity) – but because of what slow industrial expansion was doing to job opportunities: forcing people to emigrate or to remain in the countryside. But wage increases did not help employment.

Devaluation was unthinkable. Actually, it cannot ever have been far from the minds of Governors of the Bank of England, seeing how difficult they found it to maintain their gold reserves throughout the whole of our period. But it was for them a threat rather than a potential refuge, and was irrelevant to the Bank's difficulties, which arose not from an adverse balance of payments on current account, but partly from a tendency to over-lending in boom years, and mainly from the Bank's own stubborn unwillingness to hold adequate gold reserves.

We cannot be sure what difference devaluation would have made to relative prices. It would presumably have stimulated money wage demands, but we know, especially from French experience, that it is possible to devalue without dissipating all the effect in higher domestic money incomes. Britain's problem would have been greater than France's because of greater dependence on imports entering into the cost of living, but the overseas suppliers depended so largely on the British market that their prices would have fallen somewhat as Britain devalued. More doubtful is the reaction of the competing industrial countries. Would they have permitted Britain to devalue relative to other core currencies? British devaluation in 1931 was followed by US devaluation in 1933, and by French devaluation in 1936; and when the USA wanted to devalue in 1971, it had the greatest difficulty in persuading the Western European nations to permit it to do so. A good date for a British devaluation would have been about 1885; whether the other members of the core would have permitted this we cannot say.

If Britain could neither hold down wages nor devalue, she could have imposed an import tariff. A large school of industrialists and conservative politicians advocated this step, which all other core members had already taken by 1890. But the economic theory of the day did not recognise 'involuntary unemployment', and could easily prove that tariffs were not in the national interest. In any case a tariff is only a half-substitute for devaluation. The other half is a system of export subsidies. This also was unthinkable; the best liberal minds of the day were, on the contrary, devoted to trying to secure international agreement against dumping.

5.09 Thus Britain was caught in a set of ideological traps. All the strategies available to her were blocked off in one way or another. She could not lower costs by cutting wages because of the unions, or switch to American-type technology because of the slower pace of British workers. She could not reduce her propensity to import by imposing a tariff or by devaluing her currency, or increase her propensity to export by devaluing or by paying export subsidies. She could not pioneer in developing new commodities because this now required a scientific base which did not accord with her humanistic snobbery. So instead she invested her savings abroad; the economy decelerated, the average level of unemployment increased and her young people emigrated.

If she could have broken into this succession of negatives at any one point, the whole situation could have been different. We are more conscious than our forefathers were of the importance of spiralling (upwards or downwards) in economic growth. They were aware of the economies of scale, and this was a part of the case then made for an industrial tariff. We are also aware of the relationship between productivity and growth. The higher the ratio of investment, the more up-to-date and productive is the equipment. Costs are therefore lower, competitive power in world markets is increased, demand is stimulated, investment increases still further, and so on. The steel industry, for example, explained that its productivity was lagging because its growth rate was so low. It was not profitable to replace old processes by new ones, but if the industry were growing faster one would have both old and new, thereby raising average productivity. The British relied on the market economy to bring them into equilibrium; but the market pays no heed to external economies; instead it brought them to relative stagnation.

Chapter 6

The Rate of Growth

SYNOPSIS: 6.00 The rate of growth of the industrial core was low by modern standards, and differences in the rate of growth of productivity are even more remarkable.

6.01 The rate of transfer of labour to industry from other sectors was lower in the pre-1914 core than it has been since the Second World War in the non-core countries of the OECD. But the core countries had not yet exhausted their labour reservoirs.

6.02 Shortage of skills was not a constraint. Industrial growth was not constrained by agricultural shortage. 6.03 The relevance of literacy is uncertain; however, there is no evidence that output was constrained by illiteracy. 6.04 There was no shortage of industrial skills, except perhaps of intermediate technologists in Britain. 6.05 Shortage of entrepreneurship is more controversial but improbable.

6.06 Lack of raw materials could be relevant. It is arguable that France was handicapped by lack of coal and Britain by lack of phosphoric iron ores, but neither of these propositions is definitively established.

6.07 The theory that maturing industrial countries are driven to invest abroad does not seem to apply. The low profitability of Britain and France in the 1880s was not due to previous over-capitalisation. New industries and innovations, coupled with growing population, prevented the potential rate of return to capital from falling. 6.08 Neither was profitability menaced by lack of markets or by shortage of foreign exchange. The core taken as a whole was nearly self-sufficient, and approximated to a 'balanced growth' model of development.

6.09 Industrialisation involved urbanisation, which is costly, but the core countries did not lack the necessary resources. It is conceivable that French industrial growth was inhibited by reluctance of farmers to migrate to industrial occupations. The US industrial labour force was growing as rapidly around 1900 as the Japanese around 1960; there may be a ceiling to the profitable growth rate of complex networks. The slower growth of the German industrial labour force may have been due to cartelisation.

6.10 Productivity grew much faster after 1950 than before 1914. Both the investment ratio and the output–capital ratio seem to have been higher since the Second World War.

6.11 The output–capital ratio was probably raised by the backlog of innovations that accumulated between 1914 and 1950. Also more is now spent on research and development; the effects of this however are uncertain.

6.00 The British economy was a wounded bird; what determined the growth rate of the rest of the core, and therefore the strength of the pulsations sent to the periphery?

Until recently this question used to be asked with a sense of amazement, meaning: how did such rapid growth come about, when compared with the very slow movement of preceding millennia, as well as with the sharp retardation of the next forty years, from 1913 to say 1950? Nowadays the question has also another angle: why was the growth rate so low in the forty years before the First World War, when compared with the growth rate since the Second World War. These comparisons are made in Table 6.1. We have chosen 1883 to 1907 for the prewar core, since peaks coincide around those dates. The peaks for the OECD countries as a whole after the Second World War came in 1957 and 1969. Table 6.1 compares core growth rates over 1883 to 1907 (actually 1880 to 1911 for population) with core growth rates from 1957 to 1969, and the OECD growth rates for 1957 to 1969 (OECD includes the core).

Table 6.1 *Growth Rates (per cent per annum)*[1]

	Core 1880–1910	*Core 1957–69*	*Total OECD 1957–69*	*Rest of OECD 1959–69*
Total population	1·20	1·15	1·15	1·15
Labour force	1·45	1·00	0·90	0·80
Industrial population	1·80	0·80	1·40	2·20
Industrial output	3·65	5·00	5·65	8·10
Industrial productivity	1·85	4·20	4·25	5·80

Our analysis takes the unusual form of asking what constrained the growth rate of the core countries during our period. This involves a brief review of all the factors which books on development theory claim to be causes of growth or retardation. Since our purpose is with history rather than with theoretical systems, we shall keep the theory to a minimum.

POPULATION

6.01 The population of core countries was growing at about the same rate between 1880 and 1910 and between 1957 and 1969. What matters more to development, however, is the growth of the labour force rather than of the population. Here the divergence was spectacular. The core labour force was growing faster than population before the First World War, because of the declining birth rate. By the 1960s population structure was much more stable. Now the labour force was growing less rapidly than the population, for a variety of reasons, including a temporary upsurge in the birth rate and increasing years spent in school.

The next comparison, between the industrial population and the total labour force, is equally striking. The industrial population was growing much faster than the total labour force before the First World War. But in the 1960s the industrial population of the core grew less rapidly than the total labour force. This occurred because, as countries grow richer, their demand for services increases as fast or faster than their demand for commodities, but productivity grows faster in commodity production than in services, so employment in services grows faster than employment in commodity production. Industrial production can grow fast while there are still reservoirs of labour in agriculture, domestic service and so on; but once these reservoirs are exhausted, the proportion of persons engaged in industry tends to decline.

Other OECD countries have not yet reached this stage. As Table 6.1 shows, in the 1960s their labour force grew only at 0·8 per cent per annum, but their industrial populations grew at 2·2 per cent per annum.

It emerges therefore that other OECD countries were making very much larger transfers from other sectors to industry in the 1960s than our countries were making between 1880 and 1910. This should not be a surprise. The US agricultural population was growing rapidly until the end of the nineteenth century. The British economy was then growing comparatively slowly, for reasons we examined in Chapter 5, so the proportion of the British labour force in industry was not significantly greater in 1911 than in 1881. Only in France and Germany were large transfers taking place at this time from other sectors to industry. This immediately answers the question whether population growth was a constraint on the growth rate of core industrial production. The answer is that it cannot have been, except perhaps in France. Large labour reservoirs still existed in small-scale agriculture, in domestic service, in petty retailing and other sectors of the economy. Also female participation rates were still low; unmarried middle-class women were only just beginning to go out to work in large numbers, and the similar movement of married women would not gain momentum until the First World War.

Our quest is therefore now concentrated on two questions. Why did the industrial labour force not grow faster? And why did productivity per head not grow faster?

SKILLS

6.02 Was the growth rate of the core inhibited at this time by a shortage of human skills?

One of the chief constraints on less developed countries (LDCs) is a shortage of agricultural skills. Balanced economic growth (i.e. without foreign trade) depends on a growing industrial class (relatively) selling a growing industrial output to a diminishing agricultural class in return for an increasing agricultural surplus. If the agricultural surplus is constant, industry cannot have the labour; or if it takes the labour, it cannot get the agricultural products and has no market for the industrial output. Industry is then forced to sell abroad and faces a foreign exchange problem.

Agricultural skills were no problem to Britain or Germany, or to the USA down to about 1900. After 1900 the deceleration of US agricultural output caused the general price level to rise, and moved the terms of trade against industry. This was due not to shortage of skills but to shortage of land, and could have been made good by increased skills, as happened in the 1920s. The USA solved its foreign exchange problem with an explosive increase of exports of manufactures, but this merely shifted the problem to the core as a whole. We found no reason to believe that the Kondratiev upswing had either restrained or stimulated the industrial growth of the core. The immediate impact was an increase in world trade in manufactures, and generally in purchases by farmers, and a sharp deceleration in the real wages of industrial workers. The long-run impact would have been a decline of industrial profits as the industrial workers increased their share to keep their relative position *vis-à-vis* the agricultural classes. But the war came before these effects could work themselves out, and after the war there was another burst of agricultural output.

France had its own special problem with the *phylloxera*, to which the depression of the second half of the eighties has usually been attributed; but we have seen reasons for doubting this attribution.

We conclude that whereas greater agricultural knowledge is important in explaining why industrial output was growing faster in our period than in the eighteenth century, it does not contribute to explaining the difference from the 1960s.

6.03 Industrial skills have to be considered at four levels – artisans, supervisors, technologists and managers.

There is no evidence of any of the core countries being held up for lack of artisan skills. They all had apprenticeship systems of one kind or another. It was fashionable to say that the USA used more capital per head than the UK because it had less skill, but the proposition is doubtful.[2] From mid-century on the British trade unions acquired increasing control over numbers apprenticed to skilled trades, and from time to time employers alleged that there were shortages, but this does not seem to have limited output significantly. (The workers' decision to set themselves low output norms is a different matter.)

This is the place to note that the success of the industrial revolution seems not to have depended on widespread literacy. The transition to universal primary education was made during our period, but its contribution is hard to assess. The core countries varied greatly in the levels of education attained in the first half of the century. According to Mulhall,[3] in 1840 the percentages of adults able to write were as follows: France 47, UK 59, USA 80, Germany 82. France, the UK and Belgium (45) were out of step with the rest of north-West Europe, behind Holland (70), Scandinavia (80) and Switzerland (80), but inadequate literacy does not seem to have stood in the way of their industrialisation in the first half of the century. Factory workers need literacy, or at any rate are easier to instruct if literate, so some proportion of the population – say 20 per cent as a start – must be literate if an industrial revolution is to be launched. But it is highly doubtful whether workers with eight years of primary schooling will produce more industrial output than workers with six years of primary schooling. Some present-day economists assert that part of today's higher industrial output is due to additional manhours of primary schooling per head of the industrial population. This case has not been proved. It is better to be educated than uneducated, but more schooling does not necessarily result in greater industrial output.

6.04 We have seen that the training of technicians, supervisors and industrial scientists became an issue in Great Britain after about 1880, when observers began to note the extent to which Britain was falling behind in the new science-based industries. Other core countries were not conscious of shortages at this level, presumably because their training facilities were more adequate.

The industrial equipment used today requires a larger proportion of technically trained people than that of a century ago. Much of the requisite training can be done on the job, but the proportion of jobs requiring say the equivalent of two years' full-time training in a vocational or technical institute is also larger. For the economy as a whole it may now be as high as 20 per cent in the most advanced countries.

The need for advanced training in engineering and science is also much greater, not only because of requirements of production, but also because research and development, which were infinitesimal in 1880, are now major industries. Perhaps as much as 5 per cent of the labour force needs special training in these fields.

It is beyond question that the higher industrial productivity of today is mainly due to greater knowledge. It is not, however, clear that greater knowledge produces a faster rate of growth, or that knowledge with a direct bearing on industrial productivity is growing any faster now than it was between 1870 and 1913. We come to this in a moment.

If we confine ourselves to the question 'Was the rate of growth of core industrial production constrained in our period by lack of skills?', the answer seems to be: no, except to some extent in Great Britain, where attitude was the problem, rather than the capacity to produce skilled people (since this could easily have been expanded, given the will).

6.05 Finally we come to the level of management. Shortage of entrepreneurial know-how is always a problem for newly developing countries. In many the intensity of the shortage is due to an uncongenial social or political atmosphere. The supply of domestic entrepreneurs is a function of the profitability of the system and the security of investment. So if the government is keeping the foreign exchange rate too high for the level at which it is inflating the currency; or pushing up wages while controlling prices; or tying up the would-be investor with licences of all sorts, arbitrarily administered; or indulging in arbitrary confiscation; or if the courts do not dispense justice; or if the public peace is frequently arrested by damaging civil wars; in a word, if the investment climate is uncongenial, there will be a shortage of private entrepreneurs.

In our period the investment climate was uncongenial in many countries of the world, but not in those of our core.

But even when the institutions and traditions are congenial, a less developed country can be short of entrepreneurial know-how. This was hardly possible in the first half of the nineteenth century, though it is possible now. The skills required for establishing and managing the cotton mills, or the blast furnaces, of 1830 are available to every ordered society; but the skills required for managing, not to speak of establishing, a motor car or a computer factory have to be acquired by experience, and are still scarce in today's less developed countries. It is true that even in the first half of the nineteenth century France and Germany were importing entrepreneurs from Britain; and as late as the end of the century Britain was importing chemical and electrical engineering entrepreneurship from Germany and the USA, but these were imports of technology rather than of entrepreneurial know-how. More relevant is the fact that Britain lacked entrepreneurs with the right attitude to science, and therefore with an understanding of how to use scientists properly; but what was here at fault was the *Weltanschauung*, rather than a shortage of entrepreneurs as such.

The British shortage of entrepreneurship is a proposition that has usually to be argued with diffidence, since the proposer has to produce reasons for a fall in entrepreneurial effort, which is an improbable outcome of a century of industrialisation. That France lacked the right kind of entrepreneurship is a superficially more attractive opinion, since no reversal is involved, and it is therefore usually stated as if it were self-evident. Kindleberger reviews the extensive literature on this subject.[4] The argument is generally conducted in terms of French family structure, the keeping of managerial control tightly in family hands, the resulting small size of French units, and so on. Most writers underestimate the real achievement of the French, not realising, for instance, that after 1890 gross domestic product per head of population was growing perhaps 50 per cent faster in France than in the United Kingdom, although only perhaps two-thirds as fast as in Germany. The weakness of the proposition is that it must demonstrate that market conditions were such that new entrepreneurs more dynamic than the old families could not emerge and establish themselves. This would be difficult to demonstrate. It is easy to assume that lack of investment must be due to lack of entrepreneurship, but this case has not yet been established for France in our period.

PHYSICAL RESOURCES

6.06 Physical resource constraints – raw materials, construction capacity, capacity to produce industrial equipment – play a considerable role in trade cycle theory, so one must ask to what extent such constraints were effective in the core.

The core countries usually ran short of capital goods capacity at the height of Juglar booms, and this may have constrained their growth rates. It is hard to take this seriously as a constraint on the long-run rate of growth, since, given the necessary savings capacity, these countries could all have maintained larger capital goods capacities if the demand had been there.

Several LDCs found themselves constrained by construction capacity during the 1950s or 1960s. But the constraint lay not in the absolute level of this capacity, but in the rate at which capacity could be expanded; it takes time to train building artisans and supervisors. Chenery and Strout have suggested 10 per cent per annum as the fastest rate of growth achievable without waste.[5] Our core countries had no such problem.

The capacity to produce industrial machinery can be a constraint on the world economy as a whole at the height of a Juglar boom. At such a time it may be a disadvantage not to have a domestic machinery industry (although in some such cases producers of machinery give their foreign customers priority over domestic customers). At other times one can buy machinery with foreign exchange. There is nevertheless advantage in having a domestic industrial capacity, in that it makes it easier in the event of breakdowns to get hold of spare parts and specialists in maintenance. (Nowadays with air transport this is less of a problem than it used to be, though still expensive.) There is also advantage to a developing country in having a low import propensity, since this yields a large export multiplier, and therefore increases the rate of transfer of persons and resources from less to more valuable occupations. These reasons justify special efforts to encourage domestic production of some of the types of equipment which a country uses most heavily, subject to the usual arithmetic of comparative advantage. However, whatever the size of the engineering industry, even the most developed countries are heavy importers of machinery, so lack of equipment capacity can be a constraint on growth if the country has a foreign exchange problem. Thus, too heavy a dependency on the import of capital goods seems to have been an element in the British situation in the 1950s and 1960s.

The availability of raw materials can produce a similar situation. The core as a whole was never constrained by lack of raw materials, apart from a shortage of cotton during the American Civil War. Faster industrial growth after 1900 would have improved the terms of trade of raw material producers, and this could in due course have constrained industrial growth by squeezing profits. However, there is no reason to think that the growth rate of the core as a whole was constrained by lack of raw materials at any time between 1870 and 1913.

Industrial countries could buy raw materials with foreign exchange, and to this extent poverty in raw materials would show in lower incomes rather than in slower growth. But there were some raw materials which could not be exploited competitively if they had to be imported. These were the heavy raw materials, where transport cost was considerable in relation to their price, including especially the weight-losing raw materials, coal and iron ore. The handicap of not possessing ores is not as great today as it was in 1870, because the principal element is the cost of transport, which is now relatively to the cost of materials only a fraction of what it was then. Countries compete quite successfully today without having a fuel source of their own – even at 1975 oil prices – and the Japanese even succeed in underselling other steel producers, although they have to import both the fuel and the ore. More relevantly, it is not as important to be a steel producer as it then was; employment is generated more profitably in using steel to make machinery and so on than in producing steel, and several countries have profitable steel-using industries built on imported steel.

But between 1880 and 1913 the making of steel was the leading sector of the day, and those who fell behind in this, like the British and the French, were disadvantaged. Britain had problems with ore, and France with coal. The British are still disputing whether the German steel industry had an advantage in the accessibility of cheap phosphoric ores suitable for making basic steel by the Gilchrist–Thomas process.[6] Kindleberger examines at length the proposition that France was handicapped by insufficiency of domestic supplies of coal, but rejects it.[7] In neither case is it established that having to import the raw material was a decisive element in production costs.

MARKETS

6.07 Did the core need markets outside itself because its own home market was insufficiently profitable? There are three approaches to this question: one via diminishing returns to capital as capital per head increases; the second via the theory of under-consumption; and the third via the theory of balanced growth. We shall begin with diminishing returns.

In its simplest form the model reduces to a one-sector economy, containing only workers and capitalists. An increase in capital per worker reduces the marginal productivity of capital, the rate of return to new investment, and therefore the incentive to invest. So long as the capitalists spend all their income, whether on consumption or on capital formation, the system is stable; this follows from Say's Law, and rules out under-consumption. In any case under-consumption could not be cured simply by expanding foreign trade, since this implies an inflow of imports matching the outflow of exports. Foreign trade contributes a solution only if exports exceed imports, that is to say only to the extent that foreign investment is taking place.

If the capitalists either consume or invest all their income the system is stable, but on the assumption of diminishing returns to capital it will decelerate, as the falling rate of profit reduces the investment ratio. This event is postponed if we remove the assumption of a one-sector economy, and assume instead a dual economy, part capitalist and part traditional. The usual assumption is then that the capitalists can over some initial period recruit labour cheaply from the traditional sector, the length of the period depending partly on the rate of population growth and partly on what happens to productivity in the traditional sector itself. It is therefore very significant that in three of our countries – France, Germany and the United States – industry was still in 1913 recruiting labour from agriculture and other labour reservoirs. There was no shortage of labour putting pressure on the profit ratio. Neither was there a labour shortage in Britain, from which emigration continued high down to the First World War.

If the capitalists are investing a large proportion of the national income the onset of the labour shortage can only be postponed. Sooner or later in this model the supply of capital will outrun the labour supply, and diminishing returns to capital will set in. Capitalists will then seek higher profits by investing in other countries where returns are still high, and this diversion will diminish domestic growth even more. The slowdown of domestic investment cannot be reversed by stepping up domestic consumption (e.g. by increasing the relative share of wages) since the rising share of consumption is its very cause. If returns to investment are diminishing it is inevitable (and presumably at some point becomes appropriate) that the investment ratio will decline.

The whole analysis so far stands or falls by diminishing returns to capital. The assumption of diminishing returns stems from the further assumption that technological change is non-existent or hostile to capital's share. Economists have been expecting the rate of return on capital to decline ever since the middle of the eighteenth century, but this seems not to have happened. As we saw in Chapter 4, one cannot be certain what happened to the rate of return to capital between 1870 and 1913, but allowing for ups and downs there is no reason to suspect a secular fall; most historians indeed have suspected a rise. New technology kept on creating new opportunities for investment, and if Britain ran into technological stagnation and invested abroad instead of at home, this was due to a set of peculiar attitudes which left the economy under-capitalised rather than over-capitalised.

6.08 To reach the theory of balanced growth we abandon the implied assumption that the system produces only one consumer good. Instead, in its simplest form, it now produces two goods, industry and agriculture. If we assume that each industrial worker requires a minimum amount of agricultural commodities (food and raw materials) it follows at once that the profitability of industry will depend on the terms of trade between industry and agriculture. If industry grows rapidly while agriculture stagnates, the terms of trade will move against industry, and beyond a certain point capitalists would be paying out the whole product to workers in order to buy the minimum of agricultural products. Continual industrial expansion therefore requires a continual increase in agricultural output sufficient to prevent the choking of industrial profits by adverse terms of trade.

The alternative way out, if domestic agriculture is stagnant, is to export manufactures, and import food and raw materials in return. The system can then expand indefinitely if it masters the tricks of competition in manufactures and if the world terms of trade continue favourable.

As we have seen, the core as a whole was nearly self-sufficient in food and raw materials (cotton, iron ore, coal, copper, nickel, wheat) except to a great extent for wool and to a lesser extent for leather, timber and nitrates. Profitability was not menaced by any shortages of these, so they gave rise to no search for peripheral markets as a shield against declining profits. The core had for centuries engaged in peripheral trade in luxuries (tea, sugar, cocoa, coffee, spices, oilseeds) but though these had caused much international violence in the eighteenth century and up to 1814, they could not serve as constraints on development, since they were not basic materials for industrialisation or (except for sugar, which was in over-supply) basic mass foodstuffs. Indeed the quantitative significance of those luxury trades turns out to be remarkably small (see section 7.02) when one thinks of the romance and blood and misery which have been attached to them. It was for the materials of the 'second industrial revolution'[8] (electricity, motor cars, etc.) that the core found itself increasingly needing materials from the periphery (copper, tin, oil, bauxite, rubber) but this trade too did not amount to much before the First World War. Taken as a whole the core did not run into trouble from unbalanced growth until after 1900, when the terms of trade moved against industry in favour of agriculture. But, as we saw in Chapter 4, this movement did not affect the profitability of capital because the adverse terms of trade were shifted to the workers. Real wages decelerated or fell. Perhaps this change would ultimately have affected profits, as workers struggled to restore their position, but the question did not arise since after the war the terms of trade reversed themselves, in favour of industry.

The core as a whole was nearly self-sufficient, but individual countries were not. Technological progress was fairly rapid in the agriculture of all four countries, as the result of a combination of mechanisation, fertilisers, new varieties of wheat and beet, and some switch to livestock products. Nevertheless the three European countries depended increasingly on imports of food and raw materials, partly because of growing populations, and partly because comparative cost seemed to favour greater specialisation in industry. They had then to seek foreign markets for their manufactures in order to pay for their imports.

Since the Second World War some developing countries have claimed that their development has been retarded by inability to earn enough foreign exchange to pay for minimum required imports. There is no parallel in the development of the core countries, or indeed in the pre-war development of the peripheral countries. In the latter countries exports grew faster than output (in contrast with the 1960s) so there was no secular shortage of foreign exchange. Of course all countries were liable to have cyclical difficulties with foreign exchange; we have seen how carefully the Bank of England watched its gold supply. A secular shortage of foreign exchange is a different matter. We must first distinguish the shortage of foreign exchange which is also a shortage of domestic saving from the situation where there is potential saving that cannot be translated into foreign exchange; it is only in this latter situation that development can be described as being retarded by inability to earn foreign exchange.

Such inability may have many causes – the complex factors which retarded British exports illustrate this well – but in the last analysis these causes translate into an incompatibility of domestic and foreign prices. This situation did not arise before the First World War because it was not allowed to arise. Countries on the gold standard maintained their competitiveness by keeping their domestic prices in line; the extraordinary success of the core countries in keeping industrial wage costs per unit of output moving together was demonstrated in section 4.08. Did this require some Keynesian deflation as well as wage restraint? The answer is doubtful. The big turnaround in the US balance of payments in the second half of the nineties is associated with an economy running below capacity, though not specifically deflated for balance of payments reasons. Similarly the low levels of British and French activity in the second half of the eighties will have put pressure on wages, although again this was not the primary intention, and (since the terms of trade were improving sharply) neither country was short of foreign exchange at this time. The element of wage restraint in collective bargaining seems to be the main factor keeping domestic costs in line with international prices.

Countries not on the gold standard devalued their currencies if the cost of producing exports exceeded the price in foreign markets. These countries were controlled politically by the exporters and landowners, and used currency devaluation to throw on to their workers and the urban community the burden of declines in the gold price of exports.[9] One can always make exports more profitable by devaluing the currency, except in the rare case where the elasticity of demand for the product of the individual country is less than unity.

The difference between the situation then and now does not lie in different market structures or elasticities; it lies in the fact that domestic price levels were under control then, and (for better or worse) are not under control now. To say that a country could not earn enough foreign exchange to pay for needed imports would have made no sense to an economist of the year 1900 or earlier; but it makes plenty of sense today, as the British struggle again amply illustrates.

Once one accepts that it may be difficult to earn foreign exchange, then a country rich in natural resources relative to population should find it easier to develop than one which has to rely on unbalanced growth. Several countries expanded rapidly in the nineteenth century by opening up fertile lands for settlement; this was the case in the USA, Argentina, Australia, Gold Coast, Burma and Ceylon. Arguably such countries have a double advantage; the opening up of new lands not only provides a new market for the industrial sector, but also stimulates the whole economy pervasively, because of the high levels of internal migration and social mobility which it entails. Social rigidities are eroded, development horizons are lifted, and the population gains economic and social virility. However, the opening up of new land is not the only source of economic and social virility. As in Japan, lack of resources may be the challenge to which the nation responds. In fact when we look at the core countries it is conspicuous that the country where industrial productivity was growing fastest was not the United States but Germany. A country can grow just as fast from exploiting a technological backlog as it can from opening up new lands.

In sum, the core countries taken as a whole did not as far as we can see suffer from a declining productivity of investment, whether because of under-consumption, or increased capital per head, or unbalanced growth at home. They depended very little on peripheral countries for food or raw materials, and were not menaced by adverse terms of trade in such countries, except to a slight degree after 1900. Their investment in such countries was not due to exhaustion of technological opportunities at home. The growth rate of the core was not constrained by foreign trade.

URBANISATION

6.09 So far we have been negative. The industrial growth of the core was not constrained by natural increase of population, or by lack of skills, physical resources, foreign exchange or markets. Some of these – especially skills – help to explain why the growth rate was faster in our period than in the eighteenth century, but none explains why the core did not grow as fast in our period as in the 1960s. Now we come to matters of greater substance.

At this time industrialisation involved urbanisation, since the industrial population was augmented by recruiting people from the countryside. This was not the only source of recruits: the factory system also recruited people from the workshops and from domestic production, and the towns also had their own high rate of natural increase. As the rural surplus declined, the factories would also recruit from other urban occupations, especially domestic service, but this had not yet started. The main transfer at this time was from rural to urban occupations.[10]

We must therefore ask whether a feasible rate of urbanisation could impose a constraint on industrial growth. This constraint could be of three kinds. Urbanisation may be inhibited by the unwillingness of rural folk to leave their homes, by the cost of building towns, or by lack of capacity to organise urban expansion, even setting aside the question of cost.

The willingness of rural folk to leave their homes is influenced first and foremost by the natural rate of increase of the population, especially if farming is on a small-scale, peasant basis. The family farm is a powerful emotional magnet, all the more so if it has been in the family for many generations. One can therefore expect the peasant family to try to keep the family farm going, and this means that if the natural rate of increase is zero or less, migration from family farms will, in normal economic conditions, not differ significantly from zero. Of course family farmers may be forced to abandon their farms by catastrophe, either physical (such as prolonged drought or flood, or epidemic disease of cattle or plants) or economic (such as the collapse of farm prices). Most European farmers were subject to economic pressure in the eighties and nineties, and in addition the French vineyards had to cope with the *phylloxera*. Yet it is remarkable how little exodus there was from the rural areas. Table 6.2 shows the average annual percentage rates of change over long periods.

Table 6.2 *Population Growth Rates (per cent per annum)*

	Rural	*Urban*[11]
Germany (1880–1910)	−0·1	+2·5
England and Wales (1871–1911)	−0·2	+1·8
France (1891–1911)	−0·4	+1·0
USA (1880–1910)	+1·1	+3·7

In Germany the rural population was about constant over our period. All the natural increase of population went into the towns, except for a small trickle of emigrants to other countries.

Britain tests the rule. Its agricultural population did not consist mainly of farmers, and was therefore not so closely tied to the land emotionally. The number of farmers there remained fairly constant – the census of population puts it at 220,000 in 1851, 220,000 in 1881 and 230,000 in 1911 – whereas the number of agricultural labourers declined from 850,000 to 635,000 between 1881 and 1911.[12] Emotion restrained a decline in the number of farmers, but not in that of agricultural labourers. (The number of farmers in England and Wales still refuses resolutely to decline; the 1961 Census found 306,000 farmers and farm managers, while agricultural labourers and tractor drivers had fallen to 378,000.)

By 1891 France's rate of natural increase had fallen almost to zero, so almost the whole rise in urban population was derived from reducing the rural population. It is not inconceivable that unwillingness to leave the family farm was at this time a constraint on the rate of growth of French industry. We must not be misled by comparisons with our own day. Nowadays rural populations are subjected to powerful forces attracting them to the town. The schools teach the children about urban life, and stimulate their curiosity. The media – newspapers, radio, cinemas, television – bombard young people with news of what is happening in the towns. Rail and bus fares are relatively cheap, so young people can visit the towns for themselves and see all the attractions they offer. The days when large numbers of persons who lived in rural areas passed their whole lives without ever visiting a town or wanting to go, have gone. But this is how people were living in the last quarter of the nineteenth century, and it is not inconceivable that in France their unwillingness to leave their farms, except under strong pressures, constrained the rate of growth of industry, after about 1895.

It is true that France, like Britain, also had a lot of agricultural labourers and that their numbers declined faster than the farmers. But in Britain rural folk seem to have wanted to leave the countryside faster than domestic urban growth permitted and thus went off to the USA whenever that economy moved into a prosperous phase. In France the rural community seems to have been content with French domestic expansion and showed no desire to emigrate; indeed France was a country of net immigration.

We are therefore suggesting that industrial expansion may have been constrained in France by the labour force. Then, as we saw in the chapter on Britain, it would follow automatically that productivity, as well as numbers, would grow slowly, because it is less profitable to use capital to replace existing equipment than it is to use it to employ more persons. The relatively high level of foreign investment would follow from this. If the French industrial population had grown faster, more would have been invested at home, and equipment would on the average have been more up-to-date.

In the USA it was a different story. Here there was a population growing so rapidly (2·05 per cent per annum) through a combination of natural increase and immigration that the towns could not grow fast enough to absorb all the increase in population, and rural growth continued at a high level. In net terms the towns may be said to have recruited all the immigrants and about one-third of the natural increase of the countryside. The prosperous decades were the 1880s and the 1900s; was manufacturing industry constrained by lack of labour in those decades? There is no evidence suggesting this. The gap between earnings in agriculture and in industry was wide, although it is difficult to give this precise significance because of differences in the cost of living. In the 1880s farmers were complaining about falling prices, whereas money wages were rising in industry, and real wages were rising even faster; the rural population would probably in this decade have accepted more urban jobs if these had been available. The price situation was reversed in the 1900s; but this was also a time when workers were complaining about the pressure of immigrants on the labour market. For the time being the best conclusion seems to be that shortage of labour did not constrain industrial expansion in the USA.

The Third World today is like the USA prior to 1913 with its rural population growing so fast that the towns cannot absorb all the natural increase. In this connection the other half of our proposition about the willingness of rural folk to leave their farms comes into effect; that is to say that rural emigration will be considerable so long as natural increase exceeds zero. Assuming that the family wishes to keep the family farm intact, a high rate of natural increase can be met in the first instance by displacing hired labour with the labour of relatives. But there is still pressure to break up the farm, as it is passed down by each head of household, and this pressure can be relieved only by members of the family emigrating to seek employment in the towns.

The USA was an exception because it still had vast virgin lands to settle, and so could continue to increase the number of farms. Our proposition is more applicable to certain parts of the Third World today.

If urban areas are to absorb the whole of the natural increase in population, their required growth rate is given by the natural rate of increase divided by the proportion of the population currently living in urban areas. In the USA in 1880, this would have required the urban population to be growing by 7·3 per cent per annum (2·05 ÷ 28·2).

Here we come to a factor which must ultimately inhibit industrial growth, namely the difficulties and cost of rapid urbanisation. The human effort required to organise decent urban conditions is immense. Streets must be built, paved and lighted. Water must be laid down. Arrangements are needed for sewage disposal. Buses must be organised. The town has to be fed, and while it is relatively easy to bring in cereals, roots or meat from long distances, the daily delivery of milk and vegetables from the surrounding countryside is not so easy to arrange. In the nineteenth century and earlier the size of towns was limited by the logistics of meeting the daily requirements of half a million to a million people living in one town. Nowadays these matters are easier to organise. But perhaps even more important is that many towns have given up trying to organise decent conditions. Urban authorities used to be jealous of the numbers allowed into their cities; residential permits were required. Nowadays all may come, and any kind of squatting is tolerated. Numbers grow past three, four or five millions, collected together in squalor, with primitive water, sewage and transportation arrangements. As a result the struggle to organise decent urban conditions is no longer a constraint on the growth of urbanisation.

The cost of urbanisation, however, remains a key factor. The bulk of it is incurred in construction rather than equipment. It is true that the factories, transport systems and other sectors need equipment, but typically, two-thirds of the cost of urbanisation is devoted to construction, including residential accommodation and other infrastructure. Moreover, construction costs relatively more in towns than in the countryside. This is not merely because farmers to a greater extent build and maintain their own homes, especially in the off-season. It is also because the pay of construction workers in town is linked to the pay of factory workers. Productivity rises faster in factories than in construction, so money labour cost rises faster in construction than it does in factories. Economists urge LDCs to keep down mechanisation in construction, so as to provide more employment, but the fact is that the cost of urbanisation can be kept down only by measures which raise construction productivity.

From this analysis we derive two conclusions. First, industrialisation is more expensive when it involves transferring people from rural to urban areas than when it can be done where there is a settled population. This is part of the case for carrying industry into the countryside (as Mao's China has tried to do) rather than taking country people to the towns. Beyond this it also follows that a mature economy, which has exhausted its rural surplus and is not expanding its urban population, should get a higher rate of industrial growth from the same level of capital formation, since it need not spend so much on construction, and can therefore spend more on equipment per head. This may be an element in the increase in the growth rate of industrial productivity in the core countries since the Second World War.

Secondly, the high cost of urbanisation may be the key to the puzzle why some countries can industrialise without heavy borrowing from overseas, while others do not achieve this. Table 6.2 shows that the urban populations of Britain and France were growing in our period by less than 2·0 per cent per annum. Presumably the USA had to borrow not because it was capable of saving less (its domestic savings ratio exceeded that of the British) but because it had heavier urbanisation costs. The same would apply to the regions of new settlement (e.g. Australia, Canada, Argentina). And the same applies in our day to those Third World countries which are industrialising via rapid urbanisation. Newly industrialising countries are of course still far from the stage where it begins to be arguable that an infinite elasticity of supply has removed the constraint of capital shortage.

The following conclusion seems to emerge. Germany was a relatively small lender, with an urban growth rate of 2·5 per cent per annum, and the USA a relatively small borrower with an urban growth rate of 3·7 per cent per annum. Perhaps one could say that a semi-industrial country would save more than it needed if its urban growth rate was less than 3·0 per cent, and save less than it needed if its urban growth rate was more than 3·0 per cent per annum.

Today's urban growth rates are far from 3·0 per cent in the Third World, because Third World populations are growing at unprecedented rates. Colombia, with 52 per cent of its population urban in 1950, and a population growth rate of 3·3 per cent, would have needed an urbanisation growth rate of 6·3 per cent per annum if all the increase was to be absorbed into the towns. Actually the Colombian towns grew at 5·7 per cent between 1951 and 1964, testifying that the countryside did indeed try for a zero rate of increase. Brazil's urban population grew at 5·6 per cent per annum between 1950 and 1960, with the rural population still growing rapidly. The Third World is everywhere in trouble nowadays because its high rates of natural increase (averaging 2·5) have stimulated great migrations, with rural populations trying to keep their own growth rates near to zero, at the expense of urban growth rates of 5 to 10 per cent per annum. The USSR tests all the rules. Between 1929 and 1939 it actually reduced the rural population at 0·8 per cent per annum, and increased the urban population at 6·3 per cent per annum. These rates were obviously too high. The pretence of decent conditions in the towns was abandoned, as people were huddled into houses with sometimes as little space as one family per room.

After the war the rate of urbanisation was reduced to 4·2 per cent per annum between 1950 and 1960, a rate which is probably still faster than the urban authorities can cope with, if their towns are to offer decent living conditions.

We have suggested that unwillingness to migrate may have constrained industrial growth in France. Is it feasible that the cost of urbanisation constrained industrial growth in the USA? This seems unlikely since, except between 1890 and 1895, the USA never had difficulty in borrowing all the capital it required. Economists who try to explain the mechanism of the Kuznets cycle have to explain the breakdown at the peak (when immigration was at its maximum) in terms of over-building, rather than under-building. The cost of urbanisation is certainly a constraint on the industrial growth of today's LDCs, but it did not constrain the core countries in our period.

This does not, however, rule out the possibility that at any time there is a maximum to the rate at which an industrial system can expand while meeting the test of profitability, which requires good planning, matching market demands and supplies, training labour, good management, and so on. Such a limit must exist since, even with unlimited labour, capital and entrepreneurship a complex and inter-related system could not grow at an infinite rate. If we take expansion of the labour force as the measure, we note that in spite of the miraculous rates of expansion that we associate with Japan in the second half of this century, the rate of growth of the labour force in Japanese manufacturing and mining between 1956 and 1971 was only 3·8 per cent per annum. Different countries will have different capabilities at different times, but the US rate for 1890 to 1910, which was 3·5 per cent per annum, was not far behind the Japanese postwar rate. It is conceivable that a ratio of about 4 per cent is about as fast as the industrial labour force can grow while maintaining internal structural balance. Those development planners who have to worry about efficiency, shortages and surpluses should give thought to this possibility.

Of course such high rates are possible only in the early stages of development. In a mature closed economy the ratio of the industrial to the total labour force would be about constant: the industrial labour force would grow at the same rate as the occupied population. Demand for manufactures would grow slightly faster than income, but productivity would be rising slightly faster in manufacturing, so the proportion in manufacturing might well be constant. There is even some evidence that it may fall. In an open economy the direct link between domestic demand and the distribution of the labour force is broken, but it still remains likely that the industrial labour ratio of a mature economy would be fairly stable or declining; and this is probably the main reason why Table 6.1 shows the industrial population growing more slowly than the labour force of the core countries over 1957–69.

In 1890 our only nearly mature economy was Britain, where manufacturing and mining were absorbing 37 per cent of the labour force (Germany 30, France 28, USA 20). Here the occupied population was growing at 1·0 per cent, and the industrial population at 1·1 per cent. The British economy was growing too slowly to provide full employment for the natural increase of population, and so heavy emigration continued until 1913, in contrast with Germany and France. The constraint on British growth, as we have seen, was attributable to maladjustment to changes in world trade.

We have now pinpointed possible constraints on the rates of growth of the industrial labour forces of Britain, France (unwillingness of farmers to leave their farms) and the USA (a ceiling to the rate of ordered expansion). Only Germany is the remaining puzzle. Industry occupied only 26 per cent of the labour force there in 1875, and German industrialists could certainly have handled a faster growth rate than 2·0 per cent per annum. Does the solution of the German puzzle lie in excessively well ordered expansion? The economy became heavily cartelised, with market-sharing agreements of one kind or another. If so, this may also explain a phenomenon which puzzled us in Chapter 2, namely the smooth growth of German industry, with its relatively minor recessions after 1880, in marked contrast with those of the UK, France or the USA. The plausibility of these conjectures does not, unfortunately, establish their correctness.

CAPITAL

6.10 Our view that lack of capital was not a constraint on the industrial growth of the core does not imply that the core would not have grown faster if more capital had been invested. It merely implies that the investment ratio was what it was because of limitations on the demand for capital, rather than on the supply of capital. It is therefore legitimate to ask whether the higher industrial growth rates of the 1960s were in fact associated with a higher ratio of investment.

We have to begin by noting that the real differences in industrial growth between 1883 to 1907 and 1957 to 1969 are probably not as great as Table 6.1 suggests. Most indexes of industrial production for the period before 1913 are based to a considerable extent on raw material input rather than on counting the output. To this extent therefore they leave out the individual industry's economy in using raw materials. They also fail to record accurately increases in output derived from doing more work on the same raw material, which is especially a problem in metallurgy and engineering. It is therefore possible that one needs to add as much as 0·5 per year to prewar growth rates for purposes of comparison with the industrial production indexes of the 1960s. However, this still leaves a big gap, so the question as to the role of investment cannot be avoided.

Table 6.3 *Investment Ratios*[13]

	Net investment		GDP growth		ICOR	
	1899/1907	*1957/69*	*1899/1907*	*1957/69*	*1899/1907*	*1957/69*
USA[a]	12·4	7·7	4·1	4·9	3·0	1·6
UK	5·4	10·0	1·7	2·8	3·2	3·6
Germany	15·2	15·8	2·9	4·4	5·2	3·6
France	—	13·9	—	5·6	—	2·5
Core	—	9·5	—	4·7	—	2·0

[a] For USA the earlier date is 1892/1907.

The question cannot be answered with confidence because our figures for investment before the First World War are artefacts which do not command great confidence. We have assembled in Table 6.3 some figures bearing on this subject. For the later period we are still using 1957/69. For the earlier period we have chosen 1899/1907, except for the USA, where 1899 was not a peak year; for the USA instead we use the period 1892/1907. There are no prewar figures for France. Figures relate to gross domestic product as a whole; some separate figures exist for industry only, but they are even less reliable. The incremental capital output ratio (ICOR) is found by dividing the net investment ratio by the rate of growth of GDP.

The most suspect figures in Table 6.3 are those in the investment ratio columns, showing the British ratio so small in 1899/1907, and the German ratio so much larger than the American; and showing the American ratio so large in 1892/1907 and so small in 1957/69. More plausible ratios would push up the ICOR for the USA in 1957/69, and for the UK in 1899/1907; and pull down the ICOR for the USA in 1892/1907 and for Germany in 1899/1907. Besides this we have the problem of relative prices. The price of capital rose more than the GDP deflator in all three countries between 1907 and 1957, by ratios ranging from 15 to 33 per cent. Therefore in real terms the ICORs for 1957/69 are overstated by about the same order of magnitude.

Our guess would be that in all these countries, with the possible exception of the USA, the investment ratio was higher in the 1960s than it had been at the turn of the century. This contributed to the higher growth rates. However, the growth rate increased by more than investment, since it is probable that ICORs were somewhat lower in the 1960s. From the evidence we conclude that the core investment ratio rose from about 10 to about 12 per cent and that the core ICOR fell from about 3·4 to about 2·5.

Because urbanisation played little role in core industrialisation in the 1960s, less construction was required, and the proportion of capital formation going into industry may have increased. We cannot be absolutely certain of this, since core countries made a determined attack on housing conditions in the 1960s, and governments also devoted more capital to the social services. We can be certain that, with the fall in the growth rate of the industrial population, more of what was invested in industry went into raising capital per head, instead of multiplying the number of hands.

But the capital saved on the cost of increasing the urban population would not all go into manufacturing industry. As industry's labour reservoirs dry up, the system strives desperately to get more labour for industry by attracting workers from other sectors and occupations. Wages rise in industry to the inconvenience of all low-paid occupations. It becomes difficult to get bus conductors, sanitation workers, nurses, lift attendants, teachers, domestic servants and so on. So capital is diverted to what have previously been manual sectors in an effort to free labour for further expansion of industry. This is a boon to the workers at the bottom of the heap, who are the last to benefit from industrialisation. We have seen this process at work in Western Europe since the Second World War. The more advanced industrial countries have 'run short of labour' in most of their worst-paid jobs, and have reacted partly by mechanisation, and partly by encouraging immigration from low-wage countries.

It is not, then, certain that the somewhat higher ratio of capital formation has meant a relative increase in capital investment in industry, or more specifically an increase in the rate of growth of capital per head in industry, but we shall proceed from this assumption.

Let us make the following primitive experiment. If the production function is in Cobb–Douglas form, and if one can assume that the factors of production are paid their marginal products, one can determine for any period how much of an increase in output has been due to an increase in the quantities of the factors of production. The rest of the increase in output ('the residual') is then deemed to be due to technological progress of one kind or another. Using this technique we shall first estimate the residual for the prewar period. Secondly, we shall estimate how large an increase in the rate of growth of capital would be required to explain the increase in the rate of growth of output in the postwar period if the residual had not changed. And thirdly, we shall estimate by how much the residual has changed, given the likely increase in the rate of growth of capital. The assumptions are all questionable, but it is interesting to see where they lead.

Let us therefore begin by assuming the following Cobb–Douglas production function:

$$Q = L^{a} \,.\, K^{(1-a)} \,.\, r^{t}$$

where Q = industrial output, L = labour force in industry, K = capital in industry (all in index numbers) and r is a residual time trend. Let us assume a, the exponent of L, to be 0·55. This is lower than is customarily used in exercises of this sort, where the data are for national income as a whole, but it is typical of labour's share of value added in the Census of Manufactures of advanced industrial countries.[14] We will do the experiment separately for the two periods 1899–1907 and 1957–69. Table 6.1 gives us Q and L. If we assume K, we can calculate r from the formula, or vice versa.

For 1899–1907 we assume K and derive r. According to Kendrick,[15] in US manufacturing over the period 1892–1907 capital per head grew at about 2·7 per cent per annum. A similar calculation for Hoffmann's 'industry and trade' yields 2·8 per cent from 1883 to 1907 in Germany. Assume for the core as a whole 2·5. Then, since population was growing at 1·8 per cent, the growth rate of capital is given by 1·025 × 1·018 = 1·0465. And we have for one year's growth:

$$\log 1{\cdot}0365 = 0{\cdot}55 \log 1{\cdot}018 + 0{\cdot}45 \log 1{\cdot}0465 + \log r$$

whence r = 1·006. That is to say to a growth rate of 3·65, inputs contributed 3·05, and (presumably) greater knowledge contributed 0·6 per cent per annum.

Let us now assume for 1957–69 that r remains the same. We can therefore deduce by how much capital would have to be growing to explain the observed growth rate of production. For we have

$$\log 1{\cdot}042 = 0{\cdot}55 \log 1{\cdot}008 + 0{\cdot}45 \log K + \log 1{\cdot}006$$

whence K = 1·079. Capital would now have to be growing by 7·9 per cent per annum or 1·7 times as fast as in the earlier period. This would mean that net investment in manufacturing would have had to rise from say 4 to say 7 per cent of GDP.

This calculation attributes all the increase in output to increased capital. Suppose we assume that capital per head, instead of growing by 2·5 per cent per annum, was now growing twice as fast, that is by 5·0 per cent per annum. Then for the period 1957/69 $K = 1{\cdot}0584$. We now derive r, which comes out at 1·0145. The contribution of the residual is now 1·45 per cent per annum instead of 0·6 per cent, which is still a gap much wider than would be eliminated by assuming that industrial production was rising in the earlier period by 0·5 points more than the indexes say.

The value of these primitive games is not very great, because they require unwarranted assumptions about the production function and about the determination of the shares of labour and capital in the national income – not to speak of very uncertain aggregate statistics. But such as they are they suggest that the increase in productivity cannot all be accounted for by the increase in investment which has actually occurred; the core countries must also be using capital and labour together more productively. They do not support suggestions that most of the increase in productivity (from 1·9 to 4·2), is due to an increase in the residual, but that some change occurred in the residual is entirely plausible.

What were the sources of the increase in the domestic capital formation ratio? One source, applying especially to Britain and to France, is a sharp decline in the proportion of gross domestic product invested abroad. An increase in the propensity to save may be another source. Conceivably the working classes and the middle classes were saving relatively more of their incomes in the 1960s than they were saving earlier, but these classes are now so heavily burdened by hire purchase commitments for automobiles, television, washing machines and other durable commodities which are not included as investment in the national accounts, that one may doubt whether they are contributing relatively more to productive investment. Governments save more, especially through social security accumulations, but governments now also invest much more in public and social services, and were more probably a drain on savings in the 1960s than contributors to industrial finance. As for the share of profits in national income, both this and the investment ratio are so uncertain for 1899/1907 that we will make no progress along this line of inquiry.

It so happens that all the likely increase in the core investment ratio can be explained without assuming any fundamental change in the propensity to save, or rather in the propensity to save at full employment profits levels. The taming of the Juglar cycle must in itself have increased the average propensity to save, and the average rate of growth. If we assume gross saving capacity in the boom to be 20 per cent, and that Juglar fluctuations of the magnitude experienced before the First World War reduced the average gross investment ratio over the whole cycle to say 15 per cent, then a long period without significant fluctuation, like that of 1957 to 1969, could easily raise average investment to say 19 per cent. The difference in actual investment and the difference to be expected from the taming of the Juglar are of about the same magnitude. The cessation of fluctuations in the national income automatically increases its rate of growth.

THE GROWTH OF KNOWLEDGE

6.11 All this is subject to the existence of investment opportunities; the rate of development of technological knowledge is the ultimate constraint on the rate of growth of national income. People cannot produce more from their resources if they do not know how to produce more – and this was the normal state of humanity until the recent explosion of technological knowledge. Moreover, not having new technology to invest in shows up as a low propensity to save. Underdeveloped countries have plenty of rich people who have traditionally spent their incomes on hordes of servants, courtiers, armies and entertainers. Saving is a function of the opportunity to invest.

Is the increased rate of growth of core industry since the Second World War due to an increased rate of growth of technological knowledge? Table 6.1 shows that productivity per person is going faster (4·2 instead of 1·9 per cent per annum), and our primitive experiment suggested that the difference is not all accounted for by faster growth of capital per head. The 'residual' may well have doubled.

It still does not follow that technological knowledge is growing faster; the core may merely have been catching up on a backlog. There was a big backlog in 1950, because industrial investment had not been normal for some forty years, since the outbreak of the First World War. The USA and France had been 'normal' for about five years (1924–9); for the rest of this period up to 1950 industry in all four countries had been operating either below capacity or mainly to suit wartime needs. By 1950 many technological possibilities had accumulated. Compared with the United States, Western Europe was still very backward in such areas as telephones, motor transport and assembly line techniques; and the United States itself was yet to exploit fully the motor car, the aeroplane, computers, synthetic fibres, plastics, television and a host of domestic electrical machines. We do not need to summon up a faster rate of growth of inventions; catching up with the backlog of past inventions is probably an adequate explanation of the faster rate of growth of capital per head and of the residual.

Backlog is a familiar explanation of the tendency of new industrial countries to grow not only faster than older industrial countries at the same time, but also faster than the older industrial countries grew when they were new. For example, in Table 6.1 it is possible to compare the growth of our four core countries before the First World War with the growth of the rest of the OECD in the 1960s. Population was growing at about the same rate, but labour force was growing much more slowly in the rest of OECD, for the same reasons that it was growing more slowly in the core itself. The transfer from other sectors to industry was much larger, as we have already seen. The difference in the industrial growth rate was enormous (8·10 compared with 3·65). This was only to a small extent due to differences in the growth rates of the labour force (2·2 compared with 1·8); it was mainly due to differences in productivity per head (5·80 compared with 1·85). It is probable that capital per head was growing faster in the rest of the OECD in the 1960s than it had grown in the core in the 1900s, but the residual must also have been much larger.

The rule does not say that a new country must necessarily grow faster than an old one; India is an obvious exception to this. The rule says only that a new country may grow faster than an old one if its investment climate is right. It can expand the numbers in manufacturing more rapidly, subject to the important constraint of the speed at which its entrepreneurial capacity can grow, and because of backlog, it can make striking leaps in productivity.

Another version of the contribution of backlog to the rate of industrial growth is what is known as Verdoon's Law, which is best formulated in the form: the faster capital grows, the faster productivity per unit of capital grows.[16] This is because the capital created in each year is presumably more productive than its predecessors. Hence the faster capital grows, the greater is the proportion of new and therefore more productive capital in the existing stock. The same effect occurs whether the new capital increases the numbers employed in industry or increases capital per head. However, it is more pronounced when the increase is in capital per head because the increased productivity tends to be in equipment rather than in buildings. An increase in numbers involves a lot of new construction of houses and the general infrastructure of urbanisation, whereas the same amount of capital invested in increasing capital per head would be incorporating a larger proportion of new equipment.[17]

Thus the increase in the growth rate of core productivity in the 1960s can perhaps all be explained by a combination of backlog and the effects on the productivity of the capital stock of rising productivity per unit of capital, especially with a slower growth rate of the industrial labour force.

But it is also possible that the natural rate of growth has now increased. This argument has three elements.

First, electricity is a more flexible power source than the direct drive of machinery by belts from steam engines. The steam engine was virtually confined to the factory and the railway line (notwithstanding the 'portable' steam engines used with agricultural machinery or on the road); and even within the factory its use was considerably restricted by the system of belts which it required. Electricity can be used anywhere, raising productivity in the home, the office or the shop, no less than in the factory or field. Hardly a day goes by without some new invention for using electricity. Combined with the internal combustion engine, which is also much more portable than steam, electricity has thrown open vast possibilities of mechanisation.

The second element which may have increased the rate of growth of technology is the industrialisation of invention. This is no longer a haphazard process, depending on the ingenuity of a few geniuses. It is now a highly organised industry, with billions of dollars a year pouring into 'research and development'. There is great controversy over the effects of this change, which we are in no position to resolve.[18] We note only that it would be surprising if this vast expenditure in so many countries, harnessing so much trained manpower, were not yielding a faster rate of growth of useful invention.

The third element is improvement in the quality of industrial management. The Americans invented work study in the 1880s, and this has now burgeoned into a huge industry spending hundreds of millions of dollars on research and training, ranging from graduate business schools to the teaching of book-keeping in high schools. There have always been sceptics, and the movement was slow to cross the Atlantic. But from the First World War onwards, most other countries have come to be impressed by the allegedly superior business efficiency of Germany and the USA, and the dollars have flowed into business research and business training in ever greater volume. The effects of this cannot be measured. But it is possible that these expenditures have increased business efficiency, and that this has increased productivity and the willingness to adopt new methods. So many hundreds of millions of taxpayers can hardly be wrong!

What has certainly changed, when one compares the 1890s with the 1960s, is the status of business in the minds of the kinds of young people who receive higher education. If one desired to be accepted in higher social circles one did not go into industry in 1890. At that time banking or the stock exchange were just becoming acceptable professions, but not manufacturing industry. In the 1960s, on the other hand, graduate business schools were crowded with would-be industrialists, and the prime ambition of the students crowding the law schools was to become a corporation lawyer. The change is most visible in the USA, but is probably most profound in Britain, which in 1890 was still mainly dominated by the prejudices of the old landed aristocracy. One presumes that a change of this kind has increased the percentage of good brains entering into industrial management, but this is not certain, since the percentage of good brains which did not go to college in 1890 was very high, and it was then easier for non-college graduates to rise in industry than it is today.

In sum, we cannot be sure that the high growth rate of recent years will continue, since it included a large element of backlog, but it is none the less conceivable that the natural rate of growth of industrial productivity is now higher than it was in the forty years before the First World War.

Chapter 7

Challenge

SYNOPSIS: 7.00 The industrial revolution in the core countries challenged countries at the periphery either to industrialise or to trade.

7.01 Industrialisation requires a market and presupposes an agricultural surplus. The new industrial technology was relatively simple and cheap, and several countries met the agricultural condition; yet the diffusion of modern industry was slow. 7.02 The lag in the countries of South, East and Central Europe was especially remarkable, and highlights the political conditions for industrialisation.

7.03 The core's purchases from the rest of the world were smaller than is sometimes thought, but grew rapidly. 7.04 In the 1880s and 1890s the terms of trade moved against overseas suppliers, but thereafter improved swiftly. 7.05 The turnaround in prices affected the volume of world trade in manufactures, but is not reflected in the rate of growth of agricultural exports from the periphery. 7.06 The volume of world trade in primary products bore a constant relationship to world manufacturing production, but other elements of the international economy are much less predictable.

7.07 International investment was large and varied. 7.08 It mirrored the US Kuznets fluctuation (low in the 1870s and 1890s) rather than the Kondratiev fluctuations in the terms of trade.

7.09 The large emigration from Europe to 'new countries of temperate settlement' also mirrored the Kuznets fluctuation. Contrary to expectation, immigration led to rapid urbanisation of these new countries, rather than to rapid growth of their rural populations.

7.10 There was an equally large migration of Indians and Chinese to tropical countries, although the proportion returning home was larger.

7.11 These two streams moved on very different terms. The Asians came from countries with low agricultural productivity, and were willing to work for a shilling a day or less. The Europeans expected wages in excess of those earned in Europe, where productivity was several times higher than in Asia. The prices of tropical crops and of the temperate crops reflected these differences in the factoral terms of trade.

7.12 So the temperate settlements were rich, with large domestic markets for industrialisation, whereas the factoral terms of trade of the tropical countries were such that the trade option could support only low levels of development.

7.00 The industrialisation of the core in the first half of the nineteenth century presented two challenges to the periphery: to follow the example of the core, and to develop by selling to expanding core markets. We are now ready to pursue these themes.

THE INDUSTRIAL OPTION

7.01 The example was easy to follow. The new technology of the industrial revolution – for using steam, making textiles, mining coal and making iron – was ingenious, but simple. The first textile innovators made their own machinery of wood, with metal for the moving parts. Soon machine makers developed as a separate trade. The British tried, without success, to prohibit the export of machinery – the prohibition remained formally until 1844 – but the techniques spread all the same. By 1870 anybody who wanted to buy the new machines could have them, and credit terms as well. The machinery cost relatively little. The greater consumer of capital was the railway. Estimates of British capital formation in the 1820s, when the textile and iron revolutions were already advanced, but prior to the great railway boom, put it at only between 5 and 10 per cent of national income.[1] Almost any country could have saved that much.

Increasingly, but not initially, the new technology moved out of homes and workshops into factories. The additional expense was not considerable, since factories were not then built for the glorification of architects or the enrichment of construction unions. Neither was there a serious managerial problem; the entrepreneurship required was within the competence and experience of almost any country in the world. This constitutes quite a difference from our own day when to manage, not to speak of to build, a factory making aeroplanes or computers or synthetic fibres calls for levels of skill and experience which less developed countries acquire only with time.

In any case, if local entrepreneurship was lacking, foreign initiative was available. It was an old tradition in Europe for migrants to bring and establish new skills and industries. They were welcome, subject occasionally to restrictions ensuring that they take native apprentices.[2] So in the first half of the nineteenth century Englishmen were establishing or helping to establish factories using the new technology in France and Germany[3] and soon Frenchmen were doing the same all over Europe.[4] By the time Russia caught up with the industrial revolution, in the last quarter of the nineteenth century, this migration involved not only individuals but firms from the older countries which established subsidiaries in the new (the multinational corporation is not an invention of the 1960s), in order, among other reasons, to get behind the tariff barriers. The Russian government's welcome was warm.[5]

There was also a push factor – what we now call the 'backwash'. Any country which neglected to revolutionise its own textile and iron industries would soon see them eliminated by a flood of cheap British imports. It would then launch on what we now call import substitution. This spur affected even France, Germany and the United States. They were freeing themselves from dependence on British textiles by the middle of the century, but did not escape from dependence on British iron until about 1890. Marx dramatised the destruction of Indian spinning (not, as he said, weaving) by

British imports during the first half of the nineteenth century, but the sequel is often forgotten. India built its first modern textile plant in 1853. Progress was rapid, and by the end of the century India not only was self-sufficient in the cheaper cottons, but also had driven the cheaper British yarns out of many Far Eastern markets. As we have seen before, British yarn exports reached their peak in 1884, and then declined.

The backwash did not always work in this way. For example, throughout the eighteenth century, and for some time before, Sweden had been a major exporter of iron, based on charcoal for fuel. The new British iron, based on coal, ate into this market, more or less restricting the Swedes to high-quality irons based on charcoal which were (until cheap steel became available) still competitive. Sweden's trouble was lack of coal, and this problem was by no means confined to Sweden. The new smelting of iron ores with coal gave a decided advantage to the countries which had coal, forcing all others to switch to imported iron. For the first three-quarters of the century Britain commanded virtually all the export trade in iron, until Belgium, Germany and the United States began their rapid expansion after 1880.

Nevertheless, there was plenty of scope for following in the footsteps of the industrial revolution. The textile industry could always be taken in hand. The importation of cheap iron would restrict the charcoal-smelting trade, but it would give a boost to the fabricators and enable the whole range of metal-working industries to expand. By 1850 the sewing machine was penetrating the clothing industry, by 1880 boot and shoe machinery, and so on. Machinery was becoming more complex and expensive; factories were growing in size and entrepreneurship became more complicated. On the other hand lessons had been learnt, and information was more widely available, so even in 1880 the innovations of the industrial revolution were still relatively simple and within the competence of entrepreneurs in almost any part of the world.

The new technology was not, however, of equal interest to all; in particular it would not be of interest to countries which at that time had only very small markets for industrial goods.

In a closed economy the size of the industrial sector is a function of agricultural productivity. Agriculture has to be capable of producing the surplus food and raw materials consumed in the industrial sector, and it is the affluence of the farmers that enables them to be a market for industrial products. An industrial revolution therefore presupposes an agricultural revolution, occurring at least simultaneously, if not before, if the industrial product is to be saleable in the home market. At low levels of productivity it requires something else as well, namely the emergence of a class sufficiently affluent to be consuming manufactured products. For even where productivity is relatively high, a poor egalitarian country is likely to have less industry than a poor inegalitarian country. This can be seen in comparing say India with the eastern regions of Nigeria. In inegalitarian countries the ruling classes tax the poor in one way or another (including rents) and use the proceeds to support industrial artisans of various kinds, including makers of fine clothes and metalwares, building materials and furniture. In egalitarian countries the farmers eat more, and relatively less is spent on industrial products. So in 1890, for example, India had a relatively larger market for industrial products than had Africa. However, inegalitarianism could bolster industrial production only in market economies. Some of the large rural serf-like communities, like the Russian estate or the Brazilian *fazenda*, were virtually self-contained. They contained within themselves industrial artisans working on serf-like terms for the owners of the estates, producing cloth, furniture, metal goods and so on. If these artisans had to be supported whether they produced or not, it would not pay the gentry to displace their labour with imports. When eventually the market economy spread throughout the country many artisans would suffer the same long drawn out fate as the handloom weavers of Europe.

The link between agricultural productivity and the size of the industrial market could be one reason why the industrial revolution occurred first in Britain and not in France, despite the longer French industrial tradition; agricultural productivity had advanced far ahead in Britain, where already in 1840 it was 30 per cent higher than French productivity per man.[6]

The link between industry and agriculture meant that unless a country could base its industrialisation on exporting manufactures, the limits to its industrialisation would be set by its progress in raising agricultural productivity. Here the core countries were well placed. Productivity was already high in Britain; it rose steadily in France and Germany, at first through the adoption of British and Dutch practices, and later with the use of artificial fertilisers; and it rose even faster per head (but not per acre) in the USA, with mechanisation.[7]

But while it was helpful to have an industrial base from which to launch an industrial revolution, further progress was not necessarily limited by agricultural productivity, since progress could also be made by exporting manufactures. A trade drive, which results in capturing an ever increasing proportion of world trade in manufactured goods, may result (as we saw in Chapter 6) from technological superiority in manufacturing, as in Britain and afterwards Germany and the USA. But it may also result simply from a lagging agricultural revolution which forces a growing band of eager industrialists to look beyond their frontiers both for food and raw materials and for the markets that the domestic agriculture is unable to supply. Japan is the best example of this in the nineteenth century, and Brazil in the twentieth century. If other countries, like Russia, India, China, Mexico or nineteenth-century Brazil, did not pursue this course during our period, this was because their industrial sectors failed to cope even with the current domestic demand for manufactures, let alone with the prospect of producing manufactures for export.

We have been distinguishing between the option to develop by revolutionising the industrial sector, and the option to develop by exporting primary products as a prelude to industrialising. The option to industrialise did not preclude simultaneous development of an export capacity, either of raw materials or of manufactures. Foreign trade plays different roles in economic growth. It may be the engine or source of growth, as it was in Argentina or Malaya. It may be the result of growth, with comparative advantage in some particular sector leading to a rapid expansion of exports, like cotton manufactures in mid-nineteenth-century Britain, raw cotton in the USA in the same period, or chemicals in Germany at the end of the century. Alternatively it may be the lubricating oil of growth, without which the country's growth would run into balance of payments problems. This latter role has been much discussed since the end of the Second World War, when a number of countries have claimed that their production (essentially of manufactures for the domestic market) has been hampered by their inability to export enough to pay for the imports of food, raw materials or machinery which expansion would cause. This deficiency of exports as 'lubricating oil' has been felt in countries as different as Britain, Argentina and India although it is sometimes discussed in the literature as if it were confined to Latin America.

Sweden is a good example of a country where exports were the lubricating oil rather than the engine of growth. The country was well endowed with timber and iron ore. The backwash depressed the iron industry, as the new coal-burning technology could not be adopted for lack of domestic coal deposits. Swedish iron ore was mostly phosphoric. The invention of the Gilchrist–Thomas process after 1879 then stimulated local smelting, and created a rapidly expanding mining industry to meet an export demand for ores. Meanwhile, the European demand for forest products rose throughout the nineteenth century, first for timber and then for pulp and paper. At the end of the century innovations in generating hydroelectric power and transporting it over long distances also gave the country a cheap domestic source of power. Thus Sweden developed by having valuable natural resources, which it industrialised for export: this in turn producing an increasing home demand for industries manufacturing for the domestic market.[8]

Japan was also ready for the new technology. At the time of the Meiji restoration per capita income in Japan was between \$100 and \$150 of 1970 money – higher than that of 1970 India, but perhaps half that of Germany in 1830. In the absence of foreign trade the country had developed on balanced lines, and therefore had an industrial sector. The new rulers set about introducing both the industrial and the agricultural revolutions, over a wide range of industries and occupations. Exports of silk cocoons developed first – essentially an agricultural occupation with farm families winding the yarn, although the product appears as 'manufactured' in some trade classifications. Next cotton manufacturing broke through into the export market. The country had plenty of coal for the moment – it did not start importing coal until after the First World War – but it lacked coking coal and iron ore, so production of pig iron with coke, though launched, remained relatively small in our period. Exports grew very rapidly (twice as fast as world trade) which was not difficult when starting from so small a base. What was remarkable was that exports of manufactures (excluding raw silk) were racing upwards, and had by 1913 caught up with exports of primary products. Even so, exports were still below the level of Southern and Eastern Europe on a per capita basis, although living standards cannot have been far behind. Table 7.1 shows Japan's manufacturing output per head in 1913 lying at this time between Romania and Russia. It cannot be said that Japan was growing in response to exports; it was reconstructing every sector of production, and in the process developing its foreign trade.

To return to the main point, the industrial option in the nineteenth century was essentially open to countries which already had a sizable industrial sector. This was a larger group of countries than one might think, since it included not only the whole of Europe, but most of Latin America, and all that part of Asia where the peasants' surpluses were supporting landowning, merchant or other aristocracies consuming industrial products. It therefore included India and China, as well as Japan, although admittedly industrial consumption per head was significantly lower there than in Western Europe with its much higher agricultural productivity.

Having regard to this it is, at first sight, surprising how few nations exploited the industrial revolution during the nineteenth century.

Table 7.1 gives an indirect indication of this. The aim of this table is to divide industrial output in 1913 by population, and express the result as a proportion of US output per head. However, the exercise is fraught with difficulties. A note explains why these data should be treated merely as orders of magnitude, with wide margins of error, especially at the bottom end of the table.

Table 7.1 *Index of Output of Manufactures Per Head of Population, 1913*[9]

USA	100	Poland	13
		Russia	9
Europe		Yugoslavia	6
UK	90	Romania	6
Belgium	73	Greece	4
Germany	64		
Switzerland	64	*Other*	
Sweden	50	Canada	84
France	46	Australia	75
Denmark	46	New Zealand	66
Netherlands	44	Argentina	23
Norway	39	Chile	17
Austria	31	Japan	6
Czechoslovakia	28	Mexico	5
Finland	27	South Africa	5
Italy	20	Brazil	2
Hungary	19	India	1
Spain	15		

What emerges, however, is how small was the response, even in Europe. Western Europe, except for Spain and Portugal, follows behind the core countries, and will have been closer than the table suggests, because relative prices are lower (a unit of value added is worth physically more in manufactures). Central Europe has only just awakened. Eastern Europe is still almost untouched by the industrial revolution in 1913. The low indices reflect both the lower value added per head, which we must again to some extent discount, and also the smallness of the industrial population, relative to the whole. Russia can now be seen in perspective. Because of the country's size its industrial output was the fifth largest in the world in 1913 (for the same reason India was thirteenth in the list), and its industrial output had been growing rapidly for thirty years; but it was still an agricultural country with a tiny industrial sector.[10]

7.02 Why did the countries of East, Central and Southern Europe meet the challenge so poorly? They neither moved significantly into agricultural exports, nor developed their industrial potential.

Table 7.2 contains further data for some of these countries. They are listed in order of steel consumption per head, and data for North-West Europe and Japan are also included for comparative purposes. Steel consumption correlates well with other attributes, but the figures are not sufficiently reliable to bear much analytical comparison with each other. Also trade per head is misleading when comparing countries of different size, since the ratio of internal to external trade increases with size. Thus it is natural that Russia ranks lower on trade per head than on any of the other indexes. Figures on literacy (Mulhall's percentages of adults able to write) have been added, although their relevance is uncertain.

The comparison with the averages for North-West Europe is on firmer ground, since the differences exceed any feasible margins of error. In order to make this comparison we have indicated the median of the less

Table 7.2 *Some Less Developed European Countries*[11]

	Steel consumption per head (lb, 1913)	*Industrial production per head ($, 1913)*	*Exports per head ($, 1913)*	*Wheat yields per ha (quintals)*	*Exports growth (% p.a. 1883–1913)*	*Literacy (% 1889)*
Austria-Hungary	108	26·9	12·0	12·1	2·4	55
Romania	87	6·1	17·7	10·7	3·8	n.a.
Italy	74	20·3	13·6	9·7	2·5	47
Russia	63	8·9	4·5	6·4	3·3	15
Spain	56	15·0	9·4	9·3	1·1	28
Portugal	56	n.a.	5·5	5·1	0·9	n.a.
Greece	16	3·8	8·4	7·1	1·3	n.a.
Median	63	15·0	9·4	9·3	2·4	n.a.
North-West Europe	340	66·0	46·3	15·4	3·5	90
Japan	31	6·6	5·8	13·0	7·4	n.a.

developed countries rather than the weighted averages, which we have used for North-West Europe. The reason for doing this is that the population of Russia exceeded that of the total of the other six countries, so weighted averages would be dominated by the Russian figures.

We can start by observing how slowly the trade of these countries was growing. Reference to Table 7.4 shows that it was growing more slowly than anywhere else in the world; more slowly even than the trade of India, which is one of the slowest in that table. The countries of temperate settlement could grow rapidly by selling wheat, meat and wool; and the demand for tropical products was keeping up with economic expansion in the industrial countries. But the less developed countries of Europe were at a disadvantage in the temperate agricultural trade. As Table 7.2 shows, their yields per hectare were low. This was due partly to less appropriate climate, but also to delay in adopting new agricultural practices, including the use of fertilisers. But it was not only the low yields per hectare; US and temperate settlement yields per hectare were also low, but hectares per man were much greater, so costs per unit of output were lower. The impact of the agricultural revolution in the more advanced countries upon Central and Southern Europe was one of 'backwash'. Russia, Romania and Hungary, the potential granaries, were hit hard by the continual fall of wheat prices from 1873 to 1895, and it was only in the Kondratiev upswing that their granaries could contribute significantly to their economic growth.

Apart from grain there were also other exports of primary products, including timber from Austria-Hungary and Russia, iron ore from Spain, flax from Russia, copper from Austria-Hungary, Russia, Spain and Italy, zinc from Austria-Hungary, lead from Spain and Greece and bauxite from Italy. But as Table 7.2 shows, it did not amount to very much. Southern and Central Europe was exporting in 1913 less primary products per head not only than North Africa or Latin America, but also than North-West Europe (Table 7.4) several of whose countries had used the export of primary products as lubrication for their industrialisation, especially Sweden (timber, iron ore), Denmark (dairy products) and – not to be forgotten – the United Kingdom (coal).

We have referred to two elements in the agricultural failure of Central and Southern Europe, namely low prices and poor technology. The low prices should have stimulated resort to improved agricultural technology, as they did in Germany, Denmark, Britain and the United States, either of the kind designed to increase output per acre, such as new varieties, crop rotations, fertilisers and a shift in the balance between crops and livestock, or of the kind increasing the number of acres per man, such as agricultural machinery of various kinds. Some progress was of course made, notably in Hungary, but progress was inhibited by the social structure of agriculture. The small farmers, overburdened with debt, taxes and rents, lacked incentive to increase their yields, since higher yields would lead to higher exactions; and the great landowners of Eastern Europe, unlike those of Western Europe, still regarded land as a base for political power and economic tribute, rather than as a factor of production capable of being coaxed into higher productivity. They were more interested in distribution than in growth. In Britain the agricultural revolution had owed much to the leadership of some aristocratic landowners, who prodded their tenants into the new practices, and provided capital as well. The Prussian Junkers too made a business of their estates. The East European landowners were not all alike, but for the most part were not of this kind. In Japan at this time, as in Denmark, agricultural productivity progressed significantly because of extension work among small farmers; this also was no part of the Eastern European scene.

Relative agricultural stagnation is therefore a major factor in the poor response of the less developed countries of Europe, but it was not the only factor. These countries did have industrial sectors capable of transformation on modern lines, and they also had opportunities for import substitution. That value added in manufacturing was still in 1913 as low as $6 or $10 per head cannot be attributed entirely to low agricultural activity. It indicates also low entrepreneurial effort in manufacturing.

Table 7.2 indicates a wide range of effort, so one must beware of generalisations. The table also does not show the growth rates of manufacturing production, and should not therefore obscure the fact that some of these countries were already moving significantly by 1913. Unfortunately we have annual indexes only for four less developed European countries.[12] These show manufacturing growing at the following rates between 1890 and 1913 (per cent per annum): Italy 3·0, Austria 3·4, Sweden 4·1, Russia 5·08 (only 4·5 when small-scale industry and handicrafts are included). Italy stagnated in the 1890s; its rate from 1900 to 1913 was 3·9. For comparison we have Germany 4·3, USA 4·7, Japan 7·4. The Russian and Japanese cases are the only two which seem to support Gerschenkron's expectation that latecomers will grow more rapidly than the earlier starters,[13] but their cases can also be explained on other grounds – the Russians on the ground of rich natural resources (they made much headway in the coal–iron complex) and the Japanese on the ground of official and entrepreneurial drive. It is quite true that new countries can grow faster – we explored this phenomenon in Chapter 6 – but it is not inevitable that they will do so.

None the less the actual rates of growth achieved showed that these countries were already on the move at the end of the nineteenth century. The distinctive mark of the more backward countries of Europe in 1913, then, is not so much that they were stagnant, as that they had started later. The figures for Japan in Table 7.2 make a similar point. Japan was growing very rapidly in the spheres of industrial production, agricultural productivity and foreign trade; nevertheless in 1913 its economy was still only at the level of the very poorest in Europe, when measured in terms of industrial output per head, consumption of steel or total exports per head. Japan's victory over Russia in 1904 was due to superior competence rather than superior strength.

Japan did not build its first railway until 1870. Eastern Europe had started to develop earlier than Japan, and was some distance ahead in 1870, but even at that date had very few of the agents and instruments of industrialisation – the eager bourgeoisie, the investment banks, the joint stock companies, the railway networks, the national political leaders eager to promote industrialisation, and so on. Historians dispute whether a shortage of entrepreneurs is due to lack of opportunity, or is inherent in the value systems of backward societies, where even clearly profitable opportunities would be neglected because there was no one to exploit them;[14] we have met this kind of argument already in considering the British case. Certainly in backward Europe there was no lack of economic opportunities, in the sense of existing and potential markets for industrial products. Lack of the right political background may nevertheless have been a disadvantage, for industrialisation required governmental activity of various kinds to organise; for example, borrowing for railway construction, tariffs, modern company legislation, abolition of taxes and restrictions on the internal mobility of labour (including in Russia before 1861, the abolition of serfdom). Instead these governments long continued to be dominated by backward landed aristocracies, hostile in spirit to industrialisation, which menaced their political power and threatened to deprive them of their labour force. We have remarked before that it remains a puzzle why the landed classes in Western Europe permitted themselves to be submerged so easily by the bourgeoisie, at the cost, after 1870, of a substantial fall in rents associated with the Kondratiev downswing in the prices of cereals. This implies that the real problem is not why some countries stayed backward for so long, but rather why a much smaller number escaped from stagnation so soon.

The study of economic development is therefore as much a task for the political historian, with his interest in individual personalities and the behaviour of conflicting groups, as it is for the economist with his concentration on markets, prices and profitability. After one has studied worldwide trends and opportunities, the response of any particular country cannot be fully understood without the detailed analysis of its particular circumstances. Attempts at putting economic history into a set of dynamic equations are doomed to failure.

INTERNATIONAL TRADE

7.03 The industrial option was of interest chiefly to countries which already had sizable industrial sectors. The other option was to develop by exporting primary commodities to the core and other industrialising markets. One could, of course, use both options, as did Sweden, Denmark, Hungary and Japan. In any case, the second option led to the first, for a country which developed by exporting primary products could next move into import substitution, develop its own industrial base, and in due course itself join the ranks of exporters of manufactures.

This option was beset with difficulties. A country had first to be in a position to increase its exports of primary products. This would bring in imports, with possible backwash effects, which might either destroy or transform existing industries. The country had then to escape from those conditions – including those of its internal politics – which forced it towards over-specialisation in primary products. Many countries cleared the first fence, trebling or quadrupling their exports in the thirty years before 1913. But Table 7.1 records how few had reached even the low industrial level of Spain. The less developed countries would not begin substantial industrialisation until after the First World War.

In trying to grow by exporting primary products to the core, the first difficulty was that the core was not really importing all that much. As we have noted before, the core was more or less self-sufficient in the primary raw materials of the industrial revolution, and what it lacked it obtained from the temperate countries of recent European settlement. For example, the breakdown of total imports into the core (not simply of primary products) showed as follows in 1883:

From	*$m.*	%
Each other	1,637	37
Other Europe	1,421	32
Temperate settlements[15]	334	7
India	247	5
Rest of world	839	19
	4,478	100

Since the population of India and the 'rest of the world' was about a thousand million in 1883, this meant that the core was importing from the less developed countries only about one dollar per head at that time. The imports were not evenly distributed, so some countries would do better than others. Still, the stimulus to the economy would in the early stages lie in the rate of growth, rather than in the absolute level of exports.

We do not have a commodity breakdown of this trade for 1883, but Lamartine Yates gives a breakdown for 1913, which is reproduced in Table 7.3. The big items in this table were also the growth sectors. The big items in 1883 will have been sugar, coffee, vegetable oils and oilseeds, and hides and skins, plus a little cotton from India and Egypt. Running down the 1913 list selectively, we see that in cereals, Burma, Indo-China and Thailand had developed a large export of rice, and Argentina and India sizable exports of wheat. The principal livestock exports consist of frozen and chilled meat from Argentina, Australia and New Zealand, starting only in the 1880s. The export of coffee had increased by 80 per cent since 1883, and there was now a large export of cocoa from the Gold Coast (now Ghana). The trade in bananas was another product of refrigeration.

Table 7.3 *Exports of Primary Commodities, 1913 ($m.)*[16]

	Africa	*Asia*	*Latin America*	*Oceania*
Food	*278*	*785*	*1,019*	*181*
Cereals	30	269	244	52
Livestock products	39	29	110	99
Beverages	29	117	327	—
Oilseeds and fats	93	161	78	21
Fruit and vegetables	27	27	54	4
Sugar	14	87	144	5
Other and tobacco	46	95	62	—
Agricultural materials	*295*	*577*	*322*	*209*
Fibres	183	376	118	170
Lumber and pulp	9	15	12	6
Hides	49	57	92	33
Rubber	16	79	71	—
Other	38	50	29	—
Minerals	*112*	*185*	*204*	*65*
Petroleum	—	52	5	—
Ores and metals	23	110	78	65
Other	89	23	121	—
Total	*685*	*1,547*	*1,545*	*455*

Irrigation had trebled Egypt's export of cotton, and there was now also a large export of silk from Japan. Rubber was just taking off. Agriculture dominated the list. These three continents were just moving into mineral production, with nitrates from Chile, copper from Mexico and Chile, tin from Malaya and Bolivia, and a little oil from Indonesia. The casualties of the period were sugar, beaten down by subsidised production of beets in Europe, and two Indian trades, indigo destroyed by Germany's synthetic production of dyestuffs, and opium, eliminated by agreement with China.

The total trade was still not large in 1913, but the growth rate was not negligible. World trade as a whole grew in current prices between 1883 and 1913 at an average annual rate of 3·4 per cent per annum. In current prices the trade of the temperate settlement countries grew at 4·3 per cent per annum, and of Asia, Africa and Latin America (excluding Argentina, Chile and Uruguay) at 3·6 per cent per annum. With allowance for a 10 per cent fall in prices the latter figure becomes 4·0 per cent. Details are given in Table 7.4.

The growth rate of core industrial production between 1883 and 1913 was 3·4 per cent per annum. If trade was the engine of growth for the less developed countries, it is clear that their engine of growth was driving at least as fast as the engine of growth of the core, if not somewhat faster. Its comparative effect would depend on two elements: its size and its multiplier.

Table 7.4 *World Exports*[17]

	Exports per head, 1913			*Annual % growth rate of total 1883–1913*
	Primary $	*Manufactures* $	*Total* $	
Temperate settlements	56·6	4·7	61·3	4·3
North-West Europe	19·9	26·4	46·3	3·5
USA	15·6	9·4	24·9	3·8
Other Latin America	12·1	0·2	12·3	3·4
North Africa	11·5	0·5	12·0	3·2
South-East Europe	5·3	1·7	7·1	2·6
Japan	3·0	2·9	5·8	7·4
Other Asia	4·4	0·8	5·2	3·9
Africa (Black)	2·7	0·1	2·8	4·2
India	2·0	0·5	2·5	3·0
China	0·5	0·1	0·6	3·3

The simplest measure of size is ratio to national income. In 1913 manufacturing output was about 35 per cent of the national income of Germany, having been about 27 per cent in 1883 (at 1913 prices). Among the peripheral countries, exports ranged from about 40 per cent of national income in Argentina, through about 25 per cent in Brazil to 12 per cent in India and still less in China. The potential size of exports was therefore large, and the fact that exports were growing as fast as core industrial production cannot be dismissed on grounds of size. However, the net effects of exports on the economy would depend also on the export multiplier, which is the reciprocal of *m*, the marginal propensity to import. The lower the marginal propensity to import, the greater the extent to which the proceeds of additional exports would circulate inside the country, stimulating domestic production, before finally leaking back out as imports. The size of the marginal propensity to import was to some extent within local control; it depended on how much was done to stimulate production of food, raw materials, manufactures and services for the local market. So the element of government policy was central in determining how effective international trade could be as an engine of development. We shall return to this later.

7.04 The period from 1883 to 1913 was not homogeneous. From the standpoint of primary producing countries it opened badly but ended well. This is because the terms of trade moved adversely in the 1880s and 1890s, but improved in the 1900s.

There has been a lot of controversy about the terms of trade, but it is only predictions of the future that are controversial; what happened between 1883 and 1913 is not difficult to establish.

Thus Kindleberger has made an elaborate study of the merchandise terms of trade for Europe.[18] His annual index shows a turning point in 1881, after which the terms of trade improved 14 per cent to the next turning point in 1900, after which they deteriorated 7 per cent to 1910. The terms of trade of Europe's suppliers cannot be deduced simply by inverting the European index. Europe's terms of trade are based on the c.i.f. prices of imports and the f.o.b. prices of exports; but the suppliers' terms of trade are based on the f.o.b. prices of Europe's imports and the c.i.f. prices of Europe's exports. The difference depends on what is happening to transport costs. Since freights fell very sharply during our period, it is theoretically possible that the terms of trade improved simultaneously for both the importer and the exporter of the same commodity.

Table 7.5 is constructed from the indices of the prices of wheat and wool, which were of special interest to the countries of temperate settlement, and the index of the prices of tropical commercial crops.[19] In each case we have subtracted 10 per cent of an index of freights, in order to get f.o.b. price indices. We have also added 10 per cent of the index of freights to the index of prices of manufactures in world trade,[20] to arrive at a c.i.f. price. The ratios in Table 7.5 are obtained by dividing the agricultural indices by the manufacturing index.

Table 7.5 *Suppliers' Terms of Trade*

	1871/5	*1881/5*	*1888/92*	*1897/1901*	*1909/13*
Wheat	104	106	102	100	109
Wool	96	99	96	100	121
Coffee	125	88	218	100	147
Other tropicals	93	106	102	100	123

The dates, with the exception of 1909/13, are for five-year averages around the Juglar peaks.

The main purpose of the table is to bring out the fact that even when one makes allowances for changes in ocean freights there is still a Kondratiev swing in the terms of trade, moving against agriculture from the early 1880s to the middle or end of the 1890s, and then rising in favour of agriculture up to 1913. The only significant exception to this in world trade was the price of coffee which, for special reasons which we shall come to later, rose very high in the early 1890s. The downswing in the 1880s is not as great as the upswing to 1913, so in all cases the suppliers' terms of trade were better in 1909/13 than at any previous time from 1871/5, again with the exception of the coffee boom in the years 1888/92.

Table 7.5 also confirms (again with the exception of coffee) that the terms of trade were better in the early eighties than in the early seventies, despite the sharp decline of prices in terms of gold. That decline, as we have seen, ultimately pulled down money wages very considerably in the core countries, bringing the whole industrial price level down, and with it the prices of manufactures even more than agricultural prices. The turnaround in Europe's terms of trade does not begin until 1881.

United States data tell the same story, as can be seen in Chart 2.3. The USA was an agricultural exporter so its terms of trade run in the reverse direction to Europe's. The Canadian case is mixed. Canada's exports were diversified, and by good fortune her terms of trade improved throughout our period; but the terms of trade of her agricultural exports show the Kondratiev swing. Canada's terms of trade were as follows:[21]

	1873	*1883*	*1900*	*1913*
All exports	71	93	100	111
Agricultural exports	119	117	100	117

Is this swing in the terms of trade reflected in the volume of exports of agricultural products? It is not, we recall, reflected in the demand, in so far as core industrial production is a good proxy for the demand for primary products in world trade. Industrial production grew at a steady pace, subject to bigger or smaller depressions. Was it the same with agricultural production? The answer seems to be: yes. The volume of trade in agricultural products seems to have grown at a steady rate irrespective of the terms of trade. This answer does not hold for wheat, cotton or wool, whose deceleration produced the change in the terms of trade, but seems to hold for primary products as a whole.

We must in the first place remember that what matters to the farmer is not the price in terms of foreign currency, but the price in terms of his own currency. Some of these peripheral countries were on the gold standard, but a great many were not; either they were on silver, or they issued paper currency of varying foreign exchange value. The price of silver in terms of gold fell continually from 1871 to 1913, except in the years 1890–1, when the US Silver Purchase Act was in force. By 1889 it had fallen 30 per cent and by 1899 another 36 per cent (of the 1889 price). By now most of its adherents had abandoned silver, though not all.

The fall in the price of silver shielded the silver currency countries from the continual fall in international prices which occurred from 1873 to 1895. The course of wholesale prices in India is a good example of this, since

India did not abandon the silver standard until 1893.[22] Using the same Juglar peaks as before, we get:

1871/5	*1881/5*	*1888/92*	*1897/1901*	*1909/13*
76	75	88	100	102

Indian prices are about the same in the early 1880s as in the early 1870s, and then rise 33 per cent to 1897/1901, where the general index of tropical prices (ex-freights) has fallen 17 per cent. We noted in Chapter 6 that the internal effect of currency devaluation is to move the terms of trade in favour of farmers against landless labourers and the urban classes. Indian wage data show money wages trying but failing to keep up with rising prices throughout this 'Kondratiev' downswing. When one comes to study the effect of the swing in prices and the terms of trade on agricultural production and exports it is important to remember that the terms of trade to the country are quite a different matter from the terms of trade to the farmers, manipulated as these may be by devaluation, adverse tariffs and price controls.

7.05 This may be one reason why the Kondratiev swing in the terms of trade, which made so much difference to the rate of growth of world trade in manufactures before and after the turning point (say 1899), made remarkably little difference to the rate of growth of world trade in primary products, which was much the same in downswing and upswing. Another reason, no doubt, is that the elasticity of supply of agricultural products, taken together, is fairly low with respect to price. Taken separately, the farmer may choose one crop in preference to others if its price is favourable, but when all prices are moving together, the choice becomes to plant or not to plant. Nowadays farmers purchase inputs and therefore have considerable marginal costs, but this was not so in the peripheral countries before 1914, except on very advanced farms. Agricultural output grew in response to various factors – the building of roads and railways, the opening up of country by traders, immigration, the spread of knowledge of new commercial crops – which gave it a momentum that saw it through booms and slumps.

Chart 7.1 reproduces an index of world trade in primary products at constant prices, whose origin is explained in Appendix III. Unfortunately the index does not go back into the seventies. According to the annual data, the rate of growth was exactly the same between the peaks of 1882 and 1897 and 1897 and 1912 (3·1 per cent per annum). The five-year moving averages show a slight acceleration, from 3·05 to 3·15 per cent per annum, a degree of difference which the uncertainty of our data requires us to ignore. In the best of all worlds this curve would behave exactly like the curve of core industrial production, indicating that core industrial demand was the engine of growth for primary production; but this is an imperfect world. Specifically, as we can see from the moving average of core industrial production (Chart 2.2) industrial production was elevated around 1906 but depressed around 1913, whereas primary trade was depressed around 1906 but elevated around 1913. We note that the long-run elasticity

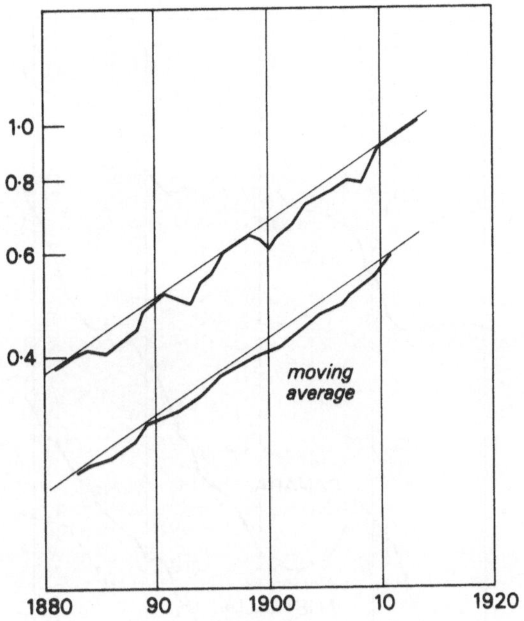

Chart 7.1 World Trade in Primary Products (Volume)

of trade with respect to core industrial production was only 0·91. Neither the magnitude nor the timing of the short-term fluctuations fulfils our expectations of close dependence.

Chart 7.2 reproduces data for the volume of agricultural production in Australia, and agricultural exports from Argentina, Canada and India.[23] (Livestock products are excluded except from Argentina.) Our interest is in the growth of the 1890s compared with the decades on either side. Argentina and Canada show no decline; Canada, on the contrary, grows faster in the 1890s after a setback in the 1880s. Australia is down in the first half of the nineties, presumably because, with the cessation of foreign investment, immigration and railway building and other construction slumped, and the opening up of new land was retarded. India also stagnated in the 1890s, but not for reasons of price, since the continuing fall in the price of silver was raising wholesale prices, as we have just seen. India suffered from appalling weather in the 1890s; there were famines in 1891–2, 1896–7, 1897–8, 1899–1900 and 1900–1. The worst famines occurred when the monsoon failed in two successive seasons, as it did in 1896–8 and 1899–1901; the last of these is estimated to have cost 10 million lives. The population of India, which grew by 10 per cent from 1881 to 1891, and by 6 per cent from 1901 to 1911, grew only by one per cent from 1891 to 1901, so the stagnation of that decade can be explained without recourse to prices.

Indian events are also relevant to our next set of data, which relate to the growth of exports from the tropical countries at constant prices; Table 7.6 gives these figures.

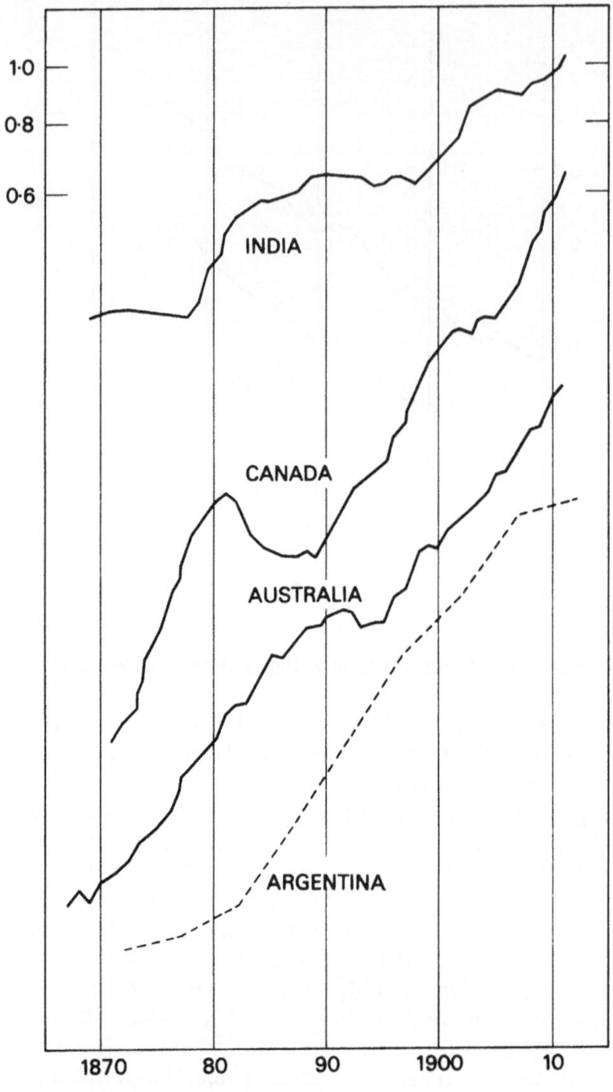

Chart 7.2 Agricultural Production or Exports

Table 7.6 *Growth Rates of Tropical Trade*[24]

	1883–99	*1899–1913*
All exports	3·4	4·1
Agricultural exports	3·0	3·4

The first point which Table 7.6 brings out is how much faster the trade in minerals and manufactures was growing than the trade in agricultural products. This pattern has continued. The share of minerals and manufactures in tropical exports rose from 9 per cent in 1883 to 23 per cent in 1913 (before oil became significant) and to 39 per cent in 1965. Demand has shifted in favour of tropical production of minerals continuously over the past century. The kinds of minerals which the tropics have in abundance (oil, bauxite, tin, copper, to mention the leading exports) were not much in demand in 1883.

The trade in tropical agricultural products, on the other hand, has never grown as fast as core industrial production. This trade is subject to well-known constraints, especially the slow population growth in Western Europe and North America, which limits the market for tea, coffee and cocoa, and also the relentless substitution of synthetics for agricultural materials, which had already made its bow before 1913 with the substitution of synthetic dyestuffs for indigo and logwood.

The increase in the growth rate of tropical trade is due partly to India and partly to the faster rise of the trades in minerals and manufactures. Without India the trade in agricultural products grew at the same rate from 1883 to 1899 and from 1899 to 1913, that is at 3·3 per cent per annum. Indian trade revived after 1899, and then grew nearly as fast as the trade of the rest of the tropical world (faster in agricultural products but more slowly in minerals).

7.06 We pause to note a mode of analysis which we are not pursuing. At this point it would be possible to attempt to make a mathematical model of the world economy. This would take the following form. The demand for primary products is a function of the growth of the industrial countries, as caused and represented by the growth of industrial production. Hence, starting with industrial production, one can derive from it the trade in primary products. Next, given the supply of primary products one can calculate the terms of trade, as we were doing more or less in Chapter 3. Given the terms of trade, and the supply of primary products we can then calculate the primary producing countries' purchase of manufactures. We could also hope to tie in international investment and international migration with the terms of trade, and so return to determining the supply of primary products.

Unfortunately one cannot get beyond the first stage of such an ambitious undertaking. In an earlier essay[25] the present writer showed that the elasticity of the volume of trade in primary products with respect to the rate of growth of world manufacturing had remained constant from about 1880 (the earliest available date) to 1929. As a rough indication, world manufacturing seems to have grown at about 3·6 per cent per annum between 1883 and 1913, and world trade in primary products at about 3·1 per cent per annum, giving an elasticity of about 0·86. Between 1950/2 and 1969/71 world manufacturing grew at 5·9 per cent per annum and world trade in primary products at 5·1 per cent per annum, yielding an elasticity of 0·87.[26] So here is one coefficient which has remained constant over nearly a century. Subsequent writers have approached this relationship in greater detail, by calculating separate import propensities for each of the leading countries; this is safer and more sophisticated.[27] We can certainly relate the volume of world trade in primary products to world industrial production or world income.

Beyond this, the model breaks down. A good fit can be found for the terms of trade for any period, but the coefficients are not stable, and different periods yield different results. Perhaps they would be stable if the general price level were constant, but it has changed dramatically over the past century.

Even if one could get beyond this barrier, the further stages also break down. So long as the share of manufactures in world trade was constant by value, as it was more or less from 1880 to 1940, one could predict the volume of world trade in manufactures from the volume of primary products and the terms of trade. This assumed that trade was mainly an exchange of manufactures against primary products, or at least that this type of trade was a constant proportion of the whole. However, since the mid-1950s the industrial countries have reduced their barriers against importing from each other, which had mounted continually from 1880 to 1950. In consequence the exchange of manufactures against manufactures has become an ever larger share of world trade. This is a fickle event; its future cannot be predicted. In order to predict world trade in manufactures we would need to see this trade settle down to a constant elasticity in relation to industrial production or national income.

Other writers have tried to make models of international investment[28] and of international migration.[29] Both these flows, as we shall see in a moment, took their pattern before the war from the US Kuznets fluctuation. They do not fit the terms of trade or yield any elasticities which could be useful for prediction. Beyond this, the rate at which peripheral countries developed varied immensely, in accordance with differences in their resources, governments, historical evolution and the emergence of dynamic leadership. The world economy is a backdrop against which the individual peripheral countries stage their very different performances. To make a model in which their rates of growth are determined primarily by events in the international economy – growth of world trade, international lending, migration, terms of trade – would be to omit the sociology of development. We are trying in this volume to paint the international backdrop, but we are leaving it to others to write the individual plays.

INTERNATIONAL INVESTMENT

7.07 The core assisted the periphery not only by providing a growing demand for its product, but also by lending money, mainly used for the development of infrastructure.

We will not repeat here the discussion of motive, which arose in Chapter 6. Briefly, countries invested abroad because this was more profitable than investing at home. The question is why it was more profitable. The answers we are rejecting turn on the investing countries already having attained maturity. This is clearly not so in the case of France, the second largest investor, technologically backward and clearly in need of much larger home investment. The case of Britain, the largest investor, is more complicated, but its failure to invest adequately at home clearly belongs in the area of unexploited opportunities. Notably output per head, excluding returns to foreign investment, grew more slowly in the countries which invested heavily abroad than in Germany or the United States.

By 1914 to invest abroad had become fashionable, and was no longer confined to Britain and France. The balance sheet, as estimated in a United Nations report, relying mainly on Feis, was as follows:[30]

Lenders	*$m.*	*Borrowers*	*$m.*
UK	18,000	Africa	4,700
France	9,000	Asia	6,000
Germany	5,800	Europe	12,000
USA	3,500	USA	6,800
Belgium, Netherlands, Switzerland	5,500	Canada	3,700
		Latin America	8,500
Other countries	2,200	Oceania	2,300
	44,000		44,000

If one divides the amount borrowed by the population of the receiving country or continent, one finds an enormous gap between lending per head to say Canada or Argentina on the one side, and say India or China on the other. But if we use instead as the divisor the trade of the recipient, the picture looks very different. This can be seen in Table 7.7.

Table 7.7 *Ratio of Foreign Debt to Trade, 1913*[31]

Canada	8·6
South Africa	6·3
Latin America	5·2
Australasia	4·8
Russia	4·8
Other Africa	4·6
India	2·4
Japan	2·3
China	2·2
Other Asia	3·3

The figures in this table follow the usual rule that 'to him that hath shall be lent', that is to say the borrowing capacity of the more developed countries exceeds that of the less developed. Turned around, the figures are also evidence for the proposition that the greater the investment, the greater will be the prosperity of the borrowing country, but this proposition is true only if the borrower's social institutions, economic structure and natural resources are such that investment can yield its full potential. Both propositions are relevant. India could have used a lot more capital productively whereas China's absorptive capacity was still on the low side.

Most of the money referred to in Table 7.7 was invested productively with minimal political interference on the part of the governments of lending countries, beyond their willingness to guarantee loans to some of their colonies – a guarantee which in the British case was most often implicit rather than explicit. Unfortunately, separate figures are not available for South-East Europe and Turkey, where most of the politically pressured loans were made, with dubious economic results.

Most of the money, but by no means all, went into infrastructure. According to Paish[32] 75 per cent of British foreign investment was in railways, electricity, telephones, tramways, gasworks, waterworks, canals and docks, and the remaining 25 per cent in mines, investment companies, banks, iron, coal, steel, oil, rubber, tin, coffee, nitrates and breweries. This underestimates the latter category, since it counts only publicly quoted company shares and omits personal investment. Tropical plantations are well represented, but industrial investment was also considerable in the temperate settlements and in Europe. In Russia, for example, foreign investment in industrial enterprises (mostly French and German) was estimated at about 1,000 million US dollars, out of a total foreign debt of $3,750 million.

7.08 The main puzzle which international investment has posed has been its timing. In preparing Chart 7.3 we have aggregated the annual data of lending by the four core countries (which for most years means adding British, French and German lending and subtracting US borrowing).[33] This net lending by the core is then reduced to constant prices by dividing by our index of prices of manufactures in world trade. Finally the result is converted to logarithms, and smoothed by a five-year moving average. It is this moving average of net core lending at constant prices that appears in Chart 7.3.

One should note, in the first place, that the rate of growth is moderate. From the peak of 1886/90 to 1909/13, the growth rate of investment in constant prices is 4·25 per cent per annum, which is not very different from that of the trade of temperate settlements and the tropical countries together in constant prices (about 4·1). This is not quite what one would expect from looking at the figures in current prices.

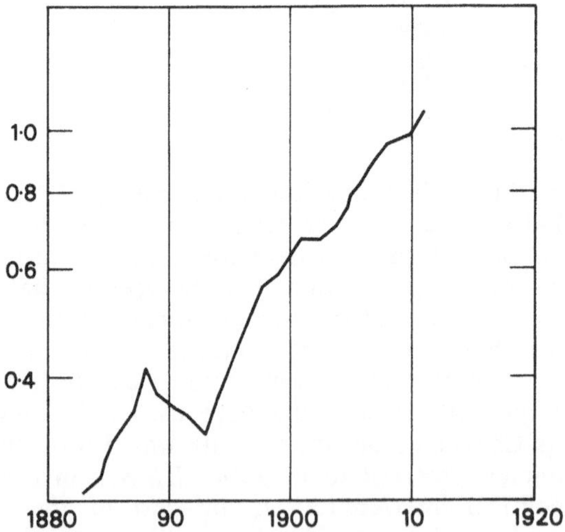

Chart 7.3 Core: Net International Investment

One should note, secondly, that the moving averages and the constant prices eliminate the year-by-year fluctuation, which tended to be substantial. For one thing these figures are compiled not from offerings on the stock exchange but by taking the difference between imports and exports (visible and invisible). These annual differences are subject to fluctuations in the volume and prices of trade which have nothing to do with foreign lending, and which are in fact offset by running down or building up short-term reserves; the moving average is therefore nearer the truth. Beyond this, British foreign lending was at the mercy of the Bank of England's method of 'managing' the gold standard, which was to keep very little gold, and to run for cover every time its gold reserves approached a predetermined minimum, as the reserves tended to do in nearly every Juglar boom. By implicit understanding with the Bank, promoters of foreign loans postponed new issues every time Bank Rate was raised, so the foreign borrower was in the front line of the Bank of England's defence. Nowadays we think of the manager of the international monetary system as a lender of last resort, who will lend money at the height of a crisis, but this was not how the Bank saw its international role. Indeed the true lenders of last resort were the Bank of France and the Reichsbank.

The graph brings out very well the big dip in foreign lending in the first half of the 1890s. Unfortunately we do not have French or German data for the 1870s. If we could take the curve back it would probably show another peak somewhere in the first half of the 1870s, with another great depression in lending in the second half of the 1870s – a Kuznets rather than a Kondratiev pattern.

Why did these collapses occur? As we have seen, the terms of trade of the peripheral countries were either better in 1890 than in 1870, or not much worse; and their fall in the 1880s was not all that great. Part of the answer is that this is a comparison centred on peaks. The fall from peak to trough was very severe, in both the 1870s and the 1890s, and such drastic and sudden changes are difficult to handle; a request for postponement is not an unnatural outcome. This is why the defaults of the 1870s, though exceptional in number, did not permanently frighten off international investment.

Of course nowadays we do not accept cyclical movements as part of a natural order. We take for granted that there should be a lender of last resort who will help countries to ride the crests and troughs of Juglar depression. The International Monetary Fund now has this function, and is gradually equipping itself to help developing countries through cyclical balance of payments disequilibrium.

Defaults due to a growing burden of debt are a different story. As we approach 1890, the problems of borrowers intensify. The steady fall in prices continually increased the real burden of debt, irrespective of the terms of trade. Prices of imports were coming down with the prices of exports, but the contractual obligations of interest and amortisation remained the same. The fall in prices was so pronounced that the average for the boom was lower than the average for the preceding trough. Here is the sequence for wool and for tropical crops (including coffee), both ex-freights.

	1871/5	*1876/80*	*1881/5*	*1888/92*	*1893/7*
Wool	100	83	78	57	55
Tropical crops	100	79	72	66	64

The troubles around 1890 did not even have to wait for a trough; the fact that prices had fallen 40 per cent over the preceding years was enough to make the debt burden difficult to carry.

Of course, once trouble began, the flow of funds for international investment would dry up rapidly. The year 1890, despite its overall prosperity, was ready for a pause in international lending. There seemed to be no end to the continual fall in the prices of primary products. Then there was the gloom spread by the Baring crisis, the associated default of Argentina, and Australia's difficulties in meeting her payments; added to which was the continual loss of gold by the USA, and doubts whether that country could remain on the gold standard. There was a large bandwagon effect in foreign lending; the clergymen, widows and orphans who mythologically were significant purchasers of foreign bonds received little hard information about the countries whose securities they were purchasing, and were the prey of rumour and fashion. With lending to the USA, Australia and Argentina out of fashion, all other countries would find themselves deprived of loans beyond any point that objective economic analysis of their own economic solutions could justify.

The real puzzle has been not why international lending dried up in the first half of the nineties, but why it attained such a high peak level in the second half of the 1880s. The prices of primary products were already falling sharply, so why was there a boom in lending at this time? Apart from the USA, the two big borrowers in the second half of the eighties were Argentina and Australia, for both of whom wool was then the staple. Reference to Chart 3.3 will show how steadily the price of wool was falling in the 1880s, even after deducting freights; any good mathematical model would generate much lower foreign investment in these two countries at that time! Australian writers have wrestled with the question why their country borrowed so much at that time. Much of the investment was actually in urban infrastructure, and may have been responding to a demographic cycle; the great inflow of population seeking gold in the 1850s was now producing a young generation marrying and creating new households.[34] Both in Australia and in Argentina most of the investment increased productive capacity in the next decade, and so paid its way. But it paid its way in the long run, rather than in the short, and was excessive in the sense that the immediate obligations were larger than could be met in a situation of declining prices.

For us there is no problem as to why the borrowers borrowed beyond their immediate financial capacity, since borrowers will always borrow if they can find lenders. Our problem is the more difficult question why the British lenders lent so much in the face of falling prices. The most plausible answer is the bandwagon effect. The biggest borrower in the first half of the 1880s was the United States, which was then experiencing the first warmth of what would be an almost uninterrupted Kuznets boom. Foreign lending was therefore in the air, and when in the second half of the 1880s US borrowing diminished, purchasers of foreign bonds were willing to be talked into buying Argentinian and Australian securities without bothering to scrutinise charts showing the trend in the price of wool since 1873.

INTERNATIONAL MIGRATION

7.09 The growth of output at the periphery was facilitated by an input of foreign labour as well as of foreign capital. Labour flowed in two separate streams: emigration from Europe, mainly to the countries of temperate settlement, and emigration from Asia, mainly to the tropical countries.

Between 1871 and 1915 some 36 million persons emigrated from Europe.[35] Nearly two-thirds of these went to the United States. The remaining 12·6 million are our present concern.

Most of these 12·6 million left Europe for four countries, Canada, Australia, Argentina and Brazil, whose total comes to about 12 million. However, the majority of these people did not stay; they moved on into other countries of Latin America, or to New Zealand or the United States, or else returned home to Europe. Net migration into those four countries between 1871 and 1915 amounts only to 5·4 million, distributed as follows:[36]

Argentina	2·50 million
Brazil	1·43
Australia	0·78
Canada	0·69
	5·40

Immigration too was subject to the great depression of the nineties. This can be seen in Chart 7.4 where the curve connects quinquennial averages of gross immigration into those four countries. Net immigration would show an even wider swing, since the emigrants left these countries in greater proportions when economic conditions were bad.

Why did so many people leave their homes? The push factor was the rising rate of natural increase, which, as we have seen earlier, tends to push people out of the countryside either into the towns, or if urban jobs are not increasing fast enough, into emigration. Death rates were falling in Western Europe in the nineteenth century. The birth rate held up in the first half of the century (except in France) and fell in the second half. So the rate of natural increase first accelerated and then decelerated. Western Europe was ahead of Eastern and Southern Europe. The relatively rapid rates of natural increase which Western Europe was experiencing in the middle of the nineteenth century had already ended by the turn of the century, when the Eastern and Southern rates of natural increase were still accelerating. This is why the big waves of emigration to the United States in the middle of the century came from Western Europe, while the big waves just before the war came from Eastern and Southern Europe. The demographic factor is of course reinforced by momentum. The number of people migrating to the United States from any particular place is a function not only of the accelerating or decelerating rate of natural increase

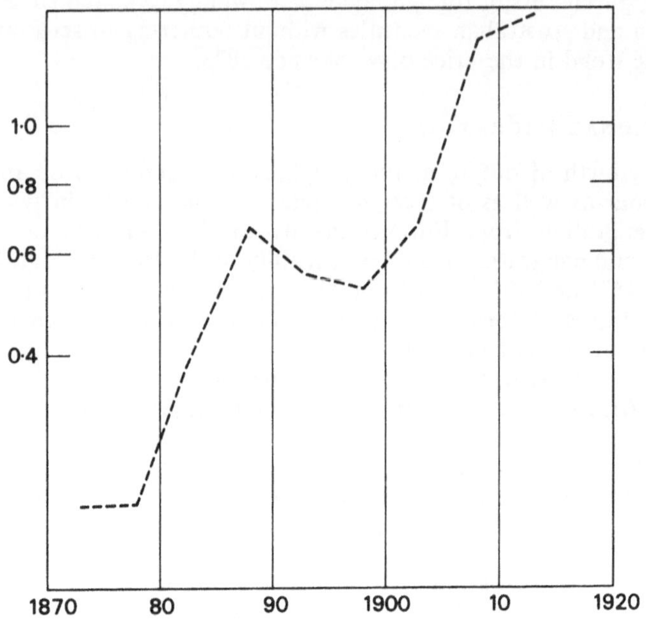

Chart 7.4 Gross Immigration to Countries of Temperate Settlement

in that place, but also of the number from that place who have already emigrated, who send back favourable news and travel funds, and who will welcome the new immigrants and find them jobs. So even after the rate of natural increase has begun to accelerate, it takes some time for the migrant flow to attain and maintain considerable volume.

Whether the people migrate to their own towns or out of their country will depend to some extent on how much investment is occurring in their towns to provide additional employment. European towns were not growing fast enough in the middle of the nineteenth century to absorb the whole of the natural increase of population, so emigration from Europe mounted.

The situation differed in France, Germany and Britain. By 1830 the population of France was already growing so slowly that there was no need for emigration. Germans were migrating and would continue to do so for some time, especially when hit by the potato blight in the mid-forties. But as their urban economy expanded rapidly, it was destined to catch up with population increase. The mid-eighties were the turning point after which German emigration slowed to a trickle. England's rate of natural increase was lower than Germany's, but so also was her rate of industrialisation, so Englishmen continued to emigrate in large numbers right down to the outbreak of the First World War.

Movements out of Europe were markedly cyclical, being heavy and light in alternate decades. Undoubtedly the main cause of this was that the United States, the principal destination, was subject to the Kuznets fluctuation. In addition, Australia's heavy investment in construction in the 1880s, followed by contraction in the 1890s, seems to have been part of a demographic cycle initiated by the big increase in population in the 1850s resulting from the gold discoveries. This coincidence with the US rhythm was accidental, but nevertheless heightened the peak and reduced the trough of international investment in the last two decades of the century. Some of the countries sending out emigrants also had demographic cycles in their rates of natural increase, Sweden being the most notable. It is even conceivable that the US Kuznets cycle was itself initiated earlier in the nineteenth century in response to immigration from Europe promoted by European demographic cycles, but the evidence for this is inconclusive.

The volume and timing of migration from any particular place was determined by a combination of push and pull factors. Take the case of England, which was the largest source of European emigrants. The push occurred at the slack periods of British industrialisation, notably from 1875 to 1895, and again in the ten years preceding the First World War. People only migrated, however, in years when the United States and other settlement countries were booming. A Kuznets great depression in the United States always cut migration sharply – not only from Britain – then a year or two after the upturn of railway investment in the USA, migrants would again begin to flow in rising numbers. Push and pull are unfortunate terms. There was no pull where there was no push; but even where there was push there was no movement except at times of pull. Thus to separate pull from push is an econometrician's headache.[37]

Push factors varied from country to country since the European countries did not synchronise their periods of greater or lesser prosperity. Taking the sum of emigration for all European countries together, the dominant factor was the pull. The emigration curve looks as it does in Chart 7.4 because in the USA and the temperate settlements the 1880s and 1900s were prosperous and the 1890s were depressed. If there is a slight anomaly it is the massive influx into the USA just before the First World War, when US production was abnormally depressed; here presumably the UK and East European pushes were too strong to be resisted.

In order to move, the migrant had also to find the fare. Personal savings and gifts and loans from relatives and friends were the main source, including especially remittances from settlers gone before, who also gave news of local economic conditions, and stood ready to help newcomers to find jobs and settle in. Apart from these personal contacts, some emigrants got help from emigration agencies, private or public, and also at times from governments of the countries to which they were emigrating, notably Australia and Brazil. The idea that people should emigrate was popular in Europe in the nineteenth century, mainly because of the Malthusian scare. It was also popular in those temperate receiving countries where there was still plenty of land suitable for agriculture or livestock farming. In many cases the land was sparsely occupied by native peoples (Indians in the Americas, aboriginal Australians, African tribes). There was no hesitation in making war on these peoples, killing them off, or confining them to reservations, so that large acreages could pass into European farming.

The figures represented by the gross migration curve in Chart 7.4 grew at an average rate of 5·0 per cent per annum between 1881–5 and 1906–10. This was beyond the absorptive capacity of these four countries, so it is not surprising that emigration was more than half as large as immigration. Net immigration into the four countries averaged 120,000 persons a year, equivalent to 0·4 per cent of their aggregate populations in 1895. There were years when immigration ran as high as one per cent of the population, but experience showed that such large movements were difficult to absorb.

The gap between gross and net immigration was widest in Canada, where emigrants exceeded immigrants in every decade between the censuses of 1871 and 1901; not until the great boom that followed the closing of the US agricultural frontier was Canada able to absorb net immigration. The gap was also wide in Australia after 1890, when that country entered into the doldrums from which it did not emerge until the mid-1900s. We do not have Brazilian emigration statistics for the whole period. Between 1899 and 1912 emigration was 65 per cent of immigration. This was a difficult period; earlier percentages will have been smaller. But Argentina held its migrants better than Brazil, and its ratio of emigrants to immigrants was 45 per cent over the whole period 1871–1915.

We associate immigration with building railways and opening up vast lands to agricultural and pastoral development, but in fact rural populations were not growing all that fast. Their natural rate of increase (excess of births over deaths) was then about 1·5 per cent per annum, and their actual increase rose significantly above this level only in Argentina. Thus, Canada's rural population was only slightly larger in 1901 than in 1881; in the next ten years of heavy immigration the rural population grew only at about 1·6 per cent per annum. Australia's rural population grew faster between 1871 and 1891 (at 1·9 per cent per annum), but thereafter fell below the rate of natural increase.[38] In Argentina between 1875 and 1914 the rural population grew at 2·1 per cent per annum.

Of course the growth rate of the rural population was affected by the rate of net immigration even where the rural population was growing more slowly than its own natural increase (that is, where net emigration to the towns was occurring). The growth of the towns was relentless, in response to the country's growing output per head, which expanded industry and services. The rural areas would have lost even more people if the towns had not been able to utilise immigration from overseas.

Rapid urbanisation is the hallmark of the development of the temperate settlements, as well as the proof of their successful response to the challenge offered by the opportunity to export primary products to the industrial countries. The urban population grew at 3·5 per cent per annum in Australia (1871–1901), at 3·9 per cent per annum in Canada (1891–1911) and at 5·3 per cent per annum in Argentina (1895–1914).

The situation was much the same in the United States, where the rural population grew between 1880 and 1900 at 1·1 per cent per annum, which was well below its natural increase, and the 3·5 per cent annual growth of the towns comprised all immigration together with all the natural increase of the towns and some immigration from the countryside.

We have commented before that these rapid rates of urbanisation are costly. They require high rates of capital formation which can be met only by importing capital. They are also costly to the human spirit, since the towns grow in ugliness of all kinds – bad housing, bad layout, shortage of water and other infrastructure, high levels of crime. The immigrants are the prey of politicians and hustlers of every sort. That more than half turn back is in no way surprising. When we say that these high rates of urbanisation proved that these countries were successful in converting a high growth rate of exports into modernised, mainly non-agricultural economies we mean precisely this and no more.

7.10 The movement of Europeans into the countries of temperate settlement was outstripped by the movement of Chinese and Indians into the tropical countries.

In 1880 about 3 million Chinese were living abroad, most of them in tropical lands (i.e. excluding North America, Japan, Formosa and other North Asian territories). By 1922 the number of Chinese living abroad was estimated at just over 8 million. For the countries which interest us at this point, the distribution was as shown in Table 7.8.

Table 7.8 *Chinese Residents*[39]

	1880	*1922*
Dutch East Indies	326,000	2,849,000
Thailand	1,500,000	1,500,000
Malaya	170,000	433,000
Other South Asia	541,000	887,000
South America	212,000	158,000
Oceania	79,000	59,000
Africa	—	5,000
	2,828,000	5,891,000

The table makes it clear that net migration was concentrated on Southern Asia. The Chinese played little part in African or Latin American development, in contrast to the Indians. We do not know how large the gross flow was, but since much of this was contract labour intending to return home, the great proportion of which left wives and children behind in China, we may expect that the gap was even wider than for European migration.

This was certainly the case with Indian migration.[40] Between 1871 and 1915 the number of emigrants was 15,809,000 of whom 11,714,000 returned to India, leaving a net migration of 4,095,000. The numbers leaving India

Table 7.9 *Indian Residents, 1930*[41]

Burma	1,300,000
Ceylon	1,133,000
Malaya	628,000
Other South Asia	28,000
West Indies	321,000
Mauritius	281,000
Africa	278,000
Australia, Fiji	79,000
	4,048,000

and China together, for all destinations, must have exceeded the number emigrating from Europe.

The Indians were more widely dispersed than the Chinese. Around 1930 the distribution of people of Indian birth in the countries which interest us was as shown in Table 7.9.

The Indians too, were mainly concentrated in Asia, but had sizable numbers also in the British sugar colonies (West Indies, Mauritius, Fiji) and in Eastern and Southern Africa. In South Asia the Indians and the Chinese overlapped only in Burma and Malaya.

In addition to Indians and Chinese there was also an outflow of Japanese. Starting only in the mid-eighties, the outflow amounted to about one million in our period. But, except for Hawaii, most of these went to temperate climates. Numbers living in the countries of interest to us around 1930 were as follows:[42]

Hawaii	134,000
Other South Asia	41,000
Brazil	103,000
	278,000

Several writers refer to this Asian movement as a substitute for or successor to the slave trade, but this is a misconception. It is true that after the abolition of slavery the sugar colonies recruited Asian labour, but this was a very small part of the flow of Indian and Chinese labour, most of which as we have seen, went to other countries in Asia, working either on European plantations or in mining and construction work.

Where land is abundant, labour is scarce; this is a tautology since it is the lack of population that makes the land abundant. Europeans did not confine their activities to areas where land was abundant. For instance, land was not abundant in Java, where sugar plantations could be introduced only by requiring the Javanese farmers to 'rent' their land to the sugar companies for (nominally) eighteen months out of every fifty-four. Even where land seemed to be abundant, as in Kenya, it usually had tribal owners, who used it in the course of a long rotation of perhaps ten to twenty years. Their rights were simply ignored.

In most cases, however, plantations were established on empty land, and had to search for labour. This problem was solved by importing Indian or Chinese labour on contract or indenture.

This labour could be had very cheaply and in unlimited quantities. India and China were already overpopulated, and subject to one or two severe famines every decade. Among the 300,000,000 Indians and 400,000,000 Chinese there was an unlimited supply of persons willing to enter 'contracts' or 'indentures', which bound them to work for a specified number of years on some plantation thousands of miles away, in a foreign country whose language they did not understand, and subjected them to criminal penalties for inadequate performance. Conditions varied from country to country. In British Guiana the contract was for five years, with entitlement to a return passage to India after ten years. Wages were much higher than in other countries,[43] at one shilling a day, with free housing of a rudimentary kind and free medical care, which nevertheless (the country was very malarial) yielded a death rate of 40 to 50 per thousand. The cost of transporting the labourer to and from India was put at about twenty pounds sterling, which, divided by ten years of 250 working days, added two pence to the daily cost.

A great deal has been written about the horrible conditions to which Asian migrant labour was subjected at the hands both of the contractors who recruited them at their home ports, transporting them abroad in overcrowded ships, and of the employers to whom they were indentured. Most of what is said is true. The Chinese got the worst treatment (especially in mid-century Peru or Cuba). Most of the Indians went to British territories where, since they were British citizens, the British government recognised some obligation to protect them by legislating codes of indenture, even though enforcement lagged behind legislation. But the overseas Chinese were all in foreign territories, where the Chinese government had little influence. From mid-century China began to negotiate treaties for the protection of Chinese labour overseas, and by the last quarter of the nineteenth century, with the Dutch East Indian government becoming more co-operative, the incidence of abuse was reduced. One test of this kind of system is the willingness of the labourer to remain in the country after the period of indentured service is completed. Increasing numbers did this – a fact which accounts for a large proportion of the 9 million Indians and Chinese living in South Asia, Africa and Latin America in 1920 – thus testifying that they thought themselves to be better off in their new countries than in their original homes (which is not saying very much). Another test was more difficult and took longer to emerge: their ability to integrate themselves into their new countries. Overseas Indians have been submitted to frightful horrors in their new countries in the second half of the twentieth century, and the future of overseas Chinese is also in doubt.

At the beginning of the nineteenth century the plantation system hardly existed in Asia. It was widespread in the Americas, where it was based on African slave labour, but Asian landowners for the most part rented out their lands to small farmers. The British introduced the system to Ceylon in the 1820s for the cultivation of coffee, whence it spread to India for cultivating tea, and to the Dutch East Indies for a number of crops, notably sugar. The system developed rapidly in the last half of the century, and especially after the opening of the Suez Canal in 1869. Anything could be grown on plantations, but in 1913 the chief plantation crops were sugar, tea, coconuts, rubber, abaca, jute and bananas. Most of the Asian coffee plantations had succumbed to disease; coffee was now primarily a Latin American crop where it was grown both on *haciendas* and by small farmers. The tropical crops essentially exported by small farmers were rice, cotton (although Egypt had some large cotton farms), cocoa, peanuts and palm oil, but small farmers grew some of everything profitably. In 1913 plantation and peasant technology were the same, and yields per acre were more or less the same (if anything, peasant yields per acre were higher). Sugar was the only tropical crop beginning to benefit from scientific research;

the new hybrid varieties were just reaching the plantations. There had been very considerable advances in the sugar mills, but the benefits of these were in theory available equally to large and small growers.

Plantation companies caught the fancy of British investors, and their shares were more welcome on the London Stock Exchange than the shares of most domestic industrial companies. Since a plantation company was really rather small in stock exchange terms, and also very far away, it needed some sort of sponsor. So the 'managing agency' system developed, in which one British firm would undertake to manage a set of companies, in which it might itself not have much capital; the investor bought shares on the strength of the managing agency's reputation.

THE FACTORAL TERMS OF TRADE

7.11 We see then that both the expansion of the temperate settlements and the growth of tropical production were aided by the migration of many millions of people. But the two streams of migration, from Europe and from Asia, moved on very different terms, and this difference was fundamental both to the challenge and to the response.

We have to start the analysis from the fact that around say 1900 the yield of wheat in Britain, which was the biggest single source of European emigration, was 1,600 lb per acre as against the tropical yield of 700 lb of grain, and that the Europeans also cultivated more acres per man. In the country to which most European immigrants went, the United States, agricultural output per man was even higher than in Europe because of greater mechanisation, and industrial productivity was also 50 to 100 per cent greater. The temperate settlements could attract and hold European emigrants, in competition with the United States, only by offering income levels higher than prevailed in North-West Europe. Since North-West Europe needed first their wool, then after 1890 their frozen meat, and ultimately after 1900 their wheat, it had to pay for these commodities prices which would yield a European standard of living.

The tropical situation was different. Any prices for tea or rubber or peanuts or sugar which offered a standard of living in excess of the 700 lb of grain per acre level were an improvement. Farmers would consider devoting idle land or time to producing such crops; and, as experience grew, would even, at somewhat higher prices, reduce their own subsistence production of food to specialise in commercial crops. But whether the small farmer reacted in this way or not, there was an unlimited supply of Indians and Chinese willing to travel to the ends of the earth to work on plantations for a shilling a day. Prices of tropical products could not get much beyond this level. We have noted that there were no significant increases in productivity, except in sugar. Moreover, increases in productivity would benefit the innovator only in an initial period. Since the supplies of land, capital and labour were all infinitely elastic, the general spread of new techniques merely reduced the price correspondingly.

In the 1880s the wage of a plantation worker was a shilling a day or less, but the wage of a 'navvy' (unskilled construction worker) in New South Wales was nine shillings a day.[44] It is true that the emigrants did not all come from Britain – many came from much poorer parts of Europe – and did not all go to Australia or the USA. But Southern Europeans could, if they wished, go to the USA, and a country like Brazil, which offered less, had more difficulty in holding its immigrants. Brazil's chief competitor was Argentina, which paid the competitive wage. To quote Professor Diaz Alejandro:

> A comparison of hourly wage rates in 1911–14 between Buenos Aires and Paris and Marseilles for seven different categories showed the Buenos Aires rates higher than those in Marseilles in all categories (by about 80 per cent) and higher than most corresponding Parisian wage rates (on average by about 25 per cent).[45]

If tea had been a temperate instead of a tropical crop, its price would have been perhaps four times as high as it actually was. And if wool had been a tropical instead of a temperate crop, it would have been had for perhaps one-fourth of the ruling price.[46]

This is a long-run rather than a short-run law. Price in the short run is determined by current demand and supply. Price in the long run moves to the level determined by alternative opportunities.

Table 7.10 shows how different tropical commodities fared. Commodities are arranged in ascending order, according to the ratio of their prices in 1913 to 1883 (the third column). The first column is the index of 1899 on 1883; the second is the index of 1913 on 1899; and the fourth column shows what percentage tropical supplies were of world supplies.

Table 7.10 *Price Index Numbers*[47]

	1899/1883	*1913/1899*	*1913/1883*	*Tropical share* (%)
Sugar	46	107	49	50
Tea	71	103	73	100
Palm oil	62	164	87	100
Cocoa	91	97	88	100
Rubber	83	111	92	100
Rice	106	91	97	95
Coffee	96	102	98	100
Cotton	66	191	125	33
Hides	72	175	126	33
Tobacco leaf	94	138	130	30
Jute	104	207	215	60

Table 7.10 makes a striking distinction. With the exception of sugar, all the commodities whose price was lower in 1913 than in 1883 were commodities produced almost wholly in the tropics. All the commodities whose prices rose over this thirty-year period were commodities in which the temperate countries produced a substantial part of total supplies. The fall in ocean freight rates affected tropical more than temperate prices, but this should not make a difference of more than five percentage points.

The prices of wholly tropical crops fell because the price of food fell (the cereals index fell by 12 per cent) and also because the tropical countries were developing rapidly. The price of wheat fell because of increases in output per head. Since farm incomes in temperate countries were related to urban incomes in those countries, a fall in the price of wheat due to productivity would not bring down the prices of other temperate agricultural products not experiencing productivity change. But it would bring down prices of tropical foodstuffs and therefore the prices of tropical cash crops competing with food for farm land or labour.

It could not have had this effect if the supply of tropical cash crops had not kept pace with the demand. In fact cash crop and cereals prices moved very closely together, as can be seen in Chart 9.1 or in Appendix III. The supply of tropical crops turned out to be highly elastic, as one would expect from the currently unlimited supplies of land and labour. Tea production spread from China to new plantations in India and Ceylon. Palm oil flowed out of West Africa, as the market economy penetrated into the rain forest. Ghana supplied virtually no cocoa in 1883, but had become the world's largest producer by 1913. Rubber in 1883 was tapped in the wild forest; by 1913 it was increasingly a plantation industry. Rice was pouring out of Burma, Thailand and Indochina. Coffee is the interesting case. In the middle of the nineteenth century supplies came mainly from Ceylon, India and Java, with an old Brazilian industry also just beginning to expand. Beginning in the 1870s the Asian plantations were hit by a new disease, which wiped out the Ceylonese plantations, and severely restricted the rest. Coffee could not have become a southern Brazilian product at Asian prices, since southern Brazil was recruiting Southern European labour that required a more than Asian standard of living. The price of coffee therefore rose sharply even at the end of the 1880s, when practically every other commodity price was plummeting. Coffee production then grew very rapidly in southern Brazil. But it also began to grow rapidly in other parts of the tropics (first northern Latin America and later Africa) where the alternative cost was not a European standard of living. So coffee began, in the 1890s, a downward slide which has continued to our day. After 1900 its price could no longer support a European standard of living, and between 1900 and 1913 emigration from Brazil was 65 per cent of immigration. Except for a brief period immediately after the Second World War there was never in the twentieth century (up to the great frost of 1975) a price at which southern Brazilians were willing to plant coffee, whereas Africans and tropical Latin Americans have continually increased their acreages.

In a word, any commodity which was, or could be, wholly produced in the tropics, had a long-run equilibrium price yielding the tropical standard of living (700 lb of grain per acre). It might take time for production to spread widely enough to bring the actual price to this level, but this was the target of market forces.

If the tropics could produce only a small proportion of the required supply, its output would not affect the price, which would then be determined by the alternatives open to temperate farmers (the 1,600 lb of grain per acre times more acres). Had tropical productivity been the same as temperate productivity this would of course have brought a European standard of living to the tropical farmers, and undoubtedly more of them would have planted the crop. Equilibrium required a price which just satisfied the tropical producers, but with which the temperate producers could still live because of superior productivity. Actually the European standard of living was rising all the time so, given that productivity was not increasing in these crops, it is not surprising that their prices rose 25 per cent above the level of 1883 (despite a fall in the price of wheat).

There are test cases. Jute was eating into the market for flax, and was in strong demand. Sugar was the only commodity in which productivity had grown very substantially, especially in European beet, so that a price profitable to the European farmer yielded nevertheless only a shilling a day to the Indian indentured labourer. The expansion of this commodity in Europe had been greatly stimulated by subsidies, but beet and cane were about competitive with each other at 1913 prices. Cotton was another test case. The USA was the principal supplier, and held its own despite great efforts by Lancashire to stimulate cotton growing in the British Empire. Yields per acre were about three times as high in the USA as in India.[48] All the same the USA could not have competed with tropical production if its southern blacks had been free to migrate to the north and to work there at white northern incomes. It was racial discrimination in the USA that kept the price of cotton so low; or to turn this around, given racial discrimination, American blacks earned so little because of the large amount of cotton that would have flowed out of Asia and Africa at a higher price.

Could not the individual tropical country break through by increasing its productivity in growing crops for export? Only if it would keep the new technology secret, and this it could not do. The most favourable case would be a breakthrough in a crop produced in the temperate world, like cotton. If India's productivity in cotton had doubled, the current price would have been highly profitable, and the Indian farmers would have poured out cotton. As the price fell, American cotton would have been displaced from world markets. However, if the new technology was not secret, tropical countries all over the world would soon have been planting cotton, with or without Indian or Chinese indentured labourers. New technology has its own backwash; those sugar plantations which failed to keep up with new varieties and large-scale milling in the last quarter of the nineteenth century simply found themselves in bankruptcy – as in Jamaica or Mauritius, in contrast to Java or Cuba. Given the unlimited reservoirs of Indian and Chinese labour, tropical wages and peasant incomes had to remain close to Indian and Chinese levels; whatever might happen to productivity, commodity prices would move to this level. The main benefit of innovation would accrue to consumers in Europe and North America.

The analysis turns on long-run infinite elasticity of supply, and therefore does not apply to minerals. The long-run price of a mineral was determined by its cost of production in the temperate world, which was still the major source of supply. When such a mineral was discovered in the tropics the labour cost of mining it would be small. A theoretical economist would say that most of the surplus belonged to rent or royalties; but in practice only small rents and royalties were extracted, and most of the surplus went into profits. Mining was not yet important in the tropics; in 1913 minerals came to only 13 per cent of tropical exports.

7.12 Much has been written about the commodity terms of trade, but changes in the commodity terms of trade are a relatively insignificant element in explaining tropical poverty. Movements in the commodity terms of trade are of the order of 15 per cent up or down over twenty years, whereas the disparity in the factoral terms of trade is of the order of several hundred per cent.

Given this difference in the factoral terms of trade, the opportunity which international trade presented to the temperate settlements was very different from the opportunity presented to the tropics. The temperate settlements were offered high income per head. From this would come immediately a large demand for manufactures, opportunities for import substitution and rapid urbanisation. Domestic saving per head would be large. Money would be available to spend on schools, at all levels, and soon these countries would have a substantial managerial and administrative élite of their own. They would thus create their own power centres, with money, education and managerial capacity, independent of and somewhat hostile to the imperial power – so that Australia, New Zealand and Canada had ceased to be colonies in any meaningful sense long before they acquired formal rights of sovereignty. The factoral terms available to them offered the opportunity for full development in every sense of the word.

The factoral terms available to the tropics, on the other hand, offered the opportunity to stay poor – at any rate until such time as the labour reservoirs of India and China might be exhausted. Nobody understood this better than the working classes in the temperate settlements themselves (and in the USA). They were always adamantly opposed to Indian or Chinese immigration into their countries because they realised that, if unchecked, it must drive wages down close to Indian and Chinese levels. In the same way white American labour did all it could to restrict the jobs available to blacks.

Indian and Chinese levels set the targets for tropical commodity prices, but prices did not sink right to those levels; there had to be some margin to bring out the required supplies. Prices had to be attractive enough to induce peasants to switch from subsistence to commercial production, or to move from India or China across thousands of miles. Just as wages were higher in the temperate settlements than in North-West Europe, so also tropical peasants and wage earners in the commercial economy earned more than the subsistence farmers in their own economies or in India. The difference was constrained by the elasticity of supply, but was nevertheless real enough to be effective. So in the developing tropics, even those at the bottom of the social hierarchy experienced a rise in their standard of living. Further up the social hierarchy a whole range of opportunities was created by economic expansion, including jobs for clerks, civil servants, lawyers and others. Opportunities for trade also developed – buying peasant produce for export, importing consumer goods for local distribution, and so on. Development considerably expanded the numbers (to use the British terminology) in the upper working, the lower middle and the middle middle classes, including both the salaried and (to use the French terminology) the *petite bourgeoisie*. However, it did not affect the number in the upper middle class, since the imperial powers kept these jobs for their own nationals, nor in the *grande bourgeoisie* because most of the big importing and exporting firms were also expatriate, and reserved managerial experience to other expatriates.

So what was offered to the tropics by the industrialisation of the core was rather limited – an opportunity to move a little way up the ladder, but thus far and no further. But it was still open to the tropics to take off from this point in the footsteps of the core itself, that is to say to have their own revolution in food production, and then to industrialise for their own local markets. The tropics, in other words, could behave as if the industrial nations did not exist, and could go through an agricultural-industrial revolution of their own. Why this did not happen we shall have to inquire.

Chapter 8

Response

SYNOPSIS: 8.00 The main concern of this chapter is to isolate the principal elements that explain why some tropical countries fared better than others. But this is preceded by a brief glance at the contrasting record of the new countries of temperate settlement.

8.01 The trade of these new countries accelerated at about the same time as tropical trade, but grew much faster than tropical, US or European trade. 8.02 As income grew they industrialised rapidly, with the exception of Argentina.

8.03 Tropical countries in 1870 had very small agricultural surpluses and industrial sectors. They took up the trade opportunity rather than the industrialisation challenge. 8.04 Because of the low technological level, the range of commodities exported was small. 8.05 Tropical trade as a whole grew rapidly, but the performance of individual countries varied widely. The countries with surplus arable wet land grew fastest. 8.06 But the measures needed for opening up surplus land were not always taken. 8.07 Colonial governments stood to gain by promoting exports, but varied very widely in their performance. There was similar variation among the governments of independent countries.

8.08 National income per head rose quite rapidly in a number of tropical countries. 8.09 Part of the increased income was used to create new infrastructure and to expand educational facilities. 8.10 Several tropical countries began to industrialise in this period; but industrial progress was inhibited by unfavourable factoral terms of trade, the domination of external trade by foreign firms, the opposition of farmers and merchants, and the hostility of governments (whether colonial or independent). 8.11 The creation of infrastructure and the modernisation of economic institutions are the important achievements of a number of tropical countries in this period.

8.00 We have now identified three different opportunities for development at the periphery which derived from the industrial revolution at the core. First, a country which already had an industrial sector could reconstruct it along the more productive technological and institutional pattern of the advanced countries whose industrial revolution had already occurred; and it could then develop from there. Secondly, countries in the temperate zones could develop primary production for export to the core and other industrial nations, in return for a European standard of living; they could then move into industrialisation for import substitution, and so build up an industrial base from which to move forward again. Thirdly, tropical countries could expand production of commercial crops, for sale at prices based on the low food-producing levels of tropical subsistence farmers; they could strengthen their infrastructure, increase productivity in food, and move towards industrialisation for home and export markets.

The second group of countries came off best; by 1913 the countries of new temperate settlement were the richest in the world. We have already seen that the countries of East, South and Central Europe did comparatively poorly. The tropical countries also had mixed results, some doing better than the more backward European countries, and some doing worse. Why in each of these categories some countries did better than others is the question that fascinates the historian.

In this chapter we shall concentrate on the tropical countries and how they fared in comparison with each other. By way of contrast we shall begin with a brief account of the performance of the new countries of temperate settlement, which shared as their engine of growth the expanding demands of world trade.

To explain why some countries do better than others within the same category is a formidable task, which needs to be approached from two directions simultaneously. One approach deals in generalisations, in theories of what stimulates and what retards industrialisation; the other deals in case studies of individual countries. Without simultaneous movement from both directions understanding is impossible. Valid generalisations cannot be formulated without deep knowledge of many (preferably all) individual cases; while the individual case cannot be understood without sound general theory.

We cannot now launch on individual histories of each of over one hundred developing countries, covering Europe, Latin America, Africa, Asia and Australasia. For this we have no competence, so we would only be promulgating error. We shall have to take for granted the works of innumerable historians who have already published individual country histories for the period 1870–1913. Regrettably the field is only covered patchily. Western Europe, Russia, the USA, Canada, Australia, Argentina, Brazil, India and Japan have attracted voluminous writing, whereas material on the developing countries of Central and Southern Europe and the rest of the developing world is only now appearing sporadically. This author's contribution to date has been to sponsor a work on the nineteenth-century history of Jamaica;[1] and even more to the point, to edit a volume of case studies of tropical development in three continents for the period 1880–1913.[2] The latter book should be read as a companion volume to the present work.

We are therefore left in this chapter with a few remarks about some factors of a general kind which facilitated or inhibited response to the economic opportunities created by new technology, expanding international trade, international lending and international migration. By 'factors of a general kind' we mean that each was characteristic of several countries. We also mean that these factors were important but not necessarily decisive (ignoring the argument whether any single event in human history is decisive). We recognise that in addition to these general factors each country was influenced by events peculiar to itself – like the great drought at the turn of the twentieth century which set back the development of Australia. We also recognise the importance to the history of each country of having the right person in the right place at the right time, a coincidence which, far from being inevitable, is sufficiently infrequent to be fascinating when it happens. We are not pretending to have the entire explanation of the rate of growth of any particular country; all we are trying to do is to identify contributing factors which were common to many countries.

THE COUNTRIES OF TEMPERATE SETTLEMENT

8.01 The countries of temperate settlement prospered in this period. By 1913 their standard of living was well in excess of that of Europe. Maizels[3] has calculated the apparent consumption of manufactures per head, at 1955 prices, for a number of selected countries. He has the following results for 1913:

	$		$
UK	175	Canada	520
France	150	Australia	330
Germany	145	New Zealand	320
Italy	95	Argentina	130

These figures almost certainly exaggerate the difference between Western Europe and the temperate settlements, but their general gist is correct: the richer temperate settlements were richer than the richer European countries, and the poorer temperate settlements were better off than Central and Southern Europe. Table 8.1 gives some basic data for the temperate settlements.

Table 8.1 *Output of Countries of Temperate Settlement*[4]

	Manufacturing per head ($, *1913*)	*Exports per head* ($, *1913*)	*Growth rate of exports 1883–1913* (% *p.a.*)
Canada	86·5	58·4	4·8
Australia	77·4	79·8	1·6
New Zealand	68·1	92·7	3·7
Argentina	23·5	66·9	7·6
Chile	17·5	41·4	2·1
South Africa	5·2	51·3	8·5
Uruguay	n.a.	19·7	3·6
Average	44·1	61·3	4·3
Brazil	2·4	12·9	4·5

Brazil does not belong to this table, and is not included in the averages. It is introduced here because during our period its net retention of European immigrants about equalled that of Australia and Canada together. However, it is a tropical country, and the fact that its exports per head were only one-fifth of Argentina's emphasises that it belongs, according to the factoral terms of trade, with the tropical countries and not with the countries of temperate settlement.

Two points stand out in comparing the countries of temperate settlement.[5] First, there is little relationship between the growth rate of trade, and the value of trade per head in 1913. This is because these countries 'took off' at different times, and then had different experiences. The second point is the great differences between them in industrialisation.

Australia was the last continent to be discovered, but it was the first temperate settlement (excluding the USA) to launch on rapid growth. This began with the introduction of merino sheep in the 1840s, but Australia took its biggest leap with the gold discoveries of the 1850s, which tripled its population in eleven years. The economy then raced ahead to about 1890, carried mainly by railways and wool. Then it stumbled. Over-borrowing for infrastructure led to financial difficulties in the first half of the 1890s. Investment was cut sharply, following the cessation of foreign borrowing, and the economy spiralled downwards from a peak in 1891 to a trough in 1897. The decisive blow, however, was not the lull in foreign investment; Australia could have ridden this as easily as Argentina. The decisive blow was the long drought, in the course of which the flock of sheep was halved. New trades were developing, especially the refrigerated meat and wheat trades; but the growth rate of Australia's exports by value between 1883 and 1913 still emerges as one of the lowest in the world. There was some compensation in rapid industrialisation for the home market, but the pace of development slowed. The national income per head of 1891 was not surpassed until about 1907.[6] All the same, in 1913 Australia still ranked with the USA and Canada for the highest national income per head.

Argentina languished until the 1860s, when the possibility of combining foreign capital, railways, immigrants and limitless fertile pampas for the production of wool began to be perceived. It took twenty years of fitful activity to gain momentum, an interval which saw the finances of the federal government established on an independent basis, a trial return to the London capital market in the early 1860s, the first 2,000 kilometres of railway, war with the Indians, and the coming to office in 1880 of General Roca, whose government London found more impressive than those of his predecessors. The 1880s then saw vast borrowing by government as well as by private companies for railway construction. The first staple was wool, supplemented by hides. But at the end of the decade the trade in refrigerated meat began, and this became a giant on its own. Add linseed, also beginning in the 1880s, and maize, which by 1913 rivalled wheat in value, and one can see why the curve for Argentinian agricultural exports (Chart 7.2) just keeps going, at an average rate of 6 per cent per annum, making Argentina compete with Japan for the title of the fastest growing country in the world between 1880 and 1913. The boom of the 1880s was checked by the depression of the first half of the nineties, and the temporary decline of international investment, but thereafter the country was off again, with astonishing inflows of migrants and capital, opening up apparently inexhaustible areas of agricultural and pastoral country. It would retain this pace until the middle 1920s, when the terms of trade again turned against primary products.

Chile also languished until the conquest of the nitrate-bearing lands in 1878. Nitrates then became the growth industry, comprising in 1913 as much as 77 per cent of total exports. Production of nitrates grew at 9 per cent per annum between 1883 and 1890, and then settled down to just over 4 per cent per annum. However, mining employed less than 5 per cent of the labour force. The country did not become a great agricultural producer, like Canada, Australia or Argentina, and did not even attract many immigrants. Its population grew between the censuses of 1895 and 1907 by 1·4 per cent per annum, and annual immigration at its highest was only 0·1 per cent of the existing population. Argentina was the magnet for immigrants to Latin America; all the other countries found it hard to compete with the opportunities and high wages which the rapid expansion of Argentina generated.

In the same way in the northern hemisphere, Canada was hard put to compete with the USA for population. A period of slow but steady growth, based on furs, timber and fish, came to a halt around 1870, and for the next three decades (i.e. to 1900) emigration exceeded immigration. The volume of exports of all commodities grew over the twenty years 1870/4 to 1890/4 only at 1·3 per cent per annum. Canada did not really take off agriculturally until the closing of the American agricultural frontier created a scarcity of wheat – a phenomenon which also had substantial impact in Australia, Argentina, Russia, Hungary and all other potential exporters of wheat. Simultaneously new wheats, more suitable to the Canadian climate, and new kinds of ploughs were introduced. From the 1890s onwards Canada took off. The new prosperity was not entirely based on wheat. Exports of metals and of livestock products also grew rapidly. And as export income expanded the domestic market, manufacturing and the service trades also raced ahead.

In sum the countries of temperate settlement were relatively late developers, in comparison with the core countries; they played no part in establishing the foundations of the industrial revolution in the core countries. The only one which was already in 1870 growing fairly fast was Australia. Argentina and Chile did not take off firmly until the 1880s, and Canada not until the 1890s; that is to say, even the countries of temperate settlement were not really drawn into the orbit of the core until after 1880, when cheap transport by rail and sea began to take effect.

8.02 The other interesting phenomenon is the differences in the degree of industrialisation, which are much wider than the differences in trade. The failure of Argentina to industrialise stands out, although it may be somewhat exaggerated in Table 8.1.[7] This failure would cost the country dearly after the First World War, when the terms of trade turned against primary products. As we have said, the option which the industrialisation of the core offered to the countries of temperate settlement was to grow rich by selling primary products, and to use the opportunity to build an industrial structure, based in the first instance on import substitution. Argentina responded well to the first part of this challenge, but neglected the second part.

Argentina was not as well endowed as Canada with industrial minerals, but was as well endowed as New Zealand. One of its gaps, the failure to establish a sizable textile industry, owed nothing to lack of materials. Some nationalists blame the failure on British interests: the exporters wanting to buy imports as cheaply as possible, the import merchants wanting to retain their commissions, and the shipping companies their freights. In fact, industrialisation would not have reduced imports, but exporters and shipping companies may not have recognised this. However, it is hard to explain a difference between Argentina and these British territories in terms of the influence of British interests, since British interests were more firmly entrenched in Canada, Australia and New Zealand than they were in Argentina. It makes more sense to speak of the power of Argentinian interests, which presumably backed exports rather than industrialisation, for the reasons given. To quote Professor Carlos Diaz Alejandro:

> It is the nearly unanimous opinion of students of Argentinian economic history that before 1930 public policy was either indifferent or hostile to the expansion of manufacturing, unless it was directly related to exports of rural origin.[8]

The crucial difference between Argentina and Australia was that Argentinian politics were dominated by an old landed aristocracy. Australia had no landed aristocracy. Its politics were dominated by its urban communities, who used their power to protect industrial profits and wages.

TROPICAL TRADE

8.03 The tropical countries were also late developers; their rapid growth did not begin until the last quarter of the nineteenth century. Many of these countries had been participating in world trade for a couple of centuries or more – notably India, Ceylon, Indonesia, Egypt, Brazil and other Latin American countries. But as we saw in Chapter 7, this trade, though romantic and the inspiration of much violence and bloodshed, was small. In the absence of cheap means of transport it had to be confined to the products of territory close to the sea or to rivers. Rapid expansion therefore had to wait for the arrival of the railways, especially since, mainly for political reasons, these territories had been by-passed by the earlier transportation revolutions, the building of canals and of macadamised roads. It is true that one could get some distance without either roads or railways; at the turn of the century it was thought in West Africa that human porterage was economic up to a distance of fifty miles from a seaport.[9] However, the railway to open up the interior, and the iron ship (iron was more crucial than steam in the shipping revolution) were the two preconditions of a large tropical trade.

But why did tropical development depend on trade? The industrial revolution offered another option: to revolutionise one's manufacturing sector along the lines of the new techniques. All the Latin American and Asian countries had manufacturing sectors; why did they not begin there?

There is an obvious answer for colonies: the imperial powers did not encourage, and in a few cases actively discouraged, their industrialisation.

There was also a small group of 'open door' countries of varying degrees of sovereign independence, which were nevertheless forbidden by treaty to raise their tariffs above specified levels (the Ottoman Empire, 3 per cent up to 1861, 8 per cent to 1907, 11 per cent thereafter; Iran, 5 per cent from 1826; China, 5 per cent from 1842; Siam, 3 per cent from 1855). Theoretically lack of tariff autonomy could be decisive, but in practice it seems not to have been so. For one thing, the Indian cotton factories were denied protection, but nevertheless flourished; tropical wages were low enough for a range of tropical manufacturing to be able to compete without tariff protection, at least in domestic markets already protected by transport costs. It is also notable that the independent sovereign states, especially the Latin Americans, did not do much better than the colonies. In the middle of the nineteenth century no political forces in Europe or North America were deciding that Europe was to be industrialised, but Brazil was to develop by exporting coffee or Indochina by exporting rice. The importance of the economic factors must not be neglected.

We have already seen some of the economic reasons that put the tropics on the path of exporting agricultural products instead of industrialising. Low agricultural productivity was a crucial factor. In the absence of an agricultural revolution the agricultural surplus was small; the manufacturing sector thus remained small. Some of this manufacturing was protected by distance: the same internal transport costs that had inhibited exports also prevented imports of manufactures from reaching into the interior. Some of it was produced within a subsistence environment, and was therefore not subject to competition. Beyond this, the internal drive towards an industrial revolution was lacking – either in the form of eager entrepreneurs or in the form of development-oriented governments – even in the politically independent countries of Asia and Latin America. The only factor driving towards an industrial revolution would be the backwash of cheap iron and textiles arriving from England and putting domestic spinners and smelters out of work. But the importance of this factor depended on the size of the market, and therefore takes us back to the small agricultural surplus and the protection afforded by lack of transport.

Industrialisation needed a dynamic force which was lacking – the kinds of people, ideas and institutions that the market economies of Western Europe had been evolving for some decades. The tropics were just as capable of producing this complex, in response to external competition, but it would take time. In the meantime it was relatively easy to respond to agricultural production for export, once transport costs came down. There was no lack of traders to travel through the countryside collecting small parcels of produce from thousands of small farmers; or of capitalists ready to man plantations with imported labour. The speed of this adjustment created an illusion; it came to be an article of faith in Western Europe that the tropical countries had a comparative advantage in agriculture, when in fact, as Indian textile production soon began to show, there were much greater differences in food production per head than in modern industrial production per head as between tropical and temperate countries.

As the tropical agricultural exports expanded, the domestic market widened, and the prospects of domestic manufacturing improved. It did not, however, follow that success in exporting primary products would lead directly into the development of manufacturing for the home market. Conceivably the opposite could happen: success in exporting primary products could become an obstacle to manufacturing by entrenching the power of groups and classes dependent on the export trade, as well as by orienting the national taste excessively towards enjoyment of foreign-produced goods, ideas and institutions. We have already seen opposing examples among the countries of temperate settlement, in the contrast between Argentina and Australia. Similar contrasts exist among the tropical countries, for example between Brazil and Egypt. The development of an export trade is one thing; the development of manufacturing industry is another.

We shall therefore begin by studying the reaction of the tropical countries towards the export opportunity, and will leave discussion of industrialisation until we have seen what happened to exports.

8.04 The range of potential exports was not unlimited. To begin with, the role of minerals was small, amounting only to 13 per cent of tropical exports in 1913, compared with 29 per cent in 1965. In 1913 minerals were prominent in the exports only of Peru, Mexico, Malaya, the Congo and Indonesia. As we have noted, the minerals of the industrial revolution were iron ore and coal, which the core countries had in abundance. The demand for the kinds of minerals now prominent in tropical trade did not come to the fore until the end of the century.

More restrictive was the inability of the tropical countries to compete with the temperate countries in basic foodstuffs. Argentina and Australia grew rich on exporting wheat, maize and livestock products. India built up a small export trade in wheat, and Burma, Thailand and Indochina a considerable export trade in rice. But there was no export of maize or sorghum, two of the chief tropical foodstuffs, mainly because productivity was so low. The same applied to livestock products; livestock diseases were widespread, mortality high and milk yields low: a major technological revolution was required here (and still is).

Low productivity also accounts for the poor performance in cotton and tobacco, two crops in which the tropics were competing with the USA. Cotton turned out to be subject to innumerable tropical pests and diseases, which kept yields down even for carefully selected varieties. This was particularly unfortunate, since cotton does not require a heavy rainfall, and there were large areas of the tropics which needed just such a crop.

Another tropical resource not exploited at this time was timber. Many tropical countries had large forest areas. But they were of mixed species, and the trees suitable for timber were scattered here and there and expensive to remove. In fact timber did not become a major tropical export until after the Second World War. The technique for converting mixed hardwoods economically into pulp has also only recently been perfected, and is even now not yet in commercial operation.

The result is a fairly narrow range of tropical exports, leading to a lopsided kind of agricultural development, in which the region which produced the export crop would be comparatively prosperous, while the regions of the same country producing food-crops or livestock remained in poverty. Since exports were usually less than 20 per cent of agricultural output, these anomalies were prominent.

Thus in effect the tropics were held back by their need for a technological revolution in agriculture such as had been occurring in Western Europe over two centuries. This view, however, is not the popular one. Many writers see the tropics rather as having been captured by the industrial nations, especially in the colonial relationship, and forced to supply cheap raw materials for Europe and North America. Other writers would not speak of force; as they see it, the leaders of the tropical establishment, both native and imperial, became ideologically committed to exporting raw materials and blind to the opportunities for a revolution in food: their countries would have been more likely to undergo a food-producing revolution if they had never become involved in exporting raw materials. In either case the exporting of raw materials is seen as a trap, which confines the tropics to poverty.

But there was never any attempt to prevent tropical countries from increasing their food production. The British were just as willing to import food as to import raw materials, and encouraged Indian wheat production to the extent of financing irrigation works. Moreover the plantations everywhere – in Dutch, French or other territories – needed food for their Indian and Chinese labourers. So a large international trade in rice developed after 1870 to supply the tropical countries themselves; Burma, Thailand and Indochina became the major exporters. It is simply not true that the industrial nations stood in the way of developing food production in the tropics.

What is true is that there were no changes in tropical food technology at this time. A small amount of research was being done in Departments of Agriculture in various territories, but it was mainly misguided, being based on the application of techniques for the management of temperate soils to the management of tropical soils. Deep ploughing and clean weeding, however, destroy tropical soils, either by allowing the sun's rays to bake the soil and destroy humus and useful micro-organisms, or else by allowing the rain to wash away either the soil itself or valuable nutrients. This lesson has now been learnt, but the management of tropical soils is still a mystery. There has been other useful progress, especially in selecting varieties and breeding useful hybrids, and also in identifying pests and diseases and learning how to control them. But most of this work belongs to the twentieth century, and its practical application to tropical foodstuffs has been proved only in the second half of this century.

In sum, the tropics were seeking to prosper through trade in a limited number of commodities, instead of through technological progress. Trade offers a once-and-for-all improvement, limited in this case by the low factoral terms. In contrast technological improvement is continuous. The tropics could not really hope to 'take off' until technological change became embedded in their way of life.

8.05 Table 8.2 shows how varied was the response of the tropical countries to the opportunities created by the expansion of world trade.

Countries are listed by continent in order of trade per head, but this is a somewhat misleading index of response. The larger the country the smaller its external trade, so we cannot conclude that Thailand was more developed than India because it did twice as much trade per head. The rate of growth of trade is not subject to this disadvantage, but has its own; newcomers to world trade, like West Africa, can grow faster than older countries, like Egypt. But even when we allow for these factors, the differences between countries in Table 8.2 are still remarkable. Our first task is therefore to elucidate why the trade of some countries grew so much faster than that of other countries.

Table 8.2 *Exports of Tropical Countries*[10]

	Per head ($, 1913)	Growth rate 1883–1913 (% p.a.)
Africa		
Mauritius	27·4	−2.0
Egypt	12·9	3·1
Madagascar	3·3	6·8
British West Africa	3·2	5·7
Portuguese Africa	2·7	3·7
French West Africa	2·2	6·3
Rest of Africa	1·4	4·0
Americas		
Cuba	69·3	2·9
West Indies	21·8	−0·1
Dominican Republic	14·8	n.a.
Brazil	12·6	4·5
Venezuela	10·5	1·3
Peru	10·0	3·7
Mexico	8·4	4·3
Central America	8·1	3·7
Ecuador	8·0	5·1
Colombia	7·3	4·1
Paraguay	7·0	n.a.
Bolivia	6·5	n.a.
Haiti	4·5	1·5
Asia		
Ceylon	7·1	5·7
Indonesia	5·6	3·8
Philippines	5·4	2·5
Thailand	5·1	5·6
Indochina	3·9	6·2
India	2·5	3·0
Oceania		
Pacific Islands	11·1	4·2

The key to understanding the response of individual countries to the export opportunity lies in the availability of additional good arable wet land that could be brought into cultivation.

This is the key because at this time there was not much willingness to switch from producing food to producing commercial export crops. Food was produced mainly by small farmers who were willing enough to produce commercial crops in addition to, but not instead of, food; their exports were, as Adam Smith said, a 'vent for surplus'.[11] We have focused on surplus land, but surplus human energy was also involved, since work was now needed on food plus export crops. Also in some cases surplus energy would suffice without surplus land, where the export crop could be grown before or after the food crop on the same land.

Apart from the small farmers there were also a number of large farmers, especially in Latin America, and some plantations, especially in the sugar colonies and Ceylon, at the beginning of our period. These seldom grew food for sale: they could switch from one export crop to another. Ceylonese plantations switched to tea and to coconuts after the coffee was destroyed by disease, and some sugar plantations in the West Indies switched to cocoa or bananas after the price of sugar collapsed. But the inflexibility of plantations was also remarkable. The fact that the value of exports from Mauritius and from the West Indies fell over the thirty-year period of Table 8.2 shows how inflexible their plantations were in holding on to a crop long after conditions had turned against it.

Water was crucial. Most of the tropical crops for which world demand was expanding are heavy users of water – especially the tree crops (coffee, cocoa, rubber, oil palm, citrus) but also the shrub and annual crops (tea, bananas, rice, maize or sugar). Hence the opportunity for development was offered not to the whole of the tropics, but more especially to the wetter regions, with rainfall exceeding say 35 inches, or else with irrigation water available. Now hundreds of millions of people live in tropical regions with less than 35 inches of rain. These regions tend to have short growing seasons which are quite wet, so they can grow any annual plant which matures quickly. They grow the hardier grains, like sorghum and millet, and they can also raise crops of cotton and peanuts. But in cotton they were competing with the depressed and segregated ex-slaves of the United States, and in peanuts they were competing with the high yields of other oilseeds grown in wetter conditions, so cotton and peanuts were not roads to fortune. Below 25 inches sorghum, peanuts and cotton cannot be grown, and only millet remains, but scores of millions of tropical people live in these conditions too.

In India people live on such lands because the better lands are occupied, but in Africa before 1880 many peoples lived on these marginal lands, although plenty of better land existed not far away. There was no pressure on the land, and in the absence of commercial exports, levels of living did not vary greatly between the wetter and the drier lands. In West Africa, for example, the Sudan savannahs were actually preferred to the forest lands, because they were healthier. Millions lived in northern territories, halfway between the desert and the forest, which yielded a good subsistence living. When at the end of the century the new crops appeared, enriching the wetter countries along the coast, a differential began to widen between per capita incomes; the difference is now as much as 5 to 1. Labour then began to migrate from north to south, some seasonally and some permanently. This migration continues to this day, although in recent years the frontier controls imposed by the new independent African governments (neither the British nor the French governments interfered with African migration) have slowed it considerably. As populations grow, the northern territories will become too overcrowded even to support subsistence, and the tensions between north and south will reach breaking point. But these problems had not yet arisen in 1913.

At that time only three tropical countries were already clearly overpopulated – Egypt, India and Java.

Egypt had been tackling its problem with large expenditures on irrigation works. Thus in the course of the 1880s and 1890s the area cultivated increased by about 10 per cent, and, thanks to double cropping, the area cropped increased by about two-thirds, or substantially more than the increase of population. Unfortunately very little was spent on new irrigation works after 1900. Thereafter population grew faster than acreage cropped. The proportion of the land devoted to cotton continued to increase, but at the expense of increased imports of food. A population crisis was at hand. Real output per head was probably stationary over the ten years before the First World War, although this was masked for the time being by the big Kondratiev increase in the price of cotton.[12]

In India at least 30 per cent of the people were already living on lands marginal to agriculture, where rainfall was low or very variable. In fact the physical problems of India were such that the option to develop by exporting tropical agricultural products applied to not more than half the country, since not more than half the people lived in areas that could hope to adopt these crops and profit by them. The principal reason why India developed more slowly than almost any other country was simply lack of water.

This is subject to two observations. First, India is a continent rather than a country; some parts developed as rapidly as anywhere else. These were the wetter regions, which could grow jute, tea or rubber; or irrigated areas, like the Punjab, which developed a large export of wheat. In the second place, more irrigation would have brought even wider development. Money was put into this, and the irrigated area rose from about 29 million acres in 1880 to 47 million acres in 1913, out of about 200 million acres under cultivation. This was quite an achievement, but a lot more was needed and possible. By 1965 the irrigated area would have reached 84 million acres, and there would still be large plans in hand. This was India's most urgent problem. According to the Census Commissioner, population and cultivated acreage grew at the same rate between 1890 and 1911, but thereafter population grew faster than cultivated acreage, and by 1951 the acreage cultivated per head had fallen by a quarter. In these circumstances even land that could have grown commercial crops for export tended to be kept for growing food, since the peasant farmer still at that time gave highest priority to producing food for his own family.[13]

Overpopulation, lack of water and lack of roads combine to explain the low level and slow growth of the Indian economy at this time. Leaving aside the question of industrialisation, to which we shall return, the crux of the matter is that the Indian peasant living in the drier half of the cultivated acreage did not acquire a rich cash crop on which to prosper. The new agricultural technology of Western Europe was not applicable in his climate, as it was in the Japanese climate, so the days of steady increases in production of food per acre were still far off. The most suitable cash crops for the drier half would have been cotton, tobacco and peanuts, which did indeed make some headway; but the first two were competing with the American ex-slaves, whose yields were also much higher, and the third was competing with West African production, so these crops were not attractive substitutes for subsistence farming. The Indian farmer is often compared with the Japanese farmer, but the comparison is false, since the Japanese farmer was much richer than the Indian in 1870. Japan was less overcrowded and had a climate more favourable to agriculture and to the new European agricultural technology. The Japanese farmer also acquired a new cash crop – the cultivation of silk. The Indian farmer was more akin to the Chinese farmer, who was even more hemmed in by overpopulation and lack of roads. For both the basic need was massive investment in irrigation and in internal transport as a background to movement out of subsistence farming.

Java was overpopulated, but the Outer Islands of Indonesia were not. However, the Dutch did not originally go to Indonesia to plant; they went as traders, and stayed to reap tribute. Their focus was therefore on Java. Some land was taken up for plantations in the Outer Islands, but the military conquests of those islands was still incomplete and Java continued in our period to be the main focus of activity. There was still empty hillside land, not suitable for rice, and this was taken for plantation tree crops. But sugar became the great plantation crop of Java, and sugar required the flatlands which the Javanese were already using for rice. Under the so-called 'Culture System', which operated from about 1830 to 1870, the villages were required by law to set aside a certain proportion of their lands for commercial crops for export, usually about one-third. For sugar this involved reducing the area in food crops, to enable the government to operate plantations. After 1870 the 'Culture System' gave way to the 'Ethical System'. This meant that the government withdrew from planting in favour of private enterprise. Private plantations were not permitted to buy the villagers' lands, but they could lease the land. A private concern would make a contract, normally for twenty-one years, giving it the right to plant one-third of the village irrigated land in cane. The planting–harvesting cycle took from eighteen to twenty-four months. At the end of this period this third would revert to rice, and another third be planted in cane; after which it would revert to rice and the next third be put into cane. Thus the Indonesian output of sugar for export grew swiftly and by 1913 sugar cane was occupying about 12 per cent of the irrigated rice lands or about 8 per cent of all rice lands. Competition for land between peasant and plantation became acute. By the Agrarian Law of 1870 the government claimed for itself all uncultivated lands. Preference was given to plantations on such lands, so the indigenous farm population increased faster than the cultivable lands available to it. Plantation production rose rapidly, with peasant production trailing far behind. This is obviously part of the economics of exploitation rather than the economics of development.[14]

China is not wholly a tropical country, but can be taken here among the overpopulated parts of the world. For Adam Smith and the classical economists China represented the extreme case of a country which has developed as far as it can go with its current institutions, and has become stagnant. It was already grossly overpopulated by the middle of the nineteenth century, and scarcely able to feed itself; hardly a year passed without a famine in some part of China or other, and major disasters claiming millions of lives came at least once a decade. There was no surplus for feeding draft animals, so human labour power was used almost exclusively. The nation had perfected the labour-intensive economy, and the world marvelled at the ingenuity with which this had been achieved.

At the economic level the analysis is simple. There were virtually no roads, so beyond the reach of the rivers people lived in isolated subsistence economies, with no chance of a cash crop. This pinpoints the failure of government, as does the fact that as late as 1913 China had acquired only 25 kilometres of railway per million inhabitants, compared with India's 180 kilometres, Japan's 200 kilometres and Brazil's 900 kilometres. Why had the country fallen so far behind? Irrigation raises the same question. Small-scale irrigation was widespread, but larger works were badly needed, as well as major works to control the disastrous floods to which the country was subject. However, such action required a vigorous government, whereas China's central government was weak and commanded only small resources. The economy was ripe for an infusion of new technology not only in making roads, in industry, irrigation or agriculture, but also in organisation and administration. But its official leaders had set their minds against new ideas and new technologies from other lands. The Japanese had tried to do the same, but had changed their minds (or had them changed) after 1854, whereas the Chinese government did not altogether give up its desire for seclusion until after the defeat by Japan in 1895.

A strong and forward-looking Chinese government, like that of Japan, could have transformed the country, by building roads, railways, large irrigation works, schools and universities, and by locating and developing its mineral resources – all of which would have been a background both for exports and for domestic manufacturing. Instead the country became the prey of aggressive foreigners, both private individuals and governments, demanding concessions and threatening and making war, while its government concerned itself mainly with defending the status quo. Professor Remer has described one of the more important deficiencies as follows:

> China had, when she met the West, a government which took no practical interest in the economic state of the country. The Chinese economy had not developed public credit, and the government was slow to avail itself of the possibilities of foreign borrowing even after it possessed, in the Chinese Maritime Customs, a revenue service under such control that it might have borrowed abroad . . . The one available means of rapid economic development under Chinese control seems to [this] student to have been the importation of foreign capital through the Chinese government. The whole weight of Chinese tradition was against this.[15]

Development does not always depend on having a strong and progressive government, but such a government is certainly a help when absence of infrastructure is a major obstacle to development, as was the situation in China.

How China and its government got into this state is an interesting question, but one that is beyond the compass of this book. It is only at the economic level that the problem of China is simple.

Such then was the situation in the overpopulated countries. Counting countries these were the exceptions, but counting heads we must note that nearly half the world's population was already living in crowded conditions (China, India, Japan, Java, Egypt, Russia), either with or without the prospect of adding substantially to the cultivated area through new investments in water or transportation. Speaking historically, the industrial revolution came early to Europe, the Americas, Africa and Australia, while their populations were still small; it came late however to Asia, where numbers had been multiplying for thousands of years. Output per head was lower, the surplus smaller, and production for bare subsistence more prevalent in the Asian economies.

8.06 The tropical countries which still had plenty of suitable land divide into those which seized the opportunity to develop, and those which did not.

The opportunity for development was available both to peasants and plantations. Peasant initiative was considerable. The rice that came pouring out of Burma, Thailand and Indochina to feed the plantation labourers, was grown by small farmers; so also was the cocoa from the Gold Coast, the cotton from Uganda, the peanuts from Nigeria and Senegal, the coffee from Colombia, and the cotton and wheat from India. Even where plantations or large farms played the leading role, small farmers usually made a substantial contribution, as in the production of Ceylon's coconuts, Latin America's coffee, Egypt's cotton, Jamaica's bananas, or Malayan and Indonesian rubber. Sugar and tea were the only two commodities the exports of which owed little to small farmer production.

The initiative which some of these small farmer communities displayed is not short of astonishing, especially in view of what has often been written about the low horizons of tropical producers. Take the case of the Burmese. In Burma the flat, wet lands of the Irrawaddy delta were largely unoccupied as late as 1870, when the rising demand for rice began to make itself felt. The British Crown claimed ownership of all empty lands, but was willing to sell at nominal prices to small settlers. So Burmese moved down from Upper Burma, squatted and cultivated, and by 1913 were exporting 2½ million tons of rice from what in 1870 had been little more than swamp.[16] The Gold Coast story is equally remarkable. The land suitable for cocoa was covered by apparently useless forest. So the Akwapim farmers (with a few Krobo, Shai and Ga) moved down from their hills, bought it, cut the trees and planted cocoa. The government was asked neither for roads nor for titles, and was indeed hardly aware that the foundations of what by 1913 was already the world's largest cocoa industry were being laid under its nose.[17]

The plantations also have some remarkable achievements to record, especially in South-East Asia, and notably in rubber, tea, oil palm, coconuts and abaca. The anomaly in studying plantations is the collapse of a number of old sugar-planting regions. The price of sugar dived steeply from 1883 – it had halved by 1913 – partly because of European government subsidies to beet sugar and partly because of rising productivity. Nevertheless output of cane sugar grew over this period at the fantastic rate of 5 per cent per year, with Cuba, Java and Hawaii in the lead. At the same time north-east Brazil, the West Indian islands and Mauritius sank into stagnation. Labour was a problem in the West Indies, since the ex-slaves shunned work on sugar plantations; but slavery had been abolished over forty years earlier, indentured labour could be had from India, while Cuba, where slavery was not abolished until 1886, attracted voluntary migration from the British islands. The puzzle is not so much the failure of the older sugar territories to adopt new sugar technologies as their failure also to find satisfactory substitutes at a time when the opportunities in tropical trade were expanding quite rapidly. There was of course some adjustment, but reference to Table 8.2 shows these territories to have the slowest growth rates – actually negative for the West Indies and Mauritius. North-east Brazil simply stagnated, its people for the most part neglecting even to migrate to the more prosperous and rapidly expanding regions of south Brazil. Taking into account the similar relative stagnation of the southern United States one may surmise that slave emancipation is a traumatic experience for an economy, after which it may go into a coma for several decades. The old ruling class, contemptuous of the ex-slave population, is preoccupied with maintaining social distance, and blocks the development of human resources. Mexico and Bolivia testify that a traumatic land reform can have the same result. On the other hand land reform in Japan, Taiwan or South Korea testifies that the experience can release a new burst of development energy, given the right countervailing effort. And the case of Cuba in the years before 1913 may support the same conclusion: left to themselves the old Cuban planters might have sunk into the same somnolence after 1886 as the Southerners, the Brazilians or the Jamaican planters; the countervailing effort was provided by the immigration of a new line of vigorous American capitalists.

The small farmers themselves could have done even better if they had been given access to vacant land. This was not much of a problem in tropical Africa. Where European settlement was occurring, large areas would be reserved for Europeans at the expense of Africans (as in Southern Africa), but there was little European settlement in tropical Africa at this time, except for small communities in Kenya and Angola: the great confrontations over land would come after the First World War. In our period land for small farmers was rather a problem of Asia and of Latin America.

The problem arose in South Asia from the competition of the plantations for vacant land. None of the governments of South Asia (British, Dutch, Spanish, French) cared particularly about small farmers. With the large reservoirs of labour available from China and India, they thought primarily in terms of promoting the plantation system. Wherever they could get away with it they claimed all vacant lands as belonging to the sovereign power, and arranged to sell or lease such lands to plantations in large blocks. The pattern was not uniform: it varied from Burma, where the government showed interest in making lands available to small farmers for growing rice; via Ceylon, where the emphasis was on plantations, but small-scale land sales were also made; to Java, where virtually all unused land was reserved to the plantations.

In Latin America the problem lay rather in ownership of the land by a very small number of private magnates, in the so-called *latifundia.* This was not universal. The coffee industry of Colombia was mainly a small farmer industry, facilitated by the ease with which small farmers could buy either private or public land. Elsewhere the large landowners varied in outlook from those holding modern economic theories to traditionalists holding land for power, status and tribute rather than for production. In Brazil a large proportion were willing to make money by having their lands planted in coffee, and although the emphasis was on coffee plantations, worked by immigrants from Southern Europe, a good deal of land also spilt over into smallholder coffee farming. At the opposite extreme were the landowners of Venezuela, whose refusal either to cultivate their lands or to rent or sell them remains something of a mystery.[18] One can of course argue that it pays a group of landowners to withhold land from cultivation so as to reduce wages and increase rent. The argument is indisputable, given the appropriate elasticities of substitution, but the question is not why the landowners behaved in this monopolistic fashion, but how they managed to bring it off, when their neighbours in Colombia and Brazil were yielding ground.

To withhold land from the peasantry, whether in Latin America or elsewhere, was not only an obstacle to their acquiring and exploiting new cash crops. It could also impoverish the peasantry in face of population growth. In the healthier and less overcrowded parts of the tropics, such as Latin America and the South-East Asian islands, the natural rate of increase was already between one and one and a half per cent per annum, doubling over say sixty years. If, as in Mexico, Java or Venezuela, the farmers were multiplying faster than the acreage they cultivated, a country could be faced with growing poverty in the midst of plenty. As in Java, the plantations might be exporting more while very many of the small farmers were eating less.

Studies of access to land therefore bring us back to the importance of governments in the development process. An essential prerequisite is their interest in infrastructure, especially at this time in the building of railways. This meant that the government must have a reputation for stability sufficient either to be able to borrow on its own credit in European capital markets, or at least to be able to give acceptable guarantees to foreign capital that might invest in railways. The Spanish government lacked this interest, thereby holding up the development of the Philippines until after 1898. Next in importance comes the government's willingness to take steps to ensure the availability of land to would-be cultivators, a condition lacking in several Latin American governments. If the government was also development-minded, and like the British government in Uganda or the Dutch government in Indonesia specifically considered the rate of growth of exports to be a test of its own efficacy, then one could expect additional measures, such as the deliberate introduction of new cotton seeds into

Uganda, of rubber into Malaya or of new varieties of sugar cane into Java, which would in most cases stimulate the growth of output.

8.07 The foregoing discussion has not distinguished between colonial and non-colonial countries. This must now be done.

Our period coincided with the extension of the colonial system to its furthest extent. By 1913 all of tropical Asia (except Thailand and China) and all of tropical Africa (except Liberia and Ethiopia) were under European or American rule. Continental Latin America, in contrast, was politically independent, except for British Honduras and the three Guianas.

There are so many different kinds of colonialism that generalisations about 'the colonial system' are usually misleading. To start with its worst effects, the imperial power may pursue policies which reduce the population by war, enslavement, forced labour in subhuman conditions, or herding people into overcrowded reserves. These were standard practices in the seventeenth and eighteenth centuries. By 1870 they had almost disappeared, with certain exceptions: the Argentinians were making war on their Indians during our period; the Germans were killing off the Herreros; the death rate of forced Congolese labourers on King Leopold's plantations was almost incredible, except that it followed the earlier precedents of Indians in Spanish American mines and Chinese in the guano fields of Peru; and the British were just starting their reservation policies in Kenya and Rhodesia. However, these instances were exceptional; by 1870 it was widely recognised that policies which reduce a colonial population are likely to be unprofitable.

There were still policies which sought to produce wealth at the expense of the native population, either by pressuring them into wage labour or withholding access to land. The former policies were much in evidence in Africa. Africans had abundant land, and did not want to work on European farms or in mines for low wages. Every device was used, from conscription of labour for private employment in the French, Belgian and Portuguese territories, to curtailing the tribal lands, prohibiting cultivation of cash crops, or imposing taxes payable only in cash – which could be obtained by working for wages – that became the preferred measures in British East and Central Africa. In such cases the economic life of African farmers was disrupted without any prospect of participating in economic expansion. Fortunately European settlement in tropical Africa was still small in our time; the worst aspects of these practices were yet to come. Access to land was the problem of Asia and Latin America where, as we have seen, it determined whether the country would be developed on a plantation or a peasant basis, or even in marginal cases like Venezuela, where it determined whether it would develop at all.

However, when all this is said, wage labour was inevitably such a small part of colonial agriculture that a government that wished to exploit a colony would hardly begin at this point, unless it was dealing with empty lands to be settled by immigration of slaves or indentured labourers. The bulk of the indigenous population were small farmers, and the traditional way of exploiting small farmers is either to tax them or to extract substantial rents. However, there was very little to tax. Asian and African farmers were producing at a subsistence level so low that years of bad weather resulted in famine. To exploit the farmers a government would first have to make them productive, which in those days meant introducing cash crops and opening up land with roads or irrigation. This colonial governments conspicuously failed to do.

To say this is not to deny that there was exploitation by traders, landowners and tax gatherers, but only to put this exploitation into quantitative perspective. It is shocking to meet a situation where half the farmer's output disappears in tributes to such persons; but even the most equitable reorganisation is unlikely to add more than 20 per cent to the farmer's income, since the real costs of distribution and of government have to be met in any system. On the other hand, the introduction of new cash crops or high yielding varieties, of water or productive technology can increase the farmer's output by 100 per cent over a short period. Whether one's object was to exploit the farmers or to enrich them the plan should have been the same: in the first place to develop their productive potential, and this was not done.

The tradition of colonial involvement, from the sixteenth century onwards, was a combination of loot and trade. By the beginning of the nineteenth century the objective of loot was losing respectability. Milestones in Britain include the impeachment of Warren Hastings between 1788 and 1795, and the emancipation from slavery between 1834 and 1838; but the Dutch continued to draw large sums in tribute from Indonesia until the ending of the Culture System in 1870. In any case, the opportunities for developing trade continued to be small until our period, when the revolution of railways and shipping combined with the expanding purchasing power of the industrial nations to create the opportunity for comparatively rapid growth. Writing of India in mid-century, Professor Jenks has the following striking passage:

> The chief economic results of the first century of British rule in India had been the ruin of the cotton manufacture in the face of Manchester competition, a diversion of labour from growing grain to the raising of opium, sugar, indigo and to a slight extent of tea, and a compulsion upon the ryot to market a larger proportion of his yearly crop in order to procure silver to pay his tribute to the government.[19]

The passage is a little misleading, since the destruction of cotton manufacture and the payment of taxes were losses, while the diversion of labour to export cash crops was a gain to the peasants, but the picture which it conveys of a neglected and somewhat abused economy is just.

The prevailing posture of colonial governments continued to be one of neglect, even after the transport revolutions had opened up new possibilities. Some critics of the colonial governments blame them for having greedily developed their colonies to be cheap sources of raw materials, but the truer and better indictment would be that after 1870 they failed even to try to develop their colonies as sources of raw materials. How could it be otherwise? The Spanish and Portugese governments were neglecting their own home territories, so it would have been odd if they had put any effort into developing their colonies. The French government was not much better in France herself; France sought colonies *pour la gloire*, rather than for the crops they could produce. France did get as far as commanding some Ivory Coast farmers to grow cocoa on their holdings for export, and conscripting others for European plantations, but these devices did not spread. The Germans were more business-oriented than the French, and paid greater lip-service to colonial economic development, but in practice it made little difference. The only three countries who took this objective seriously were Britain, the Netherlands and the USA. The Americans were the last to embark on colonialism, following their victory over Spain in 1898. Their development policy hinged on foreign plantations rather than on small farmers; but they also made a direct contribution to mass welfare in the shape of exceptionally large expenditures on education, public health and infrastructure. The Dutch had been in the business for centuries, concentrating mainly on monopoly profits from trading. After 1870 their development policy also hinged on foreign plantations rather than on small farmers; but in contrast with the Americans, expenditures on mass welfare were conspicuous by their absence. The British left policy so largely to 'the man on the spot' that it varied from one extreme to the other. If the imperial powers had set out to develop their colonies as sources of raw materials, vigorously and consistently, output per head would have been significantly higher in 1913.

In general, it is not possible to say how much difference colonial status made to the rate of economic growth. Several countries which became colonies after 1870 grew faster after colonisation than before, and only one (the Congo) actually experienced a decline. But since practically all countries, colonies or not, did better after 1870 than before (except the core and the sugar colonies) this proves nothing.

There is one area where colonial status was definitely an obstacle, namely industrialisation. It would clearly have been in the interest of the imperial governments to have developed the agricultural and mineral potential of their colonies, whereas they conceived it to be in their interest to prevent colonial industrial development. We shall meet examples of this in India. Even this policy, as the Indian case also testifies, was not well articulated or vigorously applied, and in the event was not wholly effective. It was also not the only reason why colonial industrial development lagged: industrial development also lagged over most of self-governing Europe and self-governing Latin America. But it certainly was an additional hindrance in the colonial countries.

Leaving aside industrialisation, which in much of Africa and Asia would still only have been a marginal issue, after 1870 most colonial governments have to be faulted for what they failed to do rather than for what they did. But apart from government policies, much argument about the impact of the colonial system must centre on its socio-psychological effects. To an anthropologist the most important negative aspect would be the disruption of existing social systems, which continued into the twentieth century. The mere arrival of a foreign power imposing its will and its strange ways upon the social system could stunt social development, or even cause distintegration and backward tendencies. Hence the colonial system itself appears as essentially sterile and destructive of development potential. On this view the native capacity of Asian and African societies to respond to new development opportunities was reduced by the shock of colonial subjugation.

This kind of argument has to be taken seriously. Societies do go into shock; we have just noted the stagnation of ex-slave economies at the end of the nineteenth century. However, one must distinguish between what may happen and what is inevitable. Culture contact does not always bring distintegration; sometimes, as in Japan after 1854, it heralds unprecedented efflorescence. The effect of colonialism must to some extent have depended on the character of the colonial power, how it treated its subjects, and what new opportunities it opened up for them. Some ancient cultures were stagnating, and had become obstacles to further progress; while others may have lost more than they gained.

One must also not be trapped by the tendency to idealise pre-colonial cultures, and to assume that if untouched by foreigners they would have remained forever pure, or would of their own necessarily have evolved in worthy directions. Eighteenth-century societies – whether European, African, Asian or Latin American – are not worth much shedding of tears. What we value most today – the legal and political rights of the common man, pure water supplies, schools for everybody, low infant mortality, absence of famine and so on – were not known anywhere in the world at the end of the eighteenth century. Modernisation does not begin in earnest anywhere until the nineteenth century. The question whether the impact of imperialism on existing social structures helped or hindered modernisation is valid in its own right without commitment to pre-imperialist nostalgia.

Now modernisation has to have a vehicle. Like most inventions it begins in one corner of the globe, and though simultaneous invention in several places is not impossible, diffusion by migration is more common. Diffusion takes time. The normal agents are traders, religious missionaries and soldiers. All these participated in the colonial movement.

If we limit ourselves to events since 1870, probably the most important negative effect of the colonial system was to hinder the development of a native modernising cadre. The backwardness of the less developed countries of 1870 could be changed only by people prepared to alter certain customs, laws and institutions, and to shift the balance of political and economic power away from the old landowning and aristocratic classes. But the imperial powers for the most part allied themselves with the existing power blocs. They were especially hostile to educated young people, whom, by means of a colour bar, they usually kept out of positions where administrative experience might be gained, whether in the public service or in private business. Such people, they then said, could not be employed in superior positions because they lacked managerial experience, as well as the kind of cultural background in which managerial competence flourishes. One result of this was to divert into long and bitter anti-colonial struggles much brilliant talent which could have been used creatively in development sectors. Another result was to implant an inferiority complex which still today prevents some leaders of newly independent countries from achieving their full potential. After the First World War it became fashionable for imperial powers to say that they were holding their colonies in training for self-government. This was not true; but even to make such a statement represented a slight change of attitude.

If the tropical countries had been self-governing in our period some of them would have modernised faster. We cannot be sure how many or how much faster, because the performance of the self-governing less developed countries, whether in Europe, Latin America or elsewhere, was so mixed, varying from vigorous to stagnant. If we divide the world into (a) core and periphery, (b) imperialist and non-imperialist or (c) fast and slow developers, these three divisions do not coincide. The two major imperialists of the core, Britain and France, were the slowest developers in Western Europe, at any rate after 1870. The periphery included five empires or colonial powers (Spain, Portugal, Austria, Russia and Turkey) as well as numerous self-governing countries and colonies. Portugal and Turkey which were empires, did not grow faster than Thailand, Venezuela or Greece, which were self-governing, and which in turn did not do better than Burma or Uganda, which were colonies.

The missing factor in all the slow developers of our period, whether in Europe, Asia or elsewhere, was the modernising cadre. This takes time to emerge and assume economic and political power. Such people had begun to share power in North-West Europe by the beginning of the nineteenth century, but would not seize control in Eastern Europe for another hundred years, or in Latin America for a further fifty years after that. Colonialism could have speeded up this process in Africa and Asia, since the imperial governments had the power to speed up the modernisation of their colonies if they so desired. There were some positive results in the better colonies – schools, the introduction of scientific technologies, modernisation of legal systems, strengthening of administrative structures, and so on. But for the most part colonialism was an additional obstacle to modernisation, not merely because of the prevailing attitude of neglect, but also because of the preference of the imperial powers for backing and ruling through the existing hierarchies – princely, landowning or religious – at the expense of emerging liberals or radicals. We cannot say just how much difference colonialism made; modernisation would have taken many decades even without it. The relatively poor performances of the Latin American and South and East European countries are a constant reminder that colonialism is only one of the many political, social and environmental factors which determine the rate of development. It cannot carry the whole weight of explaining why some countries did better than others, and its importance varies widely from one territory to another. With or without colonialism, modernisation, being a slow social process, was bound to have taken a considerable time.

TROPICAL DEVELOPMENT

8.08 If we look simply at growth rates, the response of countries which both had empty lands and made them available is remarkable. As we have seen before, between 1883 and 1913 core industrial production grew by 3·4 per cent per annum. World trade and trade of tropical countries both grew at 3·4 per cent in current prices, or about 3·8 per cent in volume. If we take as the top fliers from Table 8.2 those countries whose exports grew by more than 4·0 per cent per annum in current prices, the list includes

West Africa (British and French), Madagascar, Brazil, Mexico, Ecuador, Colombia, Ceylon, Thailand, Indochina and the Pacific Islands; Burma would also feature if we could separate out its exports of rice to India. The rest were short of land (Egypt, India, Java); failed to open up their lands (East and Central Africa, Venezuela, Peru, Central America, Philippines), or were caught in the collapse of sugar (Mauritius and the Caribbean islands).

Reliable national income figures do not exist for this period, but there is no doubt that income per head was raised by exports. For the tropics as a whole food supply kept pace with population growth, while exports increased by 3·5 to 4 per cent per annum in terms of real purchasing power.

This remarkable result was due neither to use of more productive techniques nor to a shift of labour from less to more remunerative occupations. For the most part it was due to bringing idle resources into production – idle land, idle time of farmers, and the services of the disguised unemployed of India and China transported to plantations. The mercantilists had always maintained that the crucial problem in development was to mobilise idle resources, and results in our period bore them out.

The role of idle resources is important in view of the low factoral terms of trade. As we pointed out at the end of Chapter 7, although these factoral terms were based on Asian productivity levels, they were superior to these levels, since there would otherwise have been no incentive to transport Indian and Chinese labour around the globe. They were only a fraction of the factoral terms available to the new temperate settlements, but were high enough for tropical countries to be able to improve their condition by exporting, if they had wet lands. The existence of surplus land and labour time added another dimension to the opportunity to trade. So although national incomes per head were low, the opportunities for growth were quite substantial.

In the tropical countries at the top of the growth list, national income must have been growing as fast or faster than in Britain or France per head of population at this time (1·0 to 1·5 per cent per annum) and faster than in much of Central and South-East Europe. This must have been the case for say Ceylon, Burma, Thailand, Malaya or Gold Coast, and was certainly true of the developing regions of many other countries, such as Colombia or Mexico. Celso Furtado reaches the same conclusion for Brazil, and although this is in dispute for the average of the country as a whole, it cannot be disputed for southern Brazil.[20] Even India as a whole seems to have grown by an annual average of about one per cent per head over the fifteen years before the First World War, after a bad patch in the 1890s, and the growth rate was naturally much higher in those regions of the country where the response was concentrated – especially the irrigated parts of the Punjab, the jute cultivating and manufacturing regions of Bengal, the Assam tea area, Bombay and the region supplying its mills with cotton. If India were carved into countries of Latin American size, we would find several that matched Latin American or South-East Asian performances. What holds down the Indian average is the large population that continued to live at subsistence level on inadequately watered marginal lands, without a profitable cash crop.[21]

Of course the results were spread very unevenly, even inside the countries that did well. Most of the farmers had no cash crop, and benefited little if at all from the spread of the market economy. Wage earners may have done a little better, especially the Chinese and Indian migrants, removed from dire poverty in their own countries. But development has to proceed quite far before it creates a shortage of labour and raises wages. Apart from the few farmers and wage earners producing directly for export, benefits to the masses would come from expansion of the public services (schools, roads, water supplies, public health) which were still meagre in 1913. Presumably the biggest beneficiaries would as usual be traders, bankers, civil servants and other members of the burgeoning middle class. Some part of the proceeds would also go abroad as profits and remittances, especially from the plantation economies, although the extent of this is frequently exaggerated. Economic development begins by strengthening the middle of the social hierarchy, and except where it originates in new small farmer cash crops takes some time to reach down to the bottom. This can of course be remedied to some extent by government action, but action of this sort was not yet on the agenda of governments in the period that we are studying.

8.09 The growth of national income through exporting offered to the tropical countries the opportunity to strengthen their infrastructure, increase productivity in food, and move towards industrialisation for home and export markets. Just as they varied in their response to the expansion of world trade, so also there were wide variations in the use that was made of the proceeds.

At the start of our period these countries all lacked the basic foundations for modern economic development. In infrastructure it was not merely that they lacked railways; they had also been by-passed by the revolutions in road and canal building which had already for a century been the support of thriving internal markets in Western Europe and North America. Their framework of public services was rudimentary; their governments did little but maintain law and order, and that with varying degrees of success. Rates of illiteracy were seldom less than 90 per cent. They had a long way to go towards modernisation.

Thus the best use of the money gained from exporting would be to spend as much of it as possible on creating physical, social and human infrastructure: railways, roads, harbours, administrative networks, courts, markets, banks, hospitals, schools and water supplies. The development of the tropical countries can best be ranked according to how well they met this test.

On the whole the countries which were growing fast met it quite well, while those at the bottom of the list had less to spend on public services and spent even less than they could have afforded. The improvement in infrastructure was substantial. Transportation improved most, but the whole range of public services was affected. Public administration was strengthened, and internal peace was generalised. Towns as usual received the lion's share, with rapid expansion of houses, water supplies, hospitals and schools. A whole new range of economic institutions came into existence – shops, banks, insurance companies, joint stock companies and new commercial codes. The average tropical town of 1870 was already unrecognisable in 1913.

Where most governments fell down was in neglecting education. Ceylon, with one-third of its children in school in 1913, must have been at or near the top of the list for tropical countries. These were not days when men gave high priority to mass primary education. From the point of view of development it is perhaps more important to have an adequate outflow from the secondary schools to man managerial and administrative positions. Here the record was better; though deplorable in Africa and Indonesia, it was not all bad, by contemporary standards, in Colombia, India, Ceylon and southern Brazil. Since the creation of a modernising cadre is a first step in economic development, one can still today see the difference in development capacity between those tropical countries which had already in 1913 a good supply of secondary schools, and those which had not. In Asia and Africa the colour bar in employment was a major obstacle, since it limited the experience of talented people, and was a constraint on the development of administrative capacity. This was inherent in all the colonial régimes, as also in Latin America, though some régimes were worse than others.

Over and above the constraint of money the low horizons of tropical governments acted as another constraint at this time. Whether self-governing or colonial, very few conceived of their responsibilities in modern terms. The best of them were certainly interested in improving transportation, and perhaps also urban water supplies, and to a lesser extent education. All they wanted to do could be done for 4 or 5 per cent of the national income or less. In this they were behind the more advanced nations of Western Europe or North America, but at that time even the more advanced nations were spending less than 10 per cent of national income, in contrast with the 20 to 30 per cent which they now spend on public services. Ideas about what governments ought to do have changed along with everything else: the performances of 1900 should not be tested by the standards of 1970.

8.10 Everything we have said about the rapid growth of some tropical countries remains subject to the limitation that they could not move up into a European standard of living by exporting tropical products, since the factoral terms of trade were set by the low food productivity of tropical farmers. The terms of trade yielded enough superior income to permit these countries to lay the foundations of modernisation, especially of physical infrastructure and human skills, but if they were to reach European standards they would still have to follow the European route, of modernising their food production and industrialising.

Limited though the home market was by the poverty of food producers, there was still scope for industrialisation to substitute for imports coming in. Failure to take advantage of this would reduce the benefit of exporting primary products, by keeping the export multiplier low. In countries which already had a significant industrial sector the result of successful exporting was an influx of cheap cottons and metalwares which set back the domestic production, so the rise in exports would be partly offset by a declining output of manufactures. McGreevey has described the impact in Colombia.[22] The full benefit of trading would therefore accrue only if, as in the Indian cotton industry, the new technology was now incorporated into the industrial structure.

In addition, the domestic market for manufactures could be supplemented by developing an export of manufactured products to the industrial nations and others. For the same element that kept their domestic market small (low income and wage levels) should also have kept their manufacturing costs low and given them the edge in exporting manufactures. It is true that the industrial nations were protecting their home markets. Nevertheless their imports of manufactures were growing by 3 to 4 per cent a year, and one of their leading members, Great Britain, had no tariffs. Moreover the competition need not be confined to the markets of the core countries, since it was possible to compete on equal terms with the core in the markets of third countries.

This challenge was not altogether neglected. By 1913 India was producing two-thirds of her domestic consumption of cotton yarn and half of her domestic consumption of cotton cloth, and was now also exporting as much cotton yarn as Great Britain. Her other big industry was jute manufacture which had caught up and passed the output of Dundee; her large-scale industry was growing as fast as Germany's (4 to 5 per cent), but slower than Japan's (7 to 8 per cent), and her handicraft industries, employing about 9 per cent of the labour force, were holding their own in the economy and expanding at about the same rate as the population.[23] The weak spot was in iron and steel, and the main cause of this weakness was the opposition of the British government.

Government policy was crucial in iron and steel since the government was the largest buyer, to meet its requirements for railways, irrigation facilities, public buildings, ordnance factories and so on. Until 1875 the Indian government bought its supplies only in Britain, so Indian manufactures stood no chance in the market. The policy was thereafter gradually eroded, but the final restrictions on Indian government purchase of Indian manufactures did not disappear until 1914.

Thus when an English group built the first modern blast furnace in India in 1875, it was important to secure Indian government contracts, and the company sought a long-term understanding. The government would not co-operate. It bought a little iron from time to time, but not enough to keep the factory going. When Lord Ripon became Governor General in 1880 he bought the plant intending to develop it, but the government in London would not permit him to do so. It took thirty years for London to abandon this policy, and agree to give the Tata brothers the contract which became the basis of the plant which they opened in 1912.[24]

Another impressive performer was Brazil which by 1913 was producing more than three-quarters of its consumption of cotton manufactures. In this it was matched by Mexico. What handicapped Brazil was lack of coking coal, which prevented it from using its iron ore deposits as a basis for a large iron and steel industry. Nowadays an iron industry can be based on imported coal; but in those days the much greater requirement of coal per ton of iron made that proposition uneconomic. Alternatively, iron and steel can be imported for fabrication into metalwares and machines, but if this industry has only a domestic market, it is confined to the types of commodities that can be produced economically on a small scale. Holland or Switzerland can use imported steel as the base for industries fabricating for export, but their customers are next door. If Brazil had had the right kind of coal, it would by 1913 probably have been well on the way to becoming a major industrial power.

Iron and steel was a difficult industry to start, requiring local materials, high-level technology, and a fairly large market. Cotton manufacture was easier. The fine counts and high-quality fabrics were left to Lancashire, but the mass demand was for the cheaper materials, where Lancashire had no advantage. Indians not only mobilised their own capital resources, but organised and managed their enterprises with relatively little European help. Moreover the industry was started without tariff protection, in full competition with Lancashire, and when the British government insisted that excise taxes be imposed on it equal to customs duties imposed for revenue purposes on cotton imports, the industry took this in its stride. The fact that India's cotton and jute industries were competing successfully in foreign markets testifies that the low-wage economy should be able to develop through manufacturing, at least for its domestic market, but also for export. If further testimony were required it is supplied by Japan.

Other countries as usual varied in their responses. We do not have much data for value added in manufacturing, but for some of these countries we have data for the ratio of the industrial population (manufacturing, mining and building) to labour force. This is shown in Table 8.3, which also includes certain European and other countries for the purpose of comparison.

The data of Table 8.3 are not strictly comparable. In the first place, the size of the labour force varies with the extent to which farmers' wives are included or excluded. Secondly, the size of the industrial population depends on where the census draws the line in deciding whether to count as a farmer or a manufacturer a person who does both; presumably the low figure for Indonesia ignores the large amount of manufacturing which farmers and their families were performing in addition to agriculture. And thirdly, the industrial figure adds together handicraft workers and persons working in capital-intensive factories; for example in Table 7.1 value added per inhabitant is six times as high in Japan as in India, whereas in Table 8.3 the labour force ratio is only 1·3. Nevertheless, when all is said, Table 8.3 does indicate widespread failure of achievement. We cannot expect all other countries to have done as well as Japan. It is true that Japan was one of the latest to enter into world trade, but the country had coal, and launched an iron industry immediately. Nevertheless, the Japanese government also had a powerful urge to industrialise, which accounts for much of the difference.

There was some manufacturing everywhere, in industries which are market related like food processing, furniture and some building materials. The 'frontier' industry, testing competitive power, was cotton manufacture, especially of cheaper and medium yarns and fabrics. Among the countries moving up to self-sufficiency in cottons were Colombia, Mexico and Ceylon.

Table 8.3 *Ratio of Industrial Population to Labour Force*[25]

Developed	%	*LDC Europe*	%	*LDC Other*	%
France (1911)	31·9	Austria (1911)	21·4	Japan (1910)	16·4
Australia (1911)	28·4	Hungary (1910)	16·7	Brazil (1920)	13·0
Sweden (1910)	25·1	Greece (1920)	15·7	India (1911)	12·2
Denmark (1911)	24·2	Spain (1910)	13·8	Mexico (1910)	11·6
		Yugoslavia (1920)	11·0	Egypt (1907)	10·7
		Finland (1910)	10·6	Ceylon (1911)	10·5
		Poland (1921)	8·7	Indonesia (1905)	3·8
		Bulgaria (1910)	8·0		
		Romania (1913)	7·8		

At the other end possibly the oddest case is Egypt, at this time one of the most prosperous tropical countries, which nevertheless failed to produce a single industrialist from its rich landowning and merchant classes. It is true that Lord Cromer, again on instructions from London, imposed from 1901 excise duties on local manufacture equal to customs duties on imports, but as we have seen from the Indian case, cotton manufacturing could manage without protection. Other countries which had little industrialisation to show included Venezuela, Peru and Thailand.

Over all, the record of industrialisation is poor. We must not expect too much, because the agricultural surplus was small. Moreover the colonial territories, especially India, were hobbled by their rulers. But Latin America especially was ripe for import substitution, and could have done better. The failure in cotton textiles is particularly marked, except for Mexico and Brazil. This can be seen from the following estimates of the number of spindles per million inhabitants in 1911:[26]

Mexico	47,780	Guatemala	2,860
Brazil	40,650	Ecuador	2,500
Peru	11,610	Chile	1,390
Venezuela	3,930	Argentina	1,170
Colombia	3,640		

By way of comparison, at that time Japan had 46,820 and Germany had 172,360 spindles per million inhabitants.

We can see a number of reasons for this lag in industrialisation. The most important derive from success in exporting primary products. This success creates a demand for manufactures, and therefore should stimulate domestic manufacturing, but it may also have the opposite effect.

To begin with, success in exporting orientates an economy towards dependence on foreign commodities, institutions and ideas, giving it an unnecessarily high propensity to import, and reducing the opportunity to grow by exploiting local resources and familiar techniques. The economy thus becomes unbalanced, and is driven by its own momentum into greater over-specialisation. This line of argument has had its supporters for a very long time – at least since the Mercantilists – and was at the heart of Frederich List's *System of National Economy*, published in 1841, which became the bible of all industrialising countries in the nineteenth century, except Great Britain. It has flourished and put out many branches in the recent writings of Latin American and other Third World economists, some of whom view significant participation in international trade in raw materials as an obstacle rather than a stimulus to industrial development.[27]

The tendency to over-specialisation in primary production was aggravated in the tropical countries by the extent to which their import and export trades fell into the hands of foreign merchants. The tropical investment that earned the highest profits was that deployed in the network of wholesaling, banking, shipping and insurance. Railway, plantation, mining and manufacturing profits were much more volatile and risky. Profits are a major source of funds for reinvestment. If trading profits had been more in domestic hands there would have been more domestic reinvestment, and almost certainly more interest in developing domestic manufacturing. Foreigners played a major role in wholesale trade in all three continents, and their negative effect was even greater in Asia and in Africa than in Latin America, where there was a greater tendency for the foreigners to decide to settle permanently and become naturalised.

The reasons for the heavy participation of foreigners in trade are partly economic, partly cultural and partly political. On the economic side there was advantage in large-scale operations because of the riskiness of trading, and the ease with which small operators could be wiped out by a bad season. The trade therefore tended to concentrate in the hands of a few large enterprises. On the cultural side, Europeans had been running big shipping and trading enterprises since the seventeenth century; in this, as also in banking and insurance, they had a considerable lead over Latin Americans and Africans, though not over Chinese or Indians. The skills could be acquired – they were being learnt for example by some Brazilians, Egyptians and Yorubas – but even where there was no political interference, dislodging the foreigners was very difficult (as was found in Brazil). The political factor was a further complication, certain imperial governments deliberately favouring their nationals at the expense both of indigenous and other foreign competitors. Whatever the reason (and the mix of reasons varied from place to place) the businesses where profits were greatest (wholesaling, banking, shipping, insurance) tended to be in foreign hands, and this certainly diminished the availability of funds and enterprise for investment in domestic manufacturing.

List had a remedy: the government should throw itself on the side of industrialisation, by raising tariffs behind whose protection infant industries might grow to competitive strength. This solution, however, presupposes that the industrial party has captured the government. But the very fact of the country's success in exporting will have created a vested interest of all those who live by primary production – small farmers no less than big capitalists – who oppose measures for industrialisation, either because they may deflect resources from agriculture and raise factor prices, or because they may result in raising the prices of manufactured goods. The outcome therefore depends on the relative political strengths of the industrial and the agricultural interests.

It is not to be supposed that in this confrontation the entrenched agricultural forces will always win. On the contrary, they lost over most of

Europe and in most of the temperate countries of recent settlement, so their long-continued power in Latin America (not broken until the 1930s) has to be explained in terms peculiar to that region rather than in terms of a general theory of economic development. At issue is the degree to which in the various countries there emerged a modernising cadre, fired by economic nationalism to promote and protect industrial enterprises. There was much variation in this, with Brazil strikingly advanced in relation to its relative poverty, and Argentina strikingly backward in relation to its relative riches. We shall not have reached the heart of industrial retardation until we understand these political differences, but this interesting sphere we must leave to the political historians.

8.11 Poor performance in industrialisation, however, is not the whole story, for this does not negate the relatively high growth rates of agricultural production and trade that we have already recorded. Taken as a whole, tropical trade was growing as fast as core industrial production, and in those tropical countries which took advantage of this, output per head was growing as rapidly as in Western Europe. This is a remarkable achievement.

There were also failures. Some countries, like the sugar colonies, or the countries of Sahelian Africa, did poorly. In all countries growth was unbalanced, and some sectors were unduly underdeveloped, notably manufacturing and education. Income distribution became more unequal, since some people benefited while others did not. In general, the export trade benefited areas with valuable minerals or adequate rain; so within the same countries regional disparities widened, in line with differences in natural resources. More of the proceeds 'trickled down' when the export crop was grown by peasants than when it was grown on plantations; but even a peasant industry attracted traders, money lenders and tax collectors who gave back less than they received. Plantation economies also involved an external drain – of dividends to investors and of remittances to the families of indentured labourers. To say that a country has had a high growth rate is not to imply that it has suddenly become a social paradise.

Nevertheless the achievement, such as it was, extends beyond mere high growth rates of national income. What matters in a developing economy is to lay the foundations of future growth. What the best of the tropical countries did was to use the expansion of world trade as an opportunity to modernise; to give themselves railways, roads, harbours, water supplies; to build towns, schools, hospitals; to cultivate a professional and trading middle class; to improve their economic, legal and political institutions, and to establish new ones in the process. These were the bases for further growth, and it is in these terms rather than the figures of current production, that one must compare and assess their achievements.

In the thirty years since the Second World War we have become accustomed to seeing some tropical countries growing by 2 to 3 per cent per head, thus matching European and North American performance. This took the world by surprise, and was therefore assumed to be quite new. But it was only the resumption of a phenomenon which had already begun in the 1880s, and had lasted until the outbreak of war in 1914. With that war the tropics went into hibernation. The terms of trade moved against them in the twenties, the great depression of the thirties impoverished them, and in the forties they were isolated by the Second World War. Thirty-five years of slow or zero development is long enough for the world to forget what has happened before, and to take it for granted that nothing has happened before.

Chapter 9

Epilogue

SYNOPSIS: 9.00 This final chapter pursues some themes of tropical development beyond the year 1913.

9.01 The modest progress which some tropical countries were achieving before 1913 was interrupted by the disorder of world trade from 1913 to 1948.

9.02 After 1948 industrial countries grew at unprecedented rates and experienced labour shortages. They now became willing to import manufactures from low-wage countries, and manufactures became the fastest growing sector of tropical exports.

9.03 Production and trade of the tropical countries also grew faster than ever; but the commodity terms of trade moved against tropical countries. 9.04 Access to foreign capital was also revived, and tropical countries borrowed heavily. 9.05 However, their greatest problem has been explosion of population, which has caused heavy migration to cities and multiplication of slums and urban unemployment. 9.06 The population explosion has also impoverished those hundreds of millions of farmers who live on marginal lands, even while farmers on wet lands have been prospering.

9.07 The opportunity to trade is useful, but the fundamental challenge is to have one's own agricultural and industrial revolutions which raise output per head continually.

9.00 In this final chapter we pursue some themes which extend beyond our period 1870 to 1913.

THE GREATEST DEPRESSION 1913–48

9.01 We have seen that a number of tropical economies began to grow quite rapidly by contemporary standards during the three or four decades before the First World War. If they had maintained the growth rates achieved then, they would by 1950 have been unrecognisably affluent. Instead, most tropical countries were not significantly wealthier (in output per head) in 1950 than they had been in 1913.

The intervening three and a half decades were for the tropics a period of disaster. First there was the First World War, culminating in the great slump of 1920. Then in the 1920s the terms of trade moved against tropical products. Then came the great depression of the 1930s with sharp curtailment of demand and even more adverse terms of trade.[1] Finally there came the Second World War.

Table 9.1 records the quantity of tropical exports at constant prices of 1913, for various peak years between 1883 and 1937, and for 1955 and 1965. There are many points of interest in this table including the continual growth in the relative importance of minerals, and the marked upsurge

Table 9.1 *Exports from Tropical Countries at 1913 Prices ($m.)*[2]

	Minerals (incl. gold)	*Manufactures*	*Agricultural*	*Total*
1883	58	38	841	937
1913	365	274	2,130	2,769
1929	927	306	3,327	4,560
1937	1,134	253	3,919	5,306
1955	1,784	379	4,641	6,804
1965	2,848	893	6,728	10,469

of exports of manufactures since the Second World War. But our present interest is in the deceleration of the rates of growth. Thus the growth rates per cent per year of total exports were as follows:

1883–1913	3·7
1913–29	3·2
1929–37	1·9
1937–55	1·4
1955–65	4·4

The constant deterioration after 1913 is not reversed until after 1955.

The First World War set back European industrial production by several years, so the average rate of growth from 1913 to 1929 was well below that from 1883 to 1913. We give below the growth rates of industrial production for Western Europe and North America together,[3] and also the growth rates of tropical agricultural exports.

	Developed industrial production	*Tropical agricultural exports*
1883–1913	3·6	3·1
1913–29	2·7	2·8
1929–37	1·3	2·1
1937–55	3·7	0·9
1955–65	4·5	3·8

From the first column one may calculate that the war cost four and a half years of industrial growth, in the sense that the level attained in 1929 would have been passed in 1925 if the average growth rate of 1883 to 1913 had been maintained. The check to tropical development was not as great as the check to European industrialisation, so the terms of trade moved against tropical products in the 1920s. This can be seen in Chart 9.1,[4] where the average terms of trade price against manufactures is 7 per cent lower over the period 1920–9 than over the period 1871–1913.

The downward movement was even more violent in the 1930s, although not quite as violent as appears in the chart, which has not been adjusted for changes in freight rates. Our table of growth rates shows the reason why prices fell so much. From 1883 to 1913 industrial production grew about 10 per cent faster than tropical agricultural exports, whereas from 1929 to 1937 agricultural exports were growing much faster than industrial production (2·1; 1·3). Prices of export crops fell even more than the price of food to which, in the long run, they are closely tied because of the possibility of switching tropical land and labour from one to the other, according to relative profitability.[5]

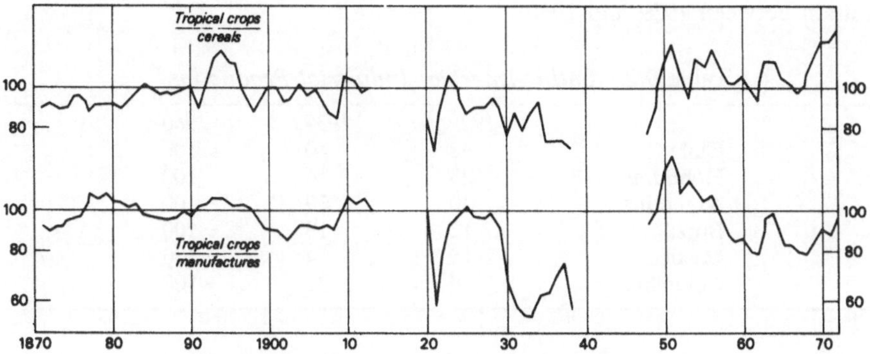

Chart 9.1 Terms of Trade of Tropical Crops

By the middle 1930s tropical development had come to a standstill. Private investment had ceased. Governments had cut back their budgets on education and welfare services, and with international investment paralysed, infrastructure could not be expanded.

The effects of this standstill persisted until well after the end of the Second World War. The growth rate of industrial production in Western Europe and North America was 3·7 per cent per annum between 1937 and 1955, but that of tropical agricultural exports was lower than ever, at 0·9 per cent per annum, well below the rate of population growth. That output was still so low some ten years after the war is not surprising, since many tropical trees take five years or more to bear. The terms of trade now swung back, and were unusually favourable in the first half of the 1950s. Thereafter they dropped back in the 1960s to below the level of the 1920s, which were themselves below the 1913 level.

This prolonged depression had only one redeeming factor: it gave a push to industrialisation in some countries of Latin America. The combination of low export earnings, adverse terms of trade and a debt burden rising sharply in real terms, left the tropical countries in general with little to spend on imports. Countries which then remained on the gold standard, without special protective measures, were subjected to a downward spiral, as the multiplier adjusted imports to exports via national income. The British colonies, for example, took heavy punishment, in comparison with those independent countries that rode the storm by devaluing their currencies or erecting barriers to imports.

In Table 9.2 we list those Latin American countries for which the relevant data are available, ranked according to the rate of growth of industrial production between 1929 and 1939. Colombia achieved 9·0 per cent per annum, Mexico 4·8, and Brazil 4·7 per cent per annum over these ten years. These three countries all maintained high growth rates up to the terminal date of the table (1960), by which time the other three countries had also emerged, the slowest (Chile) attaining a growth rate of 4·4 per cent per annum between 1939 and 1960.

Table 9.2 *Latin America: Industrial Production*[6]

	1929	*1939*	*1960*
Chile	38	40	100
Honduras	23	26	100
Argentina	30	39	100
Brazil	12	19	100
Mexico	15	24	100
Colombia	9	21	100

This long depression now forced the tropical countries to face up to the dangers of relying excessively on exporting primary products, while neglecting the domestic manufacturing opportunity at home. We pointed out in Chapter 8 that the political power of exporting interests was one of the obstacles to industrialisation. This power was broken by the experience of the years 1913–48. From 1950 onwards industrialisation has received the highest priority in all developing countries. As usual, there was overreaction. Many Third World economists concluded from the experience of the 1930s that international trade itself was finished, and would never again grow as rapidly as it had done before 1913. When after 1950 international trade actually grew more than twice as fast as it had been growing before 1913 they were unprepared for some of the opportunities which now returned to the tropical countries, and took some time to adjust their sights.

THE END OF DUALISM?

9.02 The most important new opportunity opening up to the tropical world after the Second World War was the unprecedentedly rapid growth of world trade in manufactures, associated with the decision of the leading industrial countries to reduce to very low levels their tariffs and other barriers to imports of manufactures. The volume of world trade in manufactures, which had grown at 3·5 per cent per annum between 1883 and 1913 now grew at 8·7 per cent per annum between 1957 and 1969.[7] Of special importance was the new willingness of industrial countries to import the kinds of goods that low-wage countries could manufacture cheaply because of their relatively large unskilled labour content. Previously such goods had been subjected to particularly high trade barriers.

This willingness to import manufactures from low-wage countries derives from structural changes inside the industrial nations themselves, of which we should now take note.

The analysis has to begin with the structure of the labour market. In pure models of the market economy labour of equal competence receives equal wages in all industries or occupations. This is not so in the real world, where there are protected jobs and low-wage jobs. Sometimes the difference exists between industries; unskilled labour is paid more, for example, in the motor industry than in the hospital industry. Sometimes it exists between occupations; some kinds of skilled workers, such as printers, are able to keep their wages much higher than those of persons in other occupations requiring the same degree of learning ability. Sometimes it exists between people of different races, sexes or religions. Sometimes the difference occurs even in the same industry and occupation, between employees in large-scale capital-intensive firms and employees in small labour-intensive workshops; Japan is usually cited to illustrate this.

We call this a 'dual' or 'two-sector' labour market because the natural tendency of a market economy to reach an equilibrium in which equal competence receives equal wages is arrested. Employers of workers in protected jobs would no doubt prefer to be hiring at lower wages from the low-wage sector, but they are prohibited from doing so by trade unions, by the racial, religious or sexist prejudices of some of their irreplaceable staff, by legislation, or even merely by custom.

In an economy which is developing sufficiently rapidly the number of protected jobs, especially in manufacturing and in high-level services, grows faster than the labour force. So people are recruited into the high-wage sector from or at the expense of the low-wage sector. This puts pressure on the low-wage market, creating a shortage of unskilled labour and threatening to raise wages.

The industrial countries did not run into a shortage of unskilled labour before 1913 for a number of reasons. First, industrialisation undermined the handicraft workers and threw them on to the unskilled labour market. Secondly, the fact that agricultural productivity rose faster than consumption diverted agricultural labour to urban industries. Thirdly, there was a great reservoir of labour in domestic service. Fourthly, housewives began to move into the labour market. And fifthly, there was rapid population growth, at over one per cent per annum. In these ways the low-wage sector of the economy was continually replenished.

The inter-war years were years of heavy unemployment. It was not therefore until after 1950 that this structural change began to occur in the leading industrial nations.

This had two elements: unprecedentedly rapid growth of industry and of highly paid services, and near-zero population growth. The first caused rapid expansion of the number of protected jobs. The second ended the ultimate domestic source of recruitment for low-wage jobs. As pressure mounted, the various reservoirs of low-wage labour were drained. The agricultural labour force declined swiftly. There were fewer small shopkeepers and trucking firms. Western Europe ran short of nurses, policemen, bus conductors, unskilled factory workers, and unskilled service workers (hotel staff, hospital staff, domestic workers). In the United States in 1890 only 3 per cent of white married women living with their husbands also had jobs in the labour market; by 1960 this proportion had risen to 35 per cent. But the labour market was still tight.

The economic system reacts to this situation in one of four ways: mechanising or reorganising the low-wage jobs, immigration of unskilled workers, investment in low-wage countries, or narrowing the differentials between the protected and the low-wage sector.

The drive to free labour by mechanisation or reorganisation is intensified – it is a natural reaction of any industry which is short of labour. So in recent years mechanisation has speeded up in agriculture, coal mining and construction; small enterprises and workshops which multiplied in the early stages of industrialisation now fall by the wayside unless they can raise the capital and the volume of business for the machines which substitute for labour; offices have moved to computerisation, shops and restaurants to self-service; the time of housewives is released by washing machines, dishwashers, refrigerators, canned and frozen foods, as well as day care centres and kindergartens. But still the shortage of labour persisted, with the relentless expansion of the high-wage sector.

The next stage saw the conversion of Western Europe from a region of emigration to a region of mass immigration of unskilled labour: of Indians, Pakistanis and West Indians to Britain; Turks, Italians and Yugoslavs to Germany; and southern blacks, Puerto Ricans, Mexicans and a flood of illegal immigrants to the northern states of the USA. These immigrant flows have produced resistance everywhere from the aristocrats of the labour market, not primarily because of the threat to wage levels, but for a variety of other reasons. There is concern about pressure on other resources, above all on scarce housing, but also on schools, hospitals and other public facilities. Antagonism is generated by cultural differences – language, religion, dress, eating habits, noise levels and so on – exacerbated by race prejudice where race is involved, but almost as powerful where there is no racial difference (as with South Europeans in Western Europe). Hence by 1970 powerful voices in Western Europe were already calling for an end to immigration.

A third way of coping with the shortage of low-paid labour is to invest in manufacturing industry in low-wage countries and import the product. This is a new departure, full of promise for the tropics. The main purpose of nineteenth-century foreign investment was to facilitate the export of primary products. Indeed, industrial countries took great pains to organise their tariffs so as to exclude manufactures from low-wage countries. Thus there were low tariffs on raw materials, with high tariffs on the processed version of these same materials – raw sugar, refined sugar; crude oil, gasoline; bauxite, aluminium; cotton, cloth; oilseeds, soap; cocoa, cocoa butter; coffee, instant coffee; and so on. And, as Professor Balassa showed, even after the Kennedy round the tariffs of industrial countries on the kinds of manufactures imported from developing countries were much higher than the tariffs on goods they imported from each other.[8] European and American investment in the developing countries to produce light manufactures for European and American markets is a new phenomenon of the second half of the twentieth century, responding in part to the drying up of the reservoirs of unskilled low-wage labour in the industrial countries, which had existed even over a century and a half of industrial development.

What we are observing is the attempt of the advanced market economy finally to rid itself of dualism – of a labour market divided into high-wage and low-wage sectors, unrelated to basic competence. For, given the continued expansion of the high-wage sector, this is what would happen if all the escape hatches were closed – if population ceased to grow, female participation in the labour force reached its limit, immigration ceased, and imports of low-wage goods were prohibited. The continued expansion of high-wage industrial and service jobs would create ever larger shortages in the low-paid jobs, which ultimately, after mechanisation and self-service had done their all, would be forced to pay the same wages as their competitors were offering.

The process is probably inflationary. The attitude of British trade unions is for the workers to attach as much importance to wage differentials as they do to the absolute level of wages. In New York municipal employment the sacred stone is not the absolute wage level but the demand for absolute parity between the uniformed services. Thus, as the market shortages push up low-sector wages, they will also pull up the high-sector wages which they are trying to reach. The low-sector wages may catch up ultimately, but not without a considerable increase in the general price level. This chase has probably not played much part in Western European inflation over the past two decades, because the demand for low-wage labour was being met by immigration. The major effort to eliminate dualism is still to come.

The process may also be relevant in understanding what happens to the distribution of income between labour and capital as economic development proceeds. In so far as the product-wage in industry is determined by demand and supply, it must make some difference whether industry is continuing to draw on a large reservoir of labour in agriculture, domestic services, the household, small-scale enterprise and so on, or whether this reservoir is already drained and the labour market is tight. There is some evidence that the profit ratio has fallen in Western Europe over the last dozen years or so, but whether this was initiated by labour market shortages we cannot say.

Neither can we be certain that the advanced industrial countries will continue to grow at the unprecedented pace of the 1950s and 1960s. Chart 9.2 shows that in what the United Nations calls 'the developed market economies'[9] industrial production climbed close to the ceiling all the way from 1951 to 1973. The USA behaved differently from the rest. Europe experienced no Juglar fluctuation over these two decades, until 1973. The USA, on the other hand, continued its usual volatility despite the cessation of immigration and railway construction with which it used to be linked. Indeed the US curve for 1953 to 1973 in Chart 9.2 is remarkably similar to the US curve for 1892 to 1913 in Chart 2.1. The hallmark of the US economy, its propensity to have deep recessions followed by long upswings, has not changed.

The rate of growth has been as remarkable as the relative absence of

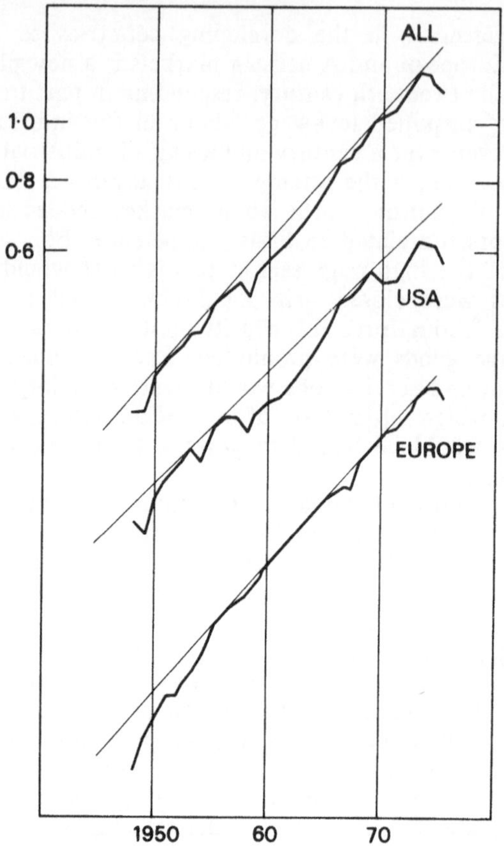

Chart 9.2 Industrial Production in Developed Countries

fluctuation for the group taken as a whole. The line along the 'All' curve in Chart 9.2 is rising at 5·1 per cent per annum. In Chapter 6 we attributed part of the pace of the 1950s and 1960s to catching up with a backlog of innovations stretching back to 1913. Europe grew particularly fast up to about 1955, catching up with postwar reconstruction, as well as draining its domestic labour reservoirs; thereafter it settled to a slower pace (5·4 per cent per annum). The element of backlog must ultimately disappear, if it has not already done so. Current business literature is beginning to be anxious as to whether the stream of invention is not drying up; and there are also apprehensions stemming from the recent tendency of the share of profits in national income to decline. The decline of production from 1973 to 1975 has been unusually sharp, worse than after 1883 or 1892 (see Chart 2.2) but not as bad as after 1907 or 1929. It is unpleasant for the group as a whole to fall off a ceiling after twenty-two years, but industrial economies have not normally travelled along the ceiling, so one must not assume that rapid growth cannot be regained.

There is more concern for the United States, where the backlog was smaller. Chart 9.2 shows that it continues to be more volatile than other industrial economies. To the common anxieties about the flow of inventions and the relative decline of profits the USA adds its own anxiety about its balance of payments, which moved adversely in the 1960s. People are asking whether the USA is not now going through the same sort of climacteric as Britain experienced after 1873. The comparison is not exact. The British growth rate declined after 1873, whereas the US growth rate was quite healthy up to 1969, allowing for the usual cyclical fluctuations. The balance of payments deficit certainly reflected challenging competition in world markets, not only from Japan and Western Europe, but also from developing country participation in the US market itself. But whereas the British for ideological reasons could not use any of the escape hatches at the end of the nineteenth century, the USA devalued its dollar in 1970 and set it afloat in 1973, so it should not be caught in the same trap. Moreover the USA was waging a sizable war in Vietnam, in which none of its industrial competitors participated.

It is too early to conclude that the US economy is in permanent trouble. If we count from the peak of 1969, US industrial production was up by only 3·0 per cent over the six years to 1975, a degree of retardation which is punishing for a country whose labour force grows by about 10 per cent over six years. But there are precedents. From 1872 to 1877 (five years) production was level; from 1892 to 1897 (five years) production was up by only 2·3 per cent; and after 1929 it took seven years for the index to rise by 2·3 per cent.

Two groups of commentators continue to ignore this point. One is the group of US economists brought up on the National Bureau of Economic Research's reference Kitchin cycles. They expect every recession to be over in eighteen months, and do not realise that it has been normal in the US economy for as many as six years to pass before the curve of production finally races to its next Kuznets peak. The unfortunate consequence of this over-optimism is that measures to end the recession are underplayed, in the expectation that the system is bound to right itself within the next few months, and this is costly to the American people. The other group are the children of the Apocalypse. Starting with Marx in 1848, every time there has been a recession critics have predicted the imminent collapse of capitalism, just as the early Christians expected the imminent arrival of Judgement Day. Capitalism will certainly pass away; all social and economic systems do. But its capacity to survive great shocks has been thoroughly demonstrated and has to be taken seriously by friend and foe alike.

The foregoing is not intended as a prediction that the industrial economies will continue to grow as fast over the next twenty years as they have grown over the last twenty years. Neither our science nor our crystal ball permits predictions of this kind. If such rapid growth continues, the industrial countries will exhaust their reservoirs of unskilled labour, and will have little difficulty in accommodating a large inflow of light manufactures from the developing countries. If they slow down, as they are often urged to do even by would-be friends of the developing countries, who see this as one way of narrowing the 'gap', their trade relations with the developing countries will be more difficult, and they will not be so ready to buy manufactured goods from these countries.

The opportunity to export manufactures is crucial for several developing countries. Already by 1975 manufactures were 33 per cent of the exports of the group of developing countries as a whole, excluding the oil countries, and if current trends continue by 1985 more than half the exports of developing countries will be manufactures. The group cannot meet its growth targets simply by exporting agricultural products because the demand of the industrial countries for such products grows too slowly. In order to pay for needed imports they need a larger share of world exports. This depends in the first instance on the developed countries reducing their barriers to imports of some agricultural and industrial products from developing countries, and this they will do only if a fast pace of industrial growth is resumed.

STRATEGY

9.03 The tropical countries also grew exceptionally fast in the 1950s and 1960s. National income of the developing countries, as classified by the United Nations, grew at an annual rate of between 4·5 and 5·5 per cent, depending on who estimates it. Even the lower estimate involves per capita growth of about 2 per cent per annum, which exceeds all historical precedents. There were, however, three difficult problems: the terms of trade, the burden of debt and population explosion.

The terms of trade deteriorated over this period of unprecedented prosperity. This is new. We saw in Chapter 7 that, after allowing for falling freights, the terms of trade of the tropical countries were higher in 1913 than at any time over the preceding forty years. This does not show in Chart 9.1 because the series there are inclusive of freights, but even there the terms of trade show no secular deterioration before 1913.

As we have noted in the first section of this chapter, tropical development came to a standstill in the 1930s and 1940s. Hence when the industrial countries began to recover after the Second World War there was a shortage of tropical crops. The terms of trade were exceptionally favourable in the first half of the 1950s, but they then declined. This also can be seen in Chart 9.1.

Two factors account for this decline. One is the speed with which the tropics were developing, and especially improving their transport facilities, which made it possible for more and more farmers to enter into producing cash crops. Despite the falling prices, tropical agricultural exports expanded at 4·4 per cent per annum between 1955 and 1965 (Table 9.1).

The second factor was the fall in the price of food, due to the immense increases in agricultural productivity in both Western Europe and North America. As Chart 9.1 shows, the prices of tropical cash crops kept pace more or less with the price of cereals. The adverse movement of the terms of trade for tropical crops with respect to the price of manufactures really derived from the fall in the price of food, which can be seen in Chart 9.3.[10] The cash crop : food ratio stayed high, but food prices brought cash crop prices down as they declined. This is in line with what we were saying in Chapter 7 about the way the factoral terms of trade between the tropics and the temperate countries are determined. After 1973, when the famine

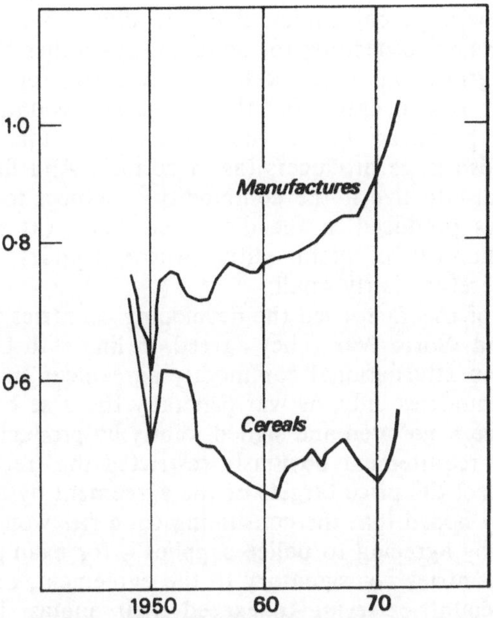

Chart 9.3 Prices in World Trade

scare drove up the price of food, the price of tropical crops also soared in sympathy. Since farmers can grow cash crops or foods, the prices of these two must tend to move together.

The adverse movement in the terms of trade in the 1950s and 1960s revived discussion of the desirability of controlling the prices of primary commodities. Developing countries speak of 'stabilising' prices, but the intention as perceived by the developed countries is that of 'maintaining' or 'raising' them. In truth tropical countries can stabilise on their own if they so desire, without needing international agreement. This they can do essentially by building up foreign exchange reserves in times of prosperity which they can spend in times of depression. There are many variants of this, including statutory marketing boards which pay fixed prices to producers, or export taxes whose rates vary directly with export prices. In addition, foreign exchange receipts can be stabilised by extending compensatory financing arrangements, of the sort now operated by the International Monetary Fund and by the European Economic Community.

International commodity agreements date back to the 1920s, and were fairly frequent in the 1930s. Experience shows that the crux of any attempt to use them to raise prices above the market level is the ability to control supplies. Brazil's effort to maintain coffee prices dates back to its valorisation scheme of 1906, and is one of the reasons why the supply of coffee has grown so rapidly in other countries. The international tea agreement, promoted by Asian suppliers, led to increasing supplies from Africa. Examples can be multiplied.

The ability to control supplies varies widely as between commodities. In general it is easier for minerals than for crops; for deep-level mining, which is done by a few large companies, than for alluvial mining, which attracts thousands of small prospectors; for annual crops rather than for tree crops; and for crops grown on large estates rather than crops grown mainly by smallholders. It is also easier for the developing countries to act if they are the major producers (as in the tea industry) than if the developed countries are also large producers (as in cotton). And fiinally it is difficult to make control effective if the commodity is subject to competition from close substitutes produced in the developed world (as with palm oil and rubber). The number of commodities whose supplies can be effectively controlled is therefore fairly small.

Recognition of this factor led the developing countries to try a new tactic after the Second World War. They agreed, in line with United Nations discussions, that an international commodity agreement should not be signed by producing countries only, as was generally the case before the war, but would instead be negotiated and signed jointly by producing and consuming countries. This requirement obviously restricted the freedom of producing countries to select the price targets of the agreement by themselves. On the other hand they hoped that the consuming countries would lend strength to the agreement by agreeing to police supplies – for example, by refusing to import from countries not signatory to the agreement, or even by refusing supplies from countries trying to exceed their quotas. In the event most international commodity negotiations have broken down on prices. Consumer and producer nations have not been able to reach agreement.

The agreement between the oil producers is a return to the pre-war mode. The consumers are not a party to the agreement, and are not consulted. The problems of the oil producers are restricted to those of their own mutual compatibility, and the possible development of competing supplies of oil or of substitute fuels.

Producing countries could circumvent the problem of controlling supplies if they agreed among themselves not on a target price or on individual quotas but simply on an export tax which they would all levy. This would raise their receipts without raising the price received by the producing firms or farmers. Thus the country would gain more without automatically giving producers an incentive to produce more. It should not be any more difficult to get producer agreement on an export tax than on prices and quotas. The problem of competition from substitutes and from new producing countries would remain; but this is inescapable, and, where significant, means that the price is best left to market forces.

It should finally be noted that most of the current discussion assumes that the terms of trade will continue to move against primary products over the next dozen years, but there is no warrant for this. In the first place we must consider the possible impact of worldwide inflation. Chart 9.3 shows that the price of manufactured goods in world trade has risen almost unceasingly since the end of the Second World War. This phenomenon takes us back to the period 1895–1913, the only other time since 1870 in which the price of manufactures has risen steadily over a long period. The pace was slower then; the price of manufactures rose at 0·6 per cent per annum between 1900 and 1913, but by 1·0 per cent per annum between 1957 and 1969, after which there was a marked acceleration (6·8 per cent per annum between 1969 and 1972) even before the general uprush stimulated by the quadrupling of oil prices in 1973. Prices were not rising because of a shortage of agricultural products; agricultural prices were lagging, as can also be seen in Chart 9.3. This has been an industrial inflation. Its hallmark is the swift rise of money wages. Thus, whereas from 1884 to 1913 US money wages in manufacturing rose at a more or less steady annual rate of 1·4 per cent (see section 4.07), the postwar rates of increase of US money wages are of a different order of magnitude: 4·7 per annum between 1948 and 1958, 2·9 per annum between 1958 and 1966, and 6·2 per annum between 1966 and 1972.[11] Prices would have been rising even faster in the 1950s and 1960s but for the unprecedentedly high rates of increase in both industrial and agricultural productivity that we have already noted.

It is possible but not likely that it was the rise in money wages that turned the terms of trade against primary products. A more likely cause is to be found in the basic conditions of production which resulted in building up large stocks of wheat and other commodities. Hence what will happen to the terms of trade over the coming decade probably depends more on what happens to underlying demand and supply than on whether runaway money wages are brought under control.

The situation changed dramatically in 1972, when heavy Russian purchases of wheat led to a famine scare which more than doubled the price of wheat over the next three years. The very sharp increase of the general price level since 1972 (the price index of manufactures in world trade rose at 17 per cent per annum over the next three years) is a response to this phenomenon, as well as to the increase in oil prices launched in 1973. The outcome of this is not predictable. Malthusian scares come in cycles, and economists, having started the round, tend to react suspiciously. On the one hand we are all aware of rising populations, of the increasing Russian demand for feed grains, and of the reduction in the farm labour force in advanced countries, reasons which lead to dire predictions of imminent famine and high food prices. We are also aware on the other hand that the Green Revolution is just beginning to take hold in Asia, Africa and Latin America, a fact which has led to equally awesome predictions of glut and farm bankruptcies. It is quite certain that we shall starve if production and population cannot be kept in line, but how this race will be run over the next twenty years is beyond prediction. If the pessimists are right the terms of trade will again move in favour of agriculture, and the concern of the tropical countries for international commodity agreements will evaporate.

9.04 The second problem for the developing countries was the burden of external debt. By the creation of special international institutions (the World Bank and the regional development banks) and also by the establishment of foreign aid programmes in the leading industrial nations, it became possible for the developing countries to borrow much more easily than before 1913. Indeed at the end of the 1960s the 'net transfer of resources' from the developed countries (including grants but subtracting repayments) was running at above 4 per cent of the total national income of the developing countries.

The corollary of this was a growing 'burden' of external debt. At the end of 1973 the external debt of the governments of the developing countries was estimated at \$90 billion, to which should be added private investment directly in enterprises, estimated at \$58 billion.[12] These two sums add to 2·1 times the value of the developing countries' exports in 1972 (the year before the quadrupling of oil prices). This ratio is low, compared with those listed in Table 7.6, which ranged from 2·2 to 8·6. However, the higher ratios in that table imply that most of the debt charge was being paid out of new borrowing, or that most of the debt was non-repayable direct investment in commercial enterprises, or that interest and dividends were mostly reinvested – since the normal debt charge on a debt of nine times exports would eat up nearly all the proceeds of the exports. High ratios for the same reason imply high vulnerability to cyclical fluctuations or to sudden cessations of foreign lending such as that of 1890 which overwhelmed Argentina and Australia and embarrassed the United States. On the other hand a ratio of debt to trade of 2·1 is quite manageable. What was troublesome about the external debt was not its size, but the speed at which it was growing. The public debt, estimated at \$47·5 billion in mid-1968, had grown at 12·3 per cent per annum, and debt charges were growing likewise.

Two elements have kept the burden manageable. In the first place the debt charges are relatively low, because of the high proportion of concessionary aid (with long amortisation periods and low interest rates). The interest paid in 1973, which was \$3·6 billion, was only 4 per cent on the amount outstanding; and the amortisation paid, \$8·8 billion, implied (if we assume the sum originally borrowed to have been about \$120 billion) that the average period of repayment of government debt, taking long- and short-term loans together, was about fourteen years.

The second element favouring the borrowers has been the continual increase in prices, which was in their favour irrespective of what happened to the terms of trade. The price index of the exports of developing countries rose by 13 per cent between 1955 and 1973, and nearly doubled between 1973 and 1975 (excluding oil) so the real cost of the debt is considerably eroded.

There is so much misconception about the 'burden' of debt that it has to be stressed that to be able to borrow is an advantage, and not a burden. If one borrows only for productive purposes, which will generate the means of repayment and more, the debt increases the national income by more than it costs. If all one's borrowing is of this kind, then the greater the 'debt burden' the better off the country will be. There is no need to worry about a ratio of debt to trade of 2·1 if the debt has been invested productively.

Some debtor countries have run into trouble for one or other of four reasons, each of which violates the condition that the investment 'will generate the means of repayment'. First, there has been a lot of unproductive expenditure, sometimes wasteful on any count, more often useful but done on an excessively lavish scale, for prestige reasons. This was especially common in the 1950s and early 1960s, when governments were still learning their business; public administration is now much improved with the emergence of planning bureaux, the spread of benefit–cost analysis and the enlightening of public opinion. Secondly, governments have invested heavily in projects which have no monetary return, or which they deliberately run at a loss, so that the investment itself does not yield cash for the debt charges, as happens with education or domestic water supplies. This would not matter if the public sector as a whole operated in such a way as to yield a surplus, but this lesson also takes time to learn. In general, governments of less developed countries do not tax enough, subsidise too heavily, and run their enterprises at a loss. Most of the governments which have escaped this trap have had no difficulty in meeting their financial obligations. However, even modest and revenue-rich governments may fail at the third obstacle, which is to translate tax or other revenues into the foreign exchange required for debt payments. Much of the investment undertaken by governments does not yield foreign exchange directly or indirectly, even though it may be highly desirable and may even yield a considerable cash income. To finance such investment out of foreign loans runs the risk that foreign exchange will not be available for the debt charges. The outcome depends on what is happening to the economy as a whole; it is safe to borrow for domestic purposes if at the same time (for whatever reason) the country's foreign exchange earning capacity is expanding adequately. In general the foreign exchange earning capacity of the developing countries increased swiftly over the 1950s and 1960s, so turning domestic revenues into foreign exchange was an intractable problem in only a few countries.[13] The fourth and most difficult problem was the practice of borrowing short and investing long, especially using five-year suppliers' credit for construction and industrial equipment with lives of between fifteen and fifty years. The industrial nations encouraged this in order to sell their manufactures, but the defaults of over a dozen countries in the 1950s and 1960s who were caught in this trap have now made the lenders more cautious. The developing countries borrowed on these foolish terms basically because not enough long-term finance was available. The expansion of the World Bank's programme has improved this situation but not solved it. Developing countries are now borrowing heavily from commercial banks in the Euro-currency and dollar markets, and this is even more risky than suppliers' credits. The basic need continues to be for an adequate flow of long-term capital through the World Bank and the regional development banks.

9.05 The third shadow that has darkened the prosperity of the 1950s and 1960s has been the growth of population, with its numerous consequences. The population of Western Europe has never grown by more than 1·25 per cent per annum, but the average for the developing countries is now approximately 2·5 per cent, whilst in several countries population is growing by more than 3 per cent per annum.

We saw when studying the core countries in Chapter 6 that a positive rate of natural increase automatically promotes migration from the countryside into the towns. If no extra cultivable land is available, the whole of the natural increase will seek refuge in the towns or overseas, if work is thought to be available. People remain at home if the towns are not expanding and there is nowhere to emigrate to; they then develop the more labour-intensive forms of cultivation, usually at a declining living standard, as Mrs Boserup has described.[14] However, if the towns are industrialising successfully and creating new jobs, their very success will bring in still more people. Rising urban unemployment is a mark of successful industrialisation in the face of population explosion; it is a tragic failure of human organisation, but it is not, as is frequently alleged, a failure of industrialisation.

It is not possible for industry to grow fast enough to absorb all the natural increase of a rapidly expanding population, unless the country is already highly industrialised. The following table shows the annual percentage rate of growth of urbanisation which will make the absolute intake into the urban areas equal to the absolute natural increase, given the current ratio of urban to total population:

	Population growth (% p.a.)				
	1·0	1·5	2·0	2·5	3·0
Urban ratio					
0·20	5·0	7·5	10·0	12·5	15·0
0·40	2·5	3·8	5·0	6·3	7·5
0·60	1·7	2·5	3·3	4·2	5·0

In 1890 Germany had an urban ratio of 0·48 and a population growth rate of 1·2. It could absorb the whole natural increase into the towns if they grew at 2·5 per cent per annum; and that was the rate at which they actually grew. In 1950 Brazil had an urban ratio of 0·36 and a population growth rate of 3·05. To absorb the whole natural increase would have required an urban growth rate of 8·4; the actual urban growth rate was 5·6. Brazil is fortunate in still having plenty of cultivable land; some Asian countries are not so well placed. Also, the larger the existing urban ratio the easier it is to absorb newcomers. Most Asian and African urban ratios are still under 20 per cent, and at 20 per cent a 3·0 per cent population growth rate would call for an urban growth rate of 15 per cent per annum. It is thus easy to see why urban growth rates exceeding 5 per cent have become so common in tropical countries.

We noted in Chapter 6 that urbanisation is very costly and that before 1913 the countries lending overseas were all urbanising at less than 3 per cent per annum, while the big borrowers (USA, Argentina, Australia) were all urbanising faster than this. High rates of urbanisation are the principal reason why the tropical countries have needed so much capital from abroad and foreign aid despite their relative prosperity. And these high rates of urbanisation are the direct consequence of explosive population growth. Economists offer some other explanations: the widening gap between urban and rural incomes; neglect of the countryside in government spending; the effect of education on raising the horizons of rural children, and so on. But the basic cause of the urban influx is population explosion.

Despite high levels of capital investment it has not in fact been possible for the tropical countries to expand urban employment at 5 per cent a year, so a massive increase in urban unemployment has resulted from the inflow of population. These countries have done well by historical standards. Industrial production has been increasing by about 6·5 per cent per year, which is higher than in the developed countries either now or in the nineteenth century. This represents an increase in employment of about

3·5 per cent and an increase in productivity of about 3·0. It is argued that the increase in productivity is too high; that it would be better to have a smaller increase in productivity combined with a larger increase in employment. The objective is laudable, but the mechanics are not clear. Much of the investment occurs in order to take advantage of potential increases in productivity, so one cannot assume that reducing the productivity would not also in some cases reduce the employment.

In any case industry employs few people in a developing economy. The rapid growth of the tropical countries has been sustained as much by a rapid growth of modern services, especially education, medical services, transportation, civil administration and so on. Such services cannot be expanded at will; they are financed out of the growth of the commodity-producing sectors of the economy.

It is fashionable to blame the governments of the developing countries and the economic system for not having provided more urban jobs over the last two decades, but it is unreasonable to expect urban occupations to grow at the 12·5 per cent per annum rate which this implies for the typical African or Asian country, or even at the 7·5 per cent rate which it implies for the less developed areas of Latin America.

There is of course only one ultimate remedy for a population explosion: family planning. In the meantime the only way to avoid mounting urban unemployment is to persuade more people to remain in the countryside. The prime objective of agricultural policy in such countries should be to bring more land under cultivation, so that more people can farm. This is one area where the study of the nineteenth century has handicapped us. Our agricultural economics is based on the assumption that numbers in agriculture will decline as economic development proceeds; our policies are therefore set towards helping to reduce the number of men per acre. Instead we shall need for the next three or four decades agricultural policies aimed at absorbing more men per acre.

In any case more people are needed in agriculture not simply to keep down urban unemployment but also in order to feed a growing population. The food production of the developing countries grew at slightly less than 3 per cent per annum in the 1950s and 1960s whereas the demand for food grew at rather more than 3 per cent. In consequence the developing world changed from being a net exporter of food into a net importer of food from the developed countries, to the tune of several billion dollars a year.

This failure was due to some extent to erroneous policies, especially as regards price controls which kept food prices down in the interest of urban populations; but it was also the result of a general neglect of rural areas, as government expenditure concentrated on improving the towns. The fact that the success of the industrial revolution in the core countries was due to its having been combined with an agrarian revolution was not widely understood in the 1950s.

Circumstances have changed. The food deficit and the balance of payments have alerted governments everywhere to the importance of increasing food production. At the same time new varieties of wheat, rice and maize are tripling and quadrupling yields per acre, and the speed with which even very small farmers have adopted these new varieties has surpassed all expectation. There are still problems. We have yet to create new higher-yielding varieties of rice suitable for rain-fed cultivation in India; and we have yet to devise cultural techniques as well as suitable varieties for the marginal dry-farming areas which support so many hundreds of millions in parts of Asia and Africa. But if the rate of success of the 1960s is repeated in the 1970s and 1980s, the food problem will be solved for the rest of this century.

This will not necessarily eliminate urban unemployment. So long as the number of jobs in the towns is increasing rapidly (significantly faster than the natural increase in population) urban incomes will continue to exceed rural incomes, and people will flock into the towns from the countryside. This can be controlled only by requiring residence permits for working in towns as is now the practice in most Communist countries, but even this system is difficult to operate and not very effective unless the penalties are severe. Ultimately the only way to eliminate urban unemployment is to bring down the rate of population growth to a level which calls for urban expansion at no more than two or three per cent a year.

9.06 The population explosion is also the prime cause of the increase in the number of people living at the barest levels of subsistence – a phenomenon which has grown worse since the Second World War. This has been particularly depressing among people living on the marginal lands with inadequate rainfall, of whom there are already many hundreds of millions in the Indian sub-continent and along the fringes of the African deserts.

This great increase in the number of the very poor is sometimes blamed on 'the failure of economic development', but given the rise in population (which was due not to economic development but to the high effectiveness of relatively cheap public health measures), the increase in poverty would have been even greater in the absence of economic development. The lesson for economic development is not that it should be less, but more, giving greater priority to the countryside and also to family planning.

It is also sometimes said, because of this great increase in the number of the very poor, that economic development has benefited only the rich and the middle classes. This is not true. Economic development has benefited the farmers who grow cash crops, such as cocoa, coffee, rice, peanuts, etc. Production of such commodities has almost doubled since the end of the war, and these small farmers are much better off, despite the terms of trade. Economic development has also benefited the urban workers, who receive much higher incomes than their rural cousins. Economic development also brings a considerable upward differentiation of the labour force, into skilled workers, supervisors, and various grades of the lower middle and middle class. It is by the expansion of the middle that development reduces inequality, and this is one reason why more developed countries are less unequal than less developed countries. It is an additional source of satisfaction to those at the bottom; the labourer himself may not be receiving higher wages, but his son has become a mechanic, and his daughter is a teacher.

It remains true, however, that the urban workers and the cash crop farmers are only a minority of the labour force in Africa and Asia (though not in Latin America). The majority of Asians and Africans are food farmers, and for them the 1950s and 1960s were a difficult time. The relentless increase in their numbers frequently exceeded the increase in good cultivable land; the terms of trade moved against them; and the Green Revolution did not gather momentum until the second half of the 1960s. The one development in their favour was the large increase in public services. The number of children in school has multiplied by three; disease is greatly reduced, and the infant mortality rate has been reduced by two-thirds; innumerable villages now have a water supply, a paved road, and regular motor transport. An index of mass welfare which included not simply the output of wage-goods, but also such things as the number of hospital beds per thousand, or the percentage of population living within one mile of a public water tap, would show that the poor have gained much more from development than it is now fashionable to believe.

Since most of the poor are farmers, the key to reducing mass poverty is an agrarian revolution which, as we have so often seen, is also the key to much else in development. The productivity of tropical food farmers is miserably low. This is intensified in some countries by their human predators – landlords, moneylenders, traders and tax-gatherers – who take a large part of the farmer's product and give little service in return. To eliminate this predatory activity would not merely increase the farmer's share of his own product, but would also give him the incentive to invest more time and resources in cultivation, and to take greater risks. Land reform is therefore at the heart of an agrarian revolution. This is not a simple matter. Mexican and Bolivian experience show that land reform can leave the farmers in poverty; while Japanese, Taiwanese and Korean land reforms show that, when accompanied by vigorous agricultural extension – with heavy emphasis on new seeds, fertilisers, water supplies and pesticides – land reform can be the prelude to astonishing rates of growth of output.

9.07 If the developed countries continue to grow as rapidly over the next two decades as they did in the 1950s and 1960s, the trading situation should be favourable to the tropical countries. Demand for their agricultural exports would continue to grow at around 4·5 per cent per year; their exports of minerals have been growing at about 7 per cent a year; and their exports of manufactures could continue a growth rate of at least 10 per cent a year. The adverse movement of the terms of trade for tropical crops could be arrested by giving greater emphasis in agricultural policy to food production. This would also reduce the balance of payments deficit for food, and help the poorest members of the economy, the small farmers who grow food.

This dependence of the tropical countries on the prosperity of the developed countries derives from the current orientation of their economies; it is not part of an inevitable natural order. The developing countries could grow rapidly, irrespective of what might happen to the developed countries, provided that among themselves their pattern was one of balanced growth. They have all the basic materials required for growth, including surpluses of fuel, iron ore and other minerals. They are capable of mastering the agricultural techniques required for feeding themselves. They are learning the tricks of manufacturing, and could save enough to finance their own growth if they gave their minds to it. Ultimately the prosperity of the tropical world does not have to depend on what happens in the developed countries.[15]

This present dependence has as its chief weakness the unfavourable factoral terms on which it is based. So long as the bulk of tropical peoples are food farmers with relatively low productivity, tropical products are available to the rest of the world on an essentially low-wage basis, except in the few cases where the tropics can exercise an effective natural monopoly. We have stressed this situation with regard to agricultural commodities (though not necessarily minerals). Now we must recognise that the opening up of the markets of the industrial countries to imports of light manufactures from the tropics is essentially of the same kind; it is an additional opportunity to sell low-wage labour.

These opportunities are not to be despised. Although the factoral terms do not compare with those ruling in trade between the developed countries or between the core and the countries of temperate settlement, they do offer the tropics a somewhat higher standard of living than would be available if they merely ceased to participate in international trade. The choice is not between trading and not trading. It is between trading on the basis of a constant low productivity, and undergoing one's own industrial and agrarian revolutions.

The low factoral terms of trade derive from the low productivity of the bulk of tropical producers: the food farmers. This low productivity is also the major constraint on industrialisation, as a country passes beyond the stage of import substitution. It is also the constraint on the tax base, which stands in the way of producing adequate schooling, public health and so on. To eliminate this constraint would make possible a balanced growth of industry, agriculture and services. There would be trade – probably much more trade than at present – but trade would be the lubricant rather than the engine of growth. Trading partners would still depend on each other's prosperity, but marginally, and not as the principal source of growth.

It is easy to exaggerate the potential contribution of foreign trade to development. To take an extreme example, India's exports are only 5 per cent of her national income. If as a result of a new international economic order India were paid five times as much for exports (without an increase in prices of imports) her national income would be raised only by 20 per cent in the first instance, say from $100 to $120 per head. The basic cause of India's poverty is not her terms of trade but the fact that an Indian farmer produces only one-eleventh as much food as an American farmer.[16] Other countries depend on foreign trade to a greater extent than India, and would benefit more directly from better terms of trade. One must also take into account the indirect effects.[17] But the main points remain: the poverty of the tropical countries is due mainly to their low productivity and only secondarily to their terms of trade. Their productivity is not low because their terms of trade are poor; their terms of trade are poor because their agricultural productivity is low.

To return to our starting point, the industrial revolution in the core challenged the periphery in two ways: to imitate it and to trade. The option to trade was of limited value, not only because the volume of trade was not all that large, but also because to trade simply at constant terms would not itself produce great wealth. The great advantage of trade was that it could create conditions for moving on to the more valuable option, that of imitating the agricultural and industrial revolutions of the core and so raising productivity. It could be helpful to start by exporting to industrial countries, because this allowed a breathing space in which to lay the foundations for development – to acquire an infrastructure, build schools, modernise economic institutions and so on. But, as in the countries of temperate settlement, this option must be seen only as a base from which to launch on self-sustaining growth, through continual improvement of output per head. The long-run engine of growth is technological change; international trade cannot substitute for this except in the initial period of laying development foundations.

Appendix I

British Statistics

The origin of the present book was this Appendix on British Statistics, which was completed and widely circulated in November 1967, though only now appearing in print. This date explains the initial aim of the undertaking, which was to try to reconcile the conflicting data on British economic activity during the forty years before the First World War.

The conflict was between Hoffmann's index of industrial production[1] and Prest's national income series,[2] as deflated by the retail price index. Hoffmann's index showed an average annual rate of growth between 1873 and 1907 (two peak years) of 1·7 per cent per annum. Prest's national income series, deflated by retail prices, showed real output increasing between the same two dates at an average rate of 2·5 per cent per annum. Given the normal expectation that industrial production grows faster than total income, Prest's result seemed to require industrial production to have been growing by about 3 per cent per annum, and was therefore not compatible with the 1·7 per cent of Hoffmann's index. This basic incompatibility hung like a cloud for twenty years over studies of this period.

There were four possibilities:

(1) that Prest's series in money rose too fast; or
(2) that Hoffmann's index rose too slowly; or
(3) that other sources of income (e.g. shipping, finance) had risen exceptionally fast; or
(4) that the price index used by Prest was inappropriate.

The first of these possibilities, that the money national income series was in error, was investigated by Jefferys and Walters[3] in 1955, by Feinstein[4] in 1961, by Deane and Cole[5] to a more limited extent in 1964, and again by Feinstein[6] in 1972. The upshot of Feinstein's latest calculation is to reduce the annual growth rate of money national income by about 0·15 points. Bigger changes are not possible if one accepts the basic components of the national income series, namely Bowley's wage series, the British Association committee's estimate of small salaries, and the returns of income declared to the income tax authorities. Bowley's series is particularly suspect because of the oversimplified way in which he gets his basic figure, the total wage bill for 1911, but a change here would affect the level of wages more than their rate of growth.[7] The growth of money national income is not investigated in this monograph.

Next we come to Hoffmann's index of industrial production. The two weaknesses of this index have been recognised for some time: that it underestimated the growth rate of products made from iron and steel, and that it omitted some industries which were growing faster than his average. It is not easy to remedy these weaknesses with confidence, since basic statistics are lacking. Our procedure is described in detail in this appendix, where the extent to which every commentator (including Hoffmann) has to rely on speculation is clear for all to see. The job has not been done before because it takes many months of tedious labour.

The outcome has been to replace four of Hoffmann's series by new ones, and to add five more series. These are shown below with their growth rates from 1873 to 1907, side by side with Hoffmann's rate; their percentage weights in the new index are also given.

	Hoffmann's rate	*New rate*	*% weight*
Revisions			
Iron and steel	2·5	2·8	5·3
Iron and steel products	2·8	2·9	14·6
Shipbuilding	2·4	3·2	3·7
Building materials[a]	1·7	2·3	3·9
Additional series			
Clothing		2·0	4·8
Textile finishing		1·4	1·9
Printing		5·6	4·7
Chemicals		5·5	3·1
Electricity		10·9[b]	1·0
Food manufacture		2·5	1·4

[a] Hoffmann's series was for timber products only.
[b] 1883–1913.

These changes raise the growth rate of the index from 1·7 to 2·1 per cent per annum (excluding building and construction). This is much less than was expected. Part of the reason is that Hoffmann had already done a good job with iron and steel products. Critics had hoped that a new index of machinery output might affect the index considerably, but in so doing they had forgotten that value added in making machinery was only 5 per cent of value added in manufacturing and mining in 1907. Critics had also hoped that additional series for industries omitted by Hoffmann would substantially raise the growth rate, but the obstacle here is the relatively low weight of the new industries in 1907. The revised index now 'represents' 91 per cent of the value added recorded in the 1907 Census of Production.

If industrial production did in fact grow so slowly, is it possible (to come to the third alternative) that the economy made up for this by having an unusually high growth rate (relative to industrial production) in other sectors? To answer this question we have made the index of gross domestic product which is presented in this appendix.

According to our new indices, between 1873 and 1907 industrial production rose by 2·1 per cent per annum, real gross domestic product by 1·8 per cent per annum, and real gross national product (GDP plus interest and dividends from abroad) by 1·9 per cent per annum. The small difference

Table A.1 *UK: New Series for Industrial Production (1913=100)*

	1 Iron and steel	2 Iron and steel products	3 Shipbuilding	4 Building materials (also construction)	5 Houses (incl. repair)	6 Commercial building (incl. repair)	7 Construction (other)	8 Clothing	9 Textile finishing	10 Printing and materials	11 Chemicals	12 Electricity	13 Food manufacture	14 Gas	15 Total (excl. construction)
1852	13·7	14·0	6·8	46·3	62·0	29·7	—	36·7	38·5	6·1	6·5	—	22·2	6·3	23·9
1853	14·7	14·6	8·9	45·5	61·5	27·0	—	39·2	41·5	6·5	6·7	—	22·8	7·1	25·6
1854	15·5	15·1	10·8	40·8	52·1	21·0	—	37·4	39·6	6·5	6·7	—	23·3	7·6	25·6
1855	16·4	15·7	16·3	37·2	47·4	12·2	—	37·6	40·5	6·4	6·9	—	23·9	8·4	25·5
1856	18·3	18·1	12·2	38·5	48·8	16·2	42·9	40·6	44·1	6·9	7·8	—	24·6	8·9	27·3
1857	18·6	19·0	12·3	37·5	48·4	17·6	39·9	39·1	42·8	7·2	8·0	—	25·1	9·2	28·4
1858	17·7	17·9	10·8	44·3	50·2	34·5	45·1	36·9	41·5	7·4	7·5	—	25·8	9·7	27·1
1859	18·9	19·1	9·5	44·7	51·6	36·5	43·6	39·2	45·2	8·4	7·8	—	26·5	10·4	28·8
1860	19·6	19·6	10·2	47·2	52·1	35·8	49·6	43·3	50·2	8·6	7·9	—	27·2	11·3	30·4
1861	19·0	19·4	9·9	50·6	52·6	17·6	67·3	39·9	46·4	8·5	7·7	—	27·8	11·7	30·0
1862	20·1	20·4	12·4	59.7	56·8	23·7	82·0	21·8	25·7	8·7	8·3	—	28·5	12·3	30·2
1863	23·1	23·1	17·6	61·7	59·2	36·5	77·8	23·7	27·6	9·3	9·5	—	29·2	12·7	30·0
1864	24·4	24·6	22·5	71·0	61·0	49·3	91·0	26·3	30·8	9·8	10·3	—	30·0	14·1	31·9
1865	24·8	24·6	22·8	78·5	59·2	48·7	110·5	31·6	37·6	10·2	10·5	—	30·6	15·1	33·9
1866	23·5	22·9	19·1	84·5	61·0	38·5	129·0	35·6	42·7	10·5	9·9	—	31·4	16·3	34·9
1867	24·7	24·0	15·2	60·5	63·9	25·7	77·1	37·4	44·8	10·4	10·3	—	32·2	17·1	34·4
1868	25·9	25·0	17·3	47·1	67·6	16·9	47·4	37·5	46·3	10·2	10·7	—	33·0	17·3	35·5

1869	28·5	25·9	19·4	42·4	70·4	21·6	31·6	34·4	43·1	10·3	11·6	—	33·8	18·1	35·3
1870	31·1	27·5	22·7	61·4	72·8	37·9	65·4	40·6	49·9	10·8	12·7	—	34·7	19·2	38·4
1871	34·9	31·6	24·4	70·5	74·2	58·1	74·4	46·4	56·2	11·5	14·5	—	35·6	20·4	41·3
1872	36·1	32·8	30·2	72·7	77·0	65·6	73·3	45·4	53·9	12·5	15·1	—	36·5	21·0	42·5
1873	35·9	33·1	28·1	64·4	74·7	50·7	63·9	49·0	56·9	13·2	15·2	—	37·4	22·1	43·7
1874	33·4	30·8	35·6	72·6	79·8	35·2	87·6	51·7	59·0	13·7	14·5	—	38·3	22·9	44·2
1875	35·7	32·7	25·4	75·9	89·7	31·8	89·5	48·7	55·6	14·9	15·9	—	39·3	23·9	44·2
1876	37·3	33·9	19·3	81·2	97·2	32·4	99·3	51·7	57·7	16·2	16·8	—	40·2	24·9	44·7
1877	38·0	33·2	25·1	71·8	94·8	29·7	76·7	51·1	56·4	17·0	16·9	—	41·2	26·0	45·4
1878	37·4	31·7	28·3	80·4	88·3	21·6	106·8	49·6	53·8	18·4	16·6	—	42·2	27·2	44·6
1879	35·6	29·7	26·4	79·1	80·3	33·1	103·8	46·5	50·9	19·2	15·6	—	43·3	28·4	42·8
1880	46·1	37·6	31·3	76·6	79·3	51·4	88·4	55·5	62·4	21·9	20·1	3·8	44·3	29·6	48·2
1881	50·7	42·8	39·9	84·7	80·8	73·0	94·4	55·3	62·7	24·4	23·4	4·0	45·4	30·9	50·9
1882	54·8	46·3	50·8	81·3	79·3	71·7	88·4	55·8	64·8	27·2	26·1	4·2	46·6	32·3	53·5
1883	54·0	43·9	58·7	81·3	80·8	56·8	95·5	55·5	66·3	29·1	25·0	4·5	47·8		54·5
1884	49·2	38·8	36·9	80·5	81·2	36·5	104·5	54·0	64·4	30·8	22·0	4·7	48·9		52·2
1885	48·0	38·0	25·2	73·1	79·3	25·7	94·4	47·0	56·6	29·8	21·7	4·9	50·2		50·4
1886	48·2	40·0	19·6	65·1	78·9	32·4	72·2	50·7	59·4	32·1	23·2	5·2	51·4		49·9
1887	55·5	49·3	24·7	71·1	81·2	43·9	78·2	54·2	62·1	33·8	28·9	5·4	52·7		53·7
1888	59·4	53·6	38·8	73·2	81·2	70·3	68·4	56·3	64·1	35·7	32·3	5·7	54·1		57·2
1889	62·7	56·7	58·2	79·1	81·7	87·2	72·6	60·0	66·8	38·9	35·4	6·0	55·4	Same as Hoffman	60·9
1890	60·9	55·0	55·0	82·6	80·8	88·6	80·8	65·7	70·6	42·2	35·4	6·3	56·8		61·8
1891	56·2	50·0	52·7	85·8	81·7	65·6	100·4	72·1	73·6	44·3	32·8	6·9	58·1		62·3
1892	51·3	46·1	50·6	84·7	85·4	43·9	106·8	61·8	61·5	45·5	30·8	7·6	59·6		59·1
1893	52·8	47·3	39·7	83·7	91·9	33·1	106·0	65·8	63·4	44·8	32·3	8·3	61·1		58·0
1894	54·3	45·8	47·0	84·7	93·9	39·2	102·6	73·8	68·9	47·3	35·4	9·2	62·6		61·8
1895	58·3	53·4	46·6	93·5	96·2	75·0	101·5	75·1	68·8	48·8	37·6	10·1	64·2		64·2
1896	68·5	63·9	53·3	104·0	105·6	94·1	108·3	80·3	72·6	54·4	46·0	11·1	65·7		68·8

Table A.1 *continued*

	1 *Iron and steel*	2 *Iron and steel products*	3 *Shipbuilding*	4 *Building materials (also construction)*	5 *Houses (incl. repair)*	6 *Commercial building (incl. repair)*	7 *Construction (other)*	8 *Clothing*	9 *Textile finishing*	10 *Printing and materials*	11 *Chemicals*	12 *Electricity*	13 *Food manufacture*	14 *Gas*	15 *Total (excl. construction)*
1897	71·5	66·1	46·1	118·8	113·1	102·8	132·4	79·8	70·9	57·7	49·0	12·2	67·4	Same as Hoffmann	69·6
1898	71·3	66·0	64·8	128·2	125·8	87·2	153·0	87·7	77·3	61·3	49·8	13·4	69·1		72·8
1899	77·2	70·8	71·0	126·0	127·7	71·7	154·9	87·8	76·8	65·1	54·4	14·8	70·8		76·3
1900	75·3	69·5	71·1	125·4	124·4	64·9	159·8	85·7	76·6	66·1	54·7	16·5	72·7		76·4
1901	75·6	69·1	73·9	135·4	124·4	60·8	185·7	76·1	68·4	69·0	56·0	18·7	74·4		75·8
1902	74·0	67·4	71·1	145·0	129·6	66·9	200·8	76·4	69·8	71·5	56·5	21·5	76·3		76·6
1903	75·6	67·4	57·3	135·3	131·9	65·6	176·7	76·2	70·8	73·5	59·2	24·7	78·2		75·5
1904	74·5	67·3	67·7	138·6	127·2	69·6	186·1	70·0	64·7	76·1	61·3	28·4	80·1		76·2
1905	84·1	77·0	81·3	135·3	128·2	98·7	161·3	84·4	78·8	79·1	72·2	32·7	82·1		81·7
1906	91·0	84·9	89·9	130·0	122·1	116·9	143·6	85·8	81·5	83·6	80·9	37·6	84·2		85·9
1907	91·5	85·7	81·2	119·6	123·0	100·7	127·5	94·7	91·5	85·7	83·7	43·2	86·3		88·7
1908	78·0	72·0	46·8	97·8	114·6	65·6	102·3	90·6	89·1	83·3	72·7	49·7	88·4		82·6
1909	84·9	78·2	49·6	92·7	115·5	44·6	101·1	86·3	83·1	83·5	80·3	57·2	90·7		83·6
1910	90·0	72·8	55·6	92·8	111·7	79·8	88·7	80·0	76·8	87·9	89·5	65·8	92·9		84·9
1911	88·5	84·9	88·9	100·5	116·4	105·5	85·0	90·1	87·6	92·0	91·4	75·6	95·3		90·8
1912	86·8	86·8	88·4	101·4	101·4	116·9	89·1	100·5	98·9	96·9	94·6	86·9	97·6		93·3
1913	100·0	100·0	100·0	100·0	100·0	100·0	100·0	100·0	100·0	100·0	100·0	100·0	100·0		100·0

between industrial production and GDP indicates that the rise of some other sectors was unusually swift, while the large difference between GDP and GNP indicates the increasing importance of income from abroad.

The sectors which grew faster than manufacturing (2·1 per cent per annum) were transport of people (3·0), catering (2·7), civilian government (2·9), professions (3·0), miscellaneous services (3·6), finance (6·0) and shipping (4·3). The first two result from rapid urbanisation, bringing the daily journey to work and the increase in commercial travel. The next three are the usual reflection of the high-income elasticity of demand for services (education, medical service, entertainment, etc.). The last two are particularly important because they earn foreign exchange. Their growth, along with that of income from foreign investment, indicates that Britain increasingly sought to earn foreign exchange by exporting services rather than goods.

The difference between our growth rate for real gross national product (1·9 per cent) and growth rates derived from deflating money national income by an index of retail prices is mainly due to the inappropriateness of this price index as a GDP deflator.[8] The retail price index reflects the changing prices of imported food and raw materials, whereas the GDP deflator represents the changing price of British products (goods and services). The retail price index is useful in measuring the changes in British consumption, but for changes in the value of British production it is inappropriate.

In sum, the original difference between Hoffmann's growth rate and Prest's growth rate deflated by retail prices was −0·8 (1·7 and 2·5). The correct difference should be +0·2 (2·1 and 1·9). This switch of 1·0 is accounted for as follows: Hoffmann's index grows too slowly by 0·4, Prest's money index rises too fast by 0·15, and the index of retail prices fell faster than the GDP deflator by the remaining 0·45 per cent per annum.

INDUSTRIAL PRODUCTION

The main problems presented by Hoffmann's series are that he underestimates the growth rate of iron and steel, and that he omits some other industries which were growing faster than his average. These problems cannot be solved simply by finding new series and incorporating them into his index. All the easily available series were known to Hoffmann, and were used by him, and although seekers may yet find some new ones, this will be due to luck rather than to diligence.

Hoffmann's series can therefore be improved only by doctoring such figures as are available, to make them better. This is, of course, an exercise in speculation. Such speculation cannot be avoided. Hoffmann's own metal series are based on speculation, since he has had to make assumptions to convert the raw data into the particular series that he presents. Any index of industrial production or of real output for any country before 1914 must incorporate a great many of the author's assumptions.

The results of the present exercise are shown in Table A.1 in the form of (a) four series to replace five given by Hoffmann (iron and steel, iron and steel products, shipbuilding and building materials, the last of which replaces both Hoffmann's 'Other Timber Products' and his 'Building'), (b) a further six new series, and (c) the figures used to complete Hoffmann's series for gas which started only in 1882. The table also contains (d) the three constituents of construction, and (e) a new total for industrial production incorporating Hoffmann's other series, but excluding building and other construction. The index now 'represents' 91 per cent of the value added in manufacturing and mining in the 1907 Census, or allowing for the Census estimate that £50m. escaped the Census, 'represents' 84 per cent of all value added.

The weights used for this new total differ from Hoffmann's. In the course of 1852 to 1913, he used three different weights, based on 1850, 1881 and 1907. The 1907 weights are from the Census of Production. He does not say where the 1850 and 1881 weights came from, but presumably they are from a combination of wage data and Census of Population data. I have not been able to reconstitute his 1850 and 1881 weights so as to include the new series, so I have used 1907 weights throughout. The results of a test in which his series were weighted with his weights and with mine showed that the change in weighting made little difference. The weights now used are shown in Table A.2.

Table A.2 *UK: Weights Used for Industrial Production (Base 1907)*

Coal	18·8	Meat	1·1
Iron ore	0·3	Confectionery	0·9
Other mining	0·2	Sugar	0·2
*Iron and steel	5·3	Beer	4·3
*Iron and steel products	14·6	Malt	0·7
Non-ferrous metals	1·7	Spirits	0·3
*Shipbuilding	3·7	Tobacco	1·0
Motor vehicles	0·3	Paper	0·8
Furniture	1·6	Leather	0·6
Cotton yarn	3·9	Leather goods	1·9
Cotton cloth	4·1	Rubber	0·5
Woollen yarn	1·1	Soap	0·5
Woollen cloth	2·2	Vegetable oils	0·2
Silk yarn	0·1	Gas	3·1
Silk cloth	0·2	*Electricity	1·0
Jute	0·5	*Clothing	4·8
Hemp	0·4	*Textile finishing	1·9
Linen yarn	0·4	*Chemicals	3·1
Linen cloth	0·6	*Printing	4·7
Flour	1·2	*Building materials	3·9
Bread	2·0	*Food manufacture	1·4
			100·0

*New series.

The following notes explain how the new series are derived.

Iron and steel

Separate series exist for the output of pig iron and of steel ingots. Combining these two is easy, since value added in making a ton of pig iron was, in 1907, slightly larger than value added in converting pig iron into a ton of steel. The trouble is that the value added derived in this way is only about 40 per cent of the value added which the 1907 Census gives for smelting iron and steel, because the big value added is in rolling and in making special steels, for which we have no continuous series. Using such data as are available, I have proceeded on the assumption that one-third of the pig iron not used in making steel[9] and three-quarters of the steel were subjected to rolling or other special processes. The final series is therefore the sum of value added in making pig iron, in converting to steel, and in 'rolling'. This series rises by 155 per cent between 1873 and 1907, in comparison with Hoffmann's 133 per cent.

Iron and steel products

This is the most important series in the index, since it carries a weight of 14·6 per cent, but since there are no direct data for making it, one has to depend on numerous assumptions. The greatest weakness of any index of British prewar production will always be at this point.

The procedure followed is first to arrive at the tonnage of iron and steel used by fabricators. This is pig iron output plus steel output minus pig iron used in making steel minus use in shipbuilding, use in making rails, and net exports of unfabricated iron and steel. The procedure is similar to that used by Cairncross, except that he subtracted net exports of all iron and steel, since he was interested in home use of iron and steel, whereas we subtract only net exports of unfabricated iron and steel, since we have to count fabricated exports as part of our net output. Cairncross's series also includes rails, which we have to exclude because the Census has classified them (as also ships' plates) in value added in smelting and rolling.[10] The resulting series is rather larger than the net use of metal by fabricators, since it includes home use of unfabricated metal other than for shipbuilding and rails; but this does not matter if the difference is small or a constant proportion of the total.

The result which one obtains by subtraction has all the errors concentrated in it, both the errors in estimating the various series subtracted, and also the errors deriving from the fact that stock changes by the other users are not taken into account. The series therefore has unlikely annual fluctuations. I have assumed that it ought to have the same fluctuations as iron and steel production; I have therefore run a nine-year moving average through both series, and have then given to iron and steel products the same percentage deviations from trend as appear in iron and steel itself.

The final adjustment is to take care of the probability that value added per ton of metal increased over this long period, as there was a shift towards more highly fabricated products. I have assumed an increase of 0·5 per cent per annum in value added per ton. Thus the final series increases by 159 per cent between 1873 and 1907, in comparison with Hoffmann's 149 per cent.

Shipbuilding

Hoffmann made no allowance for the fact that a ton of ship in 1852 (wooden, sailing) differed from a ton of ship in 1907 (steel, steam).

It is necessary to distinguish between economies in shipbuilding and in shipping. A ton of shipping (cubic capacity) could carry more weight (deadweight capacity) and travel more miles per annum in 1907 than in 1852, but these economies belong to shipping. What we want to know for shipbuilding is how much more value added was incorporated in a 1907 ton than in a 1852 ton, a near equivalent to this question being how much more it would have cost in 1907 to build the ton of 1907 than that of 1852. In the absence of evidence I have again assumed that value added per ton (whether sailing or steam) increased by 0·5 per cent per annum. Sailing ships have been converted to steam by using Cairncross's statement[11] that sailing ships sold for 60 per cent of the price of steamships, per ton. The index now rises by 180 per cent between 1873 and 1907, compared with Hoffmann's 126 per cent.

Building materials and construction

The same index is used for these two. This is justifiable only if changes in the ratio of building materials to construction exactly offset changes in the ratio of net imports of building materials (mostly timber) to home production (mostly cement, stone and clay products).

An index is produced for construction by adding together:

(a) Houses built
  (i) urban
  (ii) rural
(b) House repair
(c) Commercial property built
(d) Commercial repair
(e) Other construction represented by
  (i) railway building
  (ii) local authority loan expenditure.

For (a) (i) we have used the latest index, that of J. P. Lewis.[12] There is no index of (a) (ii), rural building, but Bernard Weber, quoted by Lewis,[13] rearranged the Census of Population data to arrive at the number of houses in rural areas (constant geographical areas) at each census date. The increases are treated as if they were the numbers built and a smoothly moving annual series is derived. (It is not feasible to use the urban series as representative of rural building because the proportionate movements from decade to decade of the increases in urban and rural houses are quite different.) Cairncross's assumption that the size of new houses is increased by 0·5 per cent per annum is adopted. The value of (b), house repair, is found by adding (a) (i) to (a) (ii), using the increase in the number of houses between 1891 and 1901 as the weight, and assuming that 1·0 per cent per annum of the value of houses is spent on house maintenance.

For (c) we first assumed that the quantity of factories, shops, offices and other commercial property in existence at the Census of Population dates was a function of the number of people occupied in manufacturing, commerce, professions and public administration. The data used here for the occupied population are those given by Mitchell and Deane.[14] They have to be reduced by 4 per cent in 1871 and earlier years, when the Census included retired persons. It is next assumed that, because of increased machinery per head and higher standards, the amount of commercial space per person employed increased by 10 per cent in each decade. One could then assume that space increased at a constant rate from census to census, but this would reduce the cyclical fluctuations of the total index of production. The amount of space fluctuates mildly with the cycle, certainly less violently than the amount of employment. We have therefore given the series the same fluctuation as that of the number of marriages in England and Wales, which is very highly correlated with production. (We multiply two series: one is space at census dates, with log linear annual interpolation; the other is percentage deviations from a nine-year moving average of marriages.) Next we take annual differences, allowing no negatives, and counting always from the preceding annual peak. Finally we run a three-year moving average through these differences, in recognition that some new building does occur even during recessions.

The value of (d) is derived from (c) by assuming that the amount spent on repairing and replacing commercial property is a constant proportion in each year of the amount of property in existence.

For (e) we have used Feinstein's and Cairncross's series of capital expenditure by the railways and loan expenditure by the local authorities, which are printed in Mitchell and Deane.[15] These are added together and deflated by Maiwald's index of the price of construction.[16]

The series (a) to (e) are added together using weights based on Cairncross's table of expenditure in 1907.[17] These weights are 1·00, 0·90, 0·61, 0·49, 2·46. This is the total used both for building materials and construction (Table A.1, series 4). Its components are also shown separately in three groups in Table A.1: housebuilding and repairs (series 5), commercial property and repairs (series 6), and other construction (series 7).

Since this index was compiled Feinstein has published a revised index of construction.[18] This is reproduced in Chart A.1, alongside our index. The main difference between the two is that since Feinstein's index makes no provision for maintenance and repair, it fluctuates more widely than ours. The difference in the mid-1860s is due to his having changed his figures for capital expenditure in railways, relying now on new calculations by Mitchell.[19]

Clothing

The preparation of this series involved much labour and many assumptions. The basic principle is to estimate the output of each type of yarn (wool, cotton, linen and silk), deduct net exports of yarn and cloth (or add net imports) and estimate what proportion of yarn remaining at home was used in clothing (in contrast with furnishings, blankets, sailcloth, etc.). The result is not very reliable.

Output of yarn is deduced from use of the raw materials, relying mainly on statistics of net imports.[20] Allowances have to be made for waste in conversion to yarn. In cotton this is taken as 6 per cent; in wool 12 per cent; in flax 33 per cent.

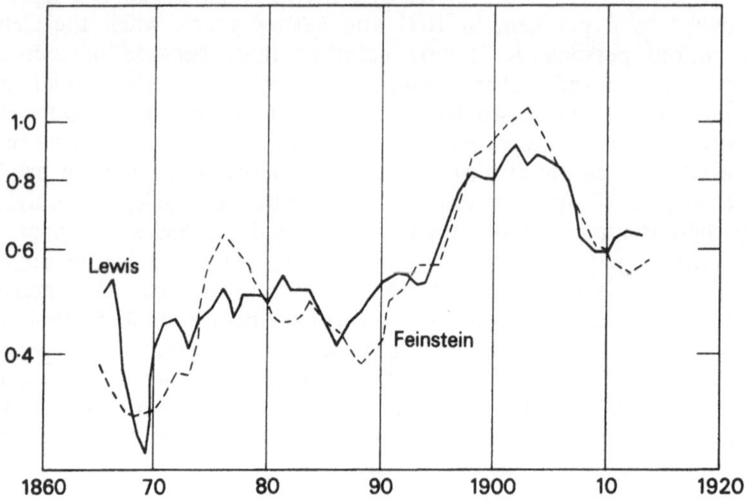

Chart A.1 UK: Construction

Imports and exports of cloth have to be converted into yarn content. Following Robson, yards of exported cloth are equated with pounds of yarn by multiplying by 0·18. Other conversion ratios are woollen cloth 0·67, worsted cloth 0·5, blankets 0·8, carpets 3·0, linen cloth 0·43, silk cloth 0·2. Since the trade statistics of the earlier years do not make all the distinctions one needs, much interpolation becomes necessary.

Not all the yarn remaining for home use goes into clothing. The proportions used in clothing are assumed to be: cotton 0·4, wool 0·75, linen 0·75, silk 1·0. Yarn used for clothing is now reconverted to yards of cloth, and added together, on the basis that value added per yard of wool or silk is twice as high as value added per yard of cotton or linen. Finally, the index is given the same cyclical fluctuation as textile finishing (q.v.) by means of nine-year moving averages.

The resulting index, it should be noted, is one of consumption, and therefore includes clothes which people make for themselves at home. An index of clothes purchased would rise faster.

Textile finishing

This is an index of yarn output, plus yarn imported, minus the export of cotton grey cloth. The different materials are weighted on the basis of the value of the work done on them by the finishing industry in 1907: silk 1·0, linen 2·7, wool 8·0, cotton 46·4.

Printing

It is assumed that printing was proportionate to the domestic use of writing paper. Spicer's annual output figures were used[21] plus net imports of writing and printing paper (excluding millboard). The series rises swiftly, but probably not fast enough, since domestic production of millboard, which rose more slowly, is included. Hoffmann objects to the annual fluctuations of Spicer's index. I have therefore taken a nine-year moving average of the result and given it the same cyclical fluctuation as the number of marriages (see the earlier reference to this procedure under building materials, (c) commercial property).

It is assumed that the production of printing materials moved proportionately with printing, so this index is weighted accordingly.

Chemicals

This index is based on the number of persons working in chemicals, etc., at the Census of Population dates, as given by Mitchell and Deane in the *Abstract of British Historical Statistics.* It is assumed that output per head increased by 1·0 per cent per annum. The index is given the same cyclical fluctuation as marriages. The assumed increase in productivity may be too high or low, but this makes little difference within the likely range since the industry was still quite small in 1907.

Electricity

Professor Prest[22] uses a series which grows by 15 per cent per annum between 1902 and 1912. Electricity developed rather slowly in the United Kingdom. It is here assumed to have grown by 5 per cent per annum between 1880 and 1890, by 10 per cent per annum between 1890 and 1900, and by 15 per cent per annum between 1900 and 1913.

Food manufacture

This series is based on the number of persons shown by the Censuses of Population working as cheesemongers, provision or fish curers, or manufacturers of condiments or aerated waters. The census figures are not quite comparable from year to year. The growth rate between 1861 and 1911 was 2·0 per annum, and this was taken for the whole period, with a further 0·5 added for an annual increase in productivity.

Gas

Hoffmann's series starts at 1882. There is a series for the Imperial Gas Company[23] for part of London only, which runs from 1850 to 1874. The growth rate of Hoffmann's series from 1883 to 1890 is 4·3 per cent per annum, and that of the Imperial Gas Company from 1866 to 1873 was 4·5 per cent. The two are therefore linked by assuming a growth rate of 4·4 per cent per annum between 1874 and 1882.

Meat

This refers to slaughtering. Hoffmann's series grows at a rate of 1·8 per cent per annum between 1868 and 1874. I have extrapolated backwards at this rate.

Comparison with Lomax

The revised index can be compared with that of K. S. Lomax[24] for the period in which they overlap. Excluding construction, the two indexes run as follows:

	Lomax	*Revised*	*Difference*
1900	76·7	76·4	−0·3
1901	76·4	75·8	−0·6
1902	78·7	76·6	−2·1
1903	79·0	75·5	−3·5
1904	79·1	76·2	−2·9
1905	83·0	81·7	−1·3
1906	85·3	85·9	+0·6
1907	87·6	88·7	+1·1
1908	85·0	82·6	−2·4
1909	85·5	83·6	−1·9
1910	87·7	84·9	−2·8
1911	91·6	90·8	−0·8
1912	93·2	93·3	+0·1
1913	100·0	100·0	—

The growth rate from 1900 to 1913 is the same for both indexes. The main difference between them is that the Juglar recession which lies between the peaks of 1899 and 1907 is less severe in the Lomax index.

GROSS DOMESTIC PRODUCT

The starting point is the year 1907, for which we have the Census of Production (manufactures and construction). All other years are derived by multiplying value added in 1907 by the appropriate annual index of real output.

GDP in 1907

Deane and Cole,[25] following Prest, put net national income of the United Kingdom in 1907 at £2,050m. I have added £50m. for depreciation, following Feinstein,[26] and deducted £144m. for interest and dividends from abroad, following Imlah.[27] This makes GDP £1,956m.

For manufacturing and construction I use the Census of Production totals, minus excise duties, plus £50m., the figure which the Census estimates for production which escaped its net. For agriculture I have used the series described below, with an addition for forestry and fishing.

Deane and Cole have a breakdown for Great Britain in 1907 which comes to £1,852m. because they have excluded Ireland. I have used their figures for rent of buildings and for transport, with adjustments for Ireland. But I have broken transport into shipping, carriage of people at home, and carriage of goods at home, using various data.[28]

All other categories are based on the numbers employed (interpolated from the 1901 and 1911 Censuses), and on wages and salaries.[29] The main divergence from the Deane and Cole estimate is in the sum of government and defence, where my figure is much closer to that given by Bowley for 1911 in *The Division of the Product of Industry* (page 25).

The breakdown chosen for 1907 depends partly on the series which are available to carry the figures back for earlier years. The series used are described below. The results are in Table A.3.

Agriculture
Ojala[30] gives value added in agriculture from 1867 to 1913, but only as averages for groups of years. Drescher[31] gives an annual series, but when this is averaged for the Ojala groups of years, there is a big divergence in the first two decades. It is here assumed that Ojala's averages are correct, and that subject to this Drescher's year-to-year fluctuation is acceptable. The two series are thus married by multiplying Drescher's series with a smoothly moving adjuster which gives it the same averages as Ojala's. By subtracting net imports at constant prices from actual consumption in the years 1867/9 and assumed consumption (based on population and income elasticity) in the years 1852/4, I deduced that output grew at about 0·4 per cent per annum over this period, and continued the index backwards at this rate.

Manufacturing and mining, construction
The indices reported in this Appendix are used.

Distribution
This corresponds to the volume of goods available for trading, which is found by adding the output of manufacturing, mining and agriculture, and the volume of imports, including re-exports, all at 1907 prices. As a check, the number of persons engaged in wholesale and retail distribution was estimated from the details of the Census of Population.[32] The population estimate yielded an increase from 1853 to 1907 of 227 per cent, while the volume of goods traded shows an increase of 225 per cent. This is a highly satisfying coincidence! The deduction from this coincidence that productivity per head in distribution was constant is plausible; but it is more likely that the number in distribution in 1853 is slightly underestimated, since the 1851 Census does not distinguish as finely between 'dealers' and 'makers' as do later censuses.

Volume of goods transported
This is assumed to vary in the same way as volume of goods traded.

Shipping
The main problem here is the changing carrying capacity of a ton of shipping. The fact that steamships could travel more miles per annum than sailing ships is usually met by counting one steam ton as equal to three sailing tons, and we have followed this tradition. Deadweight capacity also increased relatively to cubic capacity. This affected heavy goods more than light; it seems to have had relatively little effect on the net tonnage required for British imports. To allow for this, and for increasing speed, I have assumed an increase of 0·5 per cent per annum over and above the increase in tonnage.

Official statistics show tonnage on the register in each year, but what we need is tonnage in use. It is assumed that the annual fluctuation in use corresponds to the percentage deviations from a nine-year moving average of British foreign trade (Imlah's imports and exports at constant prices). The net tonnage of ships on the register in 1851 and at ten-year intervals

Table A.3 *UK: Gross Domestic Product at 1907 Prices (£m.)*

		1852	*1853*	*1854*	*1855*	*1856*	*1857*	*1858*	*1859*	*1860*	*1861*	*1862*	*1863*
(1)	Agriculture	137	137	138	139	139	140	140	141	141	142	142	143
(2)	Manufacture and mining	181	194	194	193	207	215	206	218	230	228	229	228
(3)	Construction	29	29	26	23	24	24	28	28	30	32	37	39
(4)	Shipping	4	5	5	4	5	5	5	6	6	6	6	6
(5)	Transport of people	13	13	14	14	15	15	15	16	16	17	17	18
(6)	Transport of goods	26	28	28	27	29	30	29	31	33	33	33	34
(7)	Distribution	89	96	95	93	100	102	100	105	112	113	114	115
(8)	Finance	1	1	1	1	1	1	1	1	1	1	2	2
(9)	Professions	24	25	25	26	27	28	29	30	31	32	33	34
(10)	Catering	13	13	13	14	14	14	15	15	16	16	16	16
(11)	Domestic service	52	52	53	54	54	55	56	57	57	58	59	60
(12)	Government	14	14	15	15	15	16	16	17	17	17	18	18
(13)	Defence	12	12	12	20	23	23	22	22	22	22	21	21
(14)	Rent	90	91	92	93	94	95	95	96	97	98	99	100
(15)	Miscellaneous services	10	10	10	10	10	11	11	11	11	11	11	12
(16)	GDP total[a]	694	720	720	726	758	772	769	793	820	826	839	844
(17)	GDP at current prices	—	—	—	630	657	636	624	646	682	715	728	746
(18)	GDP price, 1907 = 100	—	—	—	86·8	86·7	82·4	81·1	81·5	83·2	86·6	86·8	88·4

	1864	*1865*	*1866*	*1867*	*1868*	*1869*	*1870*	*1871*	*1872*	*1873*	*1874*	*1875*	*1876*	*1877*	*1878*	*1879*
(1) Agriculture	143	144	145	141	151	145	150	146	139	143	154	155	146	133	144	116
(2) Manufacture and mining	242	257	265	261	269	267	291	313	322	332	335	335	339	344	338	324
(3) Construction	45	49	53	38	30	27	39	44	46	40	46	48	51	45	50	50
(4) Shipping	6	7	8	7	8	8	9	10	10	10	10	11	11	12	12	13
(5) Transport of people	18	19	19	20	21	21	22	23	23	24	25	25	26	27	28	29
(6) Transport of goods	34	36	38	37	39	39	41	45	45	46	48	49	49	49	49	47
(7) Distribution	118	123	128	126	133	133	141	153	153	158	163	166	167	167	168	162
(8) Finance	2	2	3	3	3	4	4	5	5	5	6	6	6	7	7	8
(9) Professions	34	35	36	37	37	38	39	40	41	43	44	46	48	49	51	53
(10) Catering	17	17	17	17	17	18	18	18	19	19	20	21	22	22	23	24
(11) Domestic service	61	62	63	64	66	67	68	69	69	70	70	71	71	72	72	73
(12) Government	18	19	19	20	20	20	21	21	22	22	23	24	24	25	26	26
(13) Defence	20	20	20	19	19	18	18	18	18	18	18	18	18	18	17	17
(14) Rent	101	102	103	104	106	107	108	109	110	111	113	114	115	116	118	119
(15) Miscellaneous services	12	13	13	13	14	14	15	16	16	17	18	19	20	21	22	23
(16) GDP total[a]	873	905	929	907	932	926	982	1,028	1,038	1,060	1,091	1,106	1,112	1,105	1,126	1,083
(17) GDP at current prices	780	807	829	821	814	844	893	966	1,019	1,106	1,108	1,055	1,060	1,072	1,049	994
(18) GDP price, 1907=100	89·3	89·2	89·2	90·5	87·3	91·1	90·9	94·0	98·2	104·3	101·6	95·4	95·3	97·0	93·2	91·8

[a] Column may not add to total because of rounding.

Table A.3 *continued*

	1880	*1881*	*1882*	*1883*	*1884*	*1885*	*1886*	*1887*	*1888*	*1889*	*1890*	*1891*	*1892*	*1893*	*1894*	*1895*	*1896*
(1) Agriculture	140	140	133	142	145	141	146	137	140	143	145	149	144	138	141	139	139
(2) Manufacture and mining	365	386	406	413	396	382	378	407	433	462	468	472	448	440	468	487	521
(3) Construction	48	53	51	51	51	46	41	45	46	50	52	54	53	53	53	59	65
(4) Shipping	14	15	16	17	17	17	17	19	20	22	23	23	23	22	24	26	28
(5) Transport of people	29	30	31	32	33	34	35	36	37	38	39	41	42	43	44	46	47
(6) Transport of goods	53	54	56	58	56	55	55	58	61	65	65	67	65	64	68	70	74
(7) Distribution	181	184	190	198	192	189	189	198	208	222	223	228	223	217	232	241	253
(8) Finance	8	9	9	10	10	11	11	12	13	13	14	14	15	16	17	18	19
(9) Professions	55	57	59	60	62	63	65	67	69	70	72	74	76	78	80	82	84
(10) Catering	25	26	26	27	28	28	29	30	30	31	32	32	33	33	33	34	34
(11) Domestic service	73	74	74	75	76	77	77	78	79	80	80	81	81	80	80	80	79
(12) Government	27	28	29	29	30	31	32	33	33	34	35	36	37	38	39	40	41
(13) Defence	17	17	18	18	18	19	19	19	20	20	20	21	21	21	22	22	22
(14) Rent	120	122	123	124	125	126	127	128	130	131	132	133	135	136	138	140	141
(15) Miscellaneous services	24	25	26	27	28	29	30	31	32	33	35	36	37	38	39	40	41
(16) GDP total[a]	1,181	1,218	1,245	1,280	1,266	1,246	1,251	1,298	1,350	1,415	1,435	1,460	1,432	1,417	1,477	1,521	1,589
(17) GDP at current prices	1,044	1,088	1,131	1,159	1,105	1,080	1,090	1,115	1,196	1,287	1,348	1,335	1,307	1,273	1,322	1,387	1,414
(18) GDP price, 1907=100	88·4	89·3	90·8	90·5	87·3	86·7	87·1	85·9	88·6	91·0	93·9	91·4	91·3	89·8	89·5	89·2	89·0

	1897	1898	1899	1900	1901	1902	1903	1904	1905	1906	1907	1908	1909	1910	1911	1912	1913
(1) Agriculture	135	141	137	134	136	141	129	136	138	129	140	144	147	145	142	140	133
(2) Manufacture and mining	528	552	579	579	574	580	572	578	619	651	672	626	634	644	688	707	758
(3) Construction	75	80	79	79	85	91	85	87	85	82	75	61	58	58	63	64	63
(4) Shipping	28	29	30	30	31	32	33	34	36	38	40	38	39	42	44	47	49
(5) Transport of people	49	50	51	53	54	56	58	60	61	63	65	67	69	71	73	75	78
(6) Transport of goods	75	78	80	80	81	82	81	83	86	88	91	87	89	90	94	98	102
(7) Distribution	257	267	273	272	276	281	278	282	293	302	311	297	303	308	321	336	350
(8) Finance	20	21	22	23	24	25	27	28	30	31	33	35	37	39	41	43	45
(9) Professions	86	88	90	92	95	97	99	102	104	106	109	112	114	117	120	123	126
(10) Catering	35	36	36	37	37	38	40	41	42	44	45	47	48	50	51	53	55
(11) Domestic service	79	79	78	78	78	78	78	78	78	78	78	78	78	78	78	78	78
(12) Government	42	44	45	46	47	49	50	51	53	54	56	58	59	61	63	65	66
(13) Defence	23	23	23	30	37	37	30	25	26	26	27	28	28	29	30	30	31
(14) Rent	143	145	147	148	150	152	153	155	157	158	160	162	164	166	168	170	172
(15) Miscellaneous services	42	43	44	45	46	47	49	50	51	53	54	55	57	58	60	62	63
(16) GDP total[a]	1,615	1,673	1,713	1,725	1,751	1,786	1,760	1,789	1,859	1,903	1,956	1,893	1,924	1,955	2,034	2,090	2,167
(17) GDP at current prices	1,468	1,553	1,628	1,713	1,677	1,689	1,670	1,689	1,758	1,870	1,956	1,831	1,873	1,952	2,025	2,053	2,248
(18) GDP price, 1907=100	90·9	92·8	95·0	99·3	95·8	94·6	94·9	94·4	94·6	98·3	100·0	96·7	97·3	99·8	99·6	98·2	103·7

[a] Column may not add to total because of rounding.

is adjusted for the difference between steam and sail, then further adjusted upwards at a rate of 0·5 per cent per annum, and finally given the cyclical fluctuation of British foreign trade.

Transport of people
This is assumed to increase by 3·0 per cent per annum. This compares with transport of goods, whose rate of increase between 1853 and 1907 is 2·0 per cent. Passengers carried by railway increased by 3·1 per cent per annum, but passenger-miles increased more slowly because of the relative growth of suburban traffic. The figure of 3·0 per cent assumed is a compromise between the probable slower rise of railway passenger-miles and probable faster rise of omnibus plus tramway passenger-miles.

Rent of dwellings
Based on the number of houses in existence at Census of Population dates.

Defence
Based on armed services at home and abroad, assumed to increase at constant rates between census dates, except that the actual numbers are used for the years of the Crimean War and the Boer War.

Government, professions, finance, miscellaneous services
These are all based on Census of Population data, with two adjustments. (1) Numbers for 1871 and earlier years are reduced by 4 per cent, to eliminate retired persons. (2) Output per head is assumed to increase by 0·5 per cent per annum, having regard to the introduction of the typewriter and other economies in administration. Teachers are here included throughout in government. Finance includes Banking and Insurance.

Catering, domestic service
Based on Censuses of Population, adjusted for retired people in 1871 and earlier. No allowance is made for increasing productivity or for the more likely probability that the quality of service fell as relative numbers declined.

GDP at current prices
The series in Table A.3, row 17, is that given by Deane and Cole[33] for net national income of the United Kingdom, after adding Feinstein's depreciation series and subtracting Imlah's estimates of income from overseas interest and dividends. When this series is divided by GDP at constant 1907 prices, we get the national income price index number in column 18 of Table A.3.

Census of Population data
The Census of Population data (England and Wales, Scotland and Ireland) on the occupied population have been rearranged in Table A.4, after the pattern of a modern industrial classification. There are severe limitations on the comparability of the data, for the following reasons:

(1) The figures for 1851, 1861 and 1871 include retired persons.
(2) The earlier censuses do not make as fine distinctions as the later ones,

Table A.4 *UK: Occupied Population (000)*

		1851[a]	*1861*[a]	*1871*[a]	*1881*	*1891*	*1901*	*1911*
(1)	Agriculture	3,480	3,110	2,790	2,510	2,320	2,210	2,220
(2)	Fishing	50	50	60	70	70	60	60
(3)	Manufacturing	4,160	4,480	4,670	4,860	5,460	5,990	6,560
(4)	Mining	390	460	510	600	740	910	1,180
(5)	Construction	560	660	770	930	960	1,280	1,210
(6)	Distribution	770	900	1,130	1,410	1,770	2,200	2,720
(7)	Inland transport	220	330	370	520	690	990	1,090
(8)	Seamen	140	170	200	190	240	250	280
(9)	Finance	3	10	20	40	70	100	170
(10)	Professions	150	200	230	300	370	450	550
(11)	Civil administration	220	260	360	360	450	570	710
(12)	Defence	180	310	250	240	290	520	420
(13)	Catering	110	150	170	230	290	330	450
(14)	Domestic service	1,320	1,510	1,800	1,840	2,020	1,930	1,950
(15)	Miscellaneous services	90	100	130	190	260	320	420
(16)	General labourers	640	590	960	810	780	580	480
	Total	12,480[b]	13,290	14,420	15,100	16,780	18,700	20,470

[a] These figures include retired persons, except for seamen and defence.
[b] Columns may not add to totals because of rounding.

so some figures have to be split between categories as best one can. This especially affects the division between 'Manufacturing' and 'Distribution'.

(3) The proportion of persons recorded as 'General labourers' is rather high in the earlier years, with corresponding understatement of the numbers in Agriculture, Manufacturing, Mining, Construction and Transport. This is the most serious defect.

The classification used is given below, using the 'orders' of the 1911 classification of the Census of England and Wales.

Agriculture: Orders 117–129.
Fishing: 130.
Manufacturing: 63, 155–200, 203–227, 230–239, 266–272, 274–281, 283–289, 291–306, 308–322, 325–333, 335–373, 376–383, 385–389, 391–395, 397–398, 402–404, 406, 408, 410, 412–414, 417–418, 420, 422–424, 434–436, 439, 441, 448–451, 464–467.
Mining: 131–152.
Construction: 84–85, 201–202, 242–265.
Distribution: 66–73, 113–115, 153–154, 228–229, 240–241, 273, 282, 290, 307, 323–324, 334, 374–375, 384, 390, 399–401, 405, 407, 409, 411, 415–416, 419, 421, 433, 440, 442–446, 452–462.
Inland transport: 78–83, 86–104, 109–112.
Seamen: These are not the numbers shown in orders 105–108, which exclude seamen at sea at the time of the Census. The numbers here are for all seamen on British ships (including foreigners) and are taken from the annual *Statistical Abstract.*
Finance: Orders 74–77.
Professions: 19–33, 36–49.
Civil administration: 1–9, 34–35, 437–438.
Defence: This is the number serving at home and abroad, and therefore exceeds the numbers in orders 10–18.
Catering: 425–432.
Domestic service: 50–55, 61.
Miscellaneous services: 56–60, 62, 64–65, 116, 396.
General labourers: 463.

Appendix II

Core Industrial Production

This appendix describes the series used in the indexes for France, Germany and the United States, and the method of weighting of the combined index of core industrial production. The UK index is described in Appendix I.

FRANCE

The most authoritative study of French industrial production is that of T. J. Markovitch, *L'Industrie française de 1789 à 1964, Cahiers de l'Institut de Science Economique Appliquée*, AF 4, 5, 6, 7, 1965–6. Unfortunately Markovitch has published his data only in the form of decennial averages. It is useful for long-term trends, but is not a source of annual data.

Maurice Lévy-Leboyer has published an annual series in an article 'Le Croissance economique en France au XIXe siècle' in *Annales, Economies, Sociétés, Civilisations*, July–August 1968. François Crouzet has also published two annual series in 'Un Indice annual de l'industrie française au XIXe siècle', in the same journal, January–February 1970. One of Crouzet's series includes wool, linen and hemp, and the other series does not. Crouzet's indexes incorporate more information than Lévy-Leboyer's, so we have chosen Crouzet.

Markovitch's series grow from 1885/94 to 1905/13 at an annual average rate of 2·1 per cent. Crouzet's series grow by 3·0 per cent and 1·3 per cent between these dates: his fast series too fast because it overweights metal products, when compared with Markovitch (40·9 per cent in 1905/13 compared with Markovitch's 15·1 per cent), and his slow series too slowly because it overweights textiles (34·9 compared with 16·5). For our purpose we have resolved the difficulty for the time being by adding the two Crouzet series together and taking the simple average. This is tantamount to using the same series as Crouzet for industry groups, but halving the weight he assigns to wool, linen and hemp. The resulting new series grows at the same rate as Markovitch's decennial averages from 1885/94 to 1905/13. This is the series reproduced here. What we need, of course, is for Markovitch to publish an annual series.

Construction

Crouzet's series cover manufacturing and mining. The basis of an annual index for building is G. Désert's chapter, 'Aperçus sur l'industrie française du bâtiment au XIXe siècle,' in J. P. Bardet, P. Chaunu, G. Désert, P. Gouhier and H. Neveux, *Le Bâtiment*, Mouton, Paris 1973.

Désert has two series, one based on taxes paid on building materials used in towns, the other adjusted to add rural areas by assuming that consumption of building materials per head is the same in rural as in urban areas.

We have again fallen back on Markovitch, whose decennial averages for building grow at 1·15 per cent per annum from 1865/84 to 1895/1913 (long periods have to be used in averaging building). This happens, incidentally, to be about the same rate of growth as that of the urban population – a coincidence which also recurs in the UK, Germany and the USA.

Désert's urban series grows too fast (1·5 per cent per annum) and his combined series grows too slowly, because the rural population does not do as much building per head as the urban population. We have assumed instead that the absolute amount of building by the rural population was constant in each year, despite the small decline in the rural population over the period. A simple calculation then yields the constant sum which has to be added annually to Désert's index to give it the same rate of growth as Markovitch's. It gives rural building as 17·4 per cent of urban building in 1913, equivalent to 56 per cent per head of urban building per head. This adjusted index is the one reproduced in Table A.5.

Weights

Markovitch makes construction 13·2 per cent of industrial production in 1905/13. Allowing for trends to 1913, we have used weights of 1 for building to 7 for manufacturing and mining.

GERMANY

The trouble in making an index of industrial production for Germany is that the basis of recording German imports changed several times. This affects those industries for which the basic data are or include raw material imports, such as wool, cotton, silk, leather, vegetable oils, tobacco or timber. The biggest change occurred in 1879. Between 1872 and 1879 transit trade is included (but not always) in statistics of imports, but not fully in statistics of exports. The published statistics therefore show German imports falling by 25 per cent between 1879 and 1880, and Hoffmann, translating this into constant prices, shows a fall of 24 per cent (page 537). Actually 1880 was a much more prosperous year than 1879. Import figures for the 1870s have to be reduced by at least 30 per cent to make them comparable with the 1880s, and even then the series is not good because of inconsistent treatment of the transit trade.

Another major break occurs between 1888 and 1889, with the incorporation into the customs union of Bremen and most of Hamburg. This increased the published imports and reduced the published exports, because these towns had been importing more from the non-German world than the German customs area had been importing from them, and exporting less

Table A.5 *France: Industrial Production*

	I[a]	*II*[b]	*III*[c]		*I*[a]	*II*[b]	*III*[c]
1865	32·4	48·8	34·5	1890	52·1	63·4	53·5
1866	35·2	54·0	37·6	1891	55·5	67·1	57·0
1867	34·1	54·0	36·6	1892	58·3	67·6	59·5
1868	37·2	56·8	39·7	1893	56·0	67·6	57·5
1869	38·3	57·4	40·7	1894	58·4	68·4	59·7
1870	33·4	31·0	33·1	1895	55·4	69·3	57·1
1871	35·0	41·4	35·8	1896	59·3	71·7	60·9
1872	39·0	46·3	39·9	1897	63·0	73·5	64·3
1873	37·3	45·6	38·3	1898	64·6	74·9	65·9
1874	40·2	45·3	40·8	1899	67·9	81·9	69·7
1875	40·7	47·7	41·6	1900	65·6	71·4	66·3
1876	41·0	51·2	42·3	1901	64·4	68·6	64·9
1877	40·1	58·2	42·4	1902	63·4	70·0	64·2
1878	40·6	55·0	42·4	1903	67·2	73·5	68·0
1879	40·0	57·1	42·1	1904	65·1	70·7	65·8
1880	43·2	67·9	46·3	1905	72·9	70·7	72·6
1881	47·9	73·1	51·1	1906	74·0	71·4	73·7
1882	49·2	78·3	52·8	1907	77·0	74·2	76·7
1883	48·7	71·1	51·5	1908	75·8	73·8	75·6
1884	45·0	66·5	47·7	1909	81·5	76·0	80·8
1885	45·3	60·2	47·2	1910	78·5	80·8	78·8
1886	46·6	59·5	48·2	1911	88·6	88·5	88·6
1887	47·6	60·2	48·4	1912	103·0	95·5	102·1
1888	49·2	62·6	50·9	1913	100·0	100·0	100·0
1889	52·2	61·7	53·4				

[a] I = Manufacturing and mining.
[b] II = Construction.
[c] III = Manufacturing, mining and construction.

of their own produce to the non-German world than the customs union was exporting to them for their own consumption. For comparability with the 1890s, exports need to be reduced by about 10 per cent overall, and imports to be increased by about 5 per cent (adjustments which must also be carried back to the 1870s).

This is not all, since other but minor adjustments were also made in the customs area in 1882, 1884 and 1905. The truth is that a lot of work has to be done on German trade statistics if they are to become a reliable basis for economic analysis; at present they constitute a trap.

Hoffmann is aware of these defects, but decides to ignore them. This seems not to have had much effect on his index of industrial production from 1880 onwards, but it plays havoc with his results for the 1870s. Thus, according to his index, manufacturing (excluding building and mining) fell 3 per cent from 1879 to 1880, and was only 16 per cent higher in 1883 than in 1873. Neither of these is possible. For example, between 1879 and 1880 his indexes for minerals, metal production and railway traffic rose by 12, 16 and 13 per cent respectively, as we would expect from what we know of the relative prosperity of 1879 and 1880. These series were not affected by the customs statistics.

This defect does not confine itself to his index of industrial production, since it enters into other indexes which he has derived from industrial production, including elements of his building index, his index of value added in distribution, and above all his estimates of national income. Hoffmann's book is indispensable for students of German economic history, but its materials relating to the 1870s have to be used with the greatest caution.

Our solution for the purposes of this book derives from observing that an index of German coal production (including lignite) grows at the same rate as the index of manufacturing, between 1884 and 1913, and also between 1866 and 1871. We have therefore simply substituted coal production for the years 1871–84 for Hoffmann's manufacturing index between those dates. The rest of the index of manufacturing is obtained by subtracting building from Hoffmann's index of manufacturing plus building on pages 391–3, using the weights he gives there.

One result of this is that German manufacturing grows at the same rate between the peak dates 1873, 1883, 1890 and 1899. And this in turn has some effect on our ultimate conclusion that the Kondratiev price swing cannot be explained by changes in the rate of growth of the core countries.

A minor but puzzling problem concerns the year 1900. Hoffmann's index shows a rather high peak here, but on recalculation from his basic data we get the same total manufacturing output for 1900 as for 1899. We have made this adjustment.

Construction

Hoffmann's index for construction relies heavily on statistics of taxes on buildings in certain German territories, plus statistics of property insurance. Regional statistics are multiplied by a population factor to represent the whole country; and statistics in current values are adjusted by indices of the prices of buildings. Annual construction is derived by subtracting the values in each year from the values of the next year.

It is well known that fiscal statistics are an unreliable basis for annual construction indices. Similar British and French statistics have the advantage over the German statistics that they cover the whole country, and do not have to be blown up, but their results are still different from those yielded by more reliable data.

Hoffmann's series is not implausible after about 1890, but breaks down completely in the 1870s and 1880s. For example, his peak level of 1875 is not again reached until 1892. This is not possible. According to the census the urban population was growing then by 2·3 per cent per annum. Also in Hoffmann's figures the labour force in building doubled between these dates, so his figures together imply that productivity in building halved over these seventeen years.

Data for building permits do not exist, so we have turned to his data for output of construction materials. Hoffmann offers four series: bricks, cement, ceramics and timber. Ceramics is treacherous for our purpose since it includes non-building uses. Cement is a new industry, still growing logistically and too rapidly to be helpful. The brick series is not reliable before 1890, since it incorporates Hoffmann's extrapolations based on his building index. The timber series seems to be quite independent. Bricks and timber grow at the same rate after 1890. We have used timber from 1865, and added bricks from 1890 (equal weights).

Our series grows at about the right rate: from the peak of 1894 to the peak of 1910 is a growth rate of 2·55 per cent per annum. This is about the same as the rate of growth of the urban population, a surprising correspondence which we have also found in Britain, France and the USA.

The main snag is that the timber series fluctuates more widely than the brick series where they overlap. This suggests that our series overestimates the degree of the building slump in Germany in the second half of the 1870s.

Weights

We have combined manufacturing with mining, using weights of 9 to 1, and building with manufacturing plus mining, using weights of 1 to 9. So the weights are 0·9, 1·0 and 8·1.

Table A.6 *Germany: Industrial Production*

	I[a]	II[b]	III[c]		I[a]	II[b]	III[c]
1865	11·3	29·9	13·2	1890	39·0	60·2	41·1
1866	11·7	28·2	13·3	1891	39·9	61·9	42·1
1867	12·4	27·1	13·8	1892	40·4	66·3	43·0
1868	12·9	31·3	14·8	1893	42·0	60·8	43·9
1869	13·8	40·7	16·5	1894	44·4	70·1	46·9
1870	14·0	37·6	16·4	1895	48·1	65·8	49·9
1871	15·6	37·2	17·8	1896	50·0	70·9	52·1
1872	17·6	41·8	20·0	1897	52·4	71·0	54·2
1873	19·2	43·5	21·7	1898	54·6	71·1	56·2
1874	19·1	43·8	21·6	1899	56·9	74·0	58·7
1875	19·9	40·0	21·9	1900	57·4	75·2	59·2
1876	20·4	44·2	22·8	1901	57·7	76·2	59·6
1877	19·9	35·5	21·5	1902	59·0	79·5	61·1
1878	20·9	36·5	22·5	1903	63·1	86·0	65·4
1879	22·2	36·2	23·7	1904	65·7	86·6	67·8
1880	24·8	37·6	26·1	1905	68·6	86·2	70·4
1881	25·2	40·4	26·7	1906	71·7	87·7	73·3
1882	27·5	42·8	29·1	1907	76·8	89·0	78·0
1883	29·5	47·7	31·3	1908	76·5	90·8	78·0
1884	30·3	50·5	32·3	1909	80·4	95·0	81·9
1885	30·6	50·5	32·6	1910	83·8	104·7	85·9
1886	30·7	49·4	32·6	1911	89·0	99·5	90·1
1887	33·1	53·6	35·2	1912	96·2	100·5	96·6
1888	34·8	53·9	36·7	1913	100·0	100·0	100·0
1889	37·4	56·4	39·3				

[a] I = Manufacturing and mining.
[b] II = Construction.
[c] III = Manufacturing, mining and construction.

USA

The basic source for US industrial production is the index of Edwin Frickey, published in his *Production in the United States 1860–1913*, Harvard University Press, Cambridge, Mass., 1947. The version used here is that presented by Warren Nutter, incorporating amendments by Fabricant, Persons, Leong, Barger and Schorr. See Warren Nutter, *The Growth of Industrial Production in the Soviet Union,* National Bureau of Economic Research, Princeton University Press, Princeton, 1962, p. 382. It includes both manufacturing and mining.

Construction

There is a wealth of series on US construction. Most of these are reproduced in R. E. Lipsey and Doris Preston, *Source Book of Statistics Relating to Construction*, National Bureau of Economic Research, Columbia University Press, New York, 1966. We have combined three indexes, with equal weights, namely Gottlieb's index of non-farm residential housekeeping units, Long's index of non-residential building, and the American Iron and Steel Institute's index of the 'consumption' of rails. Long's index is in current values; it is converted to volume by dividing by the price index for capital expenditures of all regulated industries in M. J. Ulmer, *Capital in Transportation, Communications and Public Utilities,* National Bureau of Economic Research, Princeton University Press, Princeton, 1960, pp. 248–9.

This combined series has the merit that it grows at the same rate as the urban population. This is considered a 'merit' only because it is observed that this correspondence also exists in the British, French and German series.

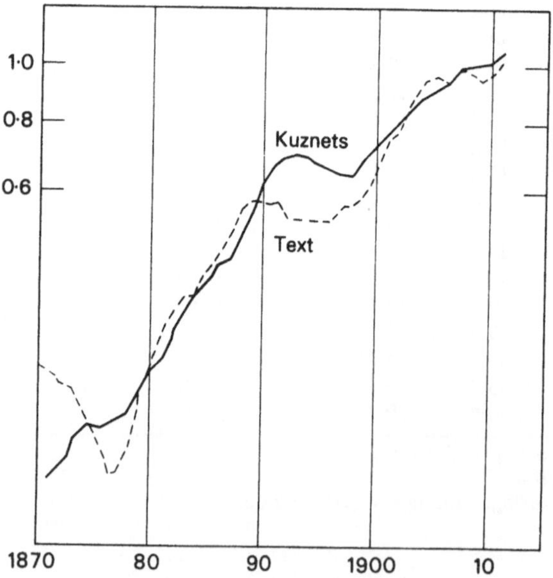

Chart A.2 USA: Construction

The US construction series probably fluctuates too widely, in comparison with these other three because, except in the case of rails, it does not include elements reflecting repair and maintenance expenditures, which are more stable than new building.

Our US construction series and Kuznets's series are compared in Chart A.2, both in five-year moving averages. Both are unrealistic in the 1870s, his for brushing aside the great depression, and ours for exaggerating it, a defect which it owes to the incredibly wide fluctuation of Long's series. An average of these two construction series for the seventies would probably be just about right. Kuznets's series also exaggerates the amount of construction in the 1890s. In consequence his ratio of gross domestic capital formulation rises from 20·6 per cent for the period 1879–88 to 23·1 per cent for the period 1889–98, falling back to 22·8 per cent for the period 1899–1908. This is most unlikely, since the 1890s were more depressed than the decades on either side. Also, if we are right, Kuznets's figures underestimate the size of the capital stock before 1899.

Table A.7 *USA: Industrial Production*

	I[a]	II[b]	III[c]		I[a]	II[b]	III[c]
1865	8·0	13·1	8·7	1890	35·0	62·5	38·9
1866	9·8	18·8	11·1	1891	36·0	52·2	38·3
1867	10·3	21·8	11·9	1892	38·8	61·8	42·1
1868	10·8	25·1	12·8	1893	34·7	51·9	37·2
1869	11·6	26·2	13·7	1894	33·7	45·3	35·4
1870	11·7	26·3	13·8	1895	39·7	59·1	42·5
1871	12·3	32·5	15·2	1896	36·9	55·0	39·5
1872	14·6	30·4	16·9	1897	39·7	60·2	42·6
1873	14·4	29·1	16·5	1898	44·7	47·5	45·1
1874	13·9	20·3	14·8	1899	49·2	62·1	51·0
1875	13·5	21·3	14·6	1900	50·6	54·3	51·1
1876	13·4	20·1	14·4	1901	56·7	80·8	60·1
1877	14·6	16·3	14·8	1902	63·2	90·0	67·0
1878	15·5	17·5	15·8	1903	65·4	88·7	68·7
1879	17·5	21·1	18·0	1904	62·3	77·3	64·4
1880	20·3	29·3	21·6	1905	73·6	104·7	78·0
1881	22·3	44·5	25·5	1906	78·9	109·0	83·2
1882	23·9	39·5	26·1	1907	80·6	99·1	83·2
1883	24·4	38·8	26·5	1908	68·0	77·4	69·3
1884	23·1	35·7	24·9	1909	80·2	103·3	83·5
1885	23·2	35·4	24·9	1910	85·3	105·7	88·2
1886	27·9	46·9	30·6	1911	82·2	98·5	84·5
1887	29·5	59·6	33·8	1912	93·7	110·6	96·1
1888	30·6	53·1	33·8	1913	100·0	100·0	100·0
1889	32·6	58·4	36·3				

[a] I = Manufacturing and mining.
[b] II = Construction.
[c] III = Manufacturing, mining and construction.

Weights

According to Kuznets's calculations (reproduced in *Historical Statistics of the United States*, p. 13), for the period 1904/13 value added in construction was 4·3 per cent and value added in manufacturing and mining was 22·2 per cent of national income. Allowing for trends to 1913, we have used weights of 1 : 6.

THE COMBINED INDEX

The index of core industrial production given in Table A.9 is found by adding together, on 1913 base, the indexes of manufacturing, mining and building of the UK, France, Germany and the USA.

Basically, the weighting is by value added in 1913. Value added is given in national currencies for the UK in Appendix I of this volume, and for Germany in Hoffmann's *Wachstum*; it can be deduced for France from Markovitch, and for the USA from various figures relating separately to manufacturing, mining and building in *Historical Statistics of the United States.*

The trouble with this combination is that it gives excessive weights to France and to the USA, in relation to the UK and Germany. This is borne out if we arrive at the weights in a different way. Svennilson (in *Growth and Stagnation in the European Economy,* United Nations, Geneva, 1954) gives for each of these countries the real dollar value of its industrial production in 1938, and index numbers linking 1938 and 1913. These results are quite different.

Table A.8 *Core: Weights for Industrial Production*

	Value added 1913	*Population*	*Productivity*	*Svennilson*	*This volume*
UK	100	100	100	100	100
France	85	69	124	55	58
Germany	122	130	94	121	122
USA	307	127	242	233	241

From the third column of Table A.8 it will be seen that our first calculation makes productivity 2·42 times as high in the USA as in the UK in 1913. This is based on value added in the censuses of manufactures. However US prices were higher than British prices. According to Rostas (*Comparative Productivity in British and American Industry*, Cambridge University Press, Cambridge, 1948, pp. 27, 42) between 1907 and 1937 productivity per man grew 47 per cent in the UK and 71 per cent in the USA, and was 2·17 higher in the USA at the later date; from which it follows that the US ratio was 1·87 in 1907, or say 1·9 in 1913. Multiplying the ratio of persons by 1·9 brings value added to 241. This figure compares well with Svennilson's 233, and we have used it (last column).

By the same process we see that the original calculations make French productivity 24 per cent higher than the British in 1913 if Markovitch's estimate of value added is used. This is not plausible. French productivity was thought to be a little below that of Germany. If we make it 85 per cent of British productivity, real value added becomes 58, which is still a little higher than Svennilson's 55. We have used 58.

The German figures raise no problem, since the productivity estimate is plausible and the Svennilson result corresponds with the values added in current prices.

The weights actually used, based on the last column of Table A.8 are:

UK	19·5
France	11·0
Germany	23·5
USA	46·0
	100·0

Table A.9 *Core: Industrial Production*

1865	18·2	1890	45·8
1866	19·9	1891	46·3
1867	19·9	1892	47·9
1868	20·8	1893	45·4
1869	21·6	1894	46·3
1870	21·7	1895	50·5
1871	23·6	1896	51·0
1872	25·6	1897	53·7
1873	25·7	1898	56·2
1874	25·4	1899	60·5
1875	25·5	1900	60·3
1876	25·9	1901	64·5
1877	25·8	1902	68·2
1878	26·5	1903	70·1
1879	27·4	1904	68·6
1880	31·0	1905	77·1
1881	34·1	1906	81·0
1882	35·5	1907	82·8
1883	36·3	1908	74·9
1884	34·9	1909	83·0
1885	34·5	1910	86·1
1886	37·0	1911	87·6
1887	39·9	1912	96·5
1888	41·6	1913	100·0
1889	44·0		

Appendix III

Miscellaneous Statistics

It is not feasible to reproduce here all the statistical series to which reference is made in the text. This appendix is confined to series produced or altered by the author, and series which may not be easily accessible to the reader.

WORLD PRODUCTION

Wheat
For world production of wheat, see Appendix IV.

Cotton
World cotton production from New York Cotton Exchange, *Cotton Year Book*, New York, 1950. Annual figures from 1870–1 here attributed to 1871. The years 1865–73 linked to a series in E. von Halle, *Baumwollproduktion und Pflanzungswirtschaft*, Berlin, 1879, vol. I. The latter series has to be adjusted for comparability, since it excludes cotton produced in India and used by Indian mills. Production in 1912–13 was 21·86 million bales of 478 lb each.

Coffee
Five-year averages of world exports from 1870 and annual exports from 1883 to 1909 are given in International Institute of Agriculture, *The World's Coffee*, Rome, 1947, pp. 96–7. For earlier years annual exports of coffee from Brazil are available in the annual *Annuario Estadistico do Café*, exports from rest of world intrapolated, using the five-year averages in *The World's Coffee*. The years from 1909 linked to a series in V. D. Wickizer, *The World's Coffee Economy*, Stanford University, Palo Alto, 1943, pp. 240–1. World production in 1913 (i.e. 1912–13) was 16·8 million bags of 60 kg each.

Wool
An annual series prepared by Professor B. P. Philpott for his Ph.D. thesis at the University of Leeds; privately communicated. See also his article based on his thesis, 'Fluctuations in Wool Prices, 1870–1953', *Yorkshire Bulletin of Economic and Social Research*, March 1955. Output in 1913 was 2,089 million lb of greasy wool.

Table A.10 *World Production (1913 = 100)*

	Cotton	*Coffee*	*Wool*
1865	14·1	—	—
1866	17·8	—	—
1867	19·2	—	—
1868	22·2	—	—
1869	20·7	—	—
1870	23·4	39·7	52·3
1871	30·8	41·1	50·7
1872	24·9	38·3	54·0
1873	27·4	34·6	53·3
1874	28·6	40·4	54·6
1875	27·9	38·2	58·4
1876	31·3	39·2	57·7
1877	29·1	40·9	60·7
1878	29·7	46·7	61·3
1879	29·3	34·6	63·6
1880	35·2	40·4	61·7
1881	39·9	42·7	66·0
1882	35·4	55·4	65·0
1883	43·9	46·9	68·6
1884	38·8	57·6	73·0
1885	38·8	49·6	72·7
1886	41·2	53·3	73·9
1887	42·4	35·4	73·5
1888	46·3	56·8	77·6
1889	47·1	43·1	79·7
1890	50·5	47·7	79·4
1891	57·1	61·3	81·8
1892	58·6	57·7	93·1
1893	48·5	48·1	90·1
1894	52·6	60·2	92·8
1895	63·5	53·1	100·6
1896	52·9	71·2	93·9
1897	59·9	82·1	92·9
1898	70·5	70·3	94·6
1899	73·7	70·6	87·8
1900	64·6	77·2	83·5
1901	66·7	100·9	90·3
1902	68·5	89·8	93·1
1903	73·5	80·5	84·8
1904	73·5	73·9	81·3
1905	87·8	75·6	86·0
1906	76·9	121·7	85·1
1907	92·9	75·8	90·0
1908	81·8	86·5	98·6
1909	93·3	97·4	102·9
1910	80·0	74·0	103·8
1911	90·9	88·8	106·3
1912	105·2	83·7	106·4
1913	100·0	100·0	100·0

PRICES

Wheat

The Sauerbeck–Statist index of the price of 'American' wheat in London, published annually in the *Journal of the Royal Statistical Society*, from 1886 onwards. The price in 1913 is given as 36s 5d per quarter.

Cotton

The Sauerbeck-Statist index for 'American Middling'. The price in 1913 was 7·01 pence per lb.

Wool

The Sauerbeck–Statist index for 'merino' wool. The price of 'Adelaide average greasy' in 1913 was 9·5 pence per lb.

Coffee

The Sauerbeck–Statist index for 'Rio Good'. The price in 1913 was 53 shillings per cwt.

Manufactures

This is an index of the f.o.b. prices of manufactures in world trade. More data for making such an index become available from time to time, so the index is continually improved. The version given here uses Schlote's index for UK exports of manufactures, Lévy-Leboyer's similar index for France, Lipsey's data on both finished and semi-finished manufactures exported from the USA (which runs only from 1879) and Hoffmann's data on both finished and semi-finished exports from Germany, which runs only from 1880, supplemented by Desai's data from 1872 to 1880. The component indexes are weighted from 1899 to 1913 and from 1880 to 1899 by the actual exports of manufactures given by Maizels for 1913 and 1899 respectively. From 1865 to 1880 the weights are from the ratios for 1883 given by W. A. Lewis, in 'International Competition in Manufactures'. (See Werner Schlote, *British Overseas Trade from 1700 to the 1930s*, Basil Blackwell, Oxford, 1952; Lévy-Leboyer, 'L'Héritage de Simiand: prix, profit et termes d'échange au XIXᵉ siècle', *Revue Historique*, January–March 1970; R. E. Lipsey, *Price and Quantity Trends in the Foreign Trade of the United States*, Princeton University Press, Princeton, NJ, 1963; W. G. Hoffmann, *Das Wachstum der Deutschen Wirtschaft seit der Mitte des 19. Jahrhunderts*, Springer-Verlag, Berlin, 1965; A. V. Desai, *Real Wages in Germany 1871–1913*, Oxford University Press, Oxford, 1968; and W. A. Lewis, 'International Competition in Manufactures', *American Economic Review*, May 1957.)

Primary products

The starting point is the separate Sauerbeck–Statist indexes for food and raw materials. These are added, using as weights the proportions of food and raw materials in world trade in 1913, which Lamartine Yates (*Forty*

Years of Foreign Trade) gives as 3 : 4. The index is required for deflating Hilgerdt's figures of world trade in primary products, which he reaches by adding together imports and exports. The trade figures are therefore an average of c.i.f. and f.o.b. values. The difference between import and export values is 10 per cent in 1913 and 15 per cent in 1881–5; and *mirabile dictu*, this is also exactly the extent of the change in the freight index. We have therefore subtracted 5 per cent of the freight index from the Sauerbeck indexes; so the index given here is an average of c.i.f. and f.o.b. prices.

Tropical crops

This index is taken from W. A. Lewis, *Aspects of Tropical Trade 1883–1965* (Almquist and Wicksell, Stockholm, 1969), where it is explained in detail. The prices are those of the British Board of Trade. The weights, which are in accordance with the value of tropical exports in 1913, are as follows:

Cocoa	3	Rice	11
Coffee	15	Rubber	10
Cotton	16	Sugar	11
Hides	9	Tea	6
Jute	7	Timber	2
Palm oil	10		
		Total	100

Cereals

This series uses the same four cereals as the United Nations' index of the price of cereals. Prices are those of the British Board of Trade. Weights are the same as used by the United Nations.

Wheat	57·9
Rice	21·6
Barley	10·3
Maize	10·2

Ocean freights

For the years 1870–1912 Cairncross's index of inward shipping freights is used. The years 1869 and 1913 are added from L. Isserlis, 'Tramp Shipping Cargoes and Freights', in the *Journal of the Royal Statistical Society*, 1938. There is no index for the years 1865–9. Taking a tip from Imlah, we have assumed that freights moved in the same ratio as prices, in this case the Sauerbeck–Statist index of British wholesale prices. Therefore on 1913 base, the index numbers we have used are:

1865	*1866*	*1867*	*1868*	*1869*
211	213	209	207	205

Table A.11 *Prices*

	Wheat	*Cotton*	*Wool*	*Coffee*	*Manufactures*	*Primary products*	*Tropical crops*	*Cereals*	*Ocean freights*
1865	116·9	270·5	121·6	109·7	156·2	—	—	—	—
1866	140·0	220·5	128·4	95·2	155·6	—	—	—	—
1867	181·5	155·1	114·7	84·4	140·6	—	—	—	—
1868	179·9	150·0	104·5	73·5	133·1	—	—	—	—
1869	136·9	173·1	89·7	80·7	133·9	—	—	—	204
1870	132·3	141·0	89·7	84·4	130·9	—	—	—	211
1871	153·8	121·8	113·6	103·6	132·7	—	120·5	136·1	211
1872	161·5	150·0	140·9	133·8	142·3	—	127·8	139·3	207
1873	173·8	128·2	134·0	161·5	139·6	—	127·1	144·0	236
1874	156·9	114·1	128·4	157·9	132·4	—	126·1	142·4	215
1875	132·3	105·1	119·3	150·6	126·4	—	120·2	125·5	203
1876	132·3	88·5	106·8	139·8	118·3	—	116·5	120·5	213
1877	150·7	89·7	106·8	144·6	113·3	—	123·1	140·1	222
1878	132·3	84·6	105·6	116·9	108·3	—	116·8	127·5	182
1879	132·3	89·7	100·0	109·7	101·6	—	112·5	123·2	171
1880	140·0	98·7	117·0	114·5	109·4	—	116·2	126·8	176
1881	143·0	91·0	104·5	92·8	106·0	96·4	110·5	124·4	186
1882	133·8	94·9	104·5	73·5	107·0	96·0	109·9	120·2	171
1883	123·0	82·0	101·1	80·7	105·0	94·8	109·2	113·2	153
1884	100·0	85·9	96·6	89·2	102·0	87·8	99·7	97·9	127
1885	95·4	79·5	82·9	73·5	96·4	83·7	93·0	94·3	112
1886	95·4	73·1	79·5	86·8	93·1	81·1	87·2	90·3	102
1887	94·8	79·5	81·8	147·0	92·4	80·1	88·0	90·1	99
1888	101·5	79·5	81·8	120·5	93·8	81·9	89·2	92·1	112

1889	96·9	84·6	93·2	143·4	94·2	83·3	93·8	94·2	131
1890	96·9	85·9	86·3	156·7	96·2	83·9	94·9	94·3	108
1891	109·2	66·7	79·5	143·4	94·2	84·3	95·3	107·6	109
1892	90·7	59·0	69·3	127·7	89·7	81·3	93·5	95·6	88
1893	76·9	65·4	68·2	153·0	87·6	80·4	94·4	81·9	89
1894	64·6	53·8	62·5	141·0	83·5	73·9	88·3	72·1	85
1895	70·7	55·1	64·8	139·8	83·2	73·0	84·8	73·0	78
1896	80·0	61·5	70·4	109·7	85·2	71·4	87·9	76·9	87
1897	95·4	55·1	67·0	77·1	83·5	72·5	85·3	87·2	86
1898	101·5	47·4	72·7	60·3	83·7	74·8	82·7	94·7	101
1899	83·0	51·3	94·3	57·8	88·9	79·7	81·2	85·5	88
1900	86·1	78·2	86·3	75·9	94·4	87·8	84·7	85·0	105
1901	83·0	67·9	70·4	66·3	91·7	83·1	82·4	82·8	72
1902	83·0	69·2	81·8	57·8	89·2	82·6	76·1	82·0	68
1903	84·6	85·9	88·6	56·6	90·2	82·6	79·9	84·4	70
1904	92·3	93·6	87·5	69·9	90·7	83·8	83·9	83·5	68
1905	93·8	73·1	95·4	74·7	91·4	86·3	83·9	87·0	71
1906	89·2	84·6	98·8	73·5	93·7	91·5	85·5	85·5	71
1907	98·4	93·6	100·0	57·8	97·6	95·1	89·6	95·4	74
1908	103·0	82·0	86·3	57·8	95·0	87·6	86·1	100·4	65
1909	113·8	89·7	98·8	66·3	92·5	88·7	88·3	105·8	70
1910	100·0	114·1	102·2	79·5	94·5	93·0	102·5	96·9	74
1911	96·9	100·0	94·3	109·7	95·9	94·7	99·5	95·9	78
1912	104·6	92·3	97·7	124·1	97·4	99·7	103·5	106·5	113
1913	100·0	100·0	100·0	100·0	100·0	100·0	100·0	100·0	100

TRADE IN PRIMARY PRODUCTS

India

Exports of agricultural products. Index number taken from George Brandau, *Ernteschwankungen und Wirtschaftliche Wechsellagen 1873–1913*, Fischer, Jena, 1936. Brandau's index runs only from 1873; earlier years calculated from the UK *Statistical Abstract Relating to British India* (annual), which was also Brandau's source. The index omits opium and indigo which were large items at the beginning but not at the end of the period; it therefore grows somewhat too fast. On the other hand exports of industrial products, also omitted, grow faster.

World trade in primary products

The value index is taken from W. A. Lewis, 'World Production, Prices and Trade', *Manchester School of Economic and Social Studies,* May 1952. This is divided by the price index in our Table A.11 to give the volume index in Table A.12.

Table A.12 *Trade in Primary Products*

	India Agricultural exports	*World Trade*	
		Value	*Volume*
1867	28·5	—	—
1868	34·4	—	—
1869	32·5	—	—
1870	31·3	—	—
1871	41·9	—	—
1872	32·7	—	—
1873	33·1	—	—
1874	34·2	—	—
1875	35·8	—	—
1876	33·6	—	—
1877	33·6	—	—
1878	30·7	—	—
1879	35·1	—	—
1880	39·7	—	—
1881	50·1	36·4	37·8
1882	57·2	37·5	39·1
1883	53·2	37·8	39·9
1884	50·9	36·0	41·0
1885	50·7	33·9	40·5
1886	54·6	33·4	41·2
1887	54·7	34·3	42·8
1888	56·4	36·2	44·2
1889	58·5	40·0	48·0
1890	62·5	41·6	49·6
1891	59·1	43·1	51·1
1892	56·2	40·7	50·1

Table A.12 *continued*

	India Agricultural exports	*World Trade*	
		Value	*Volume*
1893	54·3	39·9	49·6
1894	58·8	39·6	53·6
1895	60·4	40·4	55·3
1896	53·4	42·3	59·2
1897	56·7	44·8	61·8
1898	62·9	47·5	63·5
1899	54·3	50·4	63·2
1900	52·3	53·9	61·4
1901	70·2	53·9	64·9
1902	72·3	55·6	67·3
1903	84·6	59·5	72·0
1904	84·9	61·2	73·0
1905	79·1	65·2	75·6
1906	80·8	71·4	78·0
1907	85·1	75·1	79·0
1908	75·0	69·0	78·8
1909	87·8	76·4	86·1
1910	89·2	84·7	91·1
1911	93·7	88·2	93·1
1912	97·3	97·5	97·8
1913	100·0	100·0	100·0

POSTWAR PRICE STATISTICS

This section contains the price index numbers which have been used for Charts 9.1 and 9.3. They are continuations beyond 1913 of three series already reported in the preceding section. They are shown here to base 1913 = 100, but the weighting of the price of manufactures has changed several times since 1913, and the weighting of prices of tropical crops changed in 1953. All prices are in current US dollars.

In the case of the price of manufactures in world trade, we use the League of Nations index from 1929, and the United Nations index from 1948 onwards. The cereals index is that of the United Nations from 1950 onwards.

Table A.13 *Postwar Price Statistics*

	Manufactures	*Tropical crops*	*Cereals*
1913	100·0	100·0	100·0
1920	212·3	220·6	266·2
1921	177·0	103·0	150·5
1922	149·3	117·5	130·1
1923	143·5	133·0	124·7
1924	140·1	140·5	141·3

Table A.13 *continued*

	Manufactures	*Tropical crops*	*Cereals*
1925	146·8	149·0	171·4
1926	142·0	136·1	151·7
1927	134·2	129·3	144·2
1928	134·0	130·8	138·1
1929	133·0	118·7	132·1
1930	124·9	82·5	108·0
1931	103·9	61·6	71·5
1932	84·4	46·5	60·6
1933	93·2	51·5	61·6
1934	111·4	69·9	75·1
1935	107·5	67·1	90·3
1936	107·8	72·2	97·5
1937	114·8	84·6	113·7
1938	113·5	64·7	92·1
1948	233·9	216·4	281·8
1949	219·0	218·2	245·7
1950	194·5	242·1	215·1
1951	231·4	313·7	246·4
1952	236·3	256·9	248·9
1953	226·5	230·0	241·8
1954	224·0	252·7	215·1
1955	224·0	233·8	210·2
1956	233·9	257·7	207·8
1957	241·3	232·7	200·7
1958	238·8	208·8	198·2
1959	236·3	196·3	193·3
1960	241·3	203·5	191·8
1961	243·7	192·7	191·3
1962	243·7	186·9	201·5
1963	246·2	236·4	203·5
1964	248·7	243·5	209·6
1965	253·6	209·3	201·5
1966	261·0	214·7	209·6
1967	263·4	210·7	213·7
1968	263·4	204·7	203·5
1969	270·8	228·3	199·3
1970	288·1	254·7	195·4
1971	305·3	264·5	203·5
1972	329·9	312·1	225·9

Appendix IV

World Supply of Wheat

by MARION A. O'CONNOR

The ideal 'world' wheat series would be constructed from accounts of production or of acreage and yield contributed by all political or geographical localities for as many years as research required. This perfection, alas, does not exist, but historical world series – of an imperfect sort – do. The United States Department of Agriculture published a 'world' series beginning with the year 1890. It consists of unadjusted official data and excludes Russia and China. In 1933 the Stanford Food Research Institute published a series[1] beginning with the production year 1885. It, too, is based on official statistics to which its authors have added some excellent research done earlier in the Bureau of Statistics of the USDA by Rutter[2] and Rubinow[3] as well as the work of colleagues at the Food Research Institute, notably Timoshenko[4] and Working.[5]

The current series began with the goal of continuing the Food Research Institute series backward from 1885 to 1865 using similar methods of estimation. In the end it was not possible to construct a production series for the whole world, since production data do not exist for a number of important countries, such as India and Argentina. However, it was possible to develop a series based on the more limited concept of 'supplies available to the western world', consisting of production in most of the leading countries of the western world (including all of North America, North-West Europe, Oceania, and part of Eastern Europe) plus net exports from other producers, Argentina, India, Italy, Russia, Switzerland and Spain. For the purpose of analysing prices this is a better concept, since price is determined by supplies reaching the market, and is not much affected by what happens to farmers who produce only for their own subsistence. The resulting series is given in Table A.14 with details in Tables A.15 and A.16.

The data of the series are for production years, also referred to, in some sources, as 'crop years'. It was assumed that the calendar year for reporting of net exports was the year following the production year and so net exports were moved back one year. Thus net exports of calendar year 1866 appear in the series as net exports of production year 1865.

SOURCES

The principal sources of nineteenth-century agricultural statistics are the early copies of *The Statistical Abstract of the Principal and Other Foreign Countries* published by the British Board of Trade – especially volume 6 which contained all the currently available data from 1867 to 1875 – and the Résumés Rétrospectifs of the French *Annuaire Statistique.* The major source of production and export statistics in the last decade before the First World War are the yearbooks of the International Institute of Agriculture. These, the historical studies of the Stanford Food Research Institute, and the early yearbooks, reports and Bureau of Statistics bulletins of the United States Department of Agriculture are the principal multiple reference works for the current series.

For many countries (those of North-West Europe and North America) production series are complete for the entire period, but for others data are lacking for the earliest years or for intermittent years. Where more than one series were found, the official statistics were given preference unless there were compelling reasons for choosing an alternative. Thus, the source of the German series is Hoffmann's economic history of nineteenth-century Germany[6] and the source of the Australian series is Dunsdorfs' study of Australian wheat.[7] A number of similar choices were made in the construction of the current series and each is described in full in subsequent sections.

PRODUCTION SERIES

United States of America

Two major wheat production series were available for the United States of America: the one constructed by Working in 1926 for the Food Research Institute and the revised historical series of the USDA published in 1935.[8] Working set out to bring production estimates into agreement with apparent domestic consumption as derived from the census of manufactures. He had found that 'prior to 1901 the apparent domestic consumption of wheat in the form of flour alone was consistently above the quantity of wheat apparently available for domestic consumption for both food and feed and for waste'.[9] Beginning with estimates of per capita consumption, Working devised a production series which, when divided by official yields, resulted in revised annual acreages. Because he also assumed a constant rate of per capita consumption prior to 1880, the basic shortcoming of his wheat estimates of production is the lack of annual variability in this segment of the series. By 1935, the Department of Agriculture was prepared to publish its historical revisions, 'by which the currently published estimates have been made consistent with the decennial census figures, supplemented by state enumerations'.[10] Annual wheat production according to the USDA series is about 15 million bushels less than the Working estimates.

The new series of United States wheat production assumes (1) that Working's estimates of production levels before 1880 are correct and (2) that the annual variability in crop production as reported by the 1935 issue of the USDA *Yearbook* is a necessary and desirable feature. Accordingly, the new estimates from 1866 to 1881 are the USDA revised estimates multiplied by a series which, starting in 1882, increases backwards at 1·8 per cent a year; this yields the same geometric average as the Working series over 1868/76. The USDA series and the Working series are identical in 1882 and 1884. The Working series, however, is the source of the remaining segment of annual United States wheat production.

Both the original series for the United States begin with the production year of 1866. Therefore, in order to complete the wheat series an estimate for 1865 was derived by a backward extrapolation from the production of the next four years.

Canada

The official Canadian series records production beginning with the 'crop' year 1869: 'production actually applied to the preceding calendar year'.[11] For the sake of a complete series, new estimates were derived for the first three production years. The new estimate for Canadian wheat in 1867 is the product of an estimate of annual acreage, derived by linear interpolation between the values given for wheat acreage at the census dates 1860 and 1870, and the official yield in Minnesota in 1867. The estimate for 1866 combines the annual estimate of Canadian acreage and the official yield recorded for Wisconsin – the state closest to the Canadian spring wheat area for which there exists a record of yield in 1866. These particular yields were chosen for compatibility with Timoshenko's correlations of areas and wheat yields. The estimate for 1865 is an arithmetic compromise: it is the product of Canadian acreage for 1865 and the average of the yields for 1868 to 1872.

Timoshenko[12] found a positive correlation ($r = +0{\cdot}54$, from 1885 to 1932) between the wheat yields of the spring wheat area in the United States – Minnesota, South Dakota, North Dakota and Montana – and the prairie provinces of Canada. Because most of the Canadian wheat crop is spring wheat, the recorded yield of the spring wheat state (or a neighbouring state) closest to the Canadian prairie provinces (Manitoba, Saskatchewan and Alberta) could presumably be used for all of Canada. The choice for 1866 is limited to Wisconsin, where the average yield of wheat was 14·5 bushels per acre. By 1867, the yield for Minnesota too was recorded – 12·5 bushels per acre – and this was used as the yield for all Canada. Actually the estimates for Canada provided by the wheat yields of Wisconsin and Minnesota may be conservative. Timoshenko found the mean average yield from 1885 to 1939 in the prairie provinces of Canada to be 16·8 bushels per acre.

Australia

Crop statistics were carefully kept in Australia from the early days of settlement because the colony was expected to be agriculturally self-sufficient. Dunsdorfs' revised series of Australian wheat statistics published in 1956[13] increases the official estimates for Queensland; the remaining data are unchanged. His work is the source for Australian production in the current series.

Production in Western Europe

The current wheat series is a beneficiary of the early statistical tradition of North-West Europe. The production series for Germany, France, Norway and Sweden are complete and the data for the remaining countries are very nearly so. Because statistics for later years had duplicate sources,[14] the problem of missing data was confined to the series segment prior to 1883.

The German series is as given by Hoffmann.[15] The French series is as given in the *Annuaire Statistique.*[16] The Swedish series is as given by issues of the *Statistisk Tidskrift,*[17] from 1865 to 1882, by Rutter for 1883 and 1884 and by Bennett from 1885 to 1913. Norwegian production estimates from 1865 to 1884 are the product of acreage statistics for 1865, 1870, 1875 and 1890 as given by the British Board of Trade and five-year averages of yields as reported in the 1929 volume of *Beretning.*[18] The remainder of the series is as given by Bennett.

Early estimates of wheat production from the Netherlands, the United Kingdom, Belgium and Denmark were not immediately available but they were readily derived from ancillary material.

Netherlands

Production estimates for the Netherlands from 1870 to 1884 are as given by the United States Department of Agriculture[19] and production estimates from 1885 are as given by Bennett. The new estimates prior to 1870 were derived from the average production from 1861 to 1870 and the Belgian yields for each year from 1865 to 1869.[20]

The average production from 1865 to 1869 was taken to be equal to the average production from 1861 to 1870 but the annual variations in crop size were supplied by the Belgian yields.

United Kingdom

Production estimates for the United Kingdom are computed traditionally from official estimates of wheat acreage and wheat yields. The historical series of acreage is quite complete but official estimates of yield begin only in 1884. Prior to 1884, at least three major series of annual wheat yields are available: the yields published by *The Times*, the widely accepted series prepared by Lawes and Gilbert[21] and the series published by A. Sauerbeck in 1886.[22] The Lawes and Gilbert series was based on the recorded annual yield from experimental plots in Hertfordshire, while *The Times* series was the result of 'very numerous reports from growers and other qualified correspondents in all parts of the Kingdom'.[23] The Sauerbeck series merged three sets of yields: those prior to 1878 were 'according to Sir James Caird's valuable estimates';[24] the yields from 1879 to 1883 were provided by *The Times* series; those from 1884 onward are the official yields.[25] Since the Sauerbeck series effectively combines the estimates of a highly respected contemporary authority and the broad-based *Times* series, it was judged the most suitable in computing the production series prior to 1884.

Belgium

Belgian wheat production from 1865 to 1879 was computed from census acreages and the yields estimated for each year by the provincial commissions of agriculture and published in the Belgian *Annuaire Statistique.*[26] The new acreages between the census dates 1866 and 1880 are annual linear interpolations between the two values, 283,548 hectares and 275,932 hectares, respectively. The new acreage estimate for 1865 is the acreage of 1866. (Rutter used this technique to arrive at estimates of wheat production from 1880 to 1905.)

Denmark

The earliest statistical abstracts of the Danish kingdom published figures for grain production beginning with the year 1875.[27] Data prior to 1875 were derived from census acreages for the years 1866, 1871, and 1876 and annual estimates of yield in the Netherlands. The Netherlands yields were selected because of the relatively high correlation between the yields for the Netherlands and for Denmark between the years 1885 and 1894 ($r = +0{\cdot}64$, significant at the 5 per cent level). The regression equation of Danish yields on Netherlands yields of 1885 to 1894 and the annual Netherlands yields of 1865 to 1874 provided new estimates of yields for Denmark from 1865 to 1874. The production series generated from the Danish annual acreage and the yields obtained from the Netherlands regression equation enjoys some corroborative evidence. The average of yields for Denmark for 1875 to 1879 when estimated from the Netherlands regression is 34 bushels per acre. Official statistics for Denmark are available in this period and the average of reported yields for 1875 to 1879 is 32 bushels per acre. Since the acreages involved are quite small (usually less than 150 thousand acres), the new estimates of yield are probably adequate for present purposes.

Production from 1880 to 1905 is as given by the Bureau of Statistics of the USDA[28] and from 1905 as reported by the International Institute of Agriculture.

Production in Eastern Europe

Estimates for Eastern Europe are the sum of annual production of Austria, Hungary and Romania. It is possible to hazard a guess – but only a guess – about the wheat crops of Bulgaria, Serbia and Bosnia-Herzegovina, the area for which data are lacking. Using Bennett's estimates, the sum of production for this area between 1885 and 1894 is roughly between 10 and 15 per cent of the annual total for all six countries. And, presumably, the pattern of production growth was much the same throughout Eastern Europe. The data from 1883 to 1905 for Austria and Hungary are as given by Rutter, and from 1906 as given by the International Institute of Agriculture. Both cite the original sources.[29]

Austria

Estimates of Austrian production from 1874 to 1882 are as given by the 1883 *Report* of the USDA.

Data earlier than 1874 are fragmentary. Von Neumann-Spallart's[30] published estimate of average production between 1869 and 1876 of 12·7 million hectolitres, or 35·9 million bushels, agrees with the annual production for 1874 to 1876 as published by the British and the United States governments. An acreage estimate of 2·4 million for 1870 reported in the *Proceedings* for 1879 of the Institut Internationale de Statistique is also the average acreage between 1874 and 1880.[31] The current series for Austria assumes that the wheat acreage prior to 1874 was 2·4 million and that the average of yields from 1874 to 1879 (15·8 bushels per acre) satisfactorily represents the yield from 1865 to 1873. The average annual wheat production prior to 1874 in Austria is then estimated at 37·9 million bushels.

Hungary

Estimates of wheat production for Hungary from 1874 to 1884 are recorded in the United States Department of Agriculture *Report* of 1883.[32]

These data overlap the primary source which the current series follows to 1889.[33] The Hungarian series was then completed with the aid of estimates reported by von Matlekovitz.[34]

Von Matlekovitz published statistics of wheat production acreage and yield for the single year 1870 and averages for the five years 1871 to 1875. The new acreages for 1871, 1872 and 1873 were then computed as the arithmetic average of total acreage from 1871 to 1875 after subtracting the acreages in wheat in 1874 and 1875. The new acreages for 1865 to 1869 were estimated as the extrapolated values from an acreage curve containing all the single year's statistics of acreage (1870, 1874 and on).

The new yields for 1871, 1872 and 1873 were computed as the average of the sum of yields for 1871 to 1875, after subtracting the single-year yields for 1874 and 1875. The average yield for each of the three remaining years was then given the annual variation of the Romanian yields of the same years. An average of the yields from 1870 to 1874 was assumed to be a fair estimate of the average yield from 1865 to 1869. The new yields multiplied by the new acreage estimates provided the production estimates for the missing years.

Romania

According to official records, production data for Romania are available from 1867 to 1876 and from 1886 onward.[35] The new production estimates for 1865 and 1866 are the products of new acreages – derived from interpolated acreages between 1860 and 1870[36] – and the average of reported yields from 1867 to 1871.

The new production estimates for 1877 to 1885 were computed likewise from estimates of acreage and estimates of yield. The estimates of acreage were derived by linear interpolation and the estimates of yield were calculated from the regression equation of Hungarian and Romanian yields for the years 1886 to 1894 because Hungarian and Romanian yields have a fair positive correlation ($r = +0{\cdot}50$). Romanian wheat yields for 1877 to 1885 were then approximated by substituting the Hungarian yields of the very same years in the regression equation. The national yield for 1885 obtained by this method is 15 bushels per acre. Bennett arrived at the same estimate by taking the average of yields between 1886 and 1900. The new estimates of wheat production for 1877 to 1885 are the products of the new acreages and yields and they fit into the pattern of increasing wheat productivity evident from the official estimates before 1877 and after 1885.[37]

New Zealand
Estimates of production in New Zealand from 1868 to 1884 are as reported by the British Board of Trade in early issues of the *Statistical Abstract for Several Colonial and Other Possessions.*[38] Production data have a small gap at 1865 to 1867 and acreage at 1865 to 1866. The missing acreage was estimated by linear interpolation between 1864 and 1867 and the average yield from 1868 to 1872 was assumed to be an adequate estimate of yield in 1865, 1866 and 1867. The products of this average yield and annual acreage are the new estimates of production in 1865, 1866 and 1867. The remainder of the series from 1885 to 1913 is as given by Bennett, citing the primary source.

NET EXPORTS

At times during the preparation of the wheat series from 1865 it did not seem possible to develop sufficiently substantive estimates of national production. This proved true even in the case of three major wheat producers, Russia, India and Argentina. To complete the summary series for major producers, the net exports of the three were substituted for production estimates. Exports and imports of Russia are as given by the reports of the British Board of Trade.[39] The sources of data for India and Argentina follow. In Europe production data for Italy, Spain and Switzerland were not available. Exports and imports of wheat for all three of these countries from 1883 or thereabouts to 1902 are as given by Rutter[40] and from 1903 to 1913 as given by the yearbooks of the International Institute of Agriculture.[41] The sources of import and export data prior to the mid-eighties are described below.

India
Although statistics of wheat production are extremely scarce prior to 1884, complete export statistics are available beginning with the year 1867 from a number of sources.[42] The unique aspect of the Indian wheat trade is that it never experienced the spontaneous growth typical of the developing nations of the Americas and Australia. The Indian trade was planned and organised by financial interests in Great Britain and in India who saw in the exchange of British manufactures and Indian raw materials a policy of great mutual benefit. In India, the development first of the cotton trade and then the wheat trade were directly dependent on an official policy of railway expansion between the agricultural districts and the ports of Bombay, Calcutta and Karachi.[43] By 1878 the main wheat-growing areas were connected by rail with their ports, and 10·5 million bushels of wheat were exported. Between 1882 and 1894 annual exports averaged 34 million bushels a year (about 12 to 13 per cent of the annual crop), and in 1891 to 1892, a year of famine in southern Russia, Indian wheat exports rose to 56 million bushels. Contemporary observers[44] thought they witnessed in British India a growing threat to United States domination of international

Table A.14 *Wheat Supplies Available to the Western World, 1865–1913 (m. bushels)*[a]

		Annual production								
Year	*Total supply*[b]	*Canada*	*USA*	*Austria*	*Hungary*	*Romania*	*Western Europe*[c]	*Australia*	*New Zealand*	*Net exports*[d]
1865	809·4	*21·0	*175·0	*37·9	*47·8	*25·0	469·6	9·7	*0·9	22·6
1866	835·3	*23·8	*225·0	*37·9	*48·0	*25·6	423·0	15·4	*1·1	35·5
1867	838·9	*20·5	*275·0	*37·9	*48·3	29·0	387·9	9·3	*1·3	29·7
1868	1,072·9	22·2	*315·0	*37·9	*48·8	32·2	578·3	12·3	1·6	24·6
1869	1,085·6	22·6	*365·0	*37·9	*49·3	23·7	524·9	13·2	2·4	46·7
1870	1,022·7	16·7	*314·0	*37·9	63·2	28·0	494·6	12·1	1·8	54·3
1871	912·7	23·1	*330·0	*37·9	*47·6	26·7	389·3	11·9	2·4	43·8
1872	1,043·8	23·8	*323·0	*37·9	*37·6	18·0	552·0	18·5	3·2	29·7
1873	995·8	24·2	*376·0	*37·9	*44·6	29·0	423·0	14·6	3·4	43·2
1874	1,254·1	23·9	*410·0	42·0	61·3	33·9	618·0	18·2	3·0	43·9
1875	1,025·2	26·1	*355·0	30·9	48·9	33·6	469·1	18·8	2·9	40·0
1876	984·1	22·6	*343·0	35·1	51·7	21·4	455·1	14·6	4·1	36·6
1877	1,204·9	25·9	*432·0	39·9	76·9	*33·8	468·1	19·6	6·3	102·3
1878	1,313·6	30·4	*482·0	45·2	108·6	*40·7	506·8	20·1	6·1	73·7
1879	1,074·3	34·3	*484·0	34·5	52·2	*28·1	396·7	28·8	7·6	8·1
1880	1,263·9	32·4	*520·0	40·6	79·3	*35·1	489·1	23·5	8·1	35·7
1881	1,197·3	38·0	*413·0	41·2	88·9	*36·6	471·3	21·6	8·3	78·4
1882	1,549·7	47·8	*552·0	44·5	136·5	*48·8	589·8	21·6	10·3	98·4
1883	1,275·6	30·8	469·3	38·1	90·5	*37·4	490·1	35·9	9·8	73·6
1884	1,495·1	45·4	571·4	42·4	107·2	*40·5	541·3	30·5	6·9	109·5
1885	1,284·1	42·4	432·3	47·2	119·2	*43·5	534·6	17·9	4·2	42·5
1886	1,392·0	38·2	555·0	43·6	108·2	34·7	507·9	29·8	6·3	68·3
1887	1,562·1	39·0	558·8	51·8	151·3	47·4	548·9	38·3	9·4	117·2
1888	1,412·6	33·0	516·3	51·0	141·8	57·8	484·3	17·6	8·8	102·0
1889	1,487·8	30·8	618·4	37·5	98·4	50·2	515·4	33·9	8·4	94·8
1890	1,497·9	42·2	515·7	42·9	154·8	51·8	556·0	27·1	5·7	101·7
1891	1,573·0	60·7	787·1	39·5	145·9	48·6	400·6	25·7	10·3	54·7

1892	1,698·4	48·2	680·7	49·6	149·6	64·1	542·5	32·7	8·4	122·7
1893	1,529·3	41·3	539·4	42·7	168·8	60·7	505·9	37·3	4·9	128·4
1894	1,701·4	43·2	634·2	47·3	154·4	43·5	570·1	27·7	3·6	177·2
1895	1,725·4	55·7	668·9	40·3	171·9	68·6	558·9	18·3	6·8	136·0
1896	1,641·1	39·6	612·6	41·8	161·2	71·3	570·1	21·0	5·9	117·6
1897	1,459·6	54·4	685·0	34·5	87·2	36·7	449·1	28·8	5·7	78·1
1898	1,822·3	66·5	831·6	46·9	139·6	58·6	577·1	41·6	13·1	47·3
1899	1,736·1	59·9	682·2	50·2	150·3	25·9	594·7	39·9	8·6	124·4
1900	1,657·1	55·6	638·6	40·9	152·2	56·4	534·5	48·2	6·5	124·2
1901	1,783·3	88·3	828·9	44·0	134·6	72·4	486·8	38·4	4·0	85·7
1902	1,850·2	97·1	737·9	49·7	182·9	76·3	558·1	12·4	7·4	128·4
1903	1,923·6	81·9	681·5	46·2	176·6	73·8	597·6	74·0	7·9	184·1
1904	1,760·8	71·8	581·0	53·7	146·9	53·7	536·5	54·5	9·1	253·4
1905	2,015·4	107·0	727·2	54·5	170·6	103·4	553·8	68·6	6·8	223·6
1906	2,019·6	135·6	759·7	58·3	207·8	113·7	558·0	66·4	5·6	114·7
1907	1,730·5	93·1	636·8	52·4	130·7	42·3	600·9	44·7	5·6	124·1
1908	1,965·5	112·4	654·5	62·1	165·4	54·7	535·7	62·6	8·8	309·2
1909	2,037·4	166·7	712·7	58·5	125·0	56·6	567·0	90·2	8·7	252·1
1910	1,874·0	132·1	659·9	20·8	181·1	110·6	488·8	95·1	8·3	177·3
1911	1,997·9	231·2	621·3	58·9	190·1	93·7	570·4	71·3	7·3	153·7
1912	2,162·8	224·2	730·3	69·4	184·6	88·7	586·6	91·7	5·2	182·1
1913	2,152·0	231·7	763·4	59·6	168·2	83·4	582·8	103·1	5·2	154·5

[a] One Winchester bushel = 60 lb.
[b] The sum of entries may not equal the total because of rounding.
[c] For details of Western Europe, see Table A.15.
[d] For details of Net Exports, see Table A.16.
* New estimate.

Table A.15 *Wheat Production of Western Europe, 1865–1913 (m. bushels)*[a]

Year	*Total*[b]	*Belgium*	*Denmark*	*France*	*Germany*	*Netherlands*	*Norway*	*Sweden*	*UK*
1865	469·6	*16·1	*4·4	263·5	61·9	*5·1	*0·3	2·4	*115·9
1866	423·0	14·5	*4·1	234·4	67·4	*4·5	*0·3	2·6	*95·2
1867	387·9	*14·0	*4·1	228·5	57·2	*4·4	*0·3	1·7	*77·7
1868	578·3	*18·1	*5·0	321·9	81·6	*5·7	*0·3	1·9	*143·9
1869	524·9	*16·9	*4·8	297·6	79·8	*5·3	*0·3	2·7	*117·5
1870	494·6	*16·9	*5·2	272·6	68·6	5·8	*0·3	3·0	*122·2
1871	389·3	*11·7	*4·7	191·1	75·5	3·4	*0·3	3·0	*99·6
1872	552·0	*17·7	*5·1	332·9	85·5	5·5	*0·3	2·8	*102·2
1873	423·0	*13·2	*4·9	225·6	85·9	5·2	*0·3	3·2	*84·8
1874	618·0	*19·7	*5·9	366·7	97·8	6·8	*0·3	3·5	*117·4
1875	469·1	*15·5	4·6	277·4	82·5	6·4	*0·3	3·4	*79·0
1876	455·1	*15·0	4·0	263·1	77·3	5·4	*0·3	3·2	*86·7
1877	468·1	*16·0	4·9	275·9	92·4	5·0	*0·3	2·7	*70·9
1878	506·8	*16·8	5·4	262·7	107·3	5·7	*0·3	3·3	*105·4
1879	396·7	*14·2	5·0	218·6	94·1	5·0	*0·3	3·1	*56.4
1880	489·1	18·1	5·5	277·4	96·0	5·9	*0·3	3·6	*82·2
1881	471·3	14·9	3·1	278·1	84·8	4·7	*0·2	2·2	*83·2
1882	589·8	16·7	4·6	362·7	105·1	5·4	*0·2	3·8	*91·4
1883	490·1	15·9	4·5	291·4	96·7	5·6	*0·2	3·0	*72·8
1884	541·3	16·0	4·7	324·1	101·5	5·9	*0·2	3·7	*85·1
1885	534·6	16·6	5·1	313·0	107·2	6·3	0·3	4·1	82·0
1886	507·9	15·8	4·7	302·8	109·9	5·2	0·3	4·0	65·2
1887	548·9	17·0	5·4	320·0	116·4	6·9	0·3	4·5	78·4
1888	484·3	15·1	3·3	275·6	104·4	5·2	0·3	3·7	76·7
1889	515·4	19·1	4·2	305·7	97·7	6·5	0·3	3·8	78·1
1890	556·0	15·0	3·8	329·6	116·0	5·4	0·3	4·0	82·0

1891	400·6	11·7	4·2	215·0	96·3	3·5	0·3	4·5	65·2
1892	542·5	15·4	4·3	310·8	123·4	5·4	0·3	4·6	78·4
1893	505·9	13·2	3·9	277·8	125·1	5·0	0·3	4·0	76·7
1894	570·1	13·1	3·3	344·3	122·6	4·2	0·3	4·3	78·1
1895	558·9	12·8	3·5	339·5	116·6	4·3	0·3	3·8	78·2
1896	570·1	13·5	3·7	340·2	125·7	5·0	0·3	4·8	76·9
1897	449·1	11·7	3·6	242·1	119·9	4·3	0·3	4·7	62·5
1898	577·1	13·6	3·2	364·9	132·6	5·4	0·3	4·7	52·4
1899	594·7	11·1	4·1	365·6	141·4	5·1	0·3	4·7	62·5
1900	534·5	13·8	4·1	325·5	141·1	4·7	0·3	5·5	39·4
1901	486·8	14·1	1·0	310·9	91·8	4·2	0·3	4·5	60·0
1902	558·1	14·5	4·5	327·9	143·3	5·0	0·3	4·7	57·9
1903	597·6	12·4	4·5	363·0	130·6	4·2	0·3	5·5	77·1
1904	536·5	13·8	4·3	299·6	139·8	4·4	0·2	5·2	69·2
1905	553·8	12·4	4·1	334·8	136·0	4·8	0·3	5·3	55·9
1906	558·0	13·0	4·2	328·7	144·8	4·9	0·3	6·7	55·5
1907	600·9	15·8	4·4	381·2	127·8	5·2	0·3	6·2	60·0
1908	535·7	13·4	4·6	316·7	138·4	5·0	0·3	7·0	50·2
1909	567·0	14·6	4·3	359·2	138·0	4·1	0·3	7·4	39·0
1910	488·8	14·0	5·5	253·0	141·9	4·4	0·3	7·7	62·1
1911	570·4	15·7	5·7	322·3	149·4	5·4	0·3	8·1	63·5
1912	586·6	15·3	5·0	334·3	160·2	5·5	0·3	7·8	58·0
1913	582·8	14·8	7·2	319·4	171·1	5·1	0·3	9·5	55·5

[a] One Winchester bushel = 60 lb.
[b] The sum of entries may not equal the total because of rounding.
* New estimate.

Table A.16 *Net Exports of Wheat, Selected Countries, 1865–1913 (m. bushels)*[a]

Year	*Total*[b]	*Argentina*	*India*	*Japan*	*Italy*	*Russia*	*Spain*	*Switzerland*
1865	22·6	n.a.	n.a.	n.a.	–15·0	41·4	0·6	*–4·5
1866	35·5	n.a.	n.a.	n.a.	–13·2	51·3	2·4	*–5·0
1867	29·7	n.a.	0·5	n.a.	–6·0	40·2	*0·1	*–5·1
1868	24·6	n.a.	0·6	n.a.	–5·0	37·9	*–3·9	*–5·1
1869	46·7	n.a.	0·5	—[c]	–6·9	57·5	0·2	*–4·6
1870	54·3	–0·1	0·1	—	*–7·5	68·7	–2·0	*–4·9
1871	43·8	–0·1	0·5	—	*–8·0	58·6	–2·1	*–5·1
1872	29·7	–0·1	1·2	—	–9·2	41·5	1·0	*–4·7
1873	43·2	—[c]	0·7	0·1	–6·0	48·4	7·3	*–7·3
1874	43·9	–0·1	3·3	0·1	–11·9	56·8	2·3	*–6·7
1875	40·0	–0·2	2·0	n.a.	–9·2	55·0	–0·2	*–7·4
1876	36·6	—	4·6	—	–9·3	51·5	–1·0	*–9·2
1877	102·3	—	10·3	0·2	–5·0	102·9	1·3	*–7·3
1878	73·7	0·1	11·0	1·0	–10·5	82·9	–1·6	*–9·2
1879	8·1	0·9	1·2	0·1	–17·1	36·6	–4·4	*–9·3
1880	35·7	–0·6	4·1	—	–5·5	49·0	–1·0	*–10·2
1881	78·4	–0·4	13·9	—	–1·9	76·3	–0·6	*–8·8
1882	98·4	0·1	36·7	0·1	–2·5	83·8	–10·0	*–9·7
1883	73·6	2·2	26·0	0·9	–5·6	67·7	–8·7	*–9·0
1884	109·5	4·0	38·8	0·3	–11·7	91·8	–3·5	*–10·2
1885	42·5	2·9	29·5	0·4	–26·1	49·8	–4·1	–9·9
1886	68·3	1·4	39·2	0·3	–34·1	77·8	–5·5	–10·8
1887	117·2	8·7	41·5	0·2	–37·2	126·1	–11·5	–10·6
1888	102·0	6·6	25·3	0·3	–24·5	114·3	–8·9	–11·0
1889	94·8	0·8	32·7	0·1	–32·0	109·3	–5·3	–10·8
1890	101·7	12·0	25·6	0·1	–23·7	105·8	–5·9	–12·1
1891	54·7	14·5	26·5	—	–17·0	49·0	–5·7	–12·6

1892	122·7	17·3	55·7	—	−25·6	93·7	−5·1	−13·3
1893	128·4	37·0	27·7	—	−31·6	122·8	−15·4	−12·3
1894	177·2	59·1	22·5	—	−17·9	142·3	−15·6	−13·2
1895	136·0	37·1	12·4	0·1	−24·2	131·8	−7·4	−13·8
1896	117·6	19·5	18·2	−0·1	−25·6	128·0	−6·9	−15·5
1897	78·1	3·2	2·2	−0·3	−15·2	106·5	−5·2	−13·0
1898	47·3	23·7	4·1	−0·1	−32·2	64·3	0·3	−12·7
1899	124·4	63·0	36·1	−0·1	−17·4	70·1	−13·3	−14·0
1900	124·2	70·9	17·2	−0·5	−25·3	83·2	−8·2	−13·2
1901	85·7	33·2	−1·0	−0·2	−38·4	111·6	−5·3	−14·2
1902	128·4	23·7	13·0	−0·2	−43·3	152·9	−2·5	−15·2
1903	184·1	61·8	19·4	−2·8	−43·1	168·5	−3·3	−16·3
1904	253·4	84·7	48·3	−0·9	−29·6	176·3	−8·2	−17·2
1905	223·6	105·4	80·1	−2·2	−43·0	132·0	−32·5	−16·2
1906	114·7	82·6	33·9	−0·8	−50·5	85·0	−19·3	−16·2
1907	124·1	98·5	29·4	−2·0	−34·2	53·9	−4·3	−17·2
1908	309·2	133·6	32·3	−1·3	−29·0	188·7	−2·9	−12·1
1909	252·1	92·4	2·8	−0·8	−48·9	224·8	−3·5	−14·7
1910	177·3	69·2	39·1	−1·8	−53·0	144·3	−5·9	−14·6
1911	153·7	84·0	47·3	−2·0	−51·1	96·6	−4·9	−16·1
1912	182·1	96·6	50·9	−2·3	−65·7	122·0	−1·5	−17·8
1913	154·5	103·3	62·0	−6·2	−66·5	84·0	−2·7	−19·4

[a] One Winchester bushel = 60 lb.
[b] The sum of entries may not equal the total because of rounding.
[c] A dash = less than 0·05 million bushels.
* New estimate.

wheat trade, but India's wheat exports dropped off in the next decade and did not resume the volume of trade typical of the late 1880s until 1903–4.

Argentina

While Argentina was a Spanish colony the cultivation of principal cereals was prohibited by law. Presumably, Spain preferred the colonists to purchase grain from the mother country. It was only after independence in 1810 that agriculture began to develop, but even that development remained minimal until the constitutional era beginning in 1853.[45] Net exports for 1878 and 1879 were 93 thousand and 943 thousand bushels.[46] Wheat crops failed in 1880 and 1881, requiring increased imports again. Finally, in 1884 exports reached 4 million bushels.[47] In 1890, 12 million bushels were traded and Argentina, by this time, had become a major competitor in world wheat trade. Net exports of wheat from Argentina from 1870 to 1881 are as given by the Bureau of the American Republics, for 1882 to 1903, as given by the US Department of Agriculture, and for 1904 to 1913, as given by the International Institute of Agriculture.[48]

Italy

The Italian net exports for 1865 to 1871 were computed from official statistics of imports and exports as given by the British Board of Trade,[49] and for 1872 to 1890 from data published by the Italian Ministry of Agriculture.[50]

New estimates of net exports were derived for 1870 and 1871. No breakdown of exports, alone, by type of cereal was available for these two years. However, wheat exports from 1866 to 1870 and from 1872 to 1875 were on average 40 per cent of total grain exports (barley, malt, wheat and oats). Wheat was therefore assumed to be 40 per cent of total grain exports in 1870 and in 1871, the years for which this detailed information was lacking. The new estimates of net exports of wheat for 1870 and 1871 in Italy are the differences between the official import statistics and the new estimates of wheat exports.

Spain

The net exports of Spain were calculated from the imports and exports of wheat as given by the British Board of Trade for 1865 and 1882.[51]

The value of imported wheat rather than the quantity was recorded for 1867 and 1868. To complete the series of net exports the missing quantities were estimated from the total values and the average import price per kilogram of wheat (10·3 escudos) for the following seven years (1869 to 1875).

Switzerland

Early official statistics of the principal articles traded in Switzerland – published by the British Board of Trade – report only grain imports and no wheat exports.[52] However, von Neumann-Spallart's estimates of wheat imports from 1876 to 1880,[53] and Rutter's estimates from 1885 to 1892 indicate that wheat accounted for 75 per cent of grain imports, within a range of 73 to 79 per cent. The new estimates of wheat exports for 1866 to 1875 and for 1881 to 1884 are consequently 75 per cent of the grain imports of those years.

Wheat exports from Switzerland play a very minor role, but a seemingly constant one, with relation to wheat imports. From 1884 to 1892 exports were 0·1 per cent of imports (within a range of 0·07 to 0·13 per cent); accordingly, new estimates of exports from 1865 to 1884 are 0·1 per cent of annual imports. The new estimates of net exports are the difference between the new export and import series.

Japan

The net exports of Japan were calculated from the imports and exports of wheat published by the *Oriental Economist* in 1939.[54]

Notes

CHAPTER 1

1 Colin Clark believes that output per head in Britain in 1800 (probably then the highest in the world) was no higher than output per head in Italy around AD 300. See *The Conditions of Economic Progress*, Macmillan, London, 1957 (3rd edn), p. 677.

2 These figures are for the number of countries that had reduced farm populations from over 70 to under 50 per cent by the dates given. This achievement does not guarantee sustained growth in the future – nothing guarantees that – but does testify to considerable growth over the past, even when allowance is made for open and disguised unemployment in swollen cities. The list of countries where farm population is less than 50 per cent is as follows (listed by continent):

By 1913: Great Britain (8), Belgium (18), Switzerland (22), Germany (24), Netherlands (25), France (30), Czechoslovakia (32), Denmark (37), Norway (38), Sweden (41), Austria (41), Ireland (43), Italy (45), Hungary (45); USA (32), Canada (40); Argentina (24), Chile (40); Australia (25), New Zealand (27). (The numbers in brackets are the approximate proportions in agriculture in 1913.)

By 1939: Add Cyprus, Estonia, Finland, Greece, Latvia, Poland, Portugal, Spain, USSR; Cuba, Puerto Rico, Uruguay, Venezuela; Ceylon, Japan; South Africa.

By 1970: Add Bulgaria, Yugoslavia, Romania; Brazil, Colombia, Costa Rica, El Salvador, Mexico, Panama, Paraguay, Peru; Surinam, West Indies (Br. and Fr.); Iran, Malaya, Philippines, Seychelles, Syria, Fiji; Algeria, Libya, Mauritius, Tunisia.

Countries which had not in 1970 passed the 50 per cent mark included Turkey, India, Bangladesh, Pakistan, Indonesia, Thailand, Cambodia, Ecuador, Guatemala, Nicaragua, Morocco, Egypt and most countries of Africa south of the Sahara.

Lists for 1913 and 1939 taken mainly from a table in Colin Clark, *The Conditions of Economic Progress*, op. cit., pp. 510–20. For 1970, see *United Nations Demographic Yearbook*, 1972 and 1973.

3 See H. A. Innis, *The Fur Trade in Canada*, Yale University Press, New Haven, 1930, ch. VI.

4 Already in 1933 Sir Ronald Walker was calculating the multiplier effects of a trade recession on an export-led economy. See E. Ronald Walker, *Australia in the World Depression*, King, London, 1933, ch. VI. See also H. Belshaw, 'Stabilisation in a Dependent Economy', *Economic Record*, Supplement, April 1939.

5 Under Keynes's leadership Britain strove to get the kind of International Monetary Fund which would automatically discriminate against the dollar whenever the US economy entered a downswing.

6 D. H. Robertson, 'The Future of International Trade', *Economic Journal*, March 1938. Prebisch is credited with authorship of: United Nations Economic Commission for Latin America, *The Economic Development of Latin America and its Principal Problems*, New York, 1950.

7 The periphery is also sometimes called 'the hinterland'.

8 League of Nations, *Industrialisation and Foreign Trade*, Geneva, 1945, p. 157.

9 The precise slope of the line does not matter, since it is not used for any statistical purpose. It serves for visual differentiation between depressions of differing severity, and also to help in locating peaks.

10 In measuring growth rates one needs to know whether the points between which one is measuring stand in the same position in the trade cycle. One can measure from peak to peak (as we do in Chart 1.1) or from trough to trough, or from one average of years to another average of the same status in the cycle (peak, trough or complete cycle). Our history books are full of measurements between

years whose cyclical status is either different or unknown; such is the dearth of statistical data that historians take any years they can find. The resulting growth rates can mislead, unless the time period is long (say in excess of fifty years) in relation to the cyclical fluctuations of the series. Kuznets has presented his US national income data in the form of decade averages, and Markovitch has followed suit with his data for French industrial production. Since the trade cycle status of decades is very different (e.g. in the USA the 1880s have more boom years and the 1890s more recession years) decade averages yield misleading results unless they are used with care.

11 Clément Juglar published his first short piece on the trade cycle in 1856. His main work, *Des Crises commerciales*, was written as a prize essay in 1862, but was not published until 1889, in a volume which included some of his other writings.

12 The timing of business cycles is examined by Oskar Morgenstern in *International Financial Transactions and Business Cycles*, Princeton University Press, Princeton, 1954. Working with the peaks and troughs of NBER reference cycles (based on monthly data) he finds that:

(1) The three European reference cycles exhibit a high degree of correlation, whereas the corresponding American cycle is not so highly correlated with the rest (p. 53).
(2) In general in the prewar period the United States cycle led those of the three European countries at both peaks and troughs. No consistent timing relationship appears among the three European countries (p. 51).

However, as he points out, the reference cycle dating is based on financial rather than production data. One would expect very close timing of changes in short-term interest rates, foreign exchange rates and even stock exchange prices; whereas private investment, government expenditure and industrial production should move with greater independence.

13 These trend lines join the average output of construction in an early period to the average of a later period. For Britain, France and Germany the periods are chosen to include a full construction cycle, from peak to peak or trough to trough. The periods and growth rates are: UK 1869/86 and 1886/1910, 1·9 per cent per annum; France 1865/84 and 1895/1913, 1·2 per cent per annum; Germany 1870/9 and 1901/13, 2·6 per cent per annum. The US case is complicated by the fact that the building cycles at both ends are incomplete (after 1913) or distorted (before 1867). Our line rises by 3·6 per cent per annum, which is the growth rate from 1868/73 to 1901/7 (boom years); and is positioned to run through the average of the completed cycle of 1885–1900, midway between 1892 and 1893. For details of the indexes see Appendices I and II. Here also no importance attaches to the precise slope of trend lines.

14 We use the term 'edged out' for the last year in which the curve of the construction index lies above the semi-logarithmic line described in note 13. This can be read off Chart 1.2.

15 See especially two books by Brinley Thomas: *Migration and Economic Growth*, Cambridge University Press, Cambridge, 1954; and *Migration and Urban Development*, Methuen, London, 1972.

16 For formal econometric models of the US Kuznets cycle, see C. M. Franks and W. W. McCormick, 'A Self-Generating Model of Long Swings for the American Economy, 1860–1940', *Journal of Economic History*, June 1971. The theory of the Kuznets cycle is expounded by Moses Abramovitz in two articles: 'The Nature and Significance of Kuznets Cycles', *Economic Development and Cultural Exchange*, April 1961; also 'The Passing of the Kuznets Cycle', *Economica*, November 1968. For a comprehensive bibliography of the Kuznets cycle see Brinley Thomas, *Migration and Urban Development*, op. cit.

17 This is the Sauerbeck-Statist index, published annually in the *Journal of the Royal Statistical Society*. The index of ocean freights is from Cairncross, and is reproduced in Appendix III. The bottom curve is derived by subtracting 10 per cent of the freights index from the wholesale price index.

18 See the bibliographical monograph by S. B. Saul, *The Myth of the Great Depression*, Macmillan, London, 1969.

19 J. A. Schumpeter, *Business Cycles*, McGraw Hill, New York, 1939, 2 vols.
20 For example, Hans Rosenberg, 'Political and Social Consequences of the Great Depression of 1873–1896 in Central Europe', *Economic History Review*, 1943.
21 A. K. Cairncross, *Home and Foreign Investment 1870–1913*, Cambridge University Press, Cambridge, 1953, p. 176. We have reproduced this index in Table A.11.

CHAPTER 2

1 Note a difference in usage in this book between '1876/80' and '1876–80'. The former indicates that the data for each of the five years from 1876 to 1880 inclusive have been summed, and divided by the number of years; it is used for averages. The latter is used for the change in the four-year interval between the terminal years; e.g. 'the increase over 1876–80 was 25 per cent, or at an annual growth rate of 5·74 per cent'. Note that all annual percentage growth rates in this book are compounded.
2 The number of immigrants, the urban population and railway mileage are from US Department of Commerce, Bureau of the Census, *Historical Statistics of the United States, Colonial Times to 1957*, Washington, DC, 1960, Gottlieb's series are included in Robert E. Lipsey and Doris Preston, *Source Book of Statistics Relating to Construction*, NBER, Columbia University Press, New York, 1966.
3 Walther G. Hoffmann, *Das Wachstum der Deutschen Wirtschaft seit der Mitte des 19. Jahrhunderts*, Springer-Verlag, Berlin, 1965. Hereafter referred to as *Wachstum*, to avoid confusion with his book on British industry.
4 The rate of growth of the urban population rose from 1·3 per cent per annum between 1852 and 1871 to 2·5 per cent per annum between 1871 and 1880.
5 Rendigs Fels gives a detailed account in *American Business Cycles 1865–1897*, University of N. Carolina Press, Chapel Hill, 1959. Similar accounts have not as yet appeared for Britain, Germany or France.
6 The techniques of open market operations took some time to evolve. See the discussion in R. S. Sayers, *Bank of England Operations, 1890–1914*, King, London, 1936.
7 Calculated from R. S. Hawtrey, *A Century of Bank Rate.* Longmans, London, 1938, appendix II.
8 ibid., p. 65.
9 It is hard to take 1876 seriously as a British Juglar peak, although output was higher there than in 1872 or 1873. To have output sidestepping is really, from the standpoint of profits or employment, to have a recession. Thus the trade union unemployment index increased steadily from 1872, as follows:

1872	0·9 per cent	1876	3·7 per cent
1873	1·2	1877	4·7
1874	1·7	1878	6·8
1875	2·4	1879	11·4

This illustrates what was said in Chapter 1, section 1.03, about choosing dates of peaks. The unemployment figures are from B. R. Mitchell and Phyllis Deane, *Abstract of British Historical Statistics*, Cambridge University Press, Cambridge, 1962.
10 Capital export from Albert H. Imlah, *Economic Elements in the Pax Britannica*, Harvard University Press, Cambridge, Mass., 1958.
11 Werner Schlote, *British Overseas Trade from 1700 to the 1930s*, Basil Blackwell, Oxford, 1952.
12 The list of requests for rescheduling was impressively long. 1872: Honduras, Costa Rica, Santo Domingo, Paraguay. 1873: Spain. 1874: Bolivia, Guatemala, Liberia, Uruguay. 1875: Turkey, Egypt, Peru. Source: Leland H. Jenks, *The Migration of British Capital to 1875*, Jonathan Cape, London, 1938.
13 Hawtrey, op. cit.

14 Feinstein's housing peak at 1876 is more pronounced than ours because he does not allow for the stabilising effects of repair and of rural building; but his series for other construction displays the same phenomenon as ours. At 1900 prices, it grows from £39·6 million over 1872/6 to £45·4 million over 1877/81. C. H. Feinstein, *National Income and Expenditure of the United Kingdom, 1855–1965*, Cambridge University Press, Cambridge, 1972. The data used here are explained in our Appendix I.

15 The construction series we have used exaggerates the depth of the decline between 1871 and 1877; but the fact that this was the sharpest and deepest (though not the longest) decline is not disputable. See our Appendix II.

16 *Historical Statistics of the United States from Colonial Times.*

17 Monthly fluctuations in the gold value of the dollar are given in Henry A. Wallace, *Agricultural Prices*, Des Moines, 1920.

18 *Historical Statistics of the United States from Colonial Times.*

19 For money wages and real wages we use the figures of E. R. Phelps Brown with Margaret H. Browne, *A Century of Pay*, Macmillan, London, 1968.

20 Labour force figures are calculated from Stanley Lebergott, *Manpower in Economic Growth; the American Record since 1800*, McGraw-Hill, New York, 1964.

21 *Historical Statistics of the United States from Colonial Times.* The original source is R. E. Lipsey, *Price and Quantity Trends in the Foreign Trade of the United States*, Princeton University Press, Princeton, NJ, 1963.

22 Jurgen Kuczynski, *A Short History of Labour Conditions in Germany, 1800 to the Present Day*, Frederick Muller, London, 1945.

23 More statistics are available for France in the nineteenth century than for any other country. See the *Annuaire Statistique* published by Statistique Générale de la France. For population and labour force figures the authority is J. C. Toutain, *La Population de la France de 1700 à 1959*, Cahier AF3 de l'Institut de Science Economique Appliquée, Paris, 1963.

24 The classification is that used by the *Annuaire Statistique*, from which the figures are taken.

25 Alfred Maizels, *Industrial Growth and World Trade*, Cambridge University Press, Cambridge, 1969.

26 Based on a sample of some 80 commodities from the trade returns. This calculation was made before that of Lévy-Leboyer was published. His results are 113, 105, 100, compared with our 112, 107, 100. Maurice Lévy-Leboyer, 'L'Héritage de Simiand: prix, profit et termes d'échange au XIXe siècle', *Revue Historique*, January–March, 1970.

27 The British price index is from Schlote, op. cit. The French index is from Lévy-Leboyer, op. cit.

28 Léon Say, 'Le Rachat des chemins de fer', *Journal des Economistes*, December 1881.

29 Source: *Annuaire Statistique.*

30 From Appendix I. In this classification Textiles includes clothing; Science combines the relatively new and rapidly growing industries gas, electricity, chemicals, printing and paper; and Other combines building materials, furniture, rubber and leather goods.

31 Migration figures from Mitchell and Deane, op. cit. Capital export from Albert Imlah, op. cit.

32 H. J. Habakkuk, 'Fluctuations in House-building in Britain and the United States in the Nineteenth Century', *Journal of Economic History*, June 1962.

33 Source: Census of Population, 1911: England and Wales, summary tables, p. 11.

34 Source: UK Census of Population. The proportion of persons under 15 falls sharply over this period because of the declining birth rate. If one divides the number of persons by the number of houses the index falls continually after 1881; whereas if one divides the number of persons over 15 by the number of houses the index rises continually after 1881. To make sense of this one must weight the children in the index. After trying out various equations we have assumed, arbitrarily, that 1 child = 0·5 adult in terms of housing space.

35 The figures in Table 2.8 are from Werner Schlote, op. cit.

36 Value of world trade in manufactures can be calculated from W. A. Lewis, 'World Production, Prices and Trade', *Manchester School of Economic and Social Studies*,

May 1952. Translated into volume by using the index of prices of manufactures published here in Appendix III.

37 National income is Feinstein's gross domestic product at factor cost, 'compromise estimate'. Occupied population is from Appendix I below, assuming that occupied population grows at the same rate between peaks as between censuses. Money wages from Phelps Brown, op. cit.

38 The point that the British were already borrowing short and lending long is established by Peter H. Lindert, *Key Currencies and Gold 1900–13*, Princeton Studies in International Finance No. 24. Princeton University, 1969.

39 Jacob Viner, 'Clapham on the Bank of England', *Economica*, May 1945.

40 We use annual consumption of rails for railway investment and immigrants per thousand of population; this is why our lag between these two is shorter than the one found by Brinley Thomas, who uses railway mileage and numbers immigrating.

41 For blow by blow accounts of this depression see Rendigs Fels, op. cit., and Charles Hoffman, 'The Depression of the Nineties', *Journal of Economic History*, June 1956.

42 The figures are for new issues on the Stock Exchange and money called on previous issues. The United States is not shown separately. See Matthew Simon, 'New British Portfolio Foreign Investment, 1865–1914', in J. H. Adler (ed.), *Capital Movements*, Macmillan, London, 1967.

43 From J. G. Williamson, *American Growth and the Balance of Payments, 1820–1913*, University of North Carolina Press, Chapel Hill, 1964.

44 Imports, exports and terms of trade from R. E. Lipsey, op. cit. The chart is semi-logarithmic. Imports and exports are of merchandise only, excluding invisible services, and the diagram does not yield information on the balance of payments. The fact that the import and export curves are here drawn equal at 1893/7 has no statistical significance.

45 From J. G. Williamson, op. cit.

46 Calculated from R. E. Lipsey, op. cit. 'Primary products' is the sum of 'Food', 'Manufactured food' and 'Crude materials', and therefore includes minerals as well as agricultural products.

47 Stanley Lebergott, op. cit., pp. 512, 522.

48 Interstate Commerce Commission, *Railway Statistics*, Washington, DC, annually.

49 Milton J. Friedman and Anna J. Schwartz, *A Monetary History of the United States 1875–1960*, Princeton University Press, Princeton, NJ, 1963, p. 111.

50 Calculated from Frederick Strauss and Louis H. Bean, *Gross Farm Income and Indices of Farm Production in the United States 1869–1937*, Technical Bulletin No. 703, US Department of Agriculture, Washington, DC, 1940.

51 The graph of the moving averages can be seen in Chart 2.2.

52 From Table 2.4.

53 Alfred Maizels, op. cit.

54 A. K. Cairncross displays this elegantly in his book *Home and Foreign Investment, 1870–1913*, Cambridge University Press, Cambridge, 1953.

CHAPTER 3

1 These cost of living figures are calculated from E. H. Phelps Brown with Margaret Browne, *A Century of Pay*, Macmillan, London, 1968, appendix 3.

2 Figures for the UK calculated from C. H. Feinstein, *National Income and Expenditure of the United Kingdom, 1855–1965*, Cambridge University Press, Cambridge, 1972. Those for Germany from W. G. Hoffmann, *Das Wachstum der Deutschen Wirtschaft seit der Mitte des 19. Jahrhunderts*, Springer-Verlag, Berlin, 1965. Figures for the USA are Kuznets's annual data, as reproduced by J. W. Kendrick, *Productivity Trends in the United States*, Princeton University Press, Princeton, NJ, 1961; government investment is included.

3 US figures are from Warren and Pearson's index in *Historical Statistics*. French figures from the *Annuaire Statistique*. German figures from Alfred Jacobs and H. Richter, *Grosshandelspreise in Deutschland von 1792 bis 1932*, Institut für Konjunkturforschung, Sonderhefte No. 37, Berlin, 1935. UK figures are from the

Sauerbeck–Statist index. Freights deducted by subtracting 10 per cent of Cairncross's index, reproduced here in Appendix III.

4 Data for annual production of cotton, coffee and wool are reproduced and described in Appendix III; data for wheat in Appendix IV.

5 We use the estimate which Joseph Kitchin presented to the Gold Delegation of the Financial Committee of the League of Nations, and which is included in its *Interim Report*, Geneva, 1930, series II: Economic and Financial, no. 26. Kitchin assumed a figure for 1843, added annual production and subtracted absorption by industry and Oriental hoards. C. A. Hardy has challenged the series, concluding that it was about $1,045 million too low in 1913. See his *Is There Enough Gold?*, Brookings, Washington, DC, 1936.

6 Described and reproduced in Appendix III.

7 From Feinstein, op. cit.

8 Note that in Tables 3.2 to 3.5, results are from 1866 for wheat and cotton, and from 1871 for wool and coffee.

9 When the price index ex-freights is divided by the price index of manufactures, we get the following terms of trade equations:

Cotton from 1867

$$\begin{array}{llllllll} P = & -0{\cdot}579 & + & 4{\cdot}37D & - & 4{\cdot}41S & R^2 & = 0{\cdot}865 \\ & (9{\cdot}77) & & (16{\cdot}2) & & (16{\cdot}2) & \text{SEE} & = 0{\cdot}028 \end{array}$$

Wool from 1871

$$\begin{array}{llllllll} P = & 0{\cdot}247 & + & 0{\cdot}53D & - & 0{\cdot}93S & R^2 & = 0{\cdot}843 \\ & (22{\cdot}6) & & (13{\cdot}6) & & (11{\cdot}4) & \text{SEE} & = 0{\cdot}017 \end{array}$$

Coffee from 1871

$$\begin{array}{llllllll} P = & 0{\cdot}331 & + & 1{\cdot}71D & - & 2{\cdot}69S & R^2 & = 0{\cdot}553 \\ & (4{\cdot}31) & & (4{\cdot}86) & & (5{\cdot}81) & \text{SEE} & = 0{\cdot}090 \end{array}$$

Wheat from 1878

$$\begin{array}{llllllll} P = & 0{\cdot}600 & + & 1{\cdot}19D & - & 2{\cdot}89S & R^2 & = 0{\cdot}627 \\ & (12{\cdot}1) & & (6{\cdot}57) & & (6{\cdot}86) & \text{SEE} & = 0{\cdot}022 \end{array}$$

where P, D and S are logarithms of their respective indexes. Addition of a trend term sometimes improves the result a little and sometimes worsens it (by yielding unacceptable t ratios).

10 The commodity prices are from the Sauerbeck–Statist index published annually in the *Journal of the Royal Statistical Society*, and reproduced here in Appendix III. The freight index is from Cairncross, and is also reproduced in Appendix III.

11 Frederick Strauss and Louis H. Bean, *Gross Farm Income and Indices of Farm Production and Prices in the United States, 1869–1937*, US Department of Agriculture Technical Bulletin No. 703, Washington, DC, 1940, table 61.

12 Money wages from E. H. Phelps Brown with Margaret Browne, op. cit., appendix 3.

13 Writing in 1880, James Caird described the situation as follows:

> The continued rain and low temperature of 1879 not only acted destructively on the corn and green crops, but damaged the hay crop beyond measure . . . In nine years there have been seven defective harvests, the last culminating in intensity, and including in its grasp a portion of the animal in addition to the vegetable produce of the land. It is no comfort to the British farmer to be told that there is a similar depression in the agricultural districts of France and Germany . . . In England itself, where the bulk of the wheat crop of the kingdom is grown, there has been lost in the past ten years, by unfavourable seasons, a fourth more than a whole year's wheat crop.

James Caird, *The Landed Interest and the Supply of Food*, Frank Cass, London, 1967 (5th edn), p. 158. A long succession of bad harvests is infrequent in any one place, so whenever it happens the inhabitants of that place begin to suppose that the climate is changing. However, in the world as a whole a succession of bad harvests happens quite frequently in one place or another.

14 David K. Sheppard, *The Growth and Role of U.K. Financial Institutions, 1880–1962*, Methuen, London, 1971.

15 Money stock is the sum of bank deposits plus non-bank holdings of currency (ibid., p. 42, col. VII).

16 Stock of monetary gold is the sum of coin and bullion held by the Bank of England (ibid., p. 136, col. 15), plus gold coin in circulation (ibid., p. 180, col. 2).

17 Gross domestic product divided by the stock of money.

18 US stock of monetary gold is from Philip Cagan, *Determinants and Effects of Changes in the Stock of Money 1875–1960*, Columbia University Press, New York, 1965, p. 340. Stock of money and velocity of circulation from Milton Friedman and Anna J. Schwartz, *A Monetary History of the United States 1867–1960*, Princeton University Press, Princeton, NJ, 1963, pp. 704, 774.

19 See note 21 below.

20 Friedman and Schwartz, op. cit., p. 91.

21 Kuznets has published annual data for US national income from 1871 onwards in the form of five-year moving averages, both in current prices and in 1929 prices, from which a GNP deflator can be derived. Kendrick has published the year-by-year figures from 1889 onwards, so one can unravel the series backwards. The figures in our text for the GNP and the deflator of 1882 come from this unravelling, and are therefore subject to minor error. They show a significantly higher rate of growth from 1892 to 1906 than from 1882 to 1892. This is improbable, since the growth rate of industrial production was constant and the growth rate of agriculture was declining. Since the analysis in this paragraph of the text turns on money income (real income multiplied by the deflator) an adjustment to real income would be accompanied by an equal and opposite adjustment to the deflator, so our final result would be unchanged. Simon Kuznets, *Capital in the American Economy*, Princeton University Press, Princeton, NJ, 1961, pp. 561, 563: 'Gross National Product, Variant III'. John W. Kendrick, *Productivity Trends in the United States*, Princeton University Press, Princeton, NJ, 1961, p. 290, col. 1; p. 296, sum of cols. 1, 5, 8 and 9.

22 Philip Cagan, 'The Monetary Dynamics of Hyperinflation', in M. Friedman (ed.), *Studies in the Quantity Theory of Money*, University of Chicago Press, Chicago, 1956.

23 Although we use the same statistical tables (those of Friedman and Schwartz) Philip Cagan in *Determinants* (op. cit., n. 18 above) appears to get different results. His approach is different. Between 1882 and 1906 the stock of gold rose by 4·5 per cent per annum and the stock of money by 6·2 per cent per annum. Starting from these data Cagan would say that gold 'accounts for' 73 per cent of the increase in money, and would imply that gold is therefore what really matters. But the leeway between the rates of growth of money and of gold, and of money and money income leaves more than enough room for other-than-gold explanations of such small changes in the rate of change of prices as actually occurred. These other explanations are downgraded excessively in his descriptive writing (but not in his figures). Thus Cagan writes:

> Neither changes in banks' reserve ratios nor in the ratio of domestic gold stock to high-powered money account for any sizable part of the long run movements in the U.S. money stock before 1914 (page 254).

and

> The high correlation between prices and the money stock shown in Table 29 demonstrates that changes in velocity, whatever their explanation, have been comparatively small in the periods covered (page 259).

Actually the reserve ratio increased by two-thirds (from 5·6 to 8·4) and the velocity of circulation almost halved (from 4·2 to 2·3). Correlation of cyclical movements is not a good guide to secular change.

CHAPTER 4

1 E. H. Phelps Brown with Margaret Browne, *A Century of Pay*, Macmillan, London, 1968, appendix 3.
2 ibid., pp. 183–4.
3 G. T. Jones, *Increasing Return*, Cambridge University Press, Cambridge, 1933.
4 D. N. McCloskey, *Economic Maturity and Entrepreneurial Decline: British Iron and Steel Industry 1870–1913*, Harvard University Press, Cambridge, Mass., 1973. Since McCloskey strongly champions British entrepreneurship against charges of inefficiency, his argument would have gained superficial strength if productivity had turned out to be increasing.
5 Phelps Brown has produced some striking graphs of individual industries showing stagnation or decline of productivity: op. cit., pp. 179–80.
6 J. C. Toutain, *La Population de la France de 1700 à 1959*, Cahier AF3 de l'Institut de Science Economique Appliquée. Paris, 1963. Between the censuses of 1891 and 1896 the labour force, which had been more or less constant for fifteen years, suddenly jumps by 2·6 million. The jump is shared by men and women, and by all sectors, including industry. Since the number of persons aged 15 to 64 increased only by 0·2 million, the labour force has been redefined in a manner which produces a spurious increase of about 15 per cent.

If we add industry and commerce together, the annual growth rate is 0·4 per cent between 1881 and 1891, and 0·8 per cent between 1901 and 1911. Since the 1880s were depressed and the 1890s were prosperous, we have assumed that the growth rate for 1891 to 1901 was the same as that for 1901 to 1911. This implies that the figures for 1891 and earlier must be increased by 15·6 per cent which is about the same answer one gets from studying the age structure of the population.
7 John W. Kendrick, *Productivity Trends in the United States*, Princeton University Press, Princeton, NJ, 1961.

Our period 1892 to 1906 overlaps with Kendrick's. His productivity grows more slowly (1·3) because his labour force grows faster (3·5) and his output more slowly (4·8). (These figures combine his results for manufacturing and mining.) The data all come from the National Bureau of Economic Research, which revises them constantly. As explained in Appendix II we have used for output (without further revision of our own) a revised series published by Nutter in 1962. For labour we have started from Lebergott's revisions of the census, published in 1964. Also Kendrick's method of interpolation for annual employment data is more sophisticated than ours.

The cost of living was about the same in 1906 as in 1892. If real wages rose at 1·5 per cent per annum while productivity in manufacturing increased only by 1·3 per cent per annum a tremendous shift to wages is implied, which is not consistent with a rising capital-output ratio. The normal expectation that workers in manufacturing must share their productivity with other workers whose productivity is rising less rapidly does not have to be fulfilled because in Kendrick's calculations productivity per person is rising more slowly in manufacturing than in the rest of the economy. His figure for the whole private domestic economy is 1·8 per cent per annum. This is not simply a matter of people transferring from low-income to higher income sectors. His growth rate of productivity per person in manufacturing and mining (1·3) is well below those for agriculture (1·9) and transportation (2·0). These results are puzzling.

We use for labour force in manufacturing and mining the following figures; our interpolations are italicised:

1870	2·65 m.	1892	*5·13* m.
1872	*2·81*	1899	*6·34*
1880	3·57	1900	6·53
1882	*3·79*	1906	*8·13*
1890	4·83	1910	9·40

8 Gross profit here includes rent, interest, taxes and, unfortunately, expenditures on advertising and repairs. Figures for 1889 are adjusted to exclude hand and neighbourhood industries, assuming the same proportions as in 1899. Figures for 1889 and 1899 are adjusted to exclude contract work, using the same proportions as in 1904. Direct and certain comparability is not attainable, because classifications kept changing.

9 Raw materials were about 35 per cent of the price of manufactures in the 1907 Census of Production. Since a large part of the index of production comes from statistics of raw material use, and does not allow for economy of use of raw materials, the proportion to allocate to economies arising out of the changeover from more to less intensive raw material using industries is difficult to discover. See C. T. Saunders, 'The Consumption of Raw Materials in the U.K., 1851–1950', *Journal of the Royal Statistical Society*, vol. CXV, part III, 1952. The price change in manufactures to 1899 is from Werner Schlote, *British Overseas Trade from 1700 to the 1930s*, Basil Blackwell, Oxford, 1952 to 1913, from Alfred Maizels, *Industrial Growth and World Trade*, Cambridge University Press, Cambridge, 1969. Schlote's price increase to 1913 is even larger, viz. 1·315.

10 W. G. Hoffmann explains his procedures in *Das Wachstum der Deutschen Wirtschaft seit der Mitte des 19. Jahrhunderts*, Springer-Verlag, Berlin, 1965, p. 502.

11 Stanley Lebergott, *Manpower in Economic Growth; the American Record since 1800*, McGraw-Hill, New York, 1964, pp. 190–202.

12 Alfred Cowles and Associates, *Common Stock Indexes, 1871–1937*, Principia Press, Bloomington, Ind., 1938.

13 Kuznets gives investment in producer durables and also in various divisions of construction in current and 1929 prices, from which one can derive a price index. Ours is derived by adding producer durables and 'other construction'. Simon Kuznets, *Capital in the American Economy*, Princeton University Press, Princeton, NJ, 1961, tables R-30 and R-33.

14 op. cit., pp. 42–3.

15 In 1888 prices of industrial shares whose earnings are contained in this sample were 26 per cent below their 1892 level, whereas prices of all industrials were only 16 per cent below their 1892 level.

16 K. C. Smith and G. F. Horne, 'An Index Number of Securities, 1867–1914', *London and Cambridge Economic Service*, Special Memorandum No. 37, June 1934.

17 This combines, with equal weights, Feinstein's price indexes for plant and machinery and 'other building'.

18 This literature is reviewed by S. B. Saul, *The Myth of the Great Depression*, Macmillan, London, 1969.

19 Otto Donner, 'Die Kursbildung am Aktienmarkt', *Vierteljahrshefte Zur Konjunkturforschung*, Sonderheft 36, Berlin, 1934.

20 This index is formed by dividing investment in current prices by investment in 1913 prices for Hoffmann's *Gewerbe* (industry and trade). *Wachstum*, op. cit., pp. 246–7.

21 Marcel Lenoir, 'Le Mouvement des cours des valeurs mobilières françaises depuis 1856', *Bulletin de la Statistique Générale de la France*, October 1919.

22 This series is from Maurice Lévy-Leboyer, 'L'Héritage de Simiand: prix, profits et termes d'échange au XIXe siècle', *Revue Historique*, January–March 1970.

23 Adam Smith, *The Wealth of Nations*, book I, ch. 8, p. 76 of Cannan's edition.

24 What actually happened to wages in Britain in the first half of the nineteenth century is the subject of much controversy. Two indices of urban wages stretch back to and beyond the beginning of the industrial revolution – those of Phelps Brown and of Tucker. If we start with the 1780s they give more or less the same answer for the increase in real wages up to the 1820s (Tucker 12 per cent, Phelps Brown 15 per cent), after which they diverge. From 1850 onwards we have Wood's indexes of both money and real wages, which he gives both with and without upgrading of occupations. The curve in Chart 4.3 is for wages of 'unchanged grade', since the controversies and theories relate to unskilled labour. For the period in between the 1820s and the 1850s, we have used data left by Wood and Bowley, together with Tucker's index, to make another index from 1820 to 1850, which is linked with Wood's index at 1850. This composite index for 1825 to 1850 uses

Wood and Bowley's wages of cotton operatives, workers in shipbuilding and engineering, printers and builders, which with the addition of Tucker's artisans makes five groups, weighted equally.

The upper part of Chart 4.3 reproduces the Tucker index of money wages from 1785 to 1860, and also this composite Wood–Bowley–Tucker index from 1825 to 1850, followed by Wood's index. These are annual data, although the lower curve, for real wages, is a nine-year moving average.

To arrive at real wages we have used Tucker's index of the cost of living to deflate both his own index of money wages and also the portion of the composite Wood–Bowley–Tucker index running from 1820 to 1850; beyond 1850 we use Wood's cost of living index. We have not used Silberling's index because it is actually an index of wholesale prices. To repeat: the real wage curve in Chart 4.3 is a nine-year moving average, while the money wage curve shows annual data.

The figures of Wood and Bowley used from 1820 to 1850 are available in B. R. Mitchell and Phyllis Deane, *Abstract of British Historical Statistics*, Cambridge University Press, Cambridge, 1962. The other references are G. H. Wood, 'Real Wages and the Standard of Comfort since 1850', *Journal of the Royal Statistical Society*, March 1909; and 'Statistics of Wages in the Nineteenth Century, Part XIX: The Cotton Industry', same journal, June 1910. E. H. Phelps Brown and S. V. Hopkins, 'Seven Centuries of the Prices of Consumables Compared with Builders Wage Rates', *Economica*, November 1956. R. S. Tucker, 'Real Wages of Artisans in London, 1729–1935', *Journal of the American Statistical Association*, 1930. N. J. Silberling, 'British Prices and Business Cycles, 1779–1850', *Review of Economics and Statistics*, 1923. The literature is reviewed, with a bibliography, by M. W. Flinn, 'Trends in Real Wages 1752–1850', *Review of Economic History*, August 1974.

25 Between 1780 and 1860 both the industrial and the agricultural revolutions were in full swing, and productivity will have been rising much faster than the real wage of 'unchanged grade'. The difference would not all accrue to a rising share of profits and rents, since workers in industry have to share productivity increases with workers in other sectors, but a substantial shift to profits is also indicated by the doubling of the savings ratio which occurred over this period.

CHAPTER 5

1 The general tenor of the result is not affected by reasonable and consistent allocations of 'General Labourers' to manufacturing. For example, assume that by 1911 none of the General Labourers belongs to Manufacturing, since by 1911 the census takers had modernised their classifications. Assume further that in all previous censuses the percentage of 1911 (i.e. 2·3) is the 'correct' proportion of General Labourers in the occupied population, and allocate to Manufacturing half the difference between this and the actual number of General Labourers reported by the Census. Then the productivity growth rates for Manufacturing become 1·8, 1·4 and 1·0 instead of the 1·85, 1·15 and 0·9 reported in this paragraph. The main feature that interests us, the continual deceleration, remains.

2 Estimates of foreign investment here and elsewhere relate to long-term lending. Since Britain was already borrowing short (holding other countries' balances) and lending long, they slightly exaggerate the net investment.

3 The subject is surveyed by Murray Brown, *The Theory and Measurement of Technological Change*, Cambridge University Press, Cambridge, 1966.

4 For two such estimates see S. B. Saul, 'The Export Economy 1870–1914', *Yorkshire Bulletin of Economic and Social Research*, May 1965; and W. A. Lewis, 'International Competition in Manufactures', *American Economic Review*, May 1957. Estimates differ because of different definitions of what to include in manufactures, and also different treatments of the changes in the customs area reported in German statistics.

5 Despite reservations about Schlote's price indexes, we have to use his figures for manufactures at constant prices, because other calculations of British trade at constant prices do not distinguish between manufactures and other commodities.

Fortunately the contrasts we are making in this paragraph are so sharp that they would not be much affected by reasonable changes in the price indexes.

6 In order to add trade and production of manufactures either both must be in value added, or both must include the cost of materials and other elements in the wholesale price of manufactures. The solution here is to add 50 per cent to value added in production of manufactures, following Maizels.

7 For an alternative estimate of the potential effect on production of a large growth rate of exports see J. R. Meyer, 'An Input–Output Approach to Evaluating the Influence of Exports on British Industrial Production in the Late Nineteenth Century', *Explorations in Entrepreneurial History*, 1955.

8 See W. A. Lewis, 'World Production, Prices and Trade', *Manchester School of Economic and Social Studies*, May 1952.

9 See A. Maizels, *Industrial Growth and World Trade*, Cambridge University Press, Cambridge, 1969, p. 430.

10 Figures for 1913 are from Maizels; for 1883 UK figures from Schlote, Germany from Hoffmann, USA from Lipsey and France from Lévy-Leboyer. Schlote possibly understates the fall of UK prices to 1900. A major difficulty is that the commodity composition of exports differed; for example the main cause of the relative rise in British prices to 1913 was the rise of the prices of textiles, which were a relatively large component of British exports. Maizels's commodity comparisons of 1913 on 1899 base show the following:

	Germany	*UK*
Metals	126	108
Metal goods	108	104
Machinery	136	106
Transport equipment	70	95
Chemicals	81	127
Textiles and clothing	130	147
Other	103	120
Total	108	125

Britain was holding her own in the important metal and machinery trades.

11 For a full account of British reactions see R. J. S. Hoffman, *Great Britain and the German Trade Rivalry 1875–1914*, University of Pennsylvania Press, Philadelphia, 1933.

12 Flux's analysis of the 1907 UK and 1909 US censuses of manufactures led to the conclusion that American productivity was 2·5 times the British, in terms of value added. However, US prices were higher than British. See Appendix II for evidence leading to the conclusion that US productivity was 1·9 times the British. A. W. Flux, 'The Census of Production', *Journal of the Royal Statistical Society*, May 1924; also 'Industrial Productivity in Britain and the United States', *Quarterly Journal of Economics*, November 1933.

13 L. Rostas, *Comparative Productivity in British and American Industry*, Cambridge University Press, Cambridge, 1948.

14 E. H. Phelps Brown with Margaret Browne, *A Century of Pay*, Macmillan, London, 1968, pp. 185–7.

15 L. G. Sandberg, 'American Rings and English Mules: the Role of Economic Rationality', *Quarterly Journal of Economics*, February 1969.

16 See the useful essays in Derek H. Aldcroft, *The Development of British Industry and Foreign Competition 1875–1914*, University of Toronto Press, Toronto, 1968.

17 A. Maizels, op. cit., pp. 478 and 482.

18 This literature is enormous. Most of it is mentioned in the footnotes of Donald N. McCloskey (ed.), *Essays on a Mature Economy: Britain after 1840*, Methuen, London, 1971. Another source is the bibliographical monograph by S. B. Saul, *The Myth of the Great Depression*, Macmillan, London.

19 Charlotte Erickson, *British Industrialists: Steel and Hosiery, 1850–1950*, Cambridge University Press, Cambridge, 1959.

20 Michael Sanderson, *The Universities and British Industry 1850–1970*, Routledge and Kegan Paul, London, 1972.

21 W. O. Henderson, *Britain and Industrial Europe*, University of Liverpool Press, Liverpool, 1954. Rondo Cameron, *France and the Economic Development of Europe*, Princeton University Press, Princeton, NJ, 1967. Also J. P. McKay, *Pioneers for Profit: Foreign Entrepreneurs and Russian Industrialisation 1855–1913*, University of Chicago Press, Chicago, 1970.

22 Peter Temin, 'The Relative Decline of the British Steel Industry 1880 to 1913', in Henry Rosovsky (ed.), *Industrialisation in two Systems: Essays in Honour of Alexander Gerschenkron*, Wiley, New York, 1966.

CHAPTER 6

1 The OECD (Organisation for Economic Cooperation and Development) includes Japan, the USA, Canada and Australia, as well as Western Europe. Data here relate to manufacturing plus mining, excluding construction. Taken from two OECD annual publications: *Industrial Production Historical Statistics* and *Labour Force Statistics*.

2 Peter Temin, 'Labour Scarcity and the Problem of American Industrial Efficiency', *Journal of Economic History*, September 1966.

3 Mulhall does not give his sources. The British and European figures are probably the percentages of brides and bridegrooms able to sign the marriage register. There are also data for literacy percentages of conscripts into the French and Prussian armies, which are in general quite close to the literacy percentages of bridegrooms. American figures are from the Census, and include the slaves; the figure for whites would be about 90 per cent. Figures based on the ability to sign one's name probably greatly overstate the extent of functional literacy. See M. G. Mulhall, *The Dictionary of Statistics*, London, 1892, p. 231. Also C. M. Cipolla, *Literacy and Development in the West*, Penguin Books, Harmondsworth, 1969.

4 C. P. Kindleberger, *Economic Growth in France and Britain in 1851–1950*, Harvard University Press, Cambridge, Mass., 1964, ch. 6.

5 H. B. Chenery and A. M. Strout, 'Foreign Assistance and Economic Development', *American Economic Review*, September 1966.

6 D. L. Burn, *The Economic History of Steel Making 1867–1939*, Cambridge University Press, Cambridge, 1940. Peter Temin, 'The Relative Decline of the British Steel Industry 1880 to 1913', in Henry Rosovsky (ed.), *Industrialisation in Two Systems: Essays in Honour of Alexander Gerschenkron*, Wiley, New York, 1966.

7 C. P. Kindleberger, op. cit., ch. 2.

8 Britain has experienced several industrial revolutions. Miss Carus-Wilson puts the first (?) in the thirteenth century, converting Britain from an exporter of wool into an exporter of cloth. There were long secular swings in cloth exports; the latest upswing that she identifies runs from the last quarter of the fifteenth to the middle of the sixteenth century, with a growth rate of about one per cent per annum, which is very respectable for those days. Close on its heels follows another industrial revolution identified by John Nef, this time in a range of non-textile industries. Miss Carus-Wilson's introduction to her thirteenth-century revolution invites the comment *'plus ça change'*:

> [The thirteenth century] witnessed in fact an industrial revolution due to scientific discoveries and changes in technique; a revolution which brought poverty, unemployment and discontent to certain old centres of the [woollen] industry, but wealth, opportunity and prosperity to the country as a whole, and which was destined to alter the face of medieval England.

E. M. Carus-Wilson, 'An Industrial Revolution of the Thirteenth Century', *Economic History Review*, IX, 1 (1941); E. M. Carus-Wilson and Olive Coleman, *England's Export Trade, 1275–1547*, Clarendon Press, Oxford, 1963; J. U. Nef, *Industry and Government in France and England 1540–1640*, American Philosophical Society, Philadelphia, 1940.

9 The case of Argentina is analysed by A. G. Ford, *The Gold Standard 1880–1914: Britain and Argentina*, Oxford University Press, Oxford, 1962.

10 We are not arguing that industrialisation is the only cause of urbanisation. For

example Chile and Argentina were urbanising rapidly in the last quarter of the nineteenth century. Expansion of service industries, which also causes urbanisation, can just as well be sparked by wealth derived from lucrative production of primary products.

11 This is the growth rate of population in places having 2,000 or more inhabitants in France and Germany, or 2,500 in the USA. In England and Wales the definition turns on local government machinery; the rural population is that which lives in areas administered by rural district authorities. To compare the number of persons living in units of 2,000 or more from one census to another slightly overestimates the growth of the urban population, since the populations of areas passing the 2,000 mark are included in the later census figure but not in the earlier one. On the other hand, 2,000 is a poor cut-off figure for the study of industrialisation since the industrial towns were growing faster than overall urbanisation. However this is a good dividing line when the focus is on the decline of rural communities.

12 There was a slight increase in the number of male relatives of farmers between these dates (75,000 to 98,000). The number of female relatives of farmers working on the farm was put at 57,000 in 1911; apparently they were not counted in 1881.

13 The postwar growth and investment figures are from the United Nations annual *National Income Statistics.* Prewar US figures for capital from Simon Kuznets, *Capital in the American Economy*, Princeton University Press, Princeton, NJ, 1961, p. 95, and for national income from J. W. Kendrick, *Productivity Trends in the United States*, Princeton University Press, Princeton, NJ, 1961, p. 292. For Germany, from W. G. Hoffmann, *Das Wachstum der Deutschen Wirtschaft seit der Mitte des 19. Jahrhunderts*, Springer-Verlag, Berlin, 1965. For UK, investment from C. H. Feinstein, *National Income and Expenditure of the United Kingdom, 1855–1965*, Cambridge University Press, Cambridge, 1972; national income from our Appendix I. Net investment is gross domestic fixed investment minus capital consumption allowances; the denominator is gross domestic product (prewar USA: GNP; prewar Germany: NNP). Investment ratios are calculated in current prices. Growth rate of national income is from GDP at constant prices.

14 These studies typically have an exponent for capital as low as 0·25 or 0·3, and this of course automatically downgrades the contribution of capital to growth. Capital invested in churches, theatres, hospitals and such services does not cause growth; such investment occurs because growth in other sectors has raised national income. If one wishes to assess properly the contribution of capital to growth it is best to concentrate on the sectors where productivity grows most rapidly, especially industry and transport. In many of the exercises where 0·7 is used as the exponent for labour, it has been forgotten that whereas income accruing to employees in the public sector is included in labour income, capital used in the public sector and other non-profit uses is either not credited with income, or credited at low rates which do not truly represent productivity.

15 J. W. Kendrick, op. cit., calculated from p. 464.

16 P. J. Verdoon, 'Fattori che regolano lo sviluppo della produttività del lavoro', *L'Industria*, 1949.

17 This suggestion does not conflict with our earlier suggestion that investment may have been deflected from French industry in the last quarter of the nineteenth century by slow population growth. Given the level of investment, output per person is higher with slow population growth, but output per unit of capital is higher with fast population growth.

18 John Jewkes, David Sawers and Richard Stillerman, *The Sources of Invention*, Macmillan, London, 1958; Jacob Schmookler, *Invention and Economic Growth*, Harvard University Press, Cambridge, Mass., 1966; Universities-National Bureau Conference, *The Rate and Direction of Inventive Activity*, Princeton University Press, Princeton, NJ, 1962.

CHAPTER 7

1 Phyllis Deane, 'Capital Formation in Britain before the Railway Age', in François Crouzet (ed.), *Capital Formation in the Industrial Revolution*, Methuen, London,

1972. Of an earlier date she says: 'The impression gained by piecing such fragments as these together is that at the end of the eighteenth century the annual flow of new capital into the leading commercial and industrial sectors (shipping, textiles and iron) was not more than about £2 million or perhaps one per cent of national income.'

2 William Cunningham, *Alien Immigrants to England*, Macmillan, London, 1897, especially pp. 164–5.

3 W. O. Henderson, *Britain and Industrial Europe*, University of Liverpool Press, Liverpool, 1954.

4 Rondo Cameron, *France and the Economic Development of Europe*, Princeton University Press, Princeton, NJ, 1961.

5 J. P. McKay, *Pioneers for Profit: Foreign Entrepreneurs and Russian Industrialisation 1855–1913*, University of Chicago Press, Chicago, 1970.

6 Jean Marczewski, *Introduction à l'histoire quantitative*, Librairie Droz, Geneva, 1965, pp. 115–16.

7 W. N. Parker and J. L. V. Klein, 'Productivity Growth in Grain Production in the United States', in Conference on Research in Income and Wealth, *Output, Employment and Productivity in the United States after 1800*, vol. 30, National Bureau of Economic Research, New York, 1966.

8 G. A. Montgomery, *The Rise of Modern Industry in Sweden*, King, London, 1939. Also E. Lindahl, E. Dahlgren and K. Koch, *National Income of Sweden 1861–1930*, London, 1937.

9 The starting point is the proportionate share of world manufacturing output allocated to each country in the League of Nations monograph *Industrialisation and Foreign Trade*. The shares are the average of 1925/9, but are taken back to 1913 by industrial production indices. Sources of error are that the data are supposed to be 'value added', which does not exactly correspond to differences in physical output because of differences in prices; that the index numbers are uncertain and, like the values added, have in several cases since been revised; and that in the smallest cases the share is given by the League to only one significant place, which permits a margin of error in the lowest case, 0·2 per cent, of plus or minus 25 per cent. It is not clear whether the value of small-scale production was included in assessing proportions. The monograph specifically excludes handicrafts from its annual indexes of industrial production, but says nothing about whether they are included in the weighting of the world index. This is important in a country like India where in 1913 about 90 per cent of the males in manufacturing were in establishments with less than twenty persons. A rough check for India suggests that handicraft production must have been included. The total number in manufacturing, including handicrafts, was about 10 per cent of the labour force. If they contributed 15 per cent of national income, this would be about 3·0 rupees per inhabitant. The monograph's figures imply 3·5 rupees, which is near enough. The very low level of Indian prices (wages in 1913 were about 13 US cents a day, and national income per capita about 20 US dollars per year) suggests that real output was higher than is indicated by the index in Table 7.1 comparing India with other countries in terms of money value added; but the figure remains low even if multiplied by two or three to make this correction. The US ratio is overstated by using value added at current prices; see Appendix II.

10 For data and references see M. E. Falkus, *The Industrialisation of Russia 1700–1914*, Macmillan, London, 1972.

11 Steel consumption per head from Ingvar Svennilson, *Growth and Stagnation in the European Economy*, United Nations, Geneva, 1954. Industrial production per head from same source as Table 7.1. Exports from League of Nations, *Review of World Trade*, Geneva, annual. Population from League of Nations, *Statistical Year Book*, Geneva, annual. Wheat yields from International Institute of Agriculture, *International Yearbook of Agricultural Statistics*, Rome, annual. Growth rate of exports from same source as Table 7.3. Literacy figure is for Austria only; Hungary was lower. For source of literacy figures see Chapter 6, note 3. Japan's main crop was not wheat but rice; however, its wheat production was large enough to justify inclusion in this table for comparative purposes. The median of the second column is chosen on the assumption that industrial production per head was not

lower in Portugal than in Spain. In this table growth rate of exports is at current not constant prices.

12 B. R. Mitchell, *European Historical Statistics*, Columbia University Press, New York, 1975, pp. 355–7.

13 Alexander Gerschenkron, *Economic Backwardness in Historical Perspective*, Harvard University Press, Cambridge, Mass., 1962.

14 ibid., chapter 3, 'Social Attitudes, Entrepreneurship and Economic Development', reviews this discussion.

15 Here and hereafter the temperate settlements comprise Canada, Australia, New Zealand, Argentina, Uruguay, Chile and South Africa.

16 P. Lamartine Yates, *Forty Years of Foreign Trade*, George Allen & Unwin, London, 1959, p. 240, plus data for Oceania from pp. 64, 105, 227.

17 Data on total trade in 1913 from League of Nations, *Review of World Trade*, Geneva, annual. For 1883 data for tropical countries from W. A. Lewis, *Aspects of Tropical Trade 1883–1965*, Wicksell Lectures, Almquist, Stockholm, 1969. Data for temperate countries in 1883 from UK *Statistical Abstract for Foreign Countries*, annual, and UK *Statistical Abstract for Colonies*, annual. Breakdown of trade between manufactures and primary products based on Yates, op. cit., but assigning Austria-Hungary to South-East Europe, and leaving in North-West Europe, Sweden, Norway, Denmark, Germany, Belgium, France, Switzerland and UK. Netherlands excluded from this table because its transit trade, which was very large, was not separated from its special trade. 'South-East Europe' includes all the rest of Europe. Latin America includes the Caribbean islands. Growth rates are for trade in current prices, after adjusting for changes in foreign exchange rates relative to gold.

18 C. P. Kindleberger, *The Terms of Trade*, The Technology Press of Massachusetts Institute of Technology and John Wiley & Sons, New York, 1956, p. 12.

19 This index is described in W. A. Lewis, *Aspects of Tropical Trade*, op. cit., and is reproduced here in Appendix III.

20 See Appendix III.

21 Calculated from the indexes in M. C. Urquhart and K. A. H. Buckley, *Historical Statistics of Canada*, Cambridge University Press, Cambridge, 1965, pp. 299–300.

22 From M. Mukherjee, *National Income of India*, Statistical Publishing Society, Calcutta, 1969, p. 94.

23 Data exclude livestock products, except from Argentina. Canadian, Indian and Australian data are five-year moving averages; Argentinian data are quinquennial averages. All data assume constant prices. Canadian data from Urquhart and Buckley, *Historical Statistics of Canada*, op. cit. Indian and Australian data from G. Brandau, *Ernteschwankungen und Wirtschaftliche Wechsellagen, 1874–1913*, Gustav Fischer, Jena, 1936. Argentinian data from Carlos Diaz Alejandro, *Essays in the Economic History of the Argentine Republic*, Yale University Press, New Haven, 1970, p. 474; weighted by 1913 prices calculated from the official *Annuario Estadistica*, and carried backward from the same source.

24 From W. A. Lewis, *Aspects of Tropical Trade*, op. cit. The definition includes countries lying between 30° N and 30° S; Egypt is included, but not the rest of the Middle East or China. See source for details.

25 W. A. Lewis, 'World Production, Prices and Trade', *Manchester School of Economic and Social Studies*, May 1952.

26 Average growth rates from 1950/2 to 1969/71 are 5·1 per cent per annum for quantum of trade in primary products and 5·9 per cent per annum for world production of manufactures. Figures from 1950 to 1968 are in Table 13 of the United Nations *Statistical Year Book* for 1969, p. 54. Data to 1971 for manufacturing production are published quarterly in the UN *Monthly Bulletin of Statistics.* For primary products add the separate data for food, agricultural raw materials and fuel which are given in constant prices in Table 12 on page 47 of the UN *Statistical Year Book* for 1972. The elasticity is lower when the base is world industrial production than when it is core industrial production.

27 H. Neisser and F. Modigliani, *National Incomes and International Trade: A Quantitative Analysis*, Urbana, Ill., 1953; J. S. Polak, *An International Economic System*, London, 1954. For a review of existing models see G. B. Taplin, 'Models of

World Trade', *IMF Staff Papers*, 1967. OECD has done much work in this area; for an interim report see F. G. Adams, H. Eguchi and F. Meyer-zu-Schlochtern, *An Econometric Analysis of International Trade*, OECD, Paris, 1969.

28 M. Edelstein, 'The Determinants of U.K. Investment Abroad, 1870–1913: The U.S. Case', *Journal of Economic History*, December 1974.

29 See note 37 below.

30 United Nations, *International Capital Movements in the Inter-war Period*, Lake Success, 1949. The data are mainly from Herbert Feis, *Europe the World's Banker 1870–1914*, Yale University Press, New Haven, 1930.

31 Debt figures collected from Feis, ibid. Trade in 1913 from League of Nations, *Review of World Trade*, Geneva, annual.

32 Quoted in Feis, op. cit., p. 27.

33 Investment data are as assembled by Arthur I. Bloomfield, *Patterns of Fluctuation in International Investment before 1914*, Princeton Studies in International Finance No. 21, Princeton University, 1968.

34 See especially N. G. Butlin, *Investment in Australian Economic Development 1861–1900*, Cambridge University Press, Cambridge, 1964; and E. A. Boehm, *Prosperity and Depression in Australia 1887–1897*, Oxford University Press, Oxford, 1971. A. C. Kelley, 'Demographic Cycles and Economic Growth', *Journal of Economic History*, December 1969.

35 Imre Ferenczi and W. F. Willcox, *International Migrations*, vol. I, National Bureau of Economic Research, New York, 1929, pp. 230, 236.

36 Figure for Australia is the estimate of the Commonwealth Statistician Bureau. Figure for Canada is estimated from census data; see Urquhart and Buckley, *Historical Statistics of Canada*, op. cit. Figure for Argentina is official record of immigration and emigration. Details of emigrants from Brazil are recorded only from 1899 to 1912, when emigration was 65 per cent of immigration; it is here assumed to have averaged 50 per cent over the remaining years, which were more prosperous.

37 There is a large literature on this subject. For example: L. E. Callaway and R. K. Vedder, 'Emigration from the U.K. to the U.S.A. 1860–1913', *Journal of Economic History*, December 1971; A. C. Kelley, 'International Migration and Economic Growth: Australia 1865–1935', *Journal of Economic History*, September 1965; M. M. Quigley, 'A Model of Swedish Emigration', *Quarterly Journal of Economics*, February 1972; R. W. Richardson, 'British Emigration and Overseas Investment 1870–1914', *Economic History Review*, February 1972; J. A. Tomaske, 'The Determinants of Inter-Country Differences in European Migration 1881–1900', *Journal of Economic History*, December 1971; M. Wilkinson, 'European Migration to the U.S.; an Econometric Analysis of Aggregate Labour Supply and Demand', *Review of Economics and Statistics*, August 1970.

38 The data are actually only for Queensland, New South Wales and Victoria, which had about 80 per cent of Australia's population in 1901. Derived from the census figures by N. G. Butlin, op. cit., p. 184.

39 The 1880 figures are from Elisée Reclus, *The Earth and its Inhabitants: Asia*, Appleton, New York, 1884, vol. II: East Asia, p. 479. The 1922 figures are from Ferenczi and Willcox, op. cit., p. 149, quoting Ta Chen.

40 Migration figures from Kingsley Davis, *The Population of India and Pakistan*, Princeton University Press, Princeton, N.J., 1951, p. 99.

41 Radhakamal Mukerjee, *Migrant Asia*, Comitato Italiano per lo Studio dei Problemi della Popolazione, Rome, 1936, p. 281.

42 Mukerjee, ibid., p. 281.

43 Hugh Tinker, *A New System of Slavery*, Oxford University Press, London, 1974, pp. 185–6. Also J. P. Levin, *The Export Economies*, Harvard University Press, Cambridge, Mass., 1960.

44 This figure is from G. H. Wood, 'Changes in Average Wages in New South Wales, 1823–1898', *Journal of the Royal Statistical Society*, June 1901. Wood also gives a wage of 15s 4d weekly for an agricultural labourer, but this probably was in addition to food and lodging.

45 Carlos Diaz Alejandro, op. cit., p. 41.

46 Other elements in cost (management, capital) would be much the same in tropical

and in temperate countries, so the difference in commodity price would not be as great as the difference in wages.

47 Percentages from the essay by C. C. Stover in W. A. Lewis (ed.), *Tropical Development 1880–1913*, George Allen & Unwin, London, 1970, relying on Yates, op. cit.

48 P. Harnetty quotes Indian yields in the 1860s at 50 to 60 lb of lint per acre, and US yields at 160 lb: *Imperialism and Free Trade: Lancashire and India in the Mid Nineteenth Century*, University of British Columbia Press, Vancouver, 1972, p. 94.

CHAPTER 8

1 Gisela Eisner, *Jamaica 1830–1930*, Manchester University Press, Manchester, 1961.

2 W. A. Lewis (ed.), *Tropical Development 1880–1913*, George Allen & Unwin, London, 1970. This includes essays on Brazil, Colombia, Venezuela, Gold Coast, Nigeria, Kenya, Uganda, Egypt, Ceylon, India, Indonesia and the Philippines.

3 A. Maizels, *Industrial Growth and World Trade*, Cambridge University Press, Cambridge, 1969, p. 539.

4 Same sources as Table 7.2.

5 There is an enormous literature on these countries. For Australia see N. G. Butlin, *Australian Domestic Product Investment and Foreign Borrowing 1861–1938*, Cambridge University Press, Cambridge, 1962. This is amended by the same author's *Investment in Australian Economic Development 1861–1900*, Cambridge University Press, 1964. See also E. A. Boehm, *Prosperity and Depression in Australia 1887 to 1897*, Oxford University Press, London, 1971; and an outstanding book by Geoffrey Blainey, *The Tyranny of Distance*, Sun Books, Melbourne, 1966. On New Zealand, see C. S. F. Simkin, *The Instability of a Dependent Economy: Economic Fluctuations in New Zealand 1840–1914*, Oxford University Press, Oxford, 1951. On Canada, see K. Buckley, *Capital Formation in Canada 1896–1930*, Toronto, 1955; J. A. Stovel, *Canada in the World Economy*, Harvard University Press, Cambridge, Mass., 1959; and M. C. Urquhart and K. A. H. Buckley, *Historical Statistics of Canada*, Cambridge University Press, Cambridge, 1965. On Argentina the standard works in English are Carlos Diaz Alejandro, *Essays in the Economic History of the Argentine Republic*, Yale University Press, New Haven, 1970; A. G. Ford, *The Gold Standard 1880–1914: Britain and Argentina*, Oxford University Press, Oxford, 1962; and H. S. Ferns, *Britain and Argentina in the Nineteenth Century.* Arthur Smithies compares Argentina and Australia in 'Argentina and Australia', *American Economic Review*, May 1965. On Chile, two useful monographs in Spanish are R. L. Escobar, *La Industria in Chile: Antecedentes Estructurales*, and C. H. Ruiz-Tagle, *Concentracion de Poblacion y Desarrallo Economica: El Caso Chileno*, both published by Universidad de Chile Institute de Economia, Santiago, 1966.

6 Calculated from N. G. Butlin, op. cit.

7 Argentina scores better in relation to other temperate settlements if industrialisation is measured by labour force statistics instead of the League of Nation's estimate of industrial output. The proportion of the labour force in industry is given by the Census as 27 per cent in 1919, compared with 27 per cent in Canada in 1911 and 28 per cent in Australia in 1911. These figures include construction. Probably the labour force data include the numbers engaged in meat packing, refrigeration and other agricultural processing, which the League data may have excluded. There is no doubt on the one hand that the economy was highly urbanised or on the other hand that it was backward in textiles and metal working, two of the props of the industrial revolution. See spindle data on page 221.

8 Alejandro, op. cit., p. 217.

9 Reported by A. Baron Holmes in W. A. Lewis (ed.), op. cit., relying on P. R. Gould, *Development of the Transportation Pattern in Ghana*, Evanston, Ill., 1960.

10 Trade of each tropical country in 1883, 1899 and 1913 is given in W. A. Lewis (ed.), op. cit., pp. 46–9. Figures are in current US dollars, adjusted for changes in exchange rates, but not for commodity prices. Figures for India in 1883 and 1899 have been adjusted, using the current price of silver instead of the standard rupee exchange

rate which the Board of Trade Statistician used for the *Statistical Abstract*. For Venezuela see note 18 below.

11 For the significance of this controversy see Hla Myint, 'The Classical Theory of International Trade and the Underdeveloped Countries', *Economic Journal*, June 1958.

12 For details see the essay on Egypt by Russell Stone in Lewis (ed.), op. cit.

13 Figures in this paragraph are taken from the essay on India by Russell Lidman and R. I. Domrese in Lewis (ed.), op. cit.

14 See J. S. Furnivall, *Netherlands India: A Study of Plural Economy*, Cambridge University Press, Cambridge, 1939; Clifford Geertz, *Agricultural Involution*, University of California Press, Berkeley, 1963; and the summary essay by R. J. van Leeuwen on Indonesia in Lewis (ed.), op. cit.

15 C. F. Remer, *Foreign Investments in China*, Howard Fertig, New York, 1968, p. 117.

16 The story is told by J. S. Furnivall, *An Introduction to the Political Economy of Burma*, Rangoon, 1931.

17 Polly Hill, *The Migrant Cocoa Farmers of Southern Ghana*, Cambridge University Press, Cambridge, 1963.

18 See the essays by R. W. Harbison on Colombia, Donald Coes on Brazil and Frederick Norbury on Venezuela in Lewis (ed.), op. cit. Venezuela's low growth rate in Table 8.2 needs interpretation. The rate given there is probably too low, since the market value of the bolivar was depreciated to an unknown extent in 1883. According to the trade statistics, as summarised in Norbury's Table 5.1, the price of gold in bolivars rose 30 per cent between 1883/7 and 1908/12. If this were applied to our Table 8.2, which is supposed to be measuring values in gold, the growth rate of Venezuela's trade by value would become 2·2 per cent per annum. This is still a poor performance. It is depressed because gold was a major export in the early 1880s, and then declined. From Norbury's table one can calculate that the volume of exports at constant prices rose between 1883/7 and 1908/12 by 1·8 per cent per annum including gold, and by 2·5 per cent per annum excluding gold.

19 Leland H. Jenks, *The Migration of British Capital to 1875*, Nelson, New York, 1927, p. 209.

20 Celso Furtado, *The Economic Growth of Brazil*, University of California Press, Berkeley, 1963. Furtado's position is disputed by Nathaniel Leff, 'A Technique for Estimating Income Trends from Currency Data and an Application to Nineteenth Century Brazil', *Review of Income and Wealth*, December 1972.

21 This is based on the estimate by Lidman and Domrese in Lewis (ed.), op. cit. For a review of all previous estimates see M. Mukherjee, *National Income of India*, Statistical Publishing Society, Calcutta, 1969. Mukherjee's trend estimate for 1870 to 1915 works out at 0·8 per cent per annum.

22 W. P. McGreevey, *An Economic History of Colombia 1845–1930*, Cambridge University Press, Cambridge, 1971, pp. 164–73.

23 Data from Lidman and Domrese, in Lewis (ed.), op. cit.

24 The details of the government's attitudes and actions are in S. K. Sen, *Studies in Industrial Policy and Development of India, 1858–1914*, Calcutta, 1964.

25 Data from Population Censuses, as arranged by Paul Bairoch, *International Historical Statistics*, vol. I: *The Working Population and its Structure*, Université Libre de Bruxelles, Brussels, 1968. For Ceylon see Donald R. Snodgrass, *Ceylon, an Export Economy in Transition*, Irwin, Homewood, Ill., 1966.

26 Numbers of spindles and looms are given by D. C. M. Platt, *Latin American and British Trade 1806–1914*, Adams and Charles Black, London, 1972, p. 182. Platt's source is *The Times*, London, 29 August 1911, South American Supplement, p. 4.

27 See for example the writings of Samir Amin, such as his thoughtful book, *Le Développement du capitalisme en Côte d'Ivoire*, Les Editions de Minuit, Paris, 1967. Latin American writing is exemplified by Andre Gunder Frank, *Capitalism and Underdevelopment in Latin America*, Monthly Review Press, New York, 1969.

CHAPTER 9

1 We are concerned here only with some effects of the Great Depression. Its causes and course are analysed in numerous works, including W. A. Lewis, *Economic Survey, 1919–1939*, George Allen & Unwin, London, 1949.

2 The figures are from the appendix to W. A. Lewis, *Aspects of Tropical Trade 1883–1965*, Wicksell Lectures, Almquist and Wiksell, Stockholm, 1969. There are slight changes; specifically the trade of India in 1883 and 1899 is translated into dollars at the current rate for silver instead of at the rates used by the Board of Trade Statistician (so it now grows a little faster); the price index for manufactures has also been revised, as reported in Appendix III.

3 For sources of these data see W. A. Lewis, ibid., appendix. The European countries are those which belonged to the OECD in 1965. North America means the USA plus Canada. Japan and Australasia are excluded.

4 Calculations based on data in Table A.13 of Appendix III. Ocean freights have not been deducted.

5 For a more detailed analysis of the determinants of the terms of trade for tropical agricultural products, and of the changes between 1913 and 1965, see W. A. Lewis, ibid.

6 Source: United Nations Economic Commission for Latin America, *The Process of Industrial Development in Latin America: Statistical Appendix*, New York, 1966, p. 19.

7 Growth of world trade in manufactures 1883–1913 derived from data in W. A. Lewis, 'World Production, Prices and Trade', *Manchester School of Economic and Social Studies*, May 1952, and the price index in Appendix III. Data for 1957–69 from successive issues of the United Nations *Monthly Bulletin of Statistics.*

8 Bela Balassa, *The Structure of Protection in the Industrial Countries and its Effects on the Exports of Processed Goods From Developing Nations*, United Nations Conference on Trade and Development, New York, 1967, TD/B/C 2/36.

9 This excludes both 'the developing countries' and the Communist countries. Data from the United Nations *Monthly Bulletin of Statistics.*

10 The price indexes in Chart 9.3 are from Appendix III.

11 US wage data from the statistical appendix to the *Economic Report of the President*, Washington, DC, annual. These are hourly earnings adjusted to exclude the effects of overtime and of inter-industry shifts. The change in average weekly hours excluding overtime was slight: from 37·6 in 1956 to 37·0 in 1972.

12 Data on debt and debt charges from Organisation for Economic Cooperation and Development, *Development Cooperation, 1975 Review*, Paris, 1976, pp. 156, 243.

13 The terms of trade of tropical agricultural cash crops against manufactures, shown in Chart 9.1, are not the same as the terms of trade for developing countries, since these countries also export minerals and manufactures and also import food and raw materials. According to data in the United Nations *Monthly Bulletin of Statistics* the terms of trade of the developing countries deteriorated 11 per cent between 1955 and 1970. Over the same period the quantum of exports increased by 132 per cent, so real purchasing power increased by 105 per cent, or at an average annual rate of 4·9 per cent.

14 Esther Boserup, *The Conditions of Agricultural Growth*, George Allen & Unwin, London, 1965.

15 One of the conditions is greater interdependence among the developing countries themselves. We have reviewed what this involves in *Aspects of Tropical Trade*, op. cit., and will not repeat that discussion here.

16 The ingredients of this rough calculation are that it takes 2·2 per cent of population (5 per cent of labour force) to feed the US population, and 20 per cent of population to feed the Indian population; that Americans eat at least twice as well as Indians; and that the American farmer uses the services of another 1·5 per cent of population to supply farm machinery and farm chemicals.

17 The indirect effects depend in the first place on what happens to the volume of trade; presumably it would diminish at higher prices. The most important positive

indirect effect would be through the export multiplier; the rest of the economy would produce more in response to the increased purchasing power of the export sector. How much more would depend on the extent to which resources could be shifted to more valuable uses.

APPENDIX I

1 Hoffmann's index first appeared in a German periodical in 1934, and in a book published in 1939. The book was revised, translated into English and published in 1955 as *British Industry 1700–1950*, Blackwell, Oxford.
2 'The National Income of the United Kingdom 1870–1946', *Economic Journal*, March 1948.
3 'National Income and Expenditure of the United Kingdom 1870–1952', in S. Kuznets (ed.), *Income and Wealth*, series V, Cambridge University Press, Cambridge, 1955.
4 'Income and Investment in the United Kingdom 1856–1914', *Economic Journal*, June 1961.
5 P. Deane and W. A. Cole, *British Economic Growth 1688–1959*, Cambridge University Press, Cambridge, 1964.
6 C. H. Feinstein, *National Income Expenditure and Output of the United Kingdom 1855–1965*, Cambridge University Press, Cambridge, 1972.
7 The calculation is given in a few lines on page 74 of his *Wages and Income in the United Kingdom since 1860*, Cambridge University Press, Cambridge, 1937.
8 Prest's figure is net of depreciation and our figure is gross, so a change in the ratio of depreciation to national income would also account for a slight difference.
9 Cairncross gives this series from 1870 onwards. In earlier years the output of steel was very small; I have merely subtracted it from the output of pig iron for this series. A. K. Cairncross, *Home and Foreign Investment 1870–1913*, Cambridge, 1953, p. 164.
10 I have used Cairncross's series for metal used in shipbuilding, interpolating for earlier years by his method. There is a series for rails up to 1882 in T. H. Burnham and G. O. Haskins, *Iron and Steel in Britain 1870–1930*, London, 1943, pp. 158, 329. *The Annual Statistical Report* of the American Iron and Steel Association published the British figures up to 1911, including a complete series from 1876 in the issue for 1900. Another source (incomplete) is the *Journal of the Iron and Steel Institute*. Missing years can be found in the *Iron and Steel Trades Review*.
11 op. cit., p. 125.
12 *Building Cycles and Britain's Growth*, Macmillan, London, 1965, pp. 316–17.
13 ibid., p. 332.
14 B. R. Mitchell and Phyllis Deane, *Abstract of British Historical Statistics*, Cambridge University Press, Cambridge, 1962, p. 60.
15 op. cit., pp. 373–4.
16 K. Maiwald, 'An Index of Building Costs in the United Kingdom', *Economic History Review*, vol. VII, no. 2, 1954.
17 op. cit., p. 123.
18 C. H. Feinstein, *National Income Expenditure and Output of the United Kingdom, 1855–1965*, op. cit.
19 B. R. Mitchell, 'The Railway and U.K. Growth', *Journal of Economic History*, September 1964.
20 For cotton see R. Robson, *The Cotton Industry in Britain*, London, 1957. A series for wool, including the domestic clip and shoddy, is given in *Memorandum on British and Foreign Trade and Industry*, UK Parliamentary Papers, 1909, vol. CII. The output of flax is derived from the Agricultural Censuses of Ireland and of England and Wales. Wool imports are converted from greasy to clean basis by multiplying by 0·5417; domestic wool by multiplying by 0·75. Silk knubs are converted by multiplying by 0·5.
21 A. D. Spicer, *The Paper Trade*, London, 1907. Spicer's figures are linked with Hoffmann's index for the later years.
22 A. R. Prest and A. A. Adams, *Consumers' Expenditure in the United Kingdom, 1900–1919*, Cambridge, 1954.

23 Henry Chubb, 'On the Supply of Gas to the Metropolis', *Journal of the Royal Statistical Society*, June 1876.
24 K. S. Lomax, 'Production and Productivity Movements in the United Kingdom since 1900', *Journal of the Royal Statistical Society*, 1959.
25 P. Deane and W. A. Cole, op. cit., pp. 329–30.
26 His series can be deduced from Mitchell and Deane, op. cit., pp. 373–4.
27 A. H. Imlah, *Economic Elements in the Pax Britannica*, Harvard University Press, Cambridge, Mass., 1958, pp. 70–5.
28 The numbers engaged in shipping, rail and road transport are derived from: Bowley's estimate of value added by railways in *The Division of the Product of Industry*; Prest's estimate of expenditure on travel in *Consumers' Expenditure in the United Kingdom 1900–1919*, and Wood and Bowley's data on wages, in A. L. Bowley, *Wages and Income in the United Kingdom Since 1860*, and other sources listed there.
29 Data on salaries are found in the British Association Report, 'The Amount and Distribution of Income (other than wages) below the Income Tax Exemption Limit in the United Kingdom', *Journal of the Royal Statistical Society*, December 1910.
30 E. M. Ojala, *Agriculture and Economic Progress*, London, 1952.
31 L. Drescher, 'The Development of Agricultural Production in Great Britain and Ireland from the Early Nineteenth Century', *Manchester School of Economic and Social Studies*, May 1955.
32 The detailed checking of the Population Censuses was done by Professor Dermot Gately, then a doctoral candidate at Princeton University, who also made those real income calculations that are based on population data, and gave other valuable assistance. For the distribution of the occupied population see Table A.4.
33 op. cit., pp. 329–30.

APPENDIX IV

1 M. K. Bennett, 'World Wheat Crops 1885–1932', *Wheat Studies of the Food Research Institute*, vol. IX, no. 7, Stanford, 1933, appendix.
2 F. R. Rutter, *Cereal Production of Europe*, USDA Bureau of Statistics Bulletin No. 68, Washington, DC, 1908.
3 I. M. Rubinow, *Russia's Wheat Surplus*, USDA Bureau of Statistics Bulletin No. 42, Washington, DC, 1906; the same author, *Russia's Wheat Trade*, USDA Bureau of Statistics Bulletin No. 65, Washington, DC, 1908.
4 Especially: V. P. Timoshenko, *World Wheat Production*, vol. XVIII, no. 7, vol. XIX, no. 5 and vol. XX, no. 6 of *Wheat Studies of the Food Research Institute*, published under separate cover, Stanford.
5 H. Working, 'Wheat Acreage and Production in the United States since 1856: A Revision of Official Estimates', *Wheat Studies of the Food Research Institute*, vol. 2, no. 7, Stanford, 1926.
6 W. G. Hoffmann, *Das Wachstum der Deutschen Wirtschaft Seit der Mitte des 19 Jahrhunderts*, Berlin, 1965, p. 163.
7 E. Dunsdorfs, *The Australian Wheat Growing Industry, 1788 to 1948*, Melbourne, 1956, appendix.
8 USDA, *Yearbook*, 1935, Washington, DC, pp. 349–50.
9 Working, op. cit., p. 240.
10 USDA, *Yearbook*, 1935, p. 346.
11 M. C. Urquhart and K. A. H. Buckley, *Historical Statistics of Canada*, Cambridge and Toronto, 1965, p. 364.
12 Timoshenko, op. cit., p. 224.
13 Dunsdorfs, op. cit., appendix.
14 Data for 1885 to 1913 are given by Bennett; 1883 to 1907 by Rutter, *Cereal Production*; and 1903 to 1913 by the *International Yearbook of Agricultural Statistics*, 1911–12, pp. 22–3; ibid., 1915–16, pp. 22–3.
15 Hoffmann, op. cit., pp. 271ff.
16 France: Institut Internationale de la Statistique et des Etudes Economiques, *Annuaire Statistique*, 1951 (rétrospectif), vol. 58, Paris, 1951, p. 105.

17 Sweden: Statistisk Centralbyran, *Statistisk Tidskrift*, 1872, p. 17; ibid., 1880, p. 27; ibid., 1885, p. 27.

18 Norway: Landbruks Department, *Beretning*, 1929, p. 122, and UK *Statistical Abstract for the Principal and Other Foreign Countries*, no. 6 and no. 10.

19 USDA, *Report of the Commissioner of Agriculture, 1883*, Washington, DC, 1883, pp. 409–10, and Bennett, op. cit., p. 268.

20 Netherlands: Centraal Bureau Voor de Stastistiek, *Jaarcijfers*, 1892, 's Gravenhage, 1893, pp. 106–9, and Belgium: Ministère de l'Intérieur, *Annuaire Statistique de la Belgique*, 1871, Brussels, 1871, p. 206.

21 J. B. Lawes and J. H. Gilbert, 'On the Home Produce, Imports, Consumption and Price of Wheat over the Twenty-seven Harvest Years, 1852–53 to 1879–80', *Journal of the Statistical Society*, vol. XLIII, 1880, London, 1880. The Lawes and Gilbert series appear as averages in E. M. Ojala's doctoral dissertation, *Agriculture and Economic Progress*, London, 1952, and as an annual series attributed to Lawes and Gilbert in the appendix of J. A. Venn, *Foundations of Agricultural Economics*, Cambridge, 1933.

22 A. Sauerbeck, 'Prices of Commodities and the Precious Metals', *Journal of the Statistical Society*, vol. XLIX, 1886, London, 1886.

23 *Journal of the Royal Statistical Society*, 1880, p. 665.

24 ibid., 1886, p. 635.

25 B. R. Mitchell, *Abstract of British Historical Statistics*, Cambridge, 1962, p. 86.

26 *Annuaire Statistique*, 1871, p. 206; ibid., 1876, Brussels, 1876, p. 218.

27 Denmark: Le Bureau Royal de Statistique, *Résumé des Principaux Faits Statistiques du Danemark*, no. 2, Copenhagen, 1878, p. 22; Statistiske Departement, *Sammendrag af Statistiske Oplysninger*, no. 8, Copenhagen, 1880; ibid., no. 9, Copenhagen, 1885; ibid., no. 10, Copenhagen, 1889.

28 USDA, *Report*, 1883, and Rutter, op. cit., p. 73.

29 Rutter, op. cit., pp. 50, 52; *International Yearbook of Agricultural Statistics*, 1911–12, pp. 22–3, and ibid., 1915–16, pp. 22–3.

30 F. X. von Neumann-Spallart, *Uebersichten der Weltwirtschaft*, Jahrgang 1880, Stuttgart, 1881.

31 Institut Internationale de Statistique, *Bulletin de l'Institut Internationale de Statistique*, 1897, vol. XI, 1ère livraison, St Petersburg, 1899, p. 163.

32 USDA, *Report*, 1883, p. 402.

33 Hungary: Az Orszagos Magyar Kir., Statistikai Hivatal, *Magyar Statistikai Evkönyv*, 1893, vol. 1, Budapest, 1894, pp. 86–7.

34 A. von Matlekovitz, *Das Königreich Ungarns*, Leipzig, 1900, p. 229.

35 Romania: Ministerul Industriei si Comertului, *Anuarul Statistic al Romaniei*, 1915–16, Bucharest, 1919, pp. 32–3.

36 France: Bureau de la Statistique Générale, *Annuaire Statistique*, 1919–20, vol. 26, Paris, 1921, p. 220.

37 Romania: Ministerul Industriei si Comertului, op. cit.

38 UK Board of Trade, *Statistical Abstract for the Several Colonial and Other Possessions*, no. 15, London, 1879, p. 185, and no. 27, London, 1890.

39 UK Board of Trade, *Statistical Abstract for the Principal and Other Foreign Countries*.

40 F. R. Rutter, *European Grain Trade*, USDA Bureau of Statistics Bulletin No. 69, Washington, DC, 1908, pp. 33–4, 51 and 55.

41 *International Yearbook of Agricultural Statistics*, 1911–12, pp. 244–7; ibid., 1915–16, pp. 272–7.

42 The net exports for the current series are as given by: USDA, *Report*, 1886, Washington, 1887, and *A Report of the Statistician*, September and October 1892, Washington, 1893, and the *Statistical Abstract Relating to British India*, United Kingdom, House of Commons, *Sessional Papers*, 1878–9; ibid., 1883; ibid., 1899.

43 C. P. Wright, 'India as a Producer and Exporter of Wheat', *Wheat Studies of the Food Research Institute*, vol. 3, Stanford, 1926–7, pp. 378–9.

44 USDA, *Report* 1884, Washington, DC, *Report* 1886, Washington, DC, 1887, *Report* 1887, Washington, DC, 1888, *Report of the Statistician*, September and October, 1892, Washington, DC, 1893.

45 US Department of Agriculture, *Report of the Commissioner of Agriculture for 1876*, Washington, 1877.

46 Bureau of the American Republics, *Breadstuffs in Latin America*, Bulletin No. 35, March 1892.

47 F. W. Bicknell, *Wheat Production and Farm Life in Argentina*, US Department of Agriculture, Division of Statistics, Bulletin No. 27, Washington, 1904.

48 *Breadstuffs in Latin America*, p. 13; Bicknell, op. cit., p. 91, and *International Yearbook of Agricultural Statistics*, 1911–12, pp. 246–9.

49 UK Board of Trade, *Statistical Abstract for the Principal and Other Foreign Countries*, no. 5 and no. 6, in *Sessional Papers*, 1877 and 1878–9, respectively.

50 Italy: Ministero di Agricoltura, Industria e Commercio, Direzione Generale della Statistica, *Annuario Statistico Italiano*, 1897, Rome, 1897.

51 *Statistical Abstract for the Principal and Other Foreign Countries*, nos 5, 6 and 11.

52 *Statistical Abstract for the Principal and Other Foreign Countries*, nos 6 and 11.

53 Von Neumann-Spallart, op. cit., p. 119.

54 Japan: *Oriental Economist*, *Foreign Trade of Japan*, a statistical survey, Tokyo, 1935, pp. 5 and 155.

Author Index

Subject Index

Note: For details of specific countries see under the appropriate country, e.g. Germany: profits in.